T0305462

LEARNING AND KNOWING IN PRACTICE-BASED STUDIES

For a list of all Edward Elgar published titles visit our website at www.e-elgar.com

Learning and Knowing in Practice-Based Studies

Based Studies

Silvia Gherardi

University of Trento, Italy

and

Antonio Strati

University of Trento, Italy
and chercheur associé PREG-CRG (Ecole Polytechnique)
Paris, France

Edward Elgar
Cheltenham, UK • Northampton, MA, USA

Published by
Edward Elgar Publishing Limited
The Lypiatts
15 Lansdown Road
Cheltenham
Glos GL50 2JA
UK

Edward Elgar Publishing, Inc.
William Pratt House
9 Dewey Court
Northampton
Massachusetts 01060
USA

A catalogue record for this book is available from the British Library

Library of Congress Control Number: 2012946678

MIX
Paper from
responsible sources
FSC
www.fsc.org   FSC® C018575

ISBN 978 0 85793 854 1

Printed and bound by MPG Books Group, UK

Contents

PART III   METHODOLOGICAL INSIGHTS FOR A PRACTICE-BASED
           APPROACH

Acknowledgements

The editors and publishers wish to thank the authors and the following publishers who have kindly given permission for the use of copyright material.

Blackwell Publishing Ltd via Copyright Clearance Center's Rightslink Service for article: Silvia Gherardi and Davide Nicolini (2002), 'Learning in a Constellation of Interconnected Practices: Canon or Dissonance?', *Journal of Management Studies*, **39** (4), June, 419–36.

P. Cavagna for photograph: Fig 2.2 'The Student Anna Scalfi Performing in the Entrance to the Faculty' in: Antonio Strati (2005), 'Organizational Artifacts and the Aesthetic Approach', in Anat Rafaeli and Michael G. Pratt (eds), *Artifacts and Organizations: Beyond Mere Symbolism*, Chapter 2, 30.

Emerald Group Publishing for article: Silvia Gherardi (2003), 'Knowing as Desiring. Mythic Knowledge and the Knowledge Journey in Communities of Practitioners', *Journal of Workplace Learning*, **15** (7/8), 352–58.

Galleria Continua photograph: Fig 2.1 'Loris Cecchini's Insyallation *density Spectru Zone 1.0.*' in: Antonio Strati (2005), 'Organizational Artifacts and the Aesthetic Approach', in Anat Rafaeli and Michael G. Pratt (eds), *Artifacts and Organizations: Beyond Mere Symbolism*, Chapter 2, 30.

M.E. Sharpe, Inc. for excerpt: Antonio Strati (2003), 'Knowing in Practice: Aesthetic Understanding and Tacit Knowledge', in Davide Nicolini, Silvia Gherardi and Dvora Yanow (eds), *Knowing in Organizations: A Practice-Based Approach*, Chapter 3, 53–75.

SAGE Publications Ltd for excerpts: Antonio Strati (2008), 'Aesthetics in the Study of Organizational Life', in Daved Barry and Hans Hansen (eds), *The SAGE Handbook of New Approaches in Management and Organization*, Chapter 2.3, 229–38; Silvia Gherardi (2008), 'Situated Knowledge and Situated Action: What do Practice-Based Studies Promise?', in Daved Barry and Hans Hansen (eds), *The SAGE Handbook of New Approaches in Management and Organization*, Chapter 3.9, 516–25; Antonio Strati (2009), '"Do You Do Beautiful Things?": Aesthetics and Art in Qualitative Methods of Organization Studies', in David Buchanan and Alan Bryman (eds), *The SAGE Handbook of Organizational Research Methods*, Chapter 14, 230–45.

SAGE Publications via Copyright Clearance Center's Rightslink Service for articles: Silvia Gherardi (2000), 'Practice-Based Theorizing on Learning and Knowing in Organizations', *Organization*, **7** (2), 211–23; Antonio Strati (2007), 'Sensible Knowledge and Practice-Based

Learning', *Management Learning*, **38** (1), 61–77; Silvia Gherardi, Davide Nicolini and Antonio Strati (2007), 'The Passion for Knowing', *Organization*, **14** (3), 315–29; Silvia Gherardi (2009), 'Introduction: The Critical Power of the "Practice Lens"', *Management Learning*, **40** (2), 115–28; Silvia Gherardi (2009), 'Practice? It's a Matter of Taste!', *Management Learning*, **40** (5), 535–50; Gessica Corradi, Silvia Gherardi and Luca Verzelloni (2010), 'Through the Practice Lens: Where is the Bandwagon of Practice-Based Studies Heading?', *Management Learning*, **41** (3), 265–83.

Taylor and Francis LLC Books via Copyright Clearance Center's Rightslink Service for articles: Silvia Gherardi (1995), 'When Will He Say: "Today the Plates are Soft"? The Management of Ambiguity and Situated Decision-Making', *Studies in Cultures, Organizations and Societies*, **1**, 9–27; Antonio Strati (2005), 'Organizational Artifacts and the Aesthetic Approach', in Anat Rafaeli and Michael G. Pratt (eds), *Artifacts and Organizations: Beyond Mere Symbolism*, Chapter 2, 23–39, references; Attila Bruni, Silvia Gherardi and Laura Lucia Parolin (2007), 'Knowing in a System of Fragmented Knowledge', *Mind, Culture, and Activity*, **14** (1–2), 83–102.

Every effort has been made to trace all the copyright holders but if any have been inadvertently overlooked the publishers will be pleased to make the necessary arrangement at the first opportunity.

Introduction

Silvia Gherardi and Antonio Strati

The concept of 'practice' has been rediscovered within organizational studies mainly in the past decade, and the essays collected in this book have contributed, albeit only partly, to this rediscovery. These fifteen essays, published in international journals or collected volumes since 2000, illustrate, thematically and methodologically, the theoretical reflection and empirical research that we have conducted with the research group[1] at the University of Trento which has promoted the 'practice turn' in contemporary organizational analysis.

We propose these essays again in this book because together they furnish an overview on the fertility of the concept of practice in the field of organizational learning and knowing, and on how it has given rise to a specific strand of organizational studies which goes by the name of 'practice-based studies'. The book consists of a selection of texts used – besides other occasions – at the numerous doctoral schools that we have organized as Research Unit on Communication, Organizational Learning and Aesthetics on the topic of practice-based studies. The essays that follow were proposed and discussed during these doctoral schools,[2] because they represented valid as well as flexible teaching aids.

The book is structured in three parts with the purpose of giving prominence to both the concepts and methods of practice-based studies. The first part consists of five chapters that illustrate what is meant by practice-based theorizing. The second part, which consists of a further six chapters, highlights the key concepts with which to describe and interpret situated practices. The third part of the book comprises four chapters that contain methodological reflections on how to conduct empirical research in workplaces using a practice-based approach. We now provide general descriptions of each of these three parts in order to summarize the themes and problems that they will present to the reader.

The first part of the collection positions practice-based theorizing in regard to the issue of what sort of knowledge to produce, given dissatisfaction with positivism as a model to generate allegedly universal, objective, decontextualized and disembodied knowledge. The first chapter addresses this issue by representing it in the form of the dilemma between Scylla and Charybdis and the desire to choose neither alternative but instead to steer a middle course which avoids, on the one hand, the cognitivist view of knowledge and, on the other, the view of knowledge as a commodity – that is, as an object traded on the market. By means of this image from classical literature, the practice turn is positioned as an alternative to cognitivism and the commodification of knowledge. Knowledge, therefore, does not reside in people's minds, nor is it a commodity; rather, it is an activity situated in social, working and organizational practices. Thus accomplished is the shift from knowledge (object) to knowing (activity), where the latter is something that people 'do' together, collectively and socially.

This first chapter was originally published as the introduction to a special issue of the international journal *Organization*, in which authoritative theorists conversed together on the cultural conception of learning, situated learning theory, activity theory and actor–network theories. In so doing, they demonstrated the similarity of issues concerning the production of knowledge within organizations, but outside the positivist model. These traditions of research were the forerunners of practice-based studies, and others have joined them on the 'bandwagon', as will be illustrated in Chapter 5.

The rediscovery in organizational studies during the 2000s of the concept of practice, which had a long tradition in both philosophy and sociology (as well as other social disciplines), was due to two factors. 'Practice', in fact, articulates both the spatiality and the fabrication of the knowledge. Spatiality denotes the situatedness of knowing-in-practice, thus continuing the strand of situated learning theory and directing the researcher's attention to the plural and controversial nature of knowledge. Fabrication denotes the materiality of knowledge and the fact that practical knowledge is the product of a knowledgeable doing in that it is 'fabricated' through situated power/knowledge relations.

Practice-based theorizing therefore ensued from the definition of practice as a 'collective knowledgeable doing', and also from the activity of theorizing as a situated practice within a collectivity that socially sustains it.

The second chapter introduces the theme of aesthetic knowledge, leaving behind its cognitive counterpart. Knowledge is not confined to the heads of people, nor is the world known only with the head, but on the contrary with the entire body, and in particular through the senses. The aesthetic understanding of working practices sheds light on the sensory aspects of knowledge, and gives prominence to the hidden and tacit knowledge whereby practitioners are people who 'dwell' in a practice. On becoming a practitioner, learning is constitutive of organizing, just as organizing is constitutive of learning. A practice-based theorization therefore starts from the assumptions that practitioners and researchers know more than they know that they know; that their practices are as opaque to themselves as they are to those who observe them from the outside; and that their knowledge is embodied in their bodies and embedded in the materiality of the artifacts of a practice.

The theoretical and methodological approach used by practice-based studies can be clarified by answering the following question, which is posed by the third chapter in the book: why do individuals and organizations seek knowledge and engage in producing, maintaining and changing a corpus of knowledge? The answer most commonly put forward in the literature concerns the instrumental aspect of such activities, in the form of both problem solving and gaining competitive advantage. However, practice-based theorizing furnishes a complementary answer: that knowledge is pursued as a goal in itself because of passion and the desire to know; it is not merely instrumental and functional. The search for knowledge can be connected with pleasure, the fulfilment of human nature, the desire to know, and a passion that drives a constant becoming. We have here a literary image, which symbolizes the ties among knowledge, desire and passion: that of Dante's Ulysses and the journey of knowledge amid dangers and divine prohibitions. Passion therefore sustains practices and is the engine of their change; a topic subsequently developed among the keys concepts expounded in the second part of the book, and that is emphasized by the investigation of the aesthetic side of organizational life.

The aesthetic understanding of practices, in fact, constitutes the principal difference from their interpretation as a set of activities, because it adds to the dimension of doing the more subtle one of the distinction inherent in every doing and of the style of doing that makes the difference. This set of assumptions takes us to the fourth chapter in this first part of the book, which discusses what practice-based studies can contribute to organizational analysis. When organizational learning is considered a root metaphor, which makes it possible to establish analogies between organization and learning, then working, organizing, as well as innovating, can be seen as social practices within which those activities occur simultaneously and inseparably. Through participation as a practitioner, the activity of knowing is situated in action and through action. Participation and reflexivity are the two interpretative concepts which enable understanding of practical knowledge and the specificity of the theoretical and methodological approach used by practice-based studies.

In fact the purpose of the fifth chapter is to illustrate an 'epistemic community', that is, one of those communities which produce knowledge objects within organizational analysis – as in the case of the research community which gave rise to the 'practice turn'. Practice, it is observed, became a lens to reinterpret many aspects of the organizational life and a variety of organizational phenomena, and so a 'bandwagon' of practice-based research studies and theories was set in motion.

The second part of the book illustrates the key concepts of the practice-based approach and consists of six essays providing examples of empirical research in various organizational settings.

Aesthetic understanding is the concept illustrated by the first chapter, the purpose being to show how it is able to bring out the 'don't-know-what' characteristic of a large part of practical experience in organizational life. The second concept is that of 'knowing-in-practice'. This illustrates that knowing is a situated activity, which consists of the alignment of people, symbols and technologies working together within a system of fragmented knowledges. By means of this concept it is possible to interpret both the materiality of practices and the discursive practices that enable, for example, distance work.

The topic of discursive practices, which is present in the book from its first chapter onwards, is brought into focus by the next key concept, that of constant comparison among the perspectives of the world embraced by the co-participants in the production of a practice. This concept continues the process of replacing the notion of a community of practice with that of the practices of a community (Gherardi 2009) in order to show that dissent among practitioners and the negotiation of meanings constitute dynamics important for the innovation of practices, and that a minimum amount of agreement is sufficient to sustain a practice, not general endorsement of its principles. This concept enables one to see, in fact, that the above-mentioned alignment is provisional and unstable, that comparison among the perspectives of the practitioners produces tensions, discontinuities and incoherence, just as much as it produces order and negotiated meanings. In fact, both cacophony and consonance are produced at the same time, and both sustain the understanding of a practice from the point of view of those dwelling in it.

The three concepts illustrated thus far in the corresponding essays – aesthetic understanding, knowing-in-practice and constant comparison – are reprised within a broader interpretative frame by the next chapter, which specifies how the aesthetic dimension on the one hand provides a way to study organizations and, on the other, enables interpretation of the negotiating process that gives shape to the aesthetic and to its relations with the classic issues of ethos and truth. In other words, it raises the questions of how a practice can be much more than a set of activities, and therefore how a practice can be analysed to show that it is socially sustained by the community of practitioners and by the society within which these practitioners live. The book answers these questions by means of two closely interrelated key concepts: passion and taste-making.

The chapter which addresses the topic of passion was originally the introduction to a special issue of the international journal *Organization* published in 2007[3] and which, in presenting the various articles contained therein, discussed the theme of passion and pathos in organizational studies, emphasizing the importance of the emotions, affect and attachment to the object of the practice as an antidote to an instrumental vision of them. Simultaneously, the notion of the passion for knowledge yields reflexive forms of research in which:

- a non-instrumental conception of knowledge activates unconventional styles of research,
- the sociology of attachment reveals unusual aspects of the connection among those who work, the objects of their work, and the meanings of organizing work relations,
- the valorization of forms of sensible knowledge yields results interesting for the theory of organizing.

Finally, the concept of taste-making, illustrated in Chapter 11, makes it possible to describe and analyse the process whereby practices are sustained and changed through their refinement by the aesthetic judgement. The term 'taste-making' was coined to emphasize that taste does not pre-exist practice but is collectively shaped in practising, and flanks ethical and instrumental opinions in sustaining the sense of the practice and the constant negotiation of what constitutes a good or beautiful practice.

The third part of the book addresses the methodological question of how to study and understand organizational life by adopting a practice-based approach, starting from three standpoints. The first chapter focuses on how to access the hidden knowledge that characterizes practical knowledge and evades the awareness of practitioners and direct investigation by researchers. It proposes a projective research technique called 'the interview with the double' and illustrates an application of it. Then specified is the new methodological awareness comprised in the critical analysis of work and management practices in organizations through four analytical approaches in organizational aesthetics – archaeological, empathic-logical, aesthetic and artistic – which set different research questions for work in the field (Strati 2010). However different these may be, David Buchanan and Alan Bryman state in the introduction to the *Handbook of Organizational Research Methods* (2009, p. XXIX), from which this contribution to the book is drawn, that these approaches are all 'concerned with emancipation and the exercise of aesthetic judgement' and opposing 'alienating and manipulative processes' in the everyday working lives of organizations. The methodological discussion then turns to the performativity of practice, illustrating with the example of an artistic performance how artifacts can be analysed as 'artifacts being-in-use'.

The final chapter in the book reflects on the critical power of the practice lens. This essay was first published as the introduction to a special issue of the international journal *Management Learning*, in which authors addressed worries within the community of practice-based scholars that the success of the approach and the proliferation of writings adhering to the 'practice turn' had slackened the critical tension which had characterized the beginning of the 2000s, and that the study of practices as 'objects' had made scholars lose sight of practice as epistemology.

In summary, practice as epistemology articulates knowledge in and about organizing as a practical accomplishment, rather than as a transcendental account of a decontextualized reality made by a genderless and disembodied researcher. The critical power of the practice lens in regard to work and organizations explores:

- how practitioners and researchers act both aesthetically and cognitively; how they do what they do through their sensible intelligence and their rational understanding, and what their doing does;
- how working and organizing practices become institutionalized because they are sustained by a 'working consensus' (an institutional work) and a moral and aesthetic order;
- how practising is interactionally sustained by a pre-verbal understanding, a mutual orientation, and a production of mutually intelligible artifacts.

Theories of practice furnish the theoretical and methodological bases for the construction of organizational theories which flank the view of organization as planning and design (rationality from outside) with the view of organization as an unstable accomplishment in becoming which involves the senses and the aesthetic judgements, and which is based on widespread social intelligibility due to contingent and plural rationalities.

Notes

1. We refer to the Research Unit on Communication, Organizational Learning and Aesthetics, of the University of Trento (www.unitn.it/rucola), which began work on these topics in 1993. The choice of essays does not represent the work of all those who have collaborated with the research unit. Moreover, while some members are still at the University of Trento, others have moved to other universities, most notably Davide Nicolini to the University of Warwick in England and Laura Parolin to the University of Milan in Italy.
2. We wish to thank all the doctoral students who have attended the schools, stimulating and improving our theoretical analyses and empirical research. Since 2006 we have organized the following doctoral colloquia at Trento:

    9–11 April 2006, 'Knowing-in-practice: how to study it?'
    10–12 December 2007, 'Objects and knowing-in-practice'
    27–29 November 2008, 'Methodologies in practice-based studies'
    30 November–2 December 2009, 'Does body matter in organizational life?'
    23–25 May 2011, 'Practising technologies'
    23–25 May 2012, 'Transitions in professional responsibilities: ensuring quality and effective organisational and management practices'

    Some of these have been organized jointly with other universities and research groups, namely the Ecole Normale Superieure of Cachan, the PREG-CRG of the Ecole Polytechnique, the ESSEC of Paris (France), the Department of Education, Aarhus University (Denmark), the University of Stockholm, the Linnaeus Centre for Research on Learning, Interaction and Mediated Communication in Contemporary Society at the University of Gothenburg (Sweden), and the Stirling Institute of Education (UK).
3. This special issue contained various papers given at the 2005 Trento conference of the Organizational Learning, Knowledge and Capabilities network, and at its sixth annual conference, which centred on the theme of the Passion for Knowing and Learning.

References

Buchanan, D. and A. Bryman (eds) (2009). *The SAGE Handbook of Organizational Research Methods*. London: Sage.
Gherardi, S. (2009). Community of Practice or Practices of a Community? In S. Armstrong and C. Fukami, *The SAGE Handbook of Management Learning, Education, and Development*. London: Sage, pp. 514–30.
Strati, A. (2010). Aesthetic Understanding of Work and Organizational Life: Approaches and Research Developments. *Sociology Compass*, 4 (10), 880–93.

PART I

PRACTICE-BASED THEORIZING

[1]

Volume 7(2): 211–223
Copyright © 2000 SAGE
(London, Thousand Oaks, CA
and New Delhi)

Practice-based Theorizing on Learning and Knowing in Organizations

introduction

Silvia Gherardi

Trento University

Between Scylla and Charybdis

The figure of Ulysses in the *Odyssey* has been interpreted as a metaphor for humanity in search of knowledge. When Ulysses took his leave of Circe—forgoing immortality out of his desire to know and/or to return home—the sorceress revealed the dangers that awaited him and how to overcome them. Among these dangers were two sea monsters dwelling on opposite sides of what has been identified as the Strait of Messina. One of them was Scylla, a dreadful creature that lurked in a cave and devoured sailors from the ships that came within reach of one of her six necks, each bearing a head with three rows of teeth. The other monster, Charybdis, took the form of a whirlpool which sucked in and belched forth the waters of the sea three times every day.

In everyday language, reference to Scylla and Charybdis denotes a dilemma in which both options are equally undesirable. In the relationship between knowledge and organizations, Scylla and Charybdis can be represented, respectively, by a *mentalistic* vision of knowledge in organizations and by a *commodification* of knowledge. The desire to avoid the two dangers is shared by the authors of this special issue of *Organization*. The authors, Frank Blackler, Norman Crump, Seonaidh McDonald, Davide Nicolini, Lucy Suchman, Etienne Wenger, Dvora Yanow and myself, share concerns regarding knowledge and organization through the concept of *practice*. Yet, as I will further illustrate in this introduction, our intellectual orientations spring from several different traditions.

We came together two years ago through our desire to investigate and compare similarities and differences among our intellectual and professional interests. Davide Nicolini and Dvora Yanow created the context for this encounter by organizing the symposium 'Situated Learning, Local Knowledge, and Action: Social Approaches to the Study of Knowing in Organizations' at the American Academy of Management Annual Conference held in San Diego (1998). The project of producing a special issue of *Organization* has kept our small network together, through long

1350–5084[200005]7:2;211–223;012579

Organization 7(2)
Introduction

email conversations and limited constituent meetings. Our voices in the symposium have been joined here by the commentaries of Yrjö Engeström, John Law, Alessia Contu and Hugh Willmott, who have graciously agreed to offer their view on our work, and by another opinion on the matter of knowledge and organization in Helen Armstrong's 'Speaking Out'.

Given the impossibility of reproducing the vividness of our discussions throughout this time, in introducing this issue I seek to explain why and how the traditions of research we represent, activity theory (AT), actor-network theory (ANT), situated learning theory (SLT) and cultural perspectives to organizational learning (CP), can be grouped under the heading of what I call *practice-based theorizing*. My intention is not to force diverse ontological and epistemological assumptions into a single framework, nor is it to resolve controversies among them with a view towards constructing a single theory. More modestly, I attempt to show that, among the manifold conversations now in progress on the theme of knowing and organizing, there is one that has an emergent identity centring on the idea of *practice*.

Knowledge in Practice: Neither in the Head nor as a Commodity

The discourse on knowledge in organization studies arose in the 1970s from a metaphorical operation which combined the terms 'learning' and 'organization' in the concept of 'organizational learning' (even if the first mentions of the concept can be traced back to James March and Herbert Simon, in 1958). This was a highly successful operation, judging from the welter of publications on the subject and the ability of the discourse to conceal its metaphorical origins to the point of objectively asserting the identity of the Learning Organization, which continues to support functionalist organization theory.

One figure in this discourse states that knowledge resides in the heads of persons, and that it is appropriated, transmitted and stored by means of mentalistic processes. The figure works through the dichotomies of mind–body, thought–action, individual–organization. Its main catch-phrase is 'organizational learning', but also 'cognitive framework' or 'traditional cognitive learning theory' (Nicolini and Meznar, 1995; Fox, 1997; Easterby Smith et al., 1998). The images that accompany this appropriation of knowledge are those of ingestion or of capitalization (banking) with all their correlates (hooks, 1994). As if it were food or money, this perspective implies, knowledge exists prior to and independent from the knowing subject, who creates no knowledge in the act of appropriation. That is, the production, circulation and consumption of knowledge are viewed as autonomous activities.

A second figure in this discourse has been constructed by conversations in the economics of knowledge and in knowledge management. The starting point has been the identification of knowledge as a production factor distinct from the traditional ones of capital, labour and land. This distinction has led to the definition of knowledge as 'strategic' and to locate

Introduction
Silvia Gherardi

it in the head of the organization (i.e. management), through which its work determines corporate performance.

For instance, the resource-based theory of the firm has conceptualized knowledge as 'core competencies' or 'core capabilities', naturalizing the relationship by means of the metaphor of the tree of knowledge: the trunk and major limbs are core products and the root system is the core competence (Prahalad and Hamel, 1990). The reification of knowledge has grown more overt with the 'objectified transferable commodity' envisaged by the knowledge management approach, which treats knowledge as practically synonymous with information created, disseminated and embedded in products, services and systems. Operational knowledge in organizations exists at a tacit level, and organizational routines are the carriers of such knowledge. The transfer of knowledge, moreover, may be accomplished without distortion: to transfer is not to transform.

The concreteness of knowledge is what enables the routinization of activities, so that organizations are able to 'know' independently from their members. The commodification of knowledge proceeds dynamically, transforming the tacit into the explicit, although knowledge sometimes resists: it becomes 'sticky' (von Hippel, 1994), and the core capabilities may turn into core rigidities, enabling or constraining learning potential through path dependency (Leonard-Barton, 1995). The catch-phrase for this figure of discourse on knowledge, 'knowledge management', unites the image of knowledge as a commodity (or asset) with that of its intentional and deliberate control. It also defines the subject (the management) that stands in a privileged, if not exclusive, relationship with knowledge. The economics of knowledge is the political economy of knowledge as well.

Before considering a third figure in this discourse, *practice,* which is the object of this introduction, I will round off the discussion so far with a telling image garnered from a recent conversation with Pasquale Gagliardi. To explain why knowledge management cannot be based on a functionalist idea of knowledge, he used the following analogy: 'It's the difference between house architecture and garden architecture'. When a garden is laid out, the designer is aware that plants grow, that they grow and spread, and that they have lives of their own. Functionalists' views of knowledge, like those of house architecture, are based on the fixity of structure and on the control of form. But, if knowledge, like plants, is alive, then it can be talked about more like garden architecture as it becomes 'culturalized' in different discourses. That is, rather than focusing on knowledge as inert material, to be fixed and controlled, knowledge could be articulated both in its spatiality and in its fabrication, and in consideration to its transformative linkages between the human and the natural.

Knowledge as Practice: Between Spatiality and Fabrication

The term 'practice' may seem today like a buzzword, yet its power stems

Organization 7(2)
Introduction

from its long pedigree in philosophy. It is imbued with diverse traditions of thought such as phenomenological, Marxist and Wittgenstein's linguistic.

Thinking of learning through participation in a practice enables us to focus on the fact that, in everyday practices, learning takes place in the flow of experience, with or without our awareness of it. In everyday organizational life, work, learning, innovation, communication, negotiation, conflict over goals, their interpretation, and history, are co-present in practice. They are part of human existence. Heidegger (1962) and the phenomenological school used the term *Dasein* to denote this 'being-in-the-world' whereby subject and object are indistinguishable. They are both part of a situation and exist in a social and historical setting.

Winograd and Flores (1986) provide an illuminating example of this relationship among subject, object, context and knowledge. Consider a carpenter hammering a nail into a piece of wood. In the carpenter's practical activity, the hammer does not exist as an object with given properties. It is as much part of his world as the arm with which he wields it. The hammer belongs to the environment and can be unthinkingly used by the carpenter. The carpenter does not need to 'think a hammer' in order to drive in a nail. His capacity to act depends on his familiarity with the act of hammering. His use of the practical item 'hammer' is its significance to him in the setting 'hammering' and 'carpentry'. The hammer does not exist as such when it no longer works or if it is missing.

Hammering, in this case, is a paradigmatic example of pre-reflexive learning, of comprehension that takes place in situations of involvement in a practice. Closely associated with the phenomenological tradition, this form of comprehension is also related to the concept of tacit knowledge. This is what Polanyi (1962) meant when he said that we know much more than we know how we know. In order to convey what he means by 'tacit knowledge' in the practice of skills, he draws a distinction between two types of awareness: focal awareness and subsidiary awareness:

> ... when we use a hammer to drive in a nail, we attend to both nail and hammer, *but in a different way*. We *watch* the effect of our strokes on the nail and try to wield the hammer so as to hit the nail most effectively. When we bring down the hammer we do not feel that its handle has struck our palm but that its head has struck the nail. (Polanyi, 1962: 55, original emphasis)

The focal awareness is on driving in the nail, the subsidiary awareness on the feeling on the palm of the hand. We pay close attention to feelings when they are the instruments of our attention not because they are the object of our attention. The conclusion is that, in general, we do not have focal awareness of the instruments over which we have gained mastery.

The example of hammering is also paradigmatic of the knowledge that arises when breakdown occurs and reflexive activity intervenes. If the hammer breaks when the carpenter is hammering, reflexive knowledge is likely to occur. Reflexive, investigative, theoretical knowledge requires that something previously usable must now be unusable. The world of

Introduction
Silvia Gherardi

objects thus becomes 'simply present' (*Vorhanden*), no longer under-stood. Yet breakdowns are meaningful only when the carpenter has already understood the hammer in practice. When the carpenter is ham-mering unimpeded the hammer with its properties does not exist, for it is not paid attention to.

These examples, altogether, bring us back to knowledge and practice in organizational studies. In its association with the phenomenological tra-dition, the concept of *practice* reveals how comprehension of situations where one is 'thrown headlong into use' is pre-reflexive and does not draw distinctions among subject, object, thought or context. It also reveals how reflexive understanding arises at moments of breakdown. The tra-dition of action research has made much use of the method of the critical incident to stimulate reflection on the conditions that govern normality. Ethnomethodology, too, has been used to show how the breaching of rules exposes the rule-based operations that produce a 'normal' situation. These perspectives help us to see organizations as systems of practices, existing in the world of tacit knowledge. That is, tacit knowledge that is simply usable but that becomes the object of reflection when a breakdown occurs.

The phenomenological concept of practice is perhaps less well known than the Marxist use of the term, which assigns to practice an emancipa-tory force. As a notion central to Marxist epistemology, practice stands in contrast with the Cartesian notion of detached reflection, of the separ-ation between mind and body, and also stands in polemic with rational-ism, positivism and scientism. Practice, in this case, is an epistemological principle. If, as knowing subjects, we are to know that things are inde-pendent of us, we must first subject them to our own praxis. That is, in order to know how things are when they are not in contact with us, we must first enter into contact with them.

Practice is both our production of the world and the result of this process. It is always the product of specific historical conditions resulting from previous practice and transformed into present practice. The important contribution of this tradition to practice-based theorizing is its methodological insight that practice is a system of activities in which knowing is not separate from doing. Further, learning is a social and par-ticipative activity rather than merely a cognitive activity (e.g. Blackler, 1993).

Participating in a practice is consequently a way to acquire knowledge-in-action, but also to change or perpetuate such knowledge and to pro-duce and reproduce society. Ehn (1988) remarks that mind, culture and society are constantly reproduced in activity systems, which can there-fore be described in terms of practice-as-work (as regards the transform-ation of a given work process), practice-as-language (as regards professional language and interaction within a given work process), and practice-as-morality (as regards the politics and power of the different groups or social classes involved in a given work process).

215

Organization 7(2)
Introduction

From still another perspective language, as a distinctive feature of human activity systems, is also a practice that can be addressed in Wittgenstein's (1953) notion of a linguistic game. Language is a social, not a private fact; linguistic terms arise within a social practice of meaning construction. Participation in a practice entails taking part in a professional language game, mastering the rules and being able to use them. Having a concept means that one has learnt to obey rules within a given practice. Speech acts, as units of language and action are, therefore, part of a given practice rather than descriptions of that practice. It is in this sense that language is not only the expression of social relations but also the medium for their creation (e.g. Czarniawska-Joerges, 1991).

Those who participate in the practice of a linguistic game must share in the 'life form' that makes such practice possible, for sharing in a 'life form' is the prerequisite for understanding and transmitting so-called propositional knowledge. This is the type of knowledge acquired through the practical understanding of an operation. For example, carpenters participate in a professional language game, and they are able to 'tell' others about the procedures that they follow to make a chair. But the (propositional) knowledge that I can acquire in this way is different from practical understanding of the real operation of 'making a chair'. The propositional knowledge of how to make a chair, and how to describe the process, is qualitatively different from knowing how to use a hammer (practical knowledge) or from knowing when to change hammer and which type of hammer is best suited for a certain type of nails.

Finally, there is knowledge transmitted through the senses by virtue of familiarity with previous situations and a refinement of sensibilities toward those situations. This is the connoisseur's knowledge (Turner, 1988) possessed by persons, by professional communities and by industries. From this perspective, participating in a practice is to learn the logic of that practice; what Bourdieu calls *sens pratique* as opposed to the logic of discourse. Unlike the logic of discourse, which functions by making the work of thought explicit in a linear series of signs, *sens pratique* is pre-reflexive.

Bourdieu's conceptualizations provide another avenue to understanding the relationship between tacit and explicit knowledge, reflexive and pre-reflexive thought, through the notion of practice. It allows us to ask, can organization studies give due recognition to the fact that the *sens pratique* of organizing is inscribed in the bodies and in the *habitus* of practices? That it is much more than whatever can be described, for instance, in terms of standard operating procedures? Can organization studies, at the same time, recognize that reflexive thought—which nullifies the logic of practice—is necessary to theorize and understand the *habitus* itself?

The logic of practice is necessary for the order and continuity of an organization. Practical knowledge is kept within the *habitus*, which, as the historical product of previous individual and collective practices, produces historical 'anchors' and ensures the correctness of practices and

Introduction
Silvia Gherardi

their constancy over time more reliably than formal and explicit rules. At the same time, the replication of the logic of practice contributes to its transformation simply by making it explicit. Disembedding knowledge is an act of reflexive logic which betrays the logic of practice. It inserts distance, reflection and separation between subject and object where previously there was no distinction between subject and the world; both were totally present and caught up by the 'matter in hand'.

In summary, there are evidently numerous and diverse routes regarding 'knowledge' that can be followed under the umbrella-concept of practice. These routes may meet and then once again diverge. Yet, as a figure of discourse, the term 'practice' is a *topos* which articulates two common themes: spatiality and facticity. Altogether, *practice* articulates knowledge in and about organizing as practical accomplishment, rather than as a transcendental account of decontextualized reality, whether one assumes a realist ontology or a social constructionist one.

Practice Articulates Spatiality

When Etienne Wenger (1998) gave thorough treatment to the concept of 'community of practice', two largely interchangeable linguistic artifacts were in circulation: 'situated knowledge' and 'social learning'. In this sense, 'social' relates to the collective subject, to the subjective forms of participation in social practices, to learning as the epistemic link with the world, to knowledge as a social product. These views reintroduce into organization studies the concept of practice as work, which transforms identity, activity and social relations (Brown et al., 1989; Lave and Wenger, 1991; Brown and Duguid, 1991).

When the locus of knowledge and learning is situated in practice, the focus moves to the social, albeit in different ways according to the researcher. The concern may be mainly with the collective subject (community of practice, community of activity) that possesses and implements knowledge; it may be with the social as mediating among subjects who transmit knowledge and codify it in a *habitus*; or it may be with a social theory of action which addresses activity and passivity, the cognitive and the emotional. Mental and sensory perceptions become bits and pieces of the social construction of knowledge, and of the social worlds in which practices assume meanings and facticity (e.g. Gagliardi, 1990; Star, 1996; Gomart and Hennion, 1999; Gherardi, 1999; Strati, 1999).

However, it is the cultural perspective that has most thoroughly developed the concept of situated knowledge, and of interpretative practices as situated in specific contexts (e.g. Cook and Yanow, 1993). The local–global dynamic accounts for the transfer of knowledge from one context to another (Geertz, 1973), and for the problematic nature of the decontextualization of knowledge by 'science', ethnography or qualitative sociology (Marcus, 1994). It is difficult to treat the cultural approach as a homogeneous strand of thought, given that it comprises a multitude of conflicting discourses. However, a demarcation line can be drawn along

Organization 7(2)
Introduction

the boundary between modernism and postmodernism, which has consequences on the way in which context and situated knowledge are understood and defined (Fox, 1997).

Consistent with a modernist project is the view of context as pre-given, although the effects of objective social structures are not determined but take shape within socio-economic relations. On the other hand, the concept of context as 'emergent' is more in keeping with a postmodernist project.

> In the postmodern view, 'context' is no longer 'out there' in the messy, complex surface of an objective world; rather, that very surface complexity and confusion are a projection of language itself, the inconsistencies of its classifications, taxonomies, dichotomies, and more. (Fox, 1997: 741)

ANT and the sociology of science and technology entirely dissolve the concept of context, although they retain the idea of situatedness. The former operation takes place when the action–system or subject–action dichotomies are dissolved: 'actors are network effects'; they acquire the attributes of the entities which they include (Law, 1999). The latter operation comes about through the idea of 'performativity': if entities (human or non-human) achieve their form as a consequence of the relations in which they are located, and if relations do not hold fast by themselves, then they have to be performed in, by and through those relations.

It would be an unpardonable oversight (to say the least!) if this section did not recognize the authority of the feminist voice in discussion of 'situated knowledges', and in revealing the androcentrism of both the structures and the practices of knowledge through which social experience has been understood. The alleged 'objectivity' of knowledge and science has strategically concealed their gendered nature, as well as the power relations that determine what counts as knowledge. The feminist critique of science, and feminist works in the sociology of science and technology helped to show that even 'universal' knowledge is situated, while feminist objectivity simply means bodily situated knowledge (e.g. Fujimura et al., 1987; Harding, 1986; Haraway, 1991; Star, 1991; Mol, 1999). The advantage of a 'partial perspective'—the term is Donna Haraway's taken forward by Marilyn Strathern (1991)—is that knowledge always has to do with circumscribed domains, not with transcendence and the subject/object dichotomy.

Practice Articulates Fabrication

Practice connects 'knowing' with 'doing'. It conveys the image of materiality, of fabrication, of handiwork, of the craftsman's skill in the medieval *bottega d'arte*. In scientific laboratories, science is not just 'social construction'; it is construction *tout court*. From the Latin verb *facere*, Knorr-Cetina (1981) uses the term 'facticity', and Bruno Latour (1987) the 'fabrication' of scientific facts and technical artifacts. Knowledge consequently does not arise from scientific 'discoveries'; rather, it is fabricated

Introduction
Silvia Gherardi

by situated practices of knowledge production and reproduction, using the technologies of representation and mobilization employed by scientists.

The sociology of science thus deposes scientific knowledge from the pedestal upon which positivism placed it. It asserts that scientific knowledge should be treated as a culture like any other form of knowledge, and therefore that it too is subject to social control and social interests. The connection between power and knowledge is thematized together with ethical questions and issues concerning social change. The metaphor of 'ecologies of knowledge' (Star, 1995) is proposed in order to locate knowledge production in an ecosystem which rejects the dichotomies of functionalist thought, like those between nature and society, and between social and technical. It is argued that science and technology become monsters when they sever their connections with the social conditions of their production (Haraway, 1991; Law, 1991; Star, 1991).

If the practices of knowledge production are thus ennobled by the metaphor of the laboratory, then the practical knowledge intrinsic to the work is dignified as well. The study of knowing in practice can follow the same methodological principle stated by Latour (1987) for the analysis of science as practice: 'follow the actors' in order to identify the ways in which they associate the various elements that make up their social and natural world (Hughes, 1971; Callon, 1980).

The laboratory is a metaphor for the controversial nature of knowledge and its materiality. Practice conveys the contingent conditions and materiality of the world into knowledge. A practice-based theory of action dissolves, amongst other things, the distinction between order and disorder. An 'activity system', to use Engenström's as well as Blackler's term, is a disturbance-producing system, constituted by incoherences, inconsistencies, paradoxes and tensions.

Other adjectives have been used for concepts of knowledge which are partially similar and overlapping: 'historical', 'materialist', 'indeterminate'. However, for us, the point is not to go in search of a framework which comprises all these reflections in a single space, but rather to show how a practice-based theorizing arises from multiple perspectives and negotiations, and how in so doing delegitimizes a univocal narrative of scientific authority.

Conclusion or Mutual Inclusion?

While I was reflecting upon the fact that we authors who study how knowledge is produced/utilized/transmitted in the practices of 'others' pay little regard to how we ourselves produce 'expert' knowledge, there came to mind an article by a friend and colleague, Roy Jacques, the title of which talks about producing knowledge 'from the kitchen'.

Roy Jacques uses the kitchen as a place of sharing, and as a place to sustain an ethic of care in research. There we need to be present as embodied people:

219

Organization 7(2)
Introduction

> Metaphorically, I may visit you and converse in your kitchen and you may visit
> me in mine ... In my kitchen, certain values may prevail, and in yours, other
> values may be prominent; we need not transcend these differences to converse
> ... What is more important than a common framework is a mutual desire to
> connect with the other's meanings. (Jacques, 1992: 595–96)

Thinking of kitchens reminded me that a large number of organization studies consist of recipes, although the term seems pejorative. Yet, despite the recipe-like shape of many organization studies, it seems ironic that the eyes and sight are used as metaphors (in the etymological sense of carrier) for knowledge, while the mouth and taste are neglected. Nonetheless, taste is tied to memory. It conjures up memories and, as such, it is also a source of knowledge.

My mind then turned to the numerous novelists who alternate narrative with cooking recipes: Jorge Amado (1966), for example, in his *Dona Flor e seus dois maridos*, where he successfully attempts to convey the flavour of life in his stories and recipes; or Clara Sereni (1987), whose *Casalinghitudine* describes the flavours, personages and recipes of her kitchen to evoke her past as a left-wing militant, young mother and daughter of a famous Jewish and communist Senator.

What then is the flavour of this introduction? I may tell the reader that our symposium in San Diego tasted of the fish that we all ate together at dinner in the Fish Market, when our conversations interwove and we all had to lean across the table to hear and be heard. Our bodies and heads were bent forward to make an arch, while our fingers smelt of fish. I believe that our 'true' symposium—the allusion being to Plato's—took place in that restaurant, and not the next day when we put on our professional identities for performing the symposium for the public.

Yet, producing knowledge 'from the practice' is like producing knowledge 'from the kitchen': both are 'second-sexed' domains of discourse because they occupy a female position with respect to functionalist theories of knowledge. The importance of a functionalist theory is judged on the basis of its relation to objective, decontextualized truth, operating in the domain of the gaze. Practical knowledge, contingent and useful, is the Cinderella in the kitchen, that can never claim the status of the Science that 'discovers' and the Technology that 'applies'. A gender sub-text too is at work to define what counts as knowledge.

Paradoxically, a practice-based theorizing of learning and knowing in organizations cannot be synthesized like a cookery recipe, although I have tried to show its principal ingredients. A better metaphor is that of an open conversation which develops as it proceeds. In this conversation, there are a number of voices representing discursive positions which, with the inevitable inaccuracy and distortion of labels, can be called situated learning theory, cultural perspective, activity theory and actor-network theory.

Practice is the figure of discourse that allows the processes of 'knowing' at work and in organizing to be articulated as historical processes,

Introduction
Silvia Gherardi

material and indeterminate. As Barthes (1977) points out, a figure of discourse is a *topos* offered to the reader so that s/he may take possession of it, add something to it, remove what s/he does not need and pass it on to others. In this same way, knowledge-producing practices may either be annulled to sustain disembodied and disembedded scientific authority, or they may become the object of reflexive knowledge. Thus, in my view, *discursive practice* is the fundamental element in a practice-based theorizing of knowing. That is, the meaning of knowing is given in a community of listeners and speakers, and every new occasion for the use of this *topos* recast it in a more densely textured form. In short, the theories we create and the ways we talk about them are not separate.

References

Amado, Jorge (1966) *Dona Flor e seus dois maridos*. São Paulo: Livraria Martins.
Barthes, Roland (1977) *Fragments d'un discours amoureux*. Paris: Editions du Seuil.
Blackler, Frank (1993) 'Knowledge and the Theory of Organizations: Organizations as Activity Systems and the Reframing of Management', *Journal of Management Studies* 30(6): 864–84.
Bourdieu, Pierre (1990) *The Logic of Practice*. Stanford, CA: Stanford University Press.
Brown, John S. and Duguid, Paul (1991) 'Organizational Learning and Communities of Practice: Toward a Unified View of Working, Learning, and Innovation', *Organization Science* 2(1): 40–57.
Brown, John S., Collins, Allan and Duguid, Paul (1989) 'Situated Cognition and the Culture of Learning', *Educational Researcher* 18(1): 32–42.
Callon, Michel (1980) 'Struggles and Negotiations to Define what is Problematic and what is not: The Sociology of Translation', in K. Knorr, R. Krohn and R. Whitley (eds) *The Social Process of Scientific Investigation*, pp. 197–219. Boston, MA: Reidel.
Cook, Scott and Yanow, Dvora (1993) 'Culture and Organizational Learning', *Journal of Management Inquiry* 2(4): 373–90.
Czarniawska-Joerges, Barbara (1991) 'Culture is the Medium of Life', in P.J. Frost et al. (eds) *Reframing Organizational Culture*, pp. 285–97. Newbury Park, CA: Sage.
Easterby-Smith, Mark, Snell, Robin and Gherardi, Silvia (1998) 'Organizational Learning and Learning Organization: Diverging Communities of Practice?', *Management Learning* 29(3): 259–72.
Ehn, Pale (1988) *Work-oriented Design of Computer Artifacts*. Stockholm: Arbetlivscentrum.
Fox, Stephen (1997) 'Situated Learning Theory Versus Traditional Cognitive Learning Theory: Why Management Education should not Ignore Management Learning', *Systems Practice* 10(6): 727–47.
Fujimura, Joan, Star, Susan and Gerson, E. (1987) 'Méthode de recherche en sociologie des sciences: travail, pragmatisme et interactionisme symbolique', *Cahiers de Recherches Sociologiques* 5: 65–85.
Gagliardi, Pasquale (1990) 'Artifacts as Pathways and Remains of Organizational Life', in P. Gagliardi (ed.) *Symbols and Artifacts,* pp. 3–38. Berlin: de Gruyter.
Geertz, Clifford (1973) *The Interpretation of Cultures*. New York: Basic Books.

Organization 7(2)
Introduction

Gherardi, Silvia (1999) 'Learning as Problem-driven or Learning in the Face of Mystery?', *Organization Studies* 20(1): 101–24.

Gomart, Emilie and Hennion, Antoine (1999) 'A Sociology of Attachment: Music Amateurs, Drug Users', in J. Law and J. Hassard *Actor Network Theory and After*, pp. 220–47. Oxford: Blackwell.

Haraway, Donna (1991) 'Situated Knowledges: The Science Question in Feminism and the Privilege of Partial Perspectives', in D. Haraway *Simians, Cyborgs and Women: The Reinvention of Nature*, pp. 183-202. London: Free Association Books.

Harding, Sandra (1986) *The Science Question in Feminism*. Ithaca, NY: Cornell University.

Heidegger, Martin (1962) *Being and Time*. New York: Harper & Row.

hooks, belle (1994) *Teaching to Transgress: Education as the Practice of Freedom*. New York: Routledge.

Hughes, Everett (1971) *The Sociological Eye*. Chicago: Aldine.

Jacques, Roy (1992) 'Critique and Theory Building: Producing Knowledge "From the Kitchen"', *Academy of Management Review* 17(3): 582–606.

Knorr-Cetina, Katerine (1981) *The Manufacture of Knowledge. An Essay on the Constructivist and Contextual Nature of Science*. Oxford: Pergamon Press.

Latour, Bruno (1987) *Science in Action: How to Follow Scientists and Engineers through Society*. Milton Keynes: Open University Press.

Latour, Bruno (1993) *We Have Never Been Modern*. New York: Harvester Wheatsheaf.

Lave, Jean and Wenger, Etienne (1991) *Situated Learning. Legitimate Peripheral Participation*. Cambridge, MA: University Press.

Law, John, ed., (1991) *A Sociology of Monsters? Power, Technology and the Modern World*, Sociological Review Monograph No. 38. London: Routledge.

Law, John (1999) 'After ANT: Complexity, Naming and Topology', in J. Law and J. Hassard *Actor Network Theory and After*, pp. 1–14. Oxford: Blackwell.

Leonard-Barton, Dorothy (1995) *Wellsprings of Knowledge*. Boston, MA: Harvard Business School Press.

March, James and Simon, Herbert (1958) *Organizations*. New York: Wiley.

Marcus, G. (1994) 'What Comes (just) after "Post"? The Case of Ethnography', in N.K. Denzin and Y.S. Lincoln (eds) *Handbook of Qualitative Research*, pp. 563–74. London: Sage.

Mol, Annamarie (1999) 'Ontological Politics', in J. Law and J. Hassard *Actor Network Theory and After*, pp. 75–89. Oxford: Blackwell.

Nicolini, Davide and Meznar, Martin (1995) 'The Social Construction of Organizational Learning', *Human Relations* 48(7): 727–46.

Polanyi, Michel (1962) *Personal Knowledge*. London: Routledge (1st edn, 1958).

Prahalad, C.K. and Hamel, G. (1990) 'The Core Competence of the Corporation', *Harvard Business Review* (May–June): 79–91.

Sereni, Clara (1987) *Casalinghitudine*. Torino: Einaudi.

Star, Susan L. (1991) 'Power, Technologies and the Phenomenology of Standards: On being Allergic to Onions', in J. Law (ed.) *A Sociology of Monsters? Power, Technology and the Modern World*, Sociological Review Monograph No. 38. London: Routledge.

Star, Susan L. (1995) *Ecologies of Knowledge*. Albany, NY: State University of New York Press.

Star, Susan L. (1996) 'Working together: Symbolic Interactionism, Activity

Introduction
Silvia Gherardi

Theory, and Information Systems', in Y. Engeström and D. Middleton *Cognition and Communication at Work*, pp. 296–318. Cambridge: Cambridge University Press.

Strathern, Marilyn (1991) *Partial Connections*. Savage, MD: Rowman & Littlefield.

Strati, Antonio (1999) *Organization and Aesthetics*. London: Sage.

Turner, Barry A. (1988) 'Connoisseurship in the Study of Organizational Cultures', in A. Bryman (ed.) *Doing Research in Organizations*, pp. 108–22. London: Routledge.

von Hippel, E. (1994) 'Sticky Information and the Locus of Problem Solving: Implications for Innovation', *Management Science* 40(4): 429–39.

Wenger, Etienne (1998) *Communities of Practice. Learning, Meaning and Identity*. Cambridge: Cambridge University Press.

Winograd, T. and Flores, F. (1986) *Understanding Computers and Cognition: A New Foundation for Design*. Norwood: Ablex.

Wittgenstein, Ludwig (1953) *Philosophical Investigations*. Oxford: Blackwell.

Silvia Gherardi is professor of sociology of organization at the University of Trento, Italy. Her research activities focus on workplace learning and knowing. Her theoretical background is in qualitative sociology and organizational symbolism. She is working on a book—together with Davide Nicolini—which encapsulates her present research interest in a practice-based theory of learning. She also conducts research studies and training programmes for the development of women's competencies and participation in organizations. Her latest book (*Gender, Symbolism and Organizational Cultures*, Sage, 1995) is devoted to the theme of gender and organizational cultures. **Address**: Dipartimento di Sociologia e Ricerca Sociale, Via Verdi 26, 38100 Trento, Italy. [email: silvia.gherardi@soc.unitn.it]

[2]

Knowing in Practice: Aesthetic Understanding and Tacit Knowledge

Antonio Strati

Introduction

My main argument in this chapter is that an aesthetic approach to understanding the tacitness of organizational knowledge can provide the researcher with crucial insights into the interpersonal nature of knowing in practice in organizational life. Study of the dynamics of organizational learning focuses on people's work and organizational skills and the social construction of the latter by processes of organizational interaction that are not always explicit, formalizable, or even apparent. In these cases, one talks of tacit knowledge, of practical expertise, and of learning situated in the social practices that people implement within organizations or on their behalf. But one should also talk of aesthetic knowledge, for this would induce scholars to break with the dominant tradition of cognitive theory on organizational learning and managerial training. Aesthetic understanding, in fact, prompts considerations that question and undermine the exclusive reliance on cognition—on the rational and mental—by studies of social phenomena in organizational settings that take due account of our knowing in practice, as experienced and supported by the senses rather than just the way that we think.

This is the thesis argued in this chapter, which is organized as follows. I first outline what is meant by aesthetics in organizational theories and management studies and then show the close interweaving between aesthetics and tacit knowledge. I conclude with discussion of the meaning of an approach to the study of organizations that concentrates on the aesthetic dimension, and the value that derives from it for the traditional analysis of organizational learning.

Aesthetic Understanding and Organizational Studies

Aesthetic knowledge is the form of knowledge that persons acquire by activating the specific capacities of their perceptive-sensorial faculties and aesthetic judgment (Baumgarten, 1750–58; Kant, 1790; Vico, 1725) in the day-to-day lives of organizations. Aesthetics highlights and legitimates the personal sentiment as an intersubjective form of knowing (Carchia and D'Angelo, 1999: 257), that is, a sentiment which is both individual and collectively constructed in the interactive acts by individuals of experiencing, understanding and judging through senses and taste. Aesthetics has been the matter of much controversy during the last three centuries, and radical transformations occurred in the last century especially because of the interplay between the conceptualizations of artists and the studies of social scientists. Yet a common ground emerged from these debates, and it regarded the central topic of this chapter, namely the close relationship between aesthetics and knowledge.

Contemporary discussion of aesthetics draws a distinction between "continental philosophy"—which focuses on the culturally constructed subjects of study and their historical roots—and "analytical philosophy," which stresses structured and rigorous analysis and is grounded in logical positivism and empiricism. Both styles of philosophical research emphasize the contribution of aesthetics to knowledge. According to continental philosophy—which is the intellectual background to this chapter—in recent decades the aesthetic experience has been redefined as "vital to an understanding of the relationship between mind and world. The aesthetic, formerly exiled from mainstream attention, assumes centre-stage as the region to which we can turn for new cognitive possibilities and a sensibility that is critical of the divisions exercised by modern thought" (Cazeaux, 2000: xiii).

Analytic philosophers place different emphases on the contribution of aesthetics to knowledge. As regards art, for example, Eileen John comments that it is a source of cognive stimulation—thoughts, feelings, desires—which prompts conscious activity, creates or shapes categories of knowledge, and is an important resource "for studying the role of such factors as creativity, surprise, interest, and choice in the emergence of new ideas" (2001: 340).

Some three centuries ago, philosophical aesthetics was formed and debated in terms of:

(a) the antithesis to Cartesian rational explanation constituted by emphasis on mythical poetry, the *mythos*, the mythological imagination, reasoning by metaphors, or mythical thought, and the close and constant connection between what is thought and what is felt by the body's sensory and perceptive faculties (Vico, 1725);

(b) the sensitive judgment that enables assessment of feelings, phantasms, fictions, and other things that the intellectual judgment is unable to understand (Baumgarten, 1735, 1750–58). Involved here is whatever impinges on our senses and is part of our sensory experience, or in other words, the complex of representations that subsist beneath the analytical distinctions drawn by the science of sensible knowledge and the art of fine thought, the goal of which is the perfection of sensible knowledge in itself;

(c) the aesthetic judgment applied to the perfection or imperfection of a . particular thing. This is a sensible judgment that does not yield judgments, but rather evaluations of perceived perfection or imperfection that have the nature of sentiment and taste (Addison, 1712; Baumgarten, 1735; Kant, 1790) or a judgment in harmony with feelings instead of concepts.

The aesthetics addressed and discussed in organizational theories is therefore *aisthánomai, aisthetes, aisthetikós, aisthánesthai,* that is, expressions that all highlighted—in ancient Greek—the act of perceiving, and to which Baumgarten referred when coining the modern term "aesthetics." It concerns feeling the pathos of an organization's material and nonmaterial artifacts, perceiving an organization's beauty, appreciating the grandiosity of certain organizational practices, feeling disgust at certain courses of organizational action. As the act of perceiving and judging sensorially, *aesthetics is that form of organizational knowledge which is personal and collectively socially constructed at once.* To have a good eye or a refined taste is a personal sensorial faculty acting in—and shaped by—interpersonal relationships in organizational settings and in society. This is a source of differentiation among organization participants, given that not everyone sees the same things, reacts to the same odors, or has the same taste: there are those who "have an eye" for things while others do not; those who have an "ear" or a "nose," those who are "good with their hands," or "have taste." This socially constructed personal knowledge is ineradicable and irreducible: indeed, a remark on an organizational event to the effect that "I don't like this" may be unarguable, given that further reason-based negotiation on the matter is impossible. This is an aesthetic judgment and it brings to the fore the close connection between aesthetics and art in organizational understanding (Dégot, 1987; Jones, Moore, and Snyder, 1988; Strati and Guillet de Montoux, 2002).

Art has a cognitive value and can be a source of both knowledge and pleasure, since it provides insights about ourselves and our styles of living social matters (Young, 2001). Moreover, art is pure formativeness, writes Luigi Pareyson (1954), and the artistic action is a process of inventing and making that is not intended to produce speculative or practical works, but is instead addressed to the production of the form itself. Formativeness, however, refers to every human action, since all human actions are directed to forming something—the art of managing beautifully, for example—even though only in art *per se* is shape given to the form itself.

To resume, debate on art and aesthetics in organization theories has led to valorization of:

1. the *central importance of the human person* in the process of organizational knowledge;
2. the *corporeality of personal knowledge* in organizational life;
3. the *socially constructed character of aesthetic knowing* in organizational settings;
4. the *relationship between persons and forms*, since everyday life is characterized by an inexhaustible process of interpreting, inventing, and reshaping forms by its participants.

What bearing, therefore, does the study of aesthetics and organization (Dean, Ottensmeyer, and Ramirez, 1997; Gagliardi, 1996; Hatch, 1997; Linstead and Höpfl, 2000; Strati, 1999) have on organizational learning? It shows that the latter cannot be confined to the sphere of cognition and of the translation of all forms of knowledge into cognitive knowledge. Rather, due account should be taken of the personal knowledge based on the faculty of aesthetic judgment and the perceptive-sensorial capacities. On this rests the radical break with the dominant tradition of cognitive theory on organizational learning that aesthetic understanding entails. On this is grounded the interweaving between aesthetic knowing and tacit knowledge.

The practical knowledge acquired through the five senses of sight, hearing, smell, taste, and touch, and the faculty of aesthetic judgment connected to them, was also considered by Michael Polanyi (1962) when he drew the distinction between explicit knowledge and tacit knowledge: the former type of knowledge is formalized in scientific terms; the latter is constituted by the *awareness of knowing* how to do something without being able to provide an adequate analytical description of it and, therefore, without being able to translate it into formal, universalistic, and generalizable knowledge. It is for this latter form of knowledge that the aesthetic understanding is fundamental.

Aesthetics and Observations in the Field

In research and study on learning in organizations as social contexts (Strati, 2000), when attention has focused on organizational practices, the use of tacit knowledge described by Polanyi (1962) has sometimes emerged

(Baumard, 1996; Brown and Duguid, 1991; Cook and Yanow, 1993; Fox, 1997; Gherardi, 2000; Nonaka and Takeuchi, 1995). This form of knowledge constitutes the common ground between the debate on organizational aesthetics and that on organizational learning. This is one of the main themes of this chapter, and it will be examined on the basis of empirical observations of the work of stripping and re-laying a roof. These observations will be set out using an evocative rather than analytical style, given that this is the distinguishing feature of the aesthetic approach (Strati, 1992), and that style is like theory in the study of organizations since "staking out a theoretical position is unavoidably a rhetorical act" (Van Maanen, 1995: 134).

I was observing a meeting for the purposes of my research. When I looked out of the window I saw three workmen dismantling the roof of a nearby two-storey building. My attention had been drawn by the racket made by the workmen as, with an almost rhythmic cadence, they threw the tiles and other material stripped from the roof down into the yard below. Distracted but also intrigued, I watched what was happening on the roof and in the yard, and I was struck by the workmen's apparent disregard for safety systems, although these had apparently been adequately installed. For example, none of the workmen was attached to the ropes, and they ignored the hand-grips provided to move around the roof. The latter, in fact, sloped steeply, and as the building was two stories high, there was a considerable risk of injury if a workman slipped or lost his balance. But I was most struck, as I have described elsewhere (1999: 89),

> by the movements of one of the workmen. Although plump to the point of obesity, he moved up and down the roof with surprising agility. He was obviously in charge because he was gesticulating orders to the others. If he saw that one of his workmates was doing something wrong or had not understood, he went to help him, hanging onto the rope with one hand to descend the roof, hauling himself up with the rope to ascend, on some occasions even grabbing the chimney stack. Once he had reached the other workman, he took over, almost pushing him out of the way. I also gained the impression that his was the most satisfying, most difficult and most demanding job. All three workers, however, were intent on removing the old tiles from the roofing timbers. They then took the stripped materials and threw them down to the yard below. As the debris hit the ground, it made a variety of thumps and crashes, all equally annoying, and all of which disturbed the meeting.

It should be pointed out, however, that:

(a) The above observations were gathered coincidentally with an ongoing empirical study of organizational cultures in a manufacturing organization. The point of observation, the forms and time-scale of the observation, and the attention paid to the organizational practices on the roof were conditioned by this fact. I was observing a department meeting called to discuss sensitive matters, and in order to be as unobtrusive as possible I had sat in a peripheral part of the room next to the window, while my work instruments were placed on the floor or used as something to fiddle with distractedly.

(b) The considerations prompted by these observations took the form of a "first impression" rather than careful and rigorous analysis. The observation had been neither continual nor structured; nor had it involved the measurements so pervasive even in qualitative empirical research conducted in organizational settings. I had not counted the workers' hand movements as they stripped the roof, nor did I have any clear idea of how many times they had walked across the roof, how many times two of them had worked together, or how many times assistance had been requested or offered, how much work was progressively made. Nor was it possible for me to restart the observation from scratch. In short, I had no numerical data, but instead impressions, ethical evaluations and aesthetic judgments, which, instead of giving answers, asked questions.

(c) My "first impression" was informed with fear and concern, due partly to the fact that the research group of which I was a member (Research Unit on Cognition, Organizational Learning and Aesthetics) was studying safety practices in diverse organizational contexts, one of which was the building trade.

At this point the readers have sufficient information to try, should they so wish, to "put themselves in my place" and imagine (i) the awkwardness of my situation as an "absent/present observer" of the difficult departmental meeting, and (ii) the conflict caused by my unexpected fascination and interest in the organization observed outside the window as it set about stripping the roof: a second line of research that was entirely extraneous to the first. If the readers do so "put themselves" in my place, they will be in the same position as someone who conducts "imaginary participant observation" (Strati, 1999: 11–18)—that is, observation grounded on the ability to immerse oneself imaginatively in an organizational situation and based on the evocative process of knowing organizational life, which characterizes—besides the aesthetic approach—interpretative and introspective streams in "ethnography" (see, e.g., Coffey, Holbrook, and Atkinson, 1996; Henley, 1998; Walker, 1993). They may rely on exclusively intellective reflection but also, by activating their perceptive-sensorial faculties, on aesthetic judgment, emotions, and aesthetic sentiments. If they try, again using their imagination, to "sit" in my place, "looking" out of the window and "feeling" discomfort caused by awareness that the focus of their analysis is not events on the roof, experiencing the aesthetic attraction of what was seen and heard, which implied distracting themselves from previously careful planned research, then they will be in the situation of someone conducting—at the imaginative level, of course—direct and personal observation of the work of that particular organization. By virtue of participant observation conducted through the imagination, the readers "see," "hear," "perceive," and "are aware of" the research process in which they are imaginatively taking part through sensorial faculties rather than intellectual abilities.

The principal and most interesting feature of imaginary participatory observation is the following: if the readers decide to engage in this form of knowledge-gathering, the above description may prompt them to ask questions very different from the ones that I asked. They might not, for example, give particular importance to the workplace safety practices of the three workmen, or they might not be surprised by the agility of their movements as they worked on the roof. They might, for instance, focus on technological innovation and the work practices on the roof, or on organizational communication and the construction of gendered organizational discourses that might mobilize masculinity (Martin, 2001) in the context of these practices.

My questions were prompted by my strong reaction to the fact that the three workmen were engaged in organizational practices that literally removed the ground from beneath their feet, and to do so used what I found to be surprising work methods. They worked quickly, as if they had been overcome by a destructive frenzy and drew pleasure from the noise made by the pieces of roof as they hit the ground in the yard below (which obviously were been closed off). What I observed was not slow and deliberate movements but

1. confidence in footwork and posture, and manual dexterity,
2. speed, as if the roof had to be stripped as quickly as possible,
3. the rhythm of the work set by the regular cadence of the pieces of roof crashing into the yard below,
4. the focusing of attention on the task at hand,
5. organizational communication made up of gesticulations and few words,
6. the performance of several tasks, which required changing place on the roof as the work progressed, changing posture according to the operation to perform, moving across the roof to help a workmate.

Now, although some questions had been answered by my observations—for example, how the men coordinated work, which hierarchical practices were in use, how far body expressions were legitimated forms of organizational communication—there was one that was still unanswered: why did the workmen not slip or put a foot wrong? The slope of the roof, the varying nature of the materials ripped free and thrown into the yard, the alternation of individual work and cooperation, and the progressive actualization of stripping the roof—these were aspects which, taken together:

1. enhanced my concern about conceptions of safety and risk in organizations whose business is working on roofs, both dismantling them and constructing, repairing and re-laying them;
2. highlighted that my observations had not produced knowledge about how an organization of this kind could operate.

Conversations on Organizational Learning

When the meeting had finished and we were going off for lunch, I decided to stop for a moment in the yard, where the workmen were now taking their lunch break seated amid the debris from the roof, and ask them my questions: How do you do it? How is it done?

The first reaction was laughter, which may have been due to embarrassment, or to self-satisfaction, or even to scorn at the professor who could not understand. This was followed by an exchange of wisecracks in dialect that I could not follow, and then by an answer from the workman whom I took to be the leader. Stamping his feet, he said that the secret lay in "feeling the roof with your feet": in feeling, that is to say, that your feet are firmly fixed to it. This was not enough, however. You must never make awkward movements that might cause a loss of balance that your legs, even though they were well planted, could not counteract. You had to "look with your ears," because noises were a valuable source of information. You had to watch the others, see what they were doing, what point they had reached, ask how they felt, exchange views and instructions, give a hand if necessary. You needed your hands to work, not to hold onto the roof. It was your legs that kept you on the roof, which you felt firmly "attached to your feet."

During the next few days I again paused to talk to the workmen as they took their lunch break. The topic was always the same, but I changed the questions, asking how one could learn to work on the roof. What was it that one needed to know from the beginning? What was it that you had to be able to do? How could you know what you had to be able to do before you went up on the roof to do it?

"You mustn't be afraid of being up there on the roof," one of the other workmen said; "you mustn't be scared of heights," or of the "open air," or of the "view" up there. But, the foreman insisted, lack of fear "is of little use if you don't feel the roof with your feet" and if "you don't feel yourself nailed to the roof." How do you learn to feel yourself nailed to the roof? "It's something that has to come naturally," answered the foreman, something that "you have to learn the very first time" because afterwards it's too late," at which the others laughed. I saw that the grotesque and the ridiculous—the distinctive features of the aesthetic category of the "comic"—were part of the language-in-use of that roof-stripping and re-laying organization, although they did not extend it to include me as well.

The workmen noticed that I was not amused by the idea that someone who did not know that s/he did not know how to work on a roof might fall and be injured. They therefore began to talk to me seriously about what should be taught to a "male" novice roof-stripper—"you can't expect a woman doing this job." He should be taught to climb up and down ladders like a bear, looking up at the roof, always holding onto the ladder with at least one hand, moving one foot at a time and taking one rung at a time. When he is on the roof, he should not lean with the pitch of the roof, but hold his body so to counteract the slope, almost as if he were "leaning" on the air between him and the roof. He should be taught that there are good, bad, and deceptive handholds to be recognized at sight; that he should test and retest the firmness of handholds because "nothing stands still" on the roof and new handholds must constantly be found; that the roof "makes noises" that should be listened to and interpreted, both to assess the progress of the work and to avoid dangers that cannot be seen but only intuited by listening; that he should always watch what his workmates are doing, both to coordinate the work and to ensure their safety.

Yet these replies still did not thoroughly answer my questions. However precise and however important they may have been for someone learning the job of roof-stripper, the "lessons" described to me by the workmen covered only some aspects of the negotiations characteristic of organizational socialization, which concern as much rules, norms, and forms of organizational authority as the practical modes of task performance, the sense of work activities, the meaning of day-to-day life in the organization, and the management of organizational power relations. They failed to satisfy my questions because, on close consideration, the lessons taught to the male novice were grounded on something that was vague, unexpressed, and unknown.

What is there of the exact and formalized in instructions on how to work on a roof—such as "take care to distinguish and interpret noises that you have not heard before" or "lean on the air between your body and the roof"—when these things have never been done before? The instruction to "feel" as if your body is leaning on the air is only apparently definite; it is instead essentially vague and indeterminate, and so too is the instruction to "feel" as if your feet were nailed to the roof. Moreover, instructions that might appear better defined, on more careful analysis prove to be very unclear. What exactly is meant by using the information acquired by "listening" to the noises given off by the roof? According to one's personal background some of these noises will seem normal, others will seem strange; some will be familiar, others will seem new, maybe alarming: they will "seem" rather than "be." The same applies to the good, bad, and deceptive handholds pointed out by workmates during the initial phase of the novice's socialization, and then subsequently when the handholds change as the work progresses: "see them" is a generic expression, if one excludes cases in which the handholds are those fixed by the workmen for safety reasons. It is not that all the "lessons" that the workmen described to me were of this type. For example, the instructions on how to climb up and down ladders were precise. But much less clear was how the male novice should learn to abandon the bear posture to get off the ladder and onto the roof, and vice versa. Though this may seem a mere detail, the instruction to the novice always to keep watch on his workmates is certainly not: when should he watch them since it cannot be precisely "always" as they said? When he had interrupted his work? What exactly should he "see" when watching them? In this case, too, the lessons given to the novice struck me as generally useful advice, not the explicit formalization of a precisely defined instruction.

I talked to the workmen on a further occasion during their lunch break. They added that not everyone was suited to their work, and that you realized immediately whether or not you were. Once again, there was no lack of the banter typical of the "comic" in organizations: "if it doesn't come naturally to you," you'd better "find another job immediately" because if you wait to see how things turn out, they will turn out badly. But my perplexity was evident to them. How to work on a roof "is taught badly," said the foreman; the fact is that whether you are able to do so is something that "you have to feel yourself." You can't do it if you feel afraid, if you wait for the fear to pass with time, if "you feel that you're in danger" while you're up there. Instead, you should take the work differently, because "there's something beautiful about" working on a roof. And then, you "see immediately" if someone can do the work. When choosing a new worker, you "should watch him on the roof and feel confident" that he will not hurt himself. "You can't take on just anyone" for a job like this; it is "a responsibility" that you have toward everyone: the man himself, his family, your workmates, the business, the trade unions.

The Interweaving Between Aesthetic Understanding and Tacit Knowledge

Aesthetics—or the perceptive-sensorial capacities of people and their faculty of aesthetic judgment—was therefore particularly important as regards:

1. the work on the roof,
2. the decision to go in for that kind of work,
3. teaching someone how to do it,
4. selecting the personnel able to do it.

The statements reported above by the workmen, and especially their leader, show that theirs is work that cannot be done by those who principally perceive it as obliging them to work in a dangerous organizational setting. It can only be done by those who feel safe and who move with confidence, who trust and rely on their workmates and foreman, who feel it a pleasure to do the work because there is something beautiful about working on a roof.

Now, if the readers wish, they may try to imagine themselves in the shoes of someone beginning this kind of work, someone who has done it for some time, or even someone with the responsibilities of the foreman. They may ask whether they have has the personal capabilities required by the work, whether they feel able to do it, whether there is some aspect of it that attracts them, whether they would continue to do the work for a certain period of time. On the basis of their imaginations, they may experience (Gabriel, Fineman, and Sims, 2000; Sims, 1985) some of the sensations that—plausibly—are afforded by the senses of vision, hearing, smell, taste, touch, and by the aesthetic judgment: that is, sensations of aesthetic experience at the imaginative level that do not fulfill the criterion of scientific truth, in the sense that they are not due to experience actually gained by working on the roof, and that for precisely this reason can only fulfill the criterion of plausibility. A wide range of diverse initiatives in organizational settings—plans, project-teams, industrial designs, starting up, to mention a few—are experienced as plausible, or else at the level of fantasy, through the imagination, before it is known whether they can be undertaken and managed. These initiatives may be the result of rigorous rational calculation, but they can be imaginatively experienced through activation of intuition, analogical thinking, sensory capacities, and aesthetic judgment, in order to feel certain sensations beforehand.

Consequently, by activating their aesthetic faculties, the readers may use their imagination to walk across the roof, lean on the air, pay attention to noises, keep an eye on the handholds, monitor what their workmates are doing, rip away some roofing, throw it down into the yard, and hear the crash that it makes. They may assess whether they feel pleasure in doing all these things, whether they find that the work has "something beautiful about it," or whether they find it repellent, whether it gives them the shivers or a sense of vertigo. They may also see if they are able to tell—on the basis of the knowledge that they by now possesses—whether a novice is suited to the job before they starts it. When this experiential and knowledge-gathering process has concluded, the reader may be able to say whether they could do the work or, conversely, would find it impossible; or whether, if forced to, they could learn how to do it. In other words, they would know that they knew how to do it, or that they did not know how to do it, or that they knew that they could learn to do it. That is to say, *on the basis of their aesthetic forms of knowing, they would have focused on they tacit knowledge* and become aware that they know how to do the work, although it evades analytical, detailed, and scientifically rigorous description. Trust must be placed in tacit knowledge—awareness of being able to do something even though one is unable to explain how—and not in explicit, formal, and scientific knowledge.

Does this seldom happen in organizations? Does it only apply to manual work? Does it concern activities that require practical experience rather that formal instruction, university education, vocational training? Polanyi points out that it concerns a wide range of organizational settings and meaningful actions by those who work in them:

> The structural kinship of the arts of knowing and doing is indeed such that they are rarely exercised in isolation; we usually meet a blend of the two. Medical diagnosis combines them about equally. To percuss a lung is as much a muscular feat as a delicate discrimination of the sounds elicited. The palpation of a spleen or a kidney combines a skilful kneading of the region with a trained sense for the peculiar feeling of the organ's resistance. It is apposite therefore to include skilful feats among comprehensive entities. 1969: 126)

Medicine, in fact, provides an excellent example of an activity that requires years of book study and years of practical experience to gain mastery of abilities both tactile—percussing a lung—and auditory—recognizing the sound produced—that enable the doctor to understand the lung examined and to formulate a diagnosis. We can further develop the medical example. The training that refines the knowledge-gathering sensitivity of the doctor's perceptive and sensory faculties is meant to ensure that all doctors are of equal worth. But nobody would light-heartedly undergo a surgical operation, however routine, in the certainty that, given the training received by all surgeons, one of them is as good as any other. On the contrary, these are situations in which one tends to seek out information, details, tittle-tattle, and gossip in order to place one's confidence in the professional skills of one doctor rather than another. That is to say, the surgeon's "scalpel stroke" is not just the putting into practice of medical knowledge learned from anatomy textbooks or lectures on symptomatology at medical school; nor is it the result of mere medical empiricism.

In order to show the importance of aesthetics and its relationship with tacit knowledge as regards organizational learning, I shall briefly describe the complex features displayed (as a skilled organizational practice) by the scalpel stroke just mentioned—executed with a hand-held scalpel with a rapid and precise motion that imparts pressure and cuts in the direction intended. The action requires concentration, accuracy, dexterity, the right amount of pressure, speed, and certainly not least important, intellective control of the diagnosis. In this process—during which a situated organizational practice is implemented—the relationship between the surgeon and the scalpel, or in other words between the human being and the nonhuman item, is such that the scalpel is not considered in itself, but as an integral part of the body. This is the awareness of the nonhuman element. Polanyi calls it "subsidiary":

> The way we use a hammer or a blind man uses his stick, shows in fact that in both cases we shift outwards the points at which we make contact with the things that we observe as objects outside ourselves. While we rely on a tool or a probe, these are not handled as external objects. We may test the tool for its effectiveness or the probe for its suitability, e.g. in discovering the hidden details of a cavity, but the tool and the probe can never lie in the field of these operations; they remain necessarily on our side of it, forming part of ourselves, the operating persons. (1962: 59)

Subsidiary awareness, which here concerns my description of the skilled act of employing the scalpel, indicates that in relation to the scalpel stroke this nonhuman element is assimilated into the surgeon's existence and thus "missed"—as Latour (1992) puts it. The surgeon makes himself aware of the scalpel with which he is realizing the organizational practice in question, as if it were part of his body, and in particular of his eyes, arm, and hands. To return to Polanyi (1966; reprinted 1969: 148), "when we learn to use a language, or a probe, or a tool, and thus make ourselves aware of these things as we are of our body, we *interiorize* these things and *make ourselves dwell in them*. Such extensions of ourselves develop new faculties in us" that influence our vision of the world and have us experience life in terms of that vision.

Focal awareness, by contrast, is that awareness whereby we see the scalpel as a free-standing nonhuman object: it is newly made, it has a defect, it still has to be sterilized, it is not in its proper place. This is not the awareness of the scalpel-in-use—to employ a term from the phenomenology of science and knowledge (Husserl, 1913)—during the operation, given that if the surgeon focused his attention on the scalpel itself, he would remove it from the surgical practice that he is performing: focal awareness and subsidiary awareness, in fact, are "mutually exclusive" (Polanyi, 1962: 56).

With reference to my description of skilled surgical practice, the main understanding to be drawn from Polanyi's distinction between focal and subsidiary awareness is that the surgeon learns to know the scalpel by acquiring subsidiary awareness of it. By using the scalpel, he immerses himself in it and integrates it into himself as part of his corporeality. The knowledge thus acquired, therefore, is personal knowledge yielded by one's own personal faculties of sensory perception and aesthetic judgment, and, to return to Polanyi, mainly by tacit knowledge, because—contrary to logical positivism and also, less starkly, neopositivism and postpositivism—it is not possible "to establish all knowledge in terms of explicit relations between sensory data" (1966; reprinted 1969: 156). What explicit relations among sensory data can we establish with regard to the scalpel stroke? Or with regard to feeling oneself attached to the roof while stripping it? And if we are able to establish these explicit relations, will we be able to execute a scalpel stroke or strip a roof? Polanyi addresses the matter by discussing the ability to ride a bicycle:

> Again, from my interrogations of physicists, engineers and bicycle manufacturers, I have come to the conclusion that the principle by which the cyclist keeps his balance is not generally known. The rule observed by the cyclist is this. When he starts falling to the right he turns the handlebars to the right, so that the course of the bicycle is deflected along a curve towards the right. This results in a centrifugal force pushing the cyclist to the left and offsets the gravitational force dragging him down to the right. This manoeuvre presently throws the cyclist out of balance to the left, which he counteracts by turning the handlebars to the left; and so he continues to keep himself in balance by winding along a series of appropriate curvatures. (1962: 49–50)

What the cyclist actually does is this: for every angle out of equilibrium, he adjusts the curvature in inverse proportion to the square of the speed at which he is going, But, one asks, is it on the basis of this explicit knowledge that we can teach someone how to ride a bicycle? Is it really necessary to impart this knowledge to a child, an adult, or even someone getting on in years who wants to learn to ride a bicycle? The answer is "no." It is not by adjusting the curve in ratio to one's imbalance over the square of the speed that one learns this ability. There are a number of other factors involved — Polanyi warns — factors *that are not covered by the rule thus formulated*. Polanyi's conclusion is that the rules of art "can be useful, but they do not determine the practice of an art; they are maxims, which can serve as a guide to an art only if they can be integrated into the practical knowledge of the art. They cannot replace this knowledge" (1962: 50).

If we now return to knowing how to work on a roof, we can discern a number of features of the organization employing the three workmen described above. This organization:

1. relies on the putting-into-use of the workers' personal skills that enable them to "feel attached with their feet to the roof" and thus have their hands free to do the work;
2. recruits workers on the basis of its capacity to assess the abilities of a novice at the moment when he begins to learn and become socialized to organizational practices — that is, during the brief initial phase in which he tries to use his ability to work as a roof stripper;
3. does not provide training that teaches its workers how to "feel attached with their feet to the roof," to "lean on the air" between them and the roof, to recognize handholds and noises — in short, that teaches the skills required to work for the organization;
4. bases its identity in organizational practices that crucially require what Polanyi calls "personal" knowledge: that is, the workers' tacit knowledge which, as we have seen, is closely bound up with aesthetic knowledge if, as regards aesthetics in organizations, one does not consider only the faculty of aesthetic judgment but also people's perceptive and sensorial capacities.

In sum, this organization differs from other organizations by virtue of the fact that it comprises abilities specific to it that cannot be explained analytically and rationally. This raises a theoretical issue and at the same time relates to the debate between aesthetic understanding of organizational life and the search for rational explanation at any price (Strati, 1998: 324).

Ron Sanchez, for instance, asserts that "the presumption that "tacit knowledge" is likely to be the only viable source of distinctive competence and competitive advantage is unwarranted" (1997: 169–170), and that "a notion of 'knowledge that is not capable of being articulated' (as distinct from the 'knowledge that is articulable only with difficulty') appears to be epistemologically problematic" (1997: 165). "Real knowledge" — to paraphrase Gherardi and Turner's Real Men Don't Collect Soft Data (1987) — therefore has to be "articulable" or, at least, to be "enclosable" in cognitive schemata that let it be known (Gioia and Ford, 1995). Or, else, "real knowledge" has to be "includable" in the transitions between identified knowledge modes, such as the individual, collective, tacit, and explicit mode (Baumard, 1996; Eng. trans. 1999: 30–31).

Sanchez's above assertion that tacit knowledge is epistemologically problematic, as well as Spender's two-by-two matrix of modes of cognizing—the result of applying the distinction between the explicit or conscious and the implicit or automatic types of knowledge "to both the individual and collective mind" (1997: 33)—illustrates the difficulty of organizational scholars in understanding and appreciating the tacitness and corporeality of personal knowledge. Donaldson (2001: 956–957) shares this difficulty and warns us that the ineffability of tacit knowledge may lead scholars to "a remagification of organizations," and that it constitutes a mystification of the organizational world—and also that this concept is overused, since if people in organizations share ideas "through talking, then those ideas are not ineffable and the knowledge is not tacit."

Aesthetic understanding of organizational life, on the contrary, emphasizes tacitness and corporeality of knowing in practice. It supports Polanyi's philosophical distinction, considering that it is not solely based on expression of knowledge in discourse—that is, on the sayable and the unsayable (Donaldson; Sanchez)—or on the automatic and the conscious (Gioia and Ford; Spender), or on magic and formal rationality (Donaldson). From an aesthetic perspective (Ramirez, 2000; Strati, 1999), tacit knowledge is a distinctive and specific form of knowing that by both "attempt and organization" lets organizational practices be invented, performed, learned, and taught by the participants in the social construction of organizational life.

But even if one does not share an aesthetic viewpoint, the crucial importance of tacit knowledge in situated learning in organizations as social contexts can be stressed. This is the case of Nonaka and Takeuchi's study (1995), in which they refer to tacit knowledge to depict the organizational structure that enables an organization to create knowledge efficiently and continuously. In their model, the organization does not seek to translate the tacit into the explicit. Rather, it looks for the hypertext "jumps" and "links" by which the tacit and the explicit construct organizational processes of learning and dynamics that facilitate organizational knowledge creation.

The leaps and links that connect tacit and aesthetic knowledge to explicit knowledge highlight the fact that skills practices like those discussed with regard to the roof-laying and -stripping organization may be "nontranslatable," or if preferred "nontransferrable.." And their learning does not take place through the formal and institutional practices envisaged by traditional cognitive theory.

On the contrary, the process of organizational learning described by the three workmen highlighted an awareness as regards the organization in question: namely, that the knowledge required to work on a roof "is taught badly" (as the foreman said), and it is acquired through the performance of organizational practices. And the reader's imaginary participant observation may be attracted and mobilized by the uncontainability of their tacit knowledge — the impossibility of saying it — and its specifity — for it is precisely done — all at once.

This relates to the themes discussed by the theory of situated learning and of learning-in-organizing.

Conclusions: Personal Knowledge, Community of Practice, and Learning-in-Organizing

Although the roof-strippers' skills and practices constituted personal knowledge, they should be considered to be artifacts specific and peculiar to the organization for which the men worked. It was in that organizational setting, in fact, that those practices assumed the value and meaning that I have shown. In other words, it was in order to construct their organization collectively that the three workmen activated their capacities of aesthetic knowledge and put their tacit knowledge to use — besides, obviously, their explicit knowledge, although this was less essential to the purposes of the organization. Their practices should be viewed as organizational artifacts, although they were practices that were not implemented by the organization — unless we want to reify personal, tacit, and aesthetic knowledge into the social construct "organization" — but instead pertained to the persons who belonged to it. This, moreover, would mean imprisoning my "ethnography" in a conceptual frame, oversimplifying my own process of knowing.

What I observed through the window, in fact, was not an organization in action engaged with alacrity and a certain pleasure in dismantling a roof. It was instead the organizational practices of three persons, and my question about "how do you work on a roof" was prompted by seeing those bodies acting, the agility with which they moved, the nonhuman elements with which they interacted, and by my feeling intrigued and distracted by the noise that their individual and collective actions were making. Put otherwise: I did not see the social object "organization," but three persons who were "doing organization," or better, "intellectually *and aesthetically* doing" that specific organization. Consequently, there was no higher entity — the organization — on the one hand, and the three persons on the other. Nor did I observe three persons who had mixed themselves into the organization as if it were an extraneous body. I did not discover the underlying organizational structure widely envisaged by organization scholars and which Karl Weick opposes, emphasizing the metaphorical reality of organizations and arguing that people invent organization and their settings (1977). In short, what I observed were three men engaged in organizational practices on a roof. Hence, learning and organization were not distinct entities to be related to each other or somehow fitted together. Rather, *learning was constitutive of organizing, just as organizing was constitutive of learning:* otherwise what sense would the skills that I observed have had?

The organizational practices that the three workmen enacted bring out views on roofing that delineate a specific community "of practice" (Brown and Duguid, 1991; Lave and Wenger, 1991; Wenger, 1998). Precisely because it was their skills and practices that distinguished the roof-strippers, anyone who wanted to learn how to work on a roof was obliged to engage in complex interactive processes by which he gradually became part of the community, moving from an initially peripheral position to more and more central ones. Participation in communities of this kind is essential for learning, writes Etienne Wenger (2000: 229), since it is in this way that whatever constitutes "competence" is defined in social interactions.

However, it should not be thought that this is a harmonious interactive process; on the contrary, it is negotiative and sometimes conflictual. Max Weber (1922; Eng. trans. 1978: 42) stressed that "coercion of all sorts is a very common thing in even the most intimate of such communal relationships if one party is weaker in character than the other," while Robert Bellah (1997: 388) argues that "a good community is one in which there is argument, even conflict, about the meaning of the shared values and goals, and certainly about how they will be actualized in everyday life," which in our case is that conducted by working on the roof.

For that matter, points out Alessandro Ferrara (1992: liii), in the modern and contemporary context, community has to do with pluralism, and this "inevitably means a community which contains diversity which has not been entirely amalgamated by consensus." This is even more important when one considers the contemporary globalization process and the numerous facets of everyday organizational life in which globalization interrelates with the local cultures and becomes "glocal," as Robertson puts it (1995). Virtual communities (Hine, 2000; Jones, 1995; Jones, 1998; Mantovani, 1994; Smith and Kollock, 1999; Werry and Mowbray, 2001) have emerged in the symbolic-material reality (Castells, 1998) of the organizational life characterized by multitemporal landscape of organizational flows that develop in the permanent revolution of information and communication technology. Hence we can self-perceive "glocality" as diversity, multiplicity, and nonintegration (Beck, 1997), which are all facets of the sentiment of feeling like a community.

The distinctive feature of a community of practice, besides being observable in terms of organizational practices, is what Weber (1922; Eng. trans. 1978: 40) described with regard to the community: it is a social relation that rests on the subjective *feeling* of shared belonging. A community, in other words, is not a mere instrument (Taylor, 1991), and participation in it is not motivated rationally but felt subjectively. It is felt emotionally and aesthetically, and this further indicates the distance between learning-in-organizing and organizational learning understood as the mental process envisaged by traditional cognitive theory. Instead, feeling, both emotional and aesthetic, highlights the mundane and situated nature of organizational learning.

Put in these terms, organizational learning takes place in unusual ways that have been largely ignored by traditional cognitive theory. The latter, argues Fox (1997: 729–731), claims that organizational learning develops as a mental process, and that it consists mainly in acquisition through formal and institutional practices. Learning serves a higher purpose for the organization: it is intended to improve individual practices, starting with the professional practices of specialists in education—like professional educators or the theoreticians of learning—who are the first to undertake the training of people in organizations. This aim is instead opposed by aesthetic knowledge: aesthetic judgment is not end-directed; indeed, it is whatever remains free from every organizational purpose (White, 1996: 206).

Moreover, the predominance of the mind and of cognition in organizational knowledge has also been contested by situated learning theory. Of the latter, Fox (1997: 731–733) emphasizes its endeavour to overcome the mind/body dichotomy that both aesthetic understanding of organizational life and Polanyi's concept of tacit knowledge challenge, and to shift learning from the individual mind to the mind/body's relationship with the social practices experienced daily by persons. Set against the individual acquisition is the process that generates knowledge situated in everyday organizational practices constituted by social commitment, intersubjective relations, discursive practices, and the materials with which people interact in order to act. Learning as practice-based theorizing, writes Gherardi (2000: 212), is not in the head and it is not a commodity. The image of learning as the accumulation of items of knowledge—or of the mind as the container for those items—fails to convey learning-in-organizing. Bourdieu, too, emphasizes the performative nature of knowledge in his book on the practical sense (1980).

The equation that relates learning to organizing highlights the former as "situated activity, mediated by conversations, in situations involving human and non-human actors" (Gherardi, 1999: 114): that is, both persons and the missing masses discussed by Latour (1992) and constituted by the nonhuman elements with which people interact as they work in organizations and for them. Learning-in-organizing, precisely because it is situated, is less a way of knowing the world than, as Gherardi and Nicolini argue, a way of being in the world (2000: 332) and of putting a community on stage by performing it (2002).

To conclude, in this chapter I have illustrated by referring to an empirical study—where observations are based on studying workmen dismantle a roof—the crucial importance of aesthetic and tacit knowledge and its associated skills for a particular organization, for its success, its profits, its survival. Aesthetics, in fact, closely interweaves with the tacit knowledge of individuals, and they both signal the socially constructed personal way in which people interact to invent, negotiate, and recreate organizational life through practice, taste, and learning. Moreover, the relationship between aesthetic understanding of organizational life and tacit knowledge in relation to situated organizational learning, or learning-in-organizing, further problematizes the logical and rational knowledge of organizational life and cognitivist dominance in organizational learning studies.

Note

I would like to express my gratitude to all the colleagues who discussed the ideas illustrated in this essay at the 16th Egos Colloquium, Helsinki 2000, and at the seminars held at the University of Torino, June 2000, and Uppsala, October 2000. A previous version of this chapter was published as an article in the Italian journal *Studi Organizzativi* 2, 2000.

References

Addison, Joseph. (1712). "The Pleasures of the Imagination." *The Spectator*, June–July.

Baumard, Philippe. (1996). *Organisations déconcertées: La gestion stratégique de la connaissance*. Paris: Masson. Eng. trans.: *Tacit Knowledge in Organizations*. London: Sage, 1999).

Baumgarten, Alexander Gottlieb. (1735). *Meditationes philosophicae de nonnullis ad poema pertinentibus*. Halle in Magdeburgo: Grunert. Eng. trans.: *Reflections on Poetry*, ed. K. Aschenbrenner and W.B. Holter. Berkeley: University of California Press, 1954.

— — —. (1750–58). *Aesthetica I-II*. Frankfurt am Oder: Kleyb. Photostat: Olms, Hildesheim, 1986.

Beck, Ulrich. (1997). *Was ist Globalisierung? Irrtümer des Globalismus-Antworten auf Globalisierung*. Frankfurt am Main: Suhrkamp Verlag. Eng. trans.: *What Is Globalization?* Oxford: Blackwell, 1999.

Bellah, Robert N. (1997). "The Necessity of Opportunity and Community in a Good Society." *International Sociology* 12(4): 387–393.

Bourdieu, Pierre. (1980). *Le sens pratique*. Paris: Les Éditions de Minuit. Eng. trans.: *The Logic of Practice*. Cambridge: Polity Press, 1990.

Brown, John S., and Duguid, Paul. (1991). "Organizational Learning and Communities of Practice. Toward a Unified View of Working, Learning and Innovation." *Organization Science* 2(1): 40–57.

Carchia, Gianni, and D'Angelo, Paolo, eds. (1999). *Dizionario di estetica*. Roma-Bari: Laterza.

Castells, Manuel. (1998). *End of Millennium*. Malden, MA: Blackwell.

Cazeaux, Clive, ed. (2000). *The Continental Aesthetics Reader*. London: Routledge.

Coffey, Amanda; Holbrook, Beverley; and Atkinson, Paul. (1996). "Qualitative Data Analysis: Technologies and Representations." *Sociological Research Online* 1(1). Reprint 1999 in A. Bryman and R. Burgess, eds., *Qualitative Research I-IV*. London: Sage.

Cook, Scott D.N., and Yanow, Dvora. (1993). "Culture and Organizational Learning," *Journal of Management Inquiry* 2(4): 373–390.

Dean, James W., Jr.; Ottensmeyer, Edward; and Ramirez, Rafael. (1997). "An Aesthetic Perspective on Organizations." In C. Cooper and S. Jackson, eds., *Creating Tomorrow's Organizations: A Handbook for Future Research in Organizational Behavior*, 419–437. Chichester: Wiley.

Dégot, Vincent. (1987). "Portrait of the Manager as an Artist." *Dragon* 2(4): 13–50.

Donaldson, Lex. (2001). "Reflections on Knowledge and Knowledge-Intensive Firms." *Human Relations* 54(7): 955–963.

Ferrara, Alessandro. (1992). "Introduzione." In A. Ferrara, ed., *Comunitarismo e liberalismo*, ix–lvii. Roma: Editori Riuniti.

Fox, Stephen. (1997). "Situated Learning Theory Versus Traditional Cognitive Learning Theory: Why Management Education Should Not Ignore Management Learning." *Systems Practice* 10(6): 727–747.

Gabriel, Yiannis; Fineman, Stephen; and Sims, David. (2000). *Organizing and Organizations*. London: Sage (first ed., 1993).

Gagliardi, Pasquale. (1996). "Exploring the Aesthetic Side of Organizational Life." In S.R. Clegg, C. Hardy, and W.R. Nord, eds., *Handbook of Organization Studies*. London: Sage, 565–80.

Gherardi, Silvia. (1999). "Learning as Problem-driven or Learning in the Face of Mystery?" *Organization Studies* 20(1): 101–123.

———. (2000). "Practice-based Theorizing on Learning and Knowing in Organizations." Introduction to the Special Issue on Knowing in Practice. *Organization* 7(2): 211–223.

Gherardi, Silvia, and Nicolini, Davide. (2000). "Learning in a Constellation of Interconnected Practices: Canon or Dissonance?" *Journal of Management Studies* 39(4): 419–436.

———. (2002) "To Transfer Is to Transform: The Circulation of Safety Knowledge." *Organization* 7(2): 329–348.

Gherardi, Silvia, and Turner, Barry A. (1987). *Real Men Don't Collect Soft Data*. Trento: Dipartimento di Politica Sociale, Quaderno 13. Partial reprint 1999 in A. Bryman and R. Burgess, eds. *Qualitative Research*, vol. I, 103–118. London: Sage.

Gioia, Dennis, and Ford, Cameron. (1995). "Tacit Knowledge, Self-Communication, and Sensemaking in Organizations." In L. Thayer, ed., *Organization-Communication* 3, 77–96. Norwood, NJ: Ablex.

Hatch, Mary Jo. (1997). *Organization Theory. Modern, Symbolic, and Postmodern Perspectives*. Oxford: Oxford University Press.

Henley, Paul. (1998). "Film-making and Ethnographic Research." In J. Prosser, ed., *Image-based Research*. London: Falmer Press. Reprint 1999 in A. Bryman and R. Burgess, eds., *Qualitative Research*, vol. II, 302–322. London: Sage.

Hine, Christine. (2000). *Virtual Ethnography*. London: Sage.

Husserl, Edmund. [1913] (1950). *Ideen zu einer reinen Phänomenologie und phänomenologischen Philosophie*, ed. M. Biemel. *Husserliana III*. Den Haag: Nijhof.

John, Eileen. (2001). "Art and Knowledge." In B. Gaut and Lopes D. McIver Lopes, eds., *The Routledge Companion to Aesthetics*, 329–340. London: Routledge.

Jones, Michael O.; Moore, Michael D.; and Snyder, Richard C., eds. (1988). *Inside Organizations. Understanding the Human Dimension*. Newbury Park: Sage.

Jones, Quentin. (1998). "Virtual-Communities, Virtual Settlements and Cyber-Archaelogy: A Theoretical Outline." www.ascusc.org/jcmc/vol3/issue3/jones.html.

Jones, Steven G., ed. (1995). *Cybersociety. Computer-mediated Communication and Community*. Thousand Oaks, CA: Sage.

Kant, Immanuel. (1790). *Kritik der Urteilskraft*. In I. Kant, *Werke in zwölf Bänden*, Vol. X. Frankfurt am Main: Suhrkamp, 1968. Eng. trans.: *The Critique of Judgment*. Oxford: Oxford University Press, 1952.

Latour, Bruno. (1992). "Where Are the Missing Masses? Sociology of a Few Mundane Artefacts." In W.E. Bijker, J. Law, eds., *Shaping Technology-Building Society: Studies in Sociotechnical Change*, 225–258. Cambridge, MA: MIT Press.

Lave, Jean, and Wenger, Etienne. (1991). *Situated Learning. Legitimate Peripheral Participation*. Cambridge: Cambridge University Press.

Linstead, Stephen, Höpfl, Heather, eds. (2000). *The Aesthetics of Organization*. London: Sage.

Mantovani, Giuseppe. (1994). "Is Computer-Mediated Communication Intrinsically Apt to Enhance Democracy in Organizations?" *Human Relations* 47(1): 45–62.

Martin, Patricia Y. (2001). "'Mobilizing Masculinities': Women's Experiences of Men at Work," *Organization* 8(4): 587–618.

Nonaka, Ikujiro, and Takeuchi, Hirotaka. (1995). *The Knowledge-Creating Company. How Japanese Companies Create the Dynamics of Innovation*. Oxford: Oxford University Press.

Pareyson, Luigi. (1954). *Estetica. Teoria della formatività*. Torino: Giappichelli.

Polanyi, Michael. (1961). "Knowing and Being," *Mind* 70 (280): 458–470. Reprinted 1969 in M. Polanyi, *Knowing and Being, Essays by Michael Polanyi*, ed. M. Grene, 123–137. Chicago: University of Chicago Press.

———. (1962). *Personal Knowledge. Towards a Post-Critical Philosophy*. 2d ed. London: Routledge and Kegan Paul.

———. (1966). "The Logic of Tacit Inference." *Philosophy* 41: 1–18. Reprinted 1969 in M. Polanyi, *Knowing and Being, Essays by Michael Polanyi*, ed. M. Grene, 138–158. Chicago: University of Chicago Press.

Ramirez, Rafael. (2000). "Why Is Tacit Knowledge Tacit? An Aesthetic Exploration." Paper presented at the Eiasm Workshop on Organising Aesthetics, Certosa di Pontignano, Siena, Italy, May.

Robertson, Roland. (1995). "Glocalization: Time-Space and Homogeneity-Heterogeneity." In M. Featherstone, S. Lash, and R. Robertson, eds., *Global Modernities*, 25–44. London: Sage.

Sanchez, Ron. (1997). "Managing Articulated Knowledge in Competence-based Competition." In R. Sanchez, A. Heene, eds., *Strategic Learning and Knowledge Management*, 163–187. Chichester: Wiley.

Sims, David. (1985). "Fantasies and the Location of Skill." In A. Strati, ed., *The Symbolics of Skill*, 12–27. Trento: Dipartimento di Politica Sociale, Quaderno 5/6.

Smith, Mark A., and Kollock, Peter, eds. (1999). *Communities in Cyberspace*. London: Routledge.

Spender, J.-C. (1998). "The Dynamics of Individual and Organizational Knowledge." In C. Eden, J.-C. Spender, eds., *Managerial and Organizational Cognition: Theory, Methods and Research*, 13–39. London: Sage.

Strati, Antonio. (1992). "Aesthetic Understanding of Organizational Life." *Academy of Management Review*, 17(3): 568–581.

———. (1998) "(Mis)understanding Cognition in Organization Studies." *Scandinavian Journal of Management* 14(4): 309–329.

———. (1999). *Organization and Aesthetics*. London: Sage.

———. (2000). *Theory and Method in Organization Studies: Paradigms and Choices*. London: Sage.

Strati, Antonio, and Guillet de Montoux, Pierre, eds. (2002). *Human Relations* 55(7). Special Issue on Organizing Aesthetics.

Taylor, Charles. (1991). *The Malaise of Modernity*. Montreal: McGill-Queen's University Press.

Van Maanen, John. (1995). "Style as Theory." *Organization Science* 6(1): 133–143.

Vico, Giambattista. (1725). *Principi di una scienza nuova*. Naples: Mosca. Eng. trans.: *The New Science of Giambattista Vico*, ed. T.G. Bergin and M.H. Fisch. Ithaca, NY: Cornell University Press, 1968.

Walker, Rob. (1993). "Finding a Silent Voice for the Researcher: Using Photographs in Evaluation and Research." In M. Schratz, ed., *Qualitative Voices*. London: Falmer Press. Reprint 1999 in A. Bryman and R. Burgess, eds., *Qualitative Research*, vol. II, 279–301. London: Sage.

Weber, Max. (1922). *Wirtschaft und Gesellschaft. Grundriss der verstehenden Soziologie*. Tübingen: Mohr. Eng. trans.: *Economy and Society: An Outline of Interpretive Sociology*. I-II. Berkeley: University of California Press, 1978.

Weick, Karl. (1977). "Enactment Processes in Organizations." In B.W. Staw, G.R. Salancik, eds., *New Directions in Organizational Behavior*, 267–300. Chicago: St. Clair Press.

Wenger, Etienne. (1998). *Communities of Practice. Learning, Meaning, and Identity*. Cambridge: Cambridge University Press.

———. (2000). "Communities of Practice and Social Learning Systems." *Organization* 7(2): 225–246.

Werry, Chris, and Mowbray, Miranda, eds. (2001). *Online Communities: Commerce, Community Action, and the Virtual University*. Englewood Cliffs, NJ: Prentice-Hall.

White, David A. (1996). "'It's Working Beautifully!' Philosophical Reflections on Aesthetics and Organization Theory." *Organization* 3(2): 195–208.

Young, James O. (2001). *Art and Knowledge*. London: Routledge.

Knowing as desiring. Mythic knowledge and the knowledge journey in communities of practitioners

Silvia Gherardi

The author

Silvia Gherardi is from the Dipartimento di Sociologia e Ricerca Sociale, Research Unit on Organizational Cognition and Learning, Trento, Italy.

Keywords

Myths, Knowledge management, Learning organizations, Learning

Abstract

Why do people and their organizations seek out knowledge? Most of the recurrent explanations emphasise the instrumental use of knowledge: in order to solve problems, to gain competitive advantages, to exploit innovation commercially, or to contribute to the wellbeing of future generations. But besides the rationality and purposiveness of knowledge-gathering, there is another aspect that may be undervalued in organization studies: that of a search for knowledge driven by a love of knowledge for its own sake. Knowledge as an end in itself motivates people and organizations. In order to explore how desire for knowledge may operate in organizing, the paper refers to the literary figure of the "knowledge journey" and to one of the greatest of all travellers: Ulysses.

Electronic access

The Emerald Research Register for this journal is available at
http://www.emeraldinsight.com/researchregister

The current issue and full text archive of this journal is available at
http://www.emeraldinsight.com/1366-5626.htm

Journal of Workplace Learning
Volume 15 · Number 7/8 · 2003 · pp. 352-358
© MCB UP Limited · ISSN 1366-5626
DOI 10.1108/13665620310504846

Most of the recurrent explanations of organizational learning and knowledge management emphasise the instrumental use of knowledge: organizational knowledge is needed in order to solve problems and to gain competitive advantages. A "problem-driven" view of organizational learning represents the organization *qua* corporate actor, which is the subject of learning or the container of a specific form of it. But besides the rationality and purposiveness of knowledge-gathering, there is another aspect that may be undervalued in organization studies: that of a search for knowledge driven by a love of knowledge for its own sake.

In fact we can explore not only knowing as problem-driven but also knowing as mystery-driven (Gherardi, 1999). Knowing in the face of mystery conveys the idea that acquiring knowledge is not only an activity but is also passivity: its locus of control may be external to individuals. A broader view, which sees knowing as a socio-cultural phenomenon in organizations, helps us to explore a less intentional, less instrumental, more reflexive aspect of knowledge.

What we call "learning" – within a mystery-driven framework – may be seen as the product or effect of the codification, assembly and representation of social elements. These processes of codification and representation do not only describe what already exists, they also produce what it describes (Derrida, 1971; Foucault, 1966; Latour and Woolgar, 1979). The idea is that the relations which constitute the social are continuous. They do not halt at the ontological barriers that separate nature and culture, actor and structure, organization and environment: the dynamics of interaction prescind from these categories, forming a seamless web. Consequently, knowing is a collective accomplishment which depends on a range of spatially and temporally distributed local practices lying outside the control of any organisation and within a network of relationships.

Learning thus becomes an epistemic relation with the world, and it takes place as much in people's minds as in the social relations among them, in the oral, written and "visual" texts which convey ideas and knowledge from one context to another. Knowledge is in its turn both social and material. It is always unstable and precarious, located in time and space.

Knowing as desiring

Silvia Gherardi

Journal of Workplace Learning

Volume 15 · Number 7/8 · 2003 · 352-358

In organization studies, the organizational symbolism approach (Alvesson and Berg, 1992; Strati, 1998) has treated myth as a form of knowledge which not so much conveys factual knowledge as transmits a *forma mentis*: a perceptive grid used to interpret experience and which conditions the vision of the reality internal and external to both people and work communities. Myth, the knowledge embodied in stories and traditions, connects us to the humanity of the past and the future, thereby situating practical knowledge within the stock of knowledge that is our collective heritage.

In what follows I shall provide an example of how mythic knowledge may operate in exploring an organizational issue: the role of desire in practical knowledge. To do so, I shall refer to the literary figure of the "knowledge journey" and to one of the greatest of all travellers: Ulysses[1]. Knowledge as an end in itself motivates people and organizations: this is what I intend to argue in this article.

Mythic knowledge

I shall offer the *topos* of the "knowledge journey", drawing parallels with commonly occurring organizational situations in order to elicit in the reader the shared experience that myth is able to create between writer and reader. Mythic knowledge, in fact, operates by establishing social bonds among persons, generations and different contexts of use. Homer's *Odyssey* reflects one of the earliest forms of knowledge sharing through myth and narrative. Over time it has come to stand as a timeless reflection on humanity's voyage into the unknown. The men and women who work in organizations share, in my opinion, much more with Ulysses than appears at first sight. The thirst for knowing is what attracts humanity to the unknown, to discovery, to exploration, and to creativity. Obscurity and mystery draw knowledge into realization. The thirst for knowing was the force behind every vicissitude that beset Ulysses and his crew.

The myth of Ulysses as reinterpreted by Dante symbolizes humanity in search of knowledge. For Dante, the thirst for knowledge is what makes humanity human. In other words, knowing is also *poiesis*, the Greek term for this '"doing" as an end in itself. It is a desiring process, a journey whose

meaning lies in the travelling itself and not just in reaching the destination.

Dante recounts that Ulysses and his companions were old and slow when they came to the narrow passage where Hercules had set up landmarks to signal that no man should venture beyond. On the right hand they left Seville, and on the other they already had left Ceuta. That was the moment when Ulysses said:

> "O brothers", who through a hundred thousand dangers have reached the west, to this so brief vigil of our senses that remains to us, choose not to deny experience, following the sun, of the world that has no people. Consider your origin: you were not made to live as brutes, but to pursue virtue and knowledge (Dante Alighieri, *Inferno*, canto XXVI, pp. 112-20).

In the following sections I shall consider the rhetorical devices used by Ulysses to persuade his companions to do what he wanted: push forward into the unknown beyond the limits of legitimate knowledge that the Pillars of Hercules represented for the humanity of his time. My intention in doing so is to elicit the reader's mythic knowledge in order to invite reflection on the presence of desire in knowing practices.

"O brothers who through a hundred thousand dangers have reached the west"

Ulysses wished to arouse a desire for knowledge and a passion in the breasts of his companions. To do so he appealed to their identity and to the pride that accompanies a collective identity. He accorded them the status of "experts": they were men who had persisted onwards through 1,000 perils, and their survival testified to their skill as mariners and to their worth as companions. Ulysses' exhortation emphasises that their achievement was not a matter of luck but the result of mastery over specific expertise. The sailors had "made their own way"; they had subjected events to their will, giving their voyage sense and direction. They were men who had voluntarily undertaken a voyage to the West. Ulysses was therefore appealing to their expert knowledge, to their identity as "masters" proven by survival of 1,000 perils. His description of these men as brothers was therefore legitimated by the skill demonstrated in their mastery of difficult

Knowing as desiring

Silvia Gherardi

Journal of Workplace Learning

Volume 15 · Number 7/8 · 2003 · 352-358

situations and in their ability to give deliberate direction to what they did and what they knew. They resembled Ulysses because they were joined to him by comradeship and because he shared a bond of brotherhood – of deep trust – with them. They were like Ulysses and he was like them; together they reciprocally mirrored their attributes.

Mirroring in the other is a moment of fulfilment, a lull in the quest. Pleasure resides in moments of reciprocal mirroring as moments of fulfilment of desire. The collective celebration of skills and achievements within a community of practitioners not only contributes to the creation of a memory of community (Orr, 1993) but also constitutes a ritual for the fulfilment of a desire for reciprocal mirroring.

To classify in organizational terms what Ulysses accomplished by enacting a discursive practice known as "exhortation", I would call it the "transmission of passion in a community of practitioners". The undertaking of long voyages westwards across the Mediterranean was certainly not a widespread social practice in Ulysses' time. It represents more the figure of an "adventure" than that of a "practice", but it enables us to see how the *topos* of a passion for adventure yields insight into the transmission of passion in daily organizing. In fact, work groups, occupational or professional communities which for more or less long periods of time, and with a more or less stable structure of social and organizational relations, give rise to shared practices, share a practical knowledge that is not solely instrumental, and they display not only mastery of practices but also a passion, a feeling that is emotion and aesthetic understanding. Passion about what one does, and about doing it well, is a sentiment that pertains to a community of practitioners and anchors its identity. However, if this sentiment is not kept alive, celebrated, and relived in memory and stories, if it is not transmitted to novices, it will fade into routine, into passionless activity. Transmitting passion for a profession, occupation or a skill, for the mastery of practical situations, is an organizational practice for managing expert, tacit and collective knowledge. It has to do with knowledge management.

The knowledge of the expert consists of mastery over canonical and non-canonical practices, over a body of knowledge acquired

through social and cognitive learning processes. But it is also made up of passion, shared experience, collective identity – and the pride that accompanies it – pleasure and fulfilment and their opposites, pain and frustration. Inherent in the practice of mentoring – as a relation between two people with learning and development as its purpose – "is the notion of desire: the desire to learn, to support, to challenge, to achieve, to understand, to influence, to manipulate, to dominate, and the desire of physical attraction" (Megginson and Garvey, 2001, p. 7). Learning, development, and mastery are logical, emotional and social achievements situated in a personal and collective knowing trajectory.

Knowledge does not consist solely of a set of denotative statements. It also comprises the ideas of knowing how to do, live, and listen. It therefore concerns a competence which goes beyond the determination and application of the sole criterion of truth to include those of efficiency (technical qualification), justice and/or happiness (ethical wisdom), sonorous or chromatic beauty (auditory, visual sensitivity), and so on. Understood thus, knowledge coincides with an extensive "formation" of competencies. It is the unitary form embodied in a subject made up of different kinds of capabilities (Lyotard, 1984).

The story is the pre-eminent form of this knowledge, and narrative obeys rules which fix its pragmatics. For example, Lyotard argues, folk stories recount positive or negative formations – or in other words, the successes or failures of heroic endeavours – and these successes or failures legitimate particular social institutions (this is the social function of myths), or they represent positive or negative models of integration in consolidated institutions.

Consequently, when knowledge is reduced to mere instrumentality, what is lost is knowledge as a desire that takes us far from the realm of necessity, structuring and cognition as expressions of mental activity, and brings us closer to pleasure, play and aesthetic knowledge. When organizational researchers study the circulation and transmission of expert knowledge, they should investigate the transmission of passion, within the ludic spaces of work and the expression of passions in a professional identity formation.

Knowing as desiring

Silvia Gherardi

Journal of Workplace Learning

Volume 15 · Number 7/8 · 2003 · 352-358

Desiring and knowing

What sort of knowledge does desiring involve?

Discussion of desire in organizational studies shows that desire is significant in various ways to the proper understanding of organizational life. Gabriel *et al.* (2000, pp. 293-4) emphasise the usefulness of desire in providing an explanation for human motivation which differs from those based on need and incorporates "a social and psycho-sexual dimension". Desire differs from need, and also from instinct, by virtue of the meaning, fantasy, imagination and value that render it "culturally constituted". The importance of the cultures thrown into relief mainly by sociology is matched by the connection between desire and pleasure emphasised by depth psychologists, and of the discourse on "things sexual as against things unsexual" carried forward by Michel Foucault and discourse theorists.

Strati (2001, p. 3) argues that "luckily, no precise definition of desire has been formulated. Nor has it been possible to assess its exact influence on human action", despite the efforts of a large part of the human sciences, including the philosophy of mind (Schueler, 1995). Hence, the concept of desire is ambiguous and imprecise and is unable to explain the motives for social action. And yet it provides us with a rare opportunity to refer action to the inner complexity of the human personality, beginning with – in my view – its ability to develop aesthetic knowledge and to construct symbolic systems.

Deleuze and Guattari (1983, p. 25) note that an idealistic conception forces us to regard desire as primarily a lack: a lack of an object, a lack of the real object. It is idealistic because desire as a lack of a real object necessarily entails that there is a "dreamed-of behind every real object" insofar as the world does not contain each and every object that exists. Deleuze sees desire in affirmative terms as something that we can never sate nor fulfil but which somehow makes us more than we are: "Desire constantly couples continuous flows and partial objects that are by nature fragmentary and fragmented" (Deleuze and Guattari, 1983, p. 5); desire is never static or an end result; it is always a possible line of flight, a becoming.

Desire and knowledge are locked in a circle centred on fulfilment of a lack or as affirmation, even though we also experience desire as a revelation, as a rending experience beyond our control and management. Such desire without being is desire beyond knowledge; it is a desire of *non-savoir* that continually reveals *non-savoir* (O'Shea, 2001, p. 6).

For Lohmann and Steyaert (2001, p. 4) it is more appropriate to talk of desiring as an endless process of possibilities, which means that desire is defined by what it does, not by what it is. "There is not something which triggers desire to come into play, it is always in play as our world production" (Lohmann and Steyaert, 2001, p. 7).

I am most persuaded by Deleuze and Guattari's (1987, p. 14) description of desire as a "process of production without reference to any exterior agency", and by Lohmann and Steyaert's sociological view of the desiring process as a social practice enacted in the course of an action or event undertaken jointly by a group of sailors (Ulysses and his crew) or by any present-day community of practitioners. I shall take desiring to be a "moving concept" which allows us to perceive differently and draws attention to incompleteness in knowing processes.

Desiring therefore, like knowing, involves more than the construction of its object and its subject. Nor is it fulfilled by possession of that object; rather the tensions provoked by standing in an objectual relation reverberate back on the subject, the construction of which into a desiring and knowing actor comes about in the process. Desiring triggers a tension which induces personal investment in a search process. It prompts a knowledge journey across terrain where the distinction between cognitive and emotional no longer makes sense. From a social constructivist point of view, the emotions are a form of knowledge that maintains an epistemic link with the world through discursive practices that mobilize and regulate the emotional expressions appropriate to a community of practitioners. Knowing in organizations is not dispassionate; people love and hate their organizations, and they form meaningful, long-term relationships with them (Sims, 2004). As in the children's story *The Velveteen Rabbit* – the stuffed toy which remains just that until it is loved by a child – do organizations come alive when they are loved? David Sims proposes a parallel with the children's story and analyses the meaning of

Knowing as desiring	Journal of Workplace Learning
Silvia Gherardi	Volume 15 · Number 7/8 · 2003 · 352-358

loving by narrative – i.e. the relationship between love, the organization, and the narrative that links the person, the emotion, and the organization – in order to reflect on emotional knowing.

Another form of passionate knowledge is aesthetic knowledge. According to Strati (1999, p. 2), aesthetics in organizational life "concerns a form of human knowledge, and specifically the knowledge yielded by the perceptive faculties of learning, sight, touch, smell and taste, and by the capacity for aesthetic judgement". In organizational practices, aesthetic judgements and the expression of emotions are subject to social negotiation, definition and re-definition which shape the community of practitioners' identity and define its boundaries. In aesthetic knowledge, "feeling", understanding and knowing are intermeshed, and they merge into their being-in-use within the organization (Strati, 1999, p. 92). The Heideggerian notion of practice as *dasein* – absorbed capacity of knowing in practice in which the subject is not separated from the object – underscores the idea that meaningful action is embodied in its subjects and that an organizational actor is a hybrid entity made up of non-human elements inseparable from the human person and from his/her corporeality. Aesthetic understanding in the study of practices grasps the physicality of non-human elements in mediating the relationship of the knowing subjects with the instruments of their activities.

One might enquire as to the relevance of desiring as an organizing practice. By way of a reply we can return to Ulysses and his comrades and read their situation as a metaphor for a common organizational situation. Let us assume the Ulysses and his sailors are a team working on an innovation project: a community of practitioners in a laboratory or an R&D department. They are therefore men (and perhaps also women) who share a daily routine and have developed the knowledge with which to master the everyday aspects of their work. They can be identified externally as a "crew" performing its collective identity.

In situations like this we may ask how the pleasure of learning can be related to the drive to know. A possible answer is provided by Sardas (2001, p. 19), who studied demand by individuals for training in a second occupation. He argues that the pleasure of

learning may be due to: a desire for discovery (of another world hitherto "forbidden"); a desire to master (both as mastery for mastery's sake and mastery for action); and a compulsive need to understand. The desire for knowledge may therefore be rooted in unconscious motivations – if we consider desire from a psychoanalytic perspective – but it may be socially and organizationally shaped in the culture of a practice, when we consider desire as a social force leading to discovery and mastery as collective achievements.

There are consequently numerous organizational situations in which, "amid a thousand perils unto the West", work groups harbour and reproduce a practical "knowing-how": a set of relations with instruments that enable and mediate work practices; a shared understanding of the meaning of what they do. The production of knowledge itself "can be seen as desiring processes by which actors seduce (and select) new participants and meanings" (Bruni, 2001, p. 3). Situations such as these have usually been conceptualized and analysed with the categories of routine, leadership and community of practice. My proposal is that they should instead be analysed in terms of knowledge-based practices, the purpose being to show that practical reason is guided as much by the *habitus* as by desire. The former presides over tradition, style and the sense of community; the latter tends towards incompleteness, becoming and aesthetic understanding. The practical reason that prompts people and groups to invest (individually and collectively) in creative practices, to go beyond the Pillars of Hercules, is driven by passionate knowledge.

Practical reason and passionate knowledge

I have discussed elsewhere (Gherardi, 2001) the emergence of a strand of analysis definable as "practice-based theorizing on knowing and learning" in studies on knowledge process in organizations and organizational learning. In my view, the distinctive feature of this approach is its desire to understand knowing without reifying knowledge.

There are numerous reasons for singling out practice as the main unit of analysis of the social order – and therefore knowledge

Knowing as desiring	Journal of Workplace Learning
Silvia Gherardi	Volume 15 · Number 7/8 · 2003 · 352-358

practices as social practices. Here I shall emphasise only some of them:

- it enables the use of a constructionist approach based on becoming;
- it enables the use of a situated approach; and
- it enables the use of a materialist approach.

A practice-based approach to knowing and learning conceives knowledge as:

- Fabricated by situated practices of knowledge production and reproduction, using the technologies of representation and mobilization employed by human and non-human agents.
- Emergent in the process, a *bricolage* of material, mental, social and cultural resources. Because the world is not docile or passive, the problem is how to keep all these elements in alignment, in that knowledge is not given but is always an emergent process.
- Embedded in the world of the sensible and corporeal, which becomes an instrument of knowledge as it does in the aesthetic understanding (Strati, 1999) of organizational life.

From my point of view, the interesting aspect of social practices is how they are guided by a practical reason which stabilizes them as habits but is at the same time passionate reason, so that it expresses a desiring force which destabilizes the habit.

Practical understanding is the battery of bodily abilities that results from the active bricolage of material, mental, social and cultural resources that makes participation in practice possible. Skills are shared and no representation of the skills involved in performing appropriate human activity can be adequate. Practical understanding cannot be adequately formulated in words, neither by social researchers nor by actors themselves (Lynch, 2001). The incompleteness of the understanding of practical reasoning is due to the reciprocal construction of the subjects and objects of knowledge. This is especially apparent if we look at communities of practitioners whose activity is focused on knowledge itself: scientists are excellent examples of the way in which science, identity and the objects of knowledge spring from passionate practical knowledge. Epistemic objects are objects of knowledge characterized in terms of a lack of completeness of being

that takes away much of the wholeness, solidity, and the thing-like character that they have in our everyday conceptions (Knorr Cetina, 2001, p. 181). They have the capacity to unfold indefinitely. Objects of knowledge structure desire and provide for the continuation and unfolding of object-oriented practice (Knorr Cetina, 2001, p. 185).

In this regard Ulysses and his mariners are a topos in the discourse on knowledge: a figure half codified and half left open to subsequent interpretations. The epistemic object – passing beyond the Pillars of Hercules – is constructed as the object of desire by the desiring process that defines the mariners' identity as masters and experts, anchoring it in the humanness of the desire for knowledge.

The theme has also been treated by activity theory, which maintains that the object of activities is emergent and transformational (Engeström *et al.*, 2003). The intrinsic undecidability, incompleteness and indeterminacy of practices has been highlighted by ethnomethodological and organizational symbolism studies of what a practice actually is, with their conclusion that it is always indeterminate because it is at issue in what practitioners and others do. Besides this social and cognitive production of practical reason, I would stress its emotional, affective and aesthetic bases activated by desire and passion.

Note

1 A longer version of the "knowledge jourey" as a narrative form has been elaborated in Gheradi (2004).

References

Alighieri, D. (1970), *The Divine Comedy*, Routledge & Kegan Paul, London.

Alvesson, M. and Berg, P.O. (1992), *Corporate Culture and Organizational Symbolysm*, De Gruyter, Berlin.

Bruni, A. (2001), "'The knowledge era': the story of a research project and its translation", paper presented at the 17th EGOS Colloquium, Lyon, 5-7 July.

Deleuze, G. and Guattari, F. (1983) *Anti-Oedipus. Capilalisme and Schizophrenia*, University of Minnesota Press, St Paul, MN.

Deleuze, G. and Guattari, F. (1987), *A Thousand Plateaus. Capitalism and Schizophrenia*, University of Minnesota Press, St Paul, MN.

Derrida, J. (1971) *L'Écriture et la Différence*, de Seuil, Paris.

Knowing as desiring	Journal of Workplace Learning
Silvia Gherardi	Volume 15 · Number 7/8 · 2003 · 352-358

Engeström, Y., Puonti, A. and Seppänen, L. (2003), "Spatial and temporal expansion of the object as a challenge for reorganizing work", in Nicolini, D., Gherardi, S. and Yanow, D. (Eds), *Knowing in Organizations: A Practice-based Approach*, ME Sharpe, Armonk, NY.

Foucault, M. (1966), *Le mot et les Choses*, Gallimard, Paris.

Gabriel, Y., Fineman, S. and Sims, D. (2000), *Organizing and Organizations*, 1st ed., Sage, London.

Gherardi, S. (1999), "Learning as problem-driven or learning in the face of mystery?", *Organization Studies*, Vol. 20 No. 1, pp. 101-24.

Gherardi, S. (2001), "From organizational learning to practice-based knowing", *Human Relations*, Vol. 54 No. 1, pp. 131-9.

Gherardi, S. (2004), "Knowing as desire: Dante's Ulysses at the end of the known world", in Gabriel, Y. (Ed.), *Myths, Stories and Organizations: Premodern Narratives for Our Times*, Oxford University Press, Oxford.

Goodall, H.L. (1991), *Living in the Rock' n Roll Mystery: Reading Context, Self And Others as Clues*, Southern Illinois University Press, Carbondale, IL.

Knorr-Cetina, K. (2001), "Objectual practice", in Schatzki, T.R., Knorr-Cetina, K. and von Savigny, E. (Eds), *The Practice Turn in Contemporary Theory*, Routledge, London.

Latour, B. and Woolgar, S. (1979), *Laboratory Life: The Social Construction of Scientific Facts*, Sage, Beverly Hills, CA.

Lynch, M. (2001), "Ethnomethodology and the logic of practice", in Schatzki, T.R., Knorr-Cetina, K. and von Savigny, E. (Eds), *The Practice Turn in Contemporary Theory*, Routledge, London.

Lohmann, P. and Steyaert, C. (2001), "Organizational change as desiring production: change becoming change in a daily activity of waiting. A narrative of a transformation process", paper presented at the 17th EGOS Colloquium, Lyon, 5-7 July.

Lyotard, J.F. (1984), *The Postmodern Condition*, Manchester University Press, Manchester.

Megginson, D. and Garvey, B. (2001), "Odysseus, Telemachus and Mentor: stumbling into, searching for and signposting the road to desire", paper presented at the 17th EGOS Colloquium, Lyon, 5-7 July.

Orr, J. (1993), "Sharing knowledge, celebrating identity: war stories and community memory among service technicians", in Middleton, D.S. and Edwards, D. (Eds), *Collective Remembering: Memory in Society*, Sage, Beverly Hills, CA, pp. 169-89.

O'Shea, A. (2001), "Desire as non-savoir", paper presented at the 17th EGOS Colloquium, Lyon, 5-7 July.

Sardas, J.-C. (2001), "Desire for knowledge and identity dynamics: the case of multi-skills development", paper presented at the 17th EGOS Colloquium, Lyon, 5-7 July.

Schueler, G.F. (1995), *Desire. Its Role in Practical Reason and the Explanation of Action*, The MIT Press, Cambridge, MA.

Sims, D. (2004), "Knowing, loving and the Velveteen Rabbit", in Gabriel, Y. (Ed.), *Myths, Stories and Organizations: Premodern Narratives for Our Times*, Oxford University Press, Oxford.

Strati, A. (1998), "Organizational symbolism as a social construction: a perspective from the sociology of knowledge", *Human Relations*, Vol. 51 No. 11, pp. 1379-402.

Strati, A. (1999), *Organization and Aesthetics*, Sage, London.

Strati, A. (2001), "Aesthetics, tacit knowledge and symbolic understanding: going beyond the pillars of cognitivism in organization studies", paper presented at the 17th EGOS Colloquium, The Odyssey of Organizing, Lyon, 5-7 July.

[4]
Situated Knowledge and Situated Action: What do Practice-Based Studies Promise?

Silvia Gherardi

INTRODUCTION

'Knowledge is not something that people possess in their heads, but rather, something that people do together'. (Gergen, 1985: 270)

Since the 1980s, learning and knowing in organizations have been subject to lively and sometimes heated debate in the field of organization studies. More recently there is a form of new convergence around the so-called Practice-Based Studies (PBS) of learning and knowing in organizations. It is natural to enquire as to the reasons for this great interest, and explore how the focus on knowing in practice can contribute to a re-framing of the field.

The success of the theme of PBS in organizations resides, I believe, within that complex and variegated intellectual movement which in the social sciences has exposed the limitations of rationalism (Elster, 2000), and

which in organization studies has dismantled the functionalist paradigm from which the discipline sprang (Tsoukas and Knudsen, 2003). Consider, in fact, how organization theory used to be grounded on an image of the rational organization which privileged decision-making processes, first based on paradigmatic rationality and then on bounded rationality, and strategic planning predicated on *a priori* rationality. The shortcomings of the paradigm became evident as both scholars and practitioners in organizations came increasingly to realize that the theory was unable to account for contingencies and situational rationalities.

The image of an organization guided by the optimization principle was gradually replaced by an image of the organization which proceeds by trial and error, which builds on its own experience and that of others, which extracts maximum value from the knowledge in its possession, which strives after constant improvement, and which networks with other organizations and institutions in order to develop collectively the knowledge that it is unable to produce only on its own. This is an image, therefore, which depicts a more modest rationality of incremental and distributed type. It interprets the spirit of an age which views knowledge as a production factor and the knowledge society as manifesting epochal changes.

I do not wish to argue that study of organizational learning and knowledge in organizations has proceeded homogeneously in an anti-rationalist endeavour; on the contrary, contradictions between *a priori* rationality and incremental rationality, between positivist research and interpretative post-modern research, have traversed the debate. Unquestioning faith in rationality has rendered it into one of the myths most deeply rooted in the Western collective consciousness, and the consequence has been that the mind has been given primacy over the body as the almost exclusive seat of the knowledge-building process. Associated with a mentalist image of knowledge, therefore, is a research methodology which views individual or collective cognitive processes as the appropriate domain in which to investigate the mental schemes and mechanisms by which knowledge is produced and stored. But when knowledge is conceived as a mundane activity, situated in ongoing working and organizing practices, then we need a methodology appropriate to the observation of knowing in practice.

The intention of this chapter is to illustrate the contribution of PBS within a tradition critical of rationalism and cognitivism, doing so on the basis of a complex image of the relationship between working, organizing and knowing. It conceptualizes knowledge in the same manner as those analyses of social and institutional learning which assume the reciprocal constitution of the knower subject and the known object, of knowledge and knowing, and of practice and practising.

What practice-based studies promise to organizational studies is that they will link the study of working practices to the study of organizing, and that they will do so by making knowledge an observable phenomenon (Borzeix, 1998).

HOW TO DEFINE KNOWLEDGE?

Knowledge is not something that people possess in their heads; rather, it is something that people do together (Gergen, 1985: 270). From this perspective we may start our search for a methodology to study knowledge empirically as a situated activity.

As much in everyday life as in work organizations, people and groups create knowledge by negotiating the meanings of words, actions, situations and material artifacts. They all participate in and contribute to a world which is socially and culturally structured and constantly reconstituted by the activities of all those who belong to it. Cognitive and practical activity can thus be pursued only within this world, and through this social and cultural interweaving. Knowledge is not what resides in a person's head or in books or in data banks. To know is to be capable of participating with the requisite competence in the complex web of relationships among people, material artifacts and activities (Gherardi, 2001). On this definition it follows that knowing in practice is always a practical accomplishment.

Knowing is something people do together and it is done in every mundane activity, in organizations when people work together and in academic fields like organization studies, even if we make distinctions between lay, practical and theoretical knowledge. But also the practices of science – like any other social process – are situated in specific contexts of power/knowledge (Knorr-Cetina, 1981). Situated practices are both pre-reflexive (depending on unstated assumptions and shared knowledge for the mutual achievement of sense) and reflexively constitutive of the situated members' contexts from which they arise.

The term 'practice' is a *topos* that connects 'knowing' with 'doing'. It conveys the image of materiality, of fabrication, of handiwork, of the craftsman's skill. Knowledge consequently does not arise from scientific 'discoveries'; rather, it is fabricated by situated practices of knowledge production and reproduction using the technologies of representation and mobilization.

WHERE KNOWLEDGE IS?

We may say that the concept of practice has two important implications:

1 Social action and social knowledge must be regarded as activities inseparably woven together.
2 Knowing cannot be viewed as a conscious activity involving meaningful acts, for it presupposes only presumed or indirect references to norms, meanings and values that it claims to apply or to follow.

Therefore one of the most important directions taken by empirical studies which use the practice-based approach is the study of the practical organization of knowledge, in the form of methods of seeing, reasoning and acting in association of human and non-human elements. In fact, objects and their material world can be construed as materialized knowledge and matter which interrogate humans and interact with them.

Nevertheless, inspection of the literature shows that a unified theory of practice does not exist (Schatzki, 2001), nor does a unified field of practice studies. Rather I see three types of relations established between practices and knowledge:

- a relation of *containment*, in the sense that knowledge is a process that takes place within situated practices. On this view, practices are constituted as objective entities (in that they have been objectified) about which practitioners already have knowledge (i.e. they recognize them as practices) and which comprise bits and pieces of knowledge anchored in the material world and in the normative and aesthetic system that has elaborated them culturally.
- a relation of *mutual constitution*, in the sense that the activities of knowing and practising are not two distinct and separate phenomena; instead, they interact and produce each other.

- a relation of *equivalence*, in the sense that practising is knowing in practice, whether the subject is aware of it or not. Acting as a competent practitioner is synonymous with knowing how to connect successfully with the field of practices thus activated. The equivalence between knowing and practising arises when priority is denied to the knowledge that exists before the moment of its application, so that when applying it something already existent is not performed but the action instead creates the knowledge formed in the action itself and by means of it.

However, the three relations do not exclude each other, and emphasizing one of them does not prejudice the others. We may say that in order to make knowledge observable in its making and un-making we shall focus on working practices as the locus of knowledge production, and reproduction; we shall pay attention to the dynamics between practice as institutionalized knowledge and practising as institutionalizing process, and we shall assume that knowing in practice is synonymous of practising.

KNOWING IN PRACTICE AND KNOWING A PRACTICE

The study of practices by Bourdieu (1972), as well as by Garfinkel (1986) and Giddens (1976), is indebted to Schutz (1962), and to his definition of the social world as constituted by innumerable provinces of meaning viewed as particular sets of experiences, each of them manifesting a specific style and – with respect to this style – not only consistent in itself but also compatible with others. The world of everyday life is a province of meaning dominated and structured by what Schutz calls the 'natural attitude', so that the world is from the outset not the world of the private individual but an intersubjective world, shared by us all, and in which we have not a theoretical but eminently practical interest. However, individuals are usually aware that each of them has a different perception of reality. They are simultaneously aware that they have a sufficient degree of access to the perceptions of others to be able to perform their normal everyday activities. From this point of view, the meanings of our experiences of the outside world are considered for all practical purposes to be 'empirically identical' and thus give rise to the shared meanings indispensable for communication and for that particular 'accent' of reality conferred upon the world of everyday life. On this account, working represents the highest degree of interest in and attention to life, while simultaneously being the means with which individuals are able to alter the external world.

Put briefly, intersubjectivity gives rise not to a matching of meanings, but to the assumption that meanings are shared, or as Garfinkel puts it, to an agreement on methods of understanding. Accordingly, the most significant innovation by ethnomethodology with respect to traditional sociology is its replacement of cognitive categories with the categories of action, and the consequent view of the creation and transmission of knowledge as a socially important practice. Which means that also sociology has taken up Austin's assertion that "knowing is doing in everyday life, and it is doing society' (Giglioli, 1990: 85). In ethnomethodological studies, in fact, the transmission of knowledge as a social practice has been the focus of analysis by studies on work (Garfinkel, 1986). But because these studies have not overtly conceptualized working practice as 'learning', they have been largely ignored in the organizational field; only recently, in fact, has analysis of the social construction of technology and professional cultures by workplace studies resumed a number of ethnomethodological themes (Heath and Button, 2002).

Garfinkel (1967: 4) writes that one can discern the ethnomethodological method for analysis of social as well as working practices:

wherever studies of practical action and practical reasoning are concerned, these consist of the following: (1) the unsatisfied programmatic distinction between and substitutability of objective (context free) for indexical expressions; (2) the 'uninteresting' essential reflexivity of accounts of practical actions; and (3) the analysability of actions-in-context as a practical accomplishment.

The discussion thus far has highlighted three essential features -- indexicality, reflexivity and accountability – of the situated practices used by individuals to confer meaning on the social world.

The term 'indexical' was originally used in linguistics to denote expressions that are only completely comprehensible in the concrete context where they are produced and used. In ethnomethodological studies, however, the term has acquired specific connotations. The indexicality of social actions means that actors do not usually have problems in understanding each other, largely because comprehension is a constant and contingent achievement which depends on their interpretive work. Understanding situated practices therefore requires understanding of how individuals successfully use indexical behaviours and expressions whose meanings are constantly negotiated and renegotiated in the course of interaction. One meaning of 'situated' with reference to practices is that their performance depends on the manner in which indexicality is locally resolved. Also social norms are indexical, with the consequence that a rule of behaviour does not have a univocal meaning outside the concrete settings where it is applied. This thesis stresses in particular that the range of application of a rule is always constituted by an *a priori* indefinable number of different situations, so that a norm is always applied 'for another first time' (Garfinkel, 1967: 9)[1] and a work practice is always executed for 'another first time'.

Reflexivity, the second characteristic, is rooted in all order-producing social activities (Garfinkel, 1967: 67). It consists in the practices of accountability, observability, and referability of social action, by which is meant making the world comprehensible to oneself and to the other members of a collectivity. 'Reflexivity refers to the dynamic self-organizational tendency of social interaction to provide for its own constitution through practices of accountability and scenic display' (Flynn, 1991: 28). It is therefore actions themselves that 'reflexively' display their nature as meaningful to social actors. It is this feature that enables the analysis of practices, in that it renders their meanings accessible to 'outsiders' as well, or better, to 'external observers' (Fele, 2002). These observers consequently do not have to rely entirely on what people tell them – a method criticized by Zimmermann and Pollner (1970) because, they maintain, actions speak for themselves. However, this is not to imply that their meanings are abstract or decontextualized; rather, it depends on the fact that they inevitably participate in an organization of activity – they are, that is to say, embedded in a concrete situation.[2]

I finally deal with the notion of accountability. Generally used to denote a 'motive', a 'reason' or an 'explanation', the term is used by Garfinkel (1967: 1) as synonymous with 'observable-reportable, i.e. available to members as situated practices of looking-and-telling', that is, a constantly exhibited and public property of ordinary activities. In other words, accountability evinces the normal, ordinary, comprehensible and natural character of events. Consequently, social actions do not need to be 'baptized' by language for them to be intelligible and indexical to their participants. This signifies that accounts contribute to the setting of which they are part, and that they are interpreted and understood procedurally. 'Accounts, therefore, are not a terminus for social scientific investigation, they are, rather, a point of departure for it' (Heritage, 1987: 250). For that matter, Garfinkel himself maintains that large parts of our actions and interactions are not based on shared agreements but rather on a texture of tacit assumptions, neither explicated nor fully explicable, which are taken for granted. This, therefore, is yet another way to conceptualize tacit knowledge as 'taken for granted' which derives directly from Schulz (1962).

Finally, Garfinkel emphasizes the importance of social action as a moral phenomenon, where 'morality' is tied to patterns of action recognized by the entire community as those most correct, legitimate and adequate in a specific context[3] distinct from others. On this view, the members of society know the moral order when in the actions of others

they recognize those models that represent the 'natural facts of life', not internalized social norms – as Parsons instead argued when he treated social norms as initially 'external' and then integrated into the personality by socialization to take the form of dispositions. This account of morality also views rules as assumed in constitutive function of the intelligibility of concrete actions. Indeed, it is precisely the self-structuring of behaviour in accordance with the prescriptions of a norm which enables the actor to recognize that behaviour as a given type of action.

People engaged in a working practice acknowledge a set of social positions which are interrelated, which make sense, and which are enacted. Practices impart identities and selves that are displayed on appropriate occasions. People's experiences in, with and within practices become incorporated into their identities, the social positions that they occupy, the status that they display while they enact the set of practices, and also when they do not perform it. Professional identities are linked to a set of institutional practices but they are also performed outside their profession.

KNOWING IN PRACTICE AS A SITUATED ACTIVITY

For the time being, we may adopt a methodological perspective which, once the nature of an 'institution of practices' has been established, views analysis of situated 'seeing, saying and doing' as an operational means to give concrete definition to a field of empirical analysis. This methodological approach has already been used with good results by studies of gender as a socially situated practice (Bruni et al., 2004; Martin, 2003; Poggio, 2006), and of learning safety as practical knowledge enacted in appropriate situations (Gherardi, 2006).

However, we should keep in mind the multiple meanings of the term 'situated knowledge' and the multiple uses made of the expression. 'Situated' has a multiplicity of meanings (Gherardi, 2006), all of which are present when we consider the knowing process as embedded with the performance of a working practice:

- *Situated in the body.* The materiality of the knowing subject is primarily anchored in the body, and a body is sexed. The feminist critique of science and feminist work in the sociology of science and technology have helped to show that even 'universal' knowledge is situated, while feminist objectivity simply means bodily-situated knowledge (Fujimura et al., 1987; Harding, 1986; Mol, 1999). The advantage of a 'partial perspective' – the term coined by Donna Haraway (1991) and taken up by Marilyn Strathern (1991) – is that knowledge always has to do with circumscribed domains, not with transcendence and the subject/object dichotomy. Moreover, the material body – the body that works – assumes shape and location within the set of practices that constitute the work setting. The knowledge acquired via the five senses is aesthetic, not mental. It often forms the basis for specific competences. Craft trades required trained bodies – ones, that is, which have incorporated an expertise. It is through the body that 'an eye' (or 'an ear' or 'a nose') for something is acquired, so that aesthetic knowledge (Strati, 2003) also comprises the ability to develop a professional 'vision' in the broad sense.
- *Situated in the dynamics of interactions.* Knowing in practice articulates the emergent – *in situ* – nature of knowledge from interactions. The situation of an action can be defined as the set of resources available to convey the meaning of one's own actions and to interpret those of others (Suchman, 1987). And Latour (1987) suggests that people interact not only with each other but also with the non-human that makes up the remainder of the natural world.
- *Situated in language.* This specification highlights that all expressions change their meanings according to the subject uttering them and according to the context of use. The situation, therefore, not only defines the circumstances of an action, it also produces them through language. I prefer to talk of 'discursive practices', rather than communication or language, in order to emphasize that talking is doing, and to shift attention from the subject that talks and his/her communicative intent to the fact that situated talking practices have a form of their own (*qua* 'practices') and relative independence from the subjects that perform them.

- *Situated in a physical context.* Space is not an empty container for situations, nor is it a passive receptacle for the organized activities of actors-in-situation. On the contrary, subjects actively engage with space and establish relations with it (Kirsh, 1995). An organized space – a workplace – is a 'situational territory' (Goffman, 1971; Suchman, 1996) in which objects remind subjects of what they must do, prevent humans from doing things that may harm them, guide action according to intentions inscribed in their design, and make work and life comfortable, both materially and socially. Because the materiality of situations enters into relations, objects can be conceived as materializations of knowledge, as tangible knowledge which 'steers' and sustains a set of practices.

It is therefore possible to discern various currents of research concerned with 'knowing in practice', bearing in mind that what they have in common is not identification of a particular type of action but rather an endeavour to explain how knowledge organizes action in situation. As Béguin and Clôt (2004) noted, there are different disciplinary 'accents' which articulate three dynamics of this organization of action in situation: *interactionist*, which derives mainly from sociology and stresses interactions mediated by language and draws mainly on Lucy Suchman (1987); *ecological*, which has arisen mainly in psychology and draws on Gibson (1979) and his concept of 'affordance', which shows that some of the organization of action is undertaken by the environment; and *cultural*, which refers to cognitive anthropology and draws on the studies by Norman (1994) on cognitive artifacts and Hutchins (1995) on distributed cognition. Béguin and Clôt point out that these three currents on action and situated cognition seek to establish a relation (in their view an unsatisfactory one) between what is given in the situation and what the actors create in it.

The roots of the intellectual traditions of the study of practice-based studies may be represented as in Figure 3.9.1, where I illustrate its first genealogy as delineated by Conein and Jacopin (1994) in reference to the streams in situated action and activity theory and integrate it with its extension to

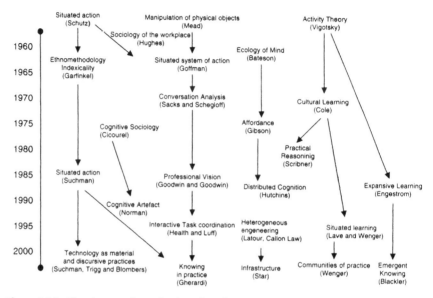

Figure 3.9.1   The streams of practice-based studies

the field of learning and knowing as practical accomplishment (Gherardi, 2000).

A METHODOLOGICAL FRAMEWORK

Once we consider the mutual constitution of practice and practising, and the situatedness of knowing as a practical accomplishment we become able to analyse knowledge as an observable phenomenon and propose a framework that focuses on knowing as a situated practice.

Imagine a work group engaged in everyday work practices which are proceeding smoothly and whose coordination is fluid and unproblematic. In this situation we observe that working is not distinct from organizing activities, and that adjusting them to a context which may change as a result of those same activities is not distinct from habitual knowledge on how to carry out those activities, or from knowing how to modify them contextually. This is therefore a situation in which working, organizing, innovating to adjust to a changing context, situated

learning and prior learning are co-present and co-produced in situation. We may therefore analyse and interpret knowledge in practice as an empirical and observable phenomenon, on the assumption that in order to perform a work practice, the context, the collectivity, the tools and technologies, and language are the resources at hand for purposive action.

It is therefore not necessary to posit the logical primacy of either the actors, or the context, or the material world, or language. Work practice as the successful outcome of the manifestation of practical knowledge in situation is *given and created* by the weaving together of knowledge anchored in the environment and the material and social world to create a texture of practice.

Within this methodological framework the focus will be on the connections-in-action established in the community of practitioners by constant conversation on the practices and the ethical and aesthetic criteria that institutionalize them within that social formation. In fact, this methodological framework proposes a conceptualization of practical activity in which practice coincides neither with routine as an analytical set of activities nor as a doing-in-situation mediated by interactions, language and technologies. The distinctive feature of this view of work practices as social and material accomplishments is the weaving together of resources within a normative conception, constantly produced and reproduced by the practitioners, about what constitutes a 'good practice', and about why one way of doing that practice is more 'attractive' than another. The concept of 'practice' is broader than those of 'activity', 'situated action' and 'routine' because it emphasises, not doing-in-situation but doing-society-in-situation.

The pragmatic dimension of doing is co-present and co-produced together with that of performing situated identities sustained by a normative and aesthetic dimension. The constant conversation that takes place among practitioners in practice and about practice produces coordination in practice and among work practices, as well as ensuring that practices continue to be such – i.e. practised – and reproduced in accordance with the social criteria that sustain them.

CONCLUSIONS: PRACTICE AS AN IN-BETWEEN CONCEPT

When we give priority to practices over mind we contribute to a transformed conception of knowledge, which is no longer possession of mind, which is mediated and propagated both by interactions between people and by the material arrangements in the world, which is discursively constructed, which is diffused, fragmented and distributed as a property of groups working within a situated material environment and within a situated and discursively sustained social world.

Practices, therefore, are modes of ordering which acquire temporal and spatial stability from provisional and unstable agreements in practice. We can say that people share a practice if their actions are appropriately regarded as answerable to norms of correct or incorrect practice, to criteria of aesthetics taste, and to standards of fairness. Therefore when

we look at situated actions in ongoing practices – seeing, saying and doing – we are making 'knowledge observable'. As Yanow (2000) noted, seeing a practice – a set of acts and interactions involving language and objects repeated over time, with patterns and variations – allow the researcher to infer back that a culture of practice is performed. And as Goodwin (1994) illustrated, practitioners learn to see and to sustain a 'professional vision' as a situated activity.

What does the concept of practice promise and why does it do so? I have argued that the 'what and the how' concern making knowledge an empirical and observable phenomenon, and I have outlined a methodological framework for the purpose. As a concluding point I shall address the 'why' question and answer it by stressing the nature of 'practice' as an in-between concept.

The concept of practice may constitute a bridge between antithetical concepts, and for this reason I have defined it elsewhere as an 'in-between concept' (Gherardi, 2003). It lies in-between habit and action in the sense that a practice has habitual features because it is based on the repetition of activities, and it also has the character of a purposeful action. But it is neither a habit nor an action. In the same sense it is an in-between concept between reproduction and production, because in practice the reproduction of society is done day by day, practice after practice, while at the same time practice is productive of its results and effects. The heuristic promise of a concept standing in-between production and reproduction, habit and action resides in its power to account for how society holds together (is reproduced) and changes in being reproduced. While production has been a much-studied phenomenon, reproduction and the endogenous dynamics of reproduction have attracted less interest. The focus is therefore on working practices and on how they are internally changed in being practised, both incrementally through application of situated rationality to the changing resources of the practice at hand, and through the social dynamics stemming from the ongoing conversation of practitioners on the normative standards of the practice. Practice-based studies make a specific contribution to the understanding of how social reproduction and its maintenance is accomplished by means of knowledgeable practices.

NOTES

1 This has two fundamental consequences: the first is that the applicability of a norm necessarily depends on the content of that norm; the second is that norms in themselves are not sufficient to direct human action because they do not exhaustively define the components constituting the behaviour to which they apply, in the sense that it is always possible to find behaviours which are not regulated by any specific rule.

2 However, Garfinkel argues that in no case is the investigation of practical actions undertaken in order that the persons involved might be able to recognize and describe what they are doing in the first place and those conducting the analysis understand the manner in which they are talking about what they are doing. This entails that the actors assume 'the reflexivity of producing, accomplishing, recognizing and demonstrating the rational and wholly practical adequacy of their procedures; they rely upon it, require it, and make use of it' (Fele, 2002: 62).

3 Note that Garfinkel does not view the context as an entity which exists before the action and determines it by means of norms; rather, it self-organizes itself with respect to the intelligible character of its manifestations. In other words, it is constantly reconstituted by actions so that it becomes at once the point of departure and arrival of the selfsame actions that constitute it (Nicotera, 1996: 53).

REFERENCES

Béguin, P. and Clôt, Y. (2004) 'L'Action Située Dans le Development de l'Activité', *@ctivités*, 1 (2): 27–49.

Borzeix, A. (1998) 'Comment Observer l'Interpretation?', in A. Borzeix, A. Bouvier and P. Pharo (eds), *Sociologie et Connaissance*, CNRS edition: Paris.

Bourdieu, P. (1972) *Esquisse d'une théorie de la pratique précédé de trois etudes de ethnologie kabyle*, Switzerland: Librairie Droz S.A. (Engl. trans. *Outline of a Theory of Practice*. Cambridge University Press, 1977).

Bruni, A., Gherardi, S. and Poggio, B. (2004) 'Doing gender, doing entrepreneurship: an ethnographic account of interwined practices', *Gender, Work and Organization*, 11 (4): 406–429.

Conein, B. and Jacopin, E. (1994) 'Action située et cognition: le savoir en place', *Sociologie du Travail*, 94 (4): 475–500.

Elster, J. (2000) *Ulysse Unbound*. Cambridge: Cambridge University Press.

Fele, G. (2002) *Etnometodologia. Introduzione allo studio delle attività ordinarie*. Roma: Carocci.

Flynn, P. (1991) *The Ethnomethodological Movement*. New York: Mouton de Gruyter.

Fujimura, J., Star, S. and Gerson, E. (1987) 'Metode de recherche en sociologie des sciences: travail, pragmatisme et interactionnisme symbolique', *Cahiers de Recherches Sociologique*, 5: 65–85.

Garfinkel, H. (1967) *Studies in Ethnomethodology*. Englewood Cliffs: Prentice-Hall.

Garfinkel, H. (1986) *Ethnomethodological Studies of Work*. London: Routledge & Kegan Paul.

Gergen, K.J. (1985) The Social Constructionist Movement in moderns psychology, American Psychologist, March 1985. pp. 266–275.

Gherardi, S. (2000) 'Practice-based theorizing on learning and knowing in organizations: an introduction', *Organization*, 7 (2): 211–223.

Gherardi, S. (2001) 'From organizational learning to practice-based knowing', *Human Relations*, 54 (1): 131–139.

Gherardi, S. (2003) 'Introduction to the workshop "Practice-based Studies": current trends and future developments'. Trento, November, 6–7.

Gherardi, S. (2006) *Organizational Knowledge: The Texture of Workplace Learning*. Blackwell, Oxford.

Gibson, J.J. (1979) *The Ecological Approach to Visual Perception*. London: Erlbaum Associates.

Giddens, A. (1976) *New Rules of Sociological Method*. London: Hutchinson.

Giglioli, P.P. (1990) *Rituale, Interazione, Vita Quotidiana*. Bologna: Il Mulino.

Goffman, E. (1971) 'The territories of the self', in E. Goffman (ed.), *Relations in Public: Microstudies of the Public Order*. New York: Harper & Row.

Goodwin, C. (1994) 'Professional vision', in *American Anthropologist*, 96 (3): 606–633.

Haraway, D. (1991) 'Situated knowledges: the science question in feminism and the privilege of partial perspectives', in D. Haraway (ed.), *Simians, Cyborgs and Women: the Reinvention of Nature*. London: Free Association Books. pp. 183–202.

Harding, S. (1986) *The Science Question in Feminism*. Ithaca: Cornell University.

Heath, C. and Button, G. (2002) 'Special issue on workplace studies: editorial introduction', *The British Journal of Sociology*, 53 (2): 157–161.

Heritage, J.C. (1987) 'Ethnomethodology', in A. Giddens and J. Turner (eds), *Social Theory Today*. Standford: Standford University Press. pp. 224–272.

Hutchins, E. (1995) *Cognition in the Wild*. Cambridge, MA: The MIT Press.

Kirsh, D. (1995) 'The intelligent use of space', *Artificial Intelligence*, 73: 36–68.

Knorr-Cetina, K. (1981) *The Manufacture of Knowledge. An Essay on the Constructivist and Contextual Nature of Science*. Oxford: Pergamon Press.

Latour, B. (1987) *Science in Action*. Cambridge, MA: Harvard University Press.

Martin, P.Y. (2003) '"Said & done" vs. "Saying & doing". Gendered practices/practising gender at work', *Gender & Society*, 17.

Mol, A. (1999) 'Ontological politics: a word and some questions', in J. Law and J. Hassard (eds), *Actor Network Theory and After*. Oxford: Blackwell.

Nicotera, F. (1996) *Etnometodologia e azione sociale*. Milano: Prometheus.

Norman, D. (1994) 'Les artefacts cognitifs', in B. Conein, N. Dodier, and L. Thévenot (eds), *Les Objects dans l'Action*. Paris: Edition de l'Ecole des Hautes Etudes en Sciences Sociales, 15–34.

Poggio, B. (2006) Introduction to the special issue 'Gender as Social Practice', *Gender, Work, and Organization*.

Schatzki, T.R. (2001) 'Introduction. Practice theory', in T.R. Schatzki, K. Knorr-Cetina and E. von Savigny (eds), *The Practice Turn in Contemporary Theory*. London and New York: Routledge. pp. 1–14.

Schutz, A. (1962) *Collected Papers I. The Problem of Social Reality*. Nijhoff: The Hague.

Strathern, M. (1991) *Partial Connections*. Savage: Rowan and Littlefield.

Strati, A. (2003) 'Knowing in practice: aesthetic understanding and tacit knowledge', in D. Nicolini, S. Gherardi and D. Yanow (eds), *Knowing in Organizations*. Armonk, NY: M.E. Sharpe, pp. 53–75.

Suchman, L. (1987) *Plans and Situated Action: The Problem of Human-Machine Communication*. Cambridge: Cambridge University Press.

Suchman, L. (1996) 'Constituting shared workspaces', in Y. Engestrom and D. Middleton (eds), *Cognition and Communication at Work*. Cambridge: Cambridge University Press.

Tsoukas, H. and Knudsen, C. (2003) 'Introduction: the need for meta-theoretical reflection in organization theory', in H. Tsoukas and C. Knudsen, *The Oxford Handbook of Organization Theory. Meta-theoretical perspectives*. Oxford: Oxford University Press. pp. 1–36.

Zimmermann, D.H. and Pollner, M. (1970) 'The everyday world as a phenomenon', in J.D. Douglas (ed.), *Understanding Everyday Life*. London: Routledge & Kegan Paul. pp. 80–103.

Yanow, D. (2000) 'Seeing organizational learning: a "Cultural" view', *Organization*, 7 (2): 329–348.

[5]

Article

Management Learning
41(3) 265–283
© The Author(s) 2010
Reprints and permission: sagepub.
co.uk/journalsPermissions.nav
DOI: 10.1177/1350507609356938
mlq.sagepub.com
$\circledS$SAGE

Through the practice lens: Where is the bandwagon of practice-based studies heading?

Gessica Corradi and Silvia Gherardi
University of Trento, Italy

Luca Verzelloni
University of Bologna, Italy

Abstract
In the last 20 years we have witnessed a return of the practice concept in studies of organizing, learning and knowing. Practice has been used as a lens for the reinterpretation of many organizational phenomena, and it seems that a bandwagon of practice-based studies has been set in motion by the coining of labels, which comprise the term 'practice'. A bandwagon can serve to institutionalize a field of studies by progressive labelling and a collective appropriation of the general label. We wonder if this has been the case for practice-based studies? The article presents seven labels and discusses their similarities and differences in order to demonstrate that, while the institutionalization of practice-based studies may be considered an achieved goal, the collective appropriation of the label has not been achieved, and therefore, the bandwagon is heading for a partition.

Keywords
epistemology; organizational learning; organizing; practice; practice-based studies

Introduction

Labels can be considered quasi-objects (Czarniaswka and Joerges, 1995) that easily travel and translate ideas from one place to another. Their capacity to transport ideas and to spread fashions resides in the equivocalness that they make possible. When a label is used, the legitimation associated with it is mobilized—by imitation—and processes of institutional isomorphism are generated. At the same time as we verify the uncertainty of an innovation, saying that we are doing what others are also doing, we are able to protect a space for experimentation, a space in which to do otherwise and perhaps to conceal failures. Isomorphism enables allomorphism (Gherardi and Lippi, 2000). Labels are therefore vectors of innovation and institutionalization that allow the translation of ideas as they diffuse them (Czarniaswka and Sévon, 2005). One label that has generated and is transporting/ translating new ideas in studies on organizational learning and knowledge management is that of

Corresponding author:
Gessica Corradi, Via G. Verdi 26, Trento, Italy, I-381222.
Email: gessica.corradi@gmail.com

'practice-based studies' (henceforth PBS). It strikes us as a platitude, as an idea whose time has come, because it seems to have been always with us.

The aim of this article is to investigate how the idea of PBS came into being, and how its entry into use started up a 'bandwagon': that is, brought together various strands of inquiry with certain features in common. The question that we shall seek to answer is where is this bandwagon heading?

The bandwagon analogy

The metaphor of the bandwagon (Fujimura, 1988, 1995) calls to mind the idea of a collective 'journey'. The concept expresses an involving activity able to bring together a heterogeneous group of subjects in pursuit of the same goal. Fujimura has studied how and why what she terms the 'bandwagon' of molecular biology has developed in cancer research. Meant by this term is a situation in which a large number of people, laboratories and organizations join their respective resources in a single approach to a problem.

The point of departure is the theory of the oncogene. When this theory was formulated by two American biologists at the beginning of the 1970s, it was nothing more than an intuition devoid of an empirical basis. Its purpose was solely to summarize in a few points what had been achieved to date in various areas of cancer research. This synthesis did not add anything further, either theoretically or experimentally, to the findings of already-completed studies. Rather, it assembled the old results under a new label which gave semantic continuity to them. Nevertheless, this idea also made it possible to integrate and give recognition to a wide array of theories and laboratory experiments performed in previous years. Thus the oncogene theory acknowledged research, disciplines and researchers that had put forward alternative explanations (mainly the viral and endogenous ones). The oncogene theory in itself did not furnish any solution to disputes, but the various schools and research centres could recognize themselves in this intuition and in the consequent methodologies (i.e. tests on DNA) and gain visibility, so that the necessary consensus was created for experiments, theories and researchers to come together under this new paradigmatic umbrella.

Fujimura then identifies two distinct phases in the start-up of a bandwagon: the first is that of *labelling*, which consists in identifying a field of meaning sufficiently wide to comprise a number of supporters able to interpret and recognize it as 'interesting'; the second is that of the *collective appropriation* of the overall label and its reproduction in local practices through adaptation and modification according to local needs and constraints, generating what Fujimura calls a 'snowball' effect.

The analogy drawn here between this famous bandwagon and PBS has the purpose of showing on the one hand how the labelling process contributes to the institutionalization of a field of interest, and on the other, how the collective appropriation of a label simultaneously serves a process of institutional isomorphism (things are done which have already been done by others in order to legitimate what one is doing) and of allomorphism (thanks to the legitimacy resources that the label confers, different things can be done). In the case of PBS, the point of departure has been a renewed interest within organization studies in the concept of practice—a concept which has a long tradition in philosophy and in sociology.

'Practice', Schatzki (1996, 2001) argues, is a term that seeks to be descriptive of fundamental phenomena in society, as encountered, for example, in the writings of philosophers and sociologist like Bourdieu (1972), Lyotard (1979), Foucault (1980), Taylor (1995), as well as ethnomethodologists (Garfinkel, 1967). In Bourdieu's case the deeper-lying structures that organize general social practices are self-reproducing dispositions; in Lyotard's discursive moves or language games; in

Foucault's genealogies of practice; in Taylor's the vocabulary embedded within the practice that marks its range of possible actions and meanings; in Garfinkel's the reflexive tendency of social interaction to provide for its own constitution through practices of accountability and scenic display.

In organization studies, the influence of practice theorists is more important as an epistemology for the study of working practices and the kind of practical and 'hidden' knowledge that supports them. In fact, a paradoxical feature is that practices are not directly accessible, observable, measurable or definable; rather, they are hidden, tacit and often linguistically inexpressible in a propositional sense. At the same time the term 'practice' has the connotation of being something transferable, teachable, transmittable or reproducible (Turner, 1994). The advent of the knowledge society and knowledge management has generated renewed interest in practical knowledge and its transmission (deliberate or otherwise); and the study of working practices, workplace interactions and activities has become central in 'bringing work back in' (Barley and Kunda, 2001), especially now that work is changing so rapidly and the traditional methods for its analysis are no longer suited to studying work as it is being done. One reason for the renewed interest in practice theories in organization studies is linked to the search for a non rational-cognitive view of knowledge. Central to the practice perspective is acknowledgement of the social, historical and structural contexts in which knowledge is manufactured. Practice allows researchers to investigate empirically how contextual elements shape knowledge and how competence is built around a contingent logic of action. Practical knowledge is a form of competent reasoning and doing. Nevertheless a unified theory of practice does not exist. With some authors, the discourse of practice is especially associated with critical theory, postmodernist and deconstructionist writing. In the work of others, we encounter a more commonplace usage of the term practice. For this reason one asks: why is it that so many aspects of organizations are now spoken of as practices?

In determining a point of departure of the bandwagon, we may state that the interest of organization studies in the concept of practice started many years before the so-called 'practice turn'(as Schatzki et al., 2001 labelled it), and as a matter of fact organization studies contributed to the practice turn in significant ways, especially through empirical studies. One can identify in studies on community of practice—and especially in the reverse of the concept—the antecedent that set the bandwagon in motion.

Studies on communities of practice have acted as pathfinders because they have introduced a plurality of concepts and innovative perspectives into the debate: for instance, the situatedness and sociality of practices; the central importance of practical know-how for work; the existence of collective identities; the importance of learning processes within a community of practitioners.

The concept of community of practice (CoP) first arose in anthropological and educational studies, and it spread particularly through the influence of Lave and Wenger's book. In light of five empirical studies on apprenticeships (obstetricians, tailors, naval officers, butchers and Alcoholics Anonymous), these authors developed the concept of the community of practice as a 'set of relations among persons, activity, and world, over time and in relation with other tangential and overlapping communities of practice' (Lave and Wenger, 1991: 98).

The notion of community of practice marks the passage from a cognitive and individual vision of learning to a social and situated one. Learning is not a phenomenon that takes place in a person's head: rather, it is a participative social process. The community is the source and the medium for socialization. It constructs and perpetuates social and working practices. The CoP can be conceived as a form of self-organization which corresponds neither to organizational boundaries nor to friendship groups. It is based on sociality among practitioners and on the sharing of practical activities. Sociality is the dimension within which interdependencies arise among people engaged in the same practices.

These interdependencies give rise to processes of legitimate and peripheral participation whereby newcomers take part in organizational life and are socialized into ways of seeing, doing and speaking. The newcomer gradually becomes a full member of the community. The knowledge at the basis of a job or a profession is transmitted, and in parallel perpetuated, through the sociality of practice.

The importance of the term 'CoP' has induced numerous authors and disciplines—mainly in organizational and managerial studies—to appropriate the concept and then, inevitably, change its meaning. The managerial literature has gradually transformed the concept of CoP (Wenger, 2000; Wenger and Snyder, 2000) into a tool used by managers to manage the knowledge of their organizations. Neglecting the risk of reifying the category, these new approaches have for years investigated how to recognize and govern the CoP.

The spread of the CoP concept has provoked numerous criticisms in recent years. Various authors have pointed out the ambiguous or ill-defined aspects of the theory (Handley et al., 2006; Roberts, 2006), concentrating mainly on elements such as the power, trust, predisposition, size, extent and duration of communities; but also on the use itself of the term 'community'. These criticisms have raised awareness that different types of CoP exist, and they have led to a proposal for translation of the label. This proposal (Gherardi et al., 1998; Brown and Duguid, 2001; Swan et al., 2002; Contu and Willmot, 2003; Roberts, 2006) suggests that the concept of community of practice (CoP) should be reversed into practices of the community (PoC). A shift has therefore come about from the notion of a CoP as the context where learning takes place to consideration of how situated and repeated actions create a context in which social relations among people, and between people and the material and cultural world, stabilize and become normatively sustained. The switch from the concept of CoP to that of PoC has generated the broad PBS debate (Gherardi, 2009a).

In order to illustrate how the bandwagon moved on we looked for the appearance of any new label, and Table 1 shows the chronological development of seven different labels and the understanding of practice within each of them. It will help us to answer to questions like: When did the label first appear? Who introduced it? What does the term practice denote?

While Table 1 will help us to trace the similarities in definitions, the next two sections will try to make sense of the differences along two lines:

1. practice as an 'empirical object': conceptual labels like practice standpoint, practice-based learning or work-based learning and research fields like strategy-as-practice or science-as-practice underline the existence of a specific empirical object. In this case, the practices (or the process within a practice) become the locus in which scholars study the activities of the practitioners;
2. practice as 'a way of seeing': conceptual labels like knowing-in-practice, practice lens, approach and perspective use, implicitly or explicitly, the metaphor of sight: practice as a way of seeing a context, and therefore an epistemology. In fact, many scholars adopt the sight metaphor as a lens for understanding the situatedness of practical reasoning and the contingent nature of organizational rationality.

Practice as empirical object

Two labels—practice-based standpoint and practice-based or work-based learning—share the feature that they consider practice to be the locus of learning and knowing although they refer to two different research communities (organization scholars and educationalists). Now briefly described is their interest in the use of the concept of practice and their principal interpretative categories. It is important to consider the years in which studies were published in order to trace the chronology of the bandwagon's setting in motion.

Table 1. A chronology of practice-based studies

Label	Who first introduced it	Definition of practice
Practice-based standpoint	Brown and Duguid (1991)	'From this **practice-based standpoint,** we view learning as the bridge between working and innovating' (Brown and Duguid, 1991: 41). 'For our purposes, then, we intend the term "practice" to refer to the coordinated activities of individuals and groups in doing their "real work" as it is informed by a particular organizational or group context. In this sense, we wish to distinguish practice from both behaviour and action. By "practice", we refer to action informed by meaning drawn from a particular group context' (Cook and Brown, 1999: 390).
Work-based learning and practice-based learning	Raelin (1997, 2007)	'This approach recognizes that practitioners in order to be proficient need to bridge the gap between explicit and tacit knowledge and between theory and practice. **Work-based learning** subscribes to a form of knowing that is context-dependent. Practitioners use theories to frame their understanding of the context but simultaneously incorporate an awareness of the social processes in which organizational activity is embedded' (Raelin, 1997: 572).
Practice 'as what people do'	Pickering (1990, 1992) Whittington (1996)	'I sought an understanding of science-as-practice, of science as a way of being in, getting on with, making sense of, and finding out about the world' (Pickering, 1990: 685). 'The practice perspective is concerned with managerial activity, how managers "do strategy"' (Whittington, 1996: 732).
Practice lens and practice-oriented research	Orlikowski (2000)	'A **practice lens** to examine how people, as they interact with a technology in their ongoing practices, enact structures which shape their emergent and situated use of that technology. Viewing the use of technology as a process of enactment enables a deeper understanding of the constitutive role of social practices in the ongoing use and change of technologies in the workplace' (Orlikowski, 2000: 404).
Knowing in practice	Gherardi (2000) Orlikowski (2002)	'**Practice** is the figure of discourse that allows the processes of knowing at work and in organizing to be articulated as historical processes, material and indeterminate' (Gherardi, 2000: 220–21). 'A perspective on **knowing in practice** which highlights the essential role of human action in knowing how to get things done in complex organizational work. The perspective suggest that knowing is not a static embedded capability, or stable disposition of actors, but rather an ongoing social accomplishment, constituted and reconstituted as actor engage the world in practice' (Orlikowski, 2002: 249).
Practice-based perspective	Sole and Edmondson (2002)	'**A practice-based perspective** emphasizes the collective, situated and provisional nature of knowledge, in contrast to a rational-cognitive view of knowledge. Practice connotes doing and involves awareness and application of both explicit (language, tools, concepts, roles, procedures) and tacit (rules of thumb, embodied capabilities, shared worldviews) elements. Central to the practice perspective is acknowledgement of the social, historical and structural contexts in which actions take place. Contextual elements are thus seen to shape how individuals learn and how they acquire knowledge and competence' (Sole and Edmondson, 2002: 18).
Practice-based approaches	Carlile (2002)	'In a **practice-based research approach,** it is crucial to be able to observe what people do, what their work is like, and what effort it takes to problem solve their respective combinations of objects and ends' (Carlile, 2002: 447).

Practice-based standpoint

An obligatory point of departure for reconstruction of the PBS bandwagon is the 1991 study by Brown and Duguid, who coined the expression 'practice-based standpoint'. Practice became the locus for understanding situated learning processes: 'from this practice-based standpoint, we view learning as the bridge between working and innovating' (Brown and Duguid, 1991: 41).

Drawing in particular on works by Orr (1987, 1990), Brown and Duguid conceive every work setting as an arena of repeated practices (canonical or otherwise) and constant innovations. Methodologically, in every context, divergences must be sought between 'espoused practice' and 'actual practice' (Brown and Duguid, 1991: 41). The dimension of espoused practice consists in the *opus operatum* characterizing the activities of each actor. This 'canonical vision' of a person's activities comprises the set of actions which every individual undertakes, formally or otherwise. Vice versa, the dimension of actual practice consists in the *modus operandi* negotiated in the every-day routine of people operating in a context: the situated doing, the composite set of 'non-canonical' activities that cannot be governed in abstract by executives. To study the often obscure dimension of work practices is to explore the complexity of situations and to trace the network of roles that constitute a work setting. It was this insight that represented the most fruitful contribution of Brown and Duguid's article to the subsequent literature, although the label 'practice-based stand-point' did not acquire significant currency. It was replaced in this group of authors' subsequent studies by the concepts of epistemology of practice and the 'generative dance' among practitio-ners, organizational knowledge and organizational knowing (Cook and Brown, 1999; Brown and Duguid, 2001).

Knowledge can be depicted through two very distinct 'visions': the epistemology of possession, and the epistemology of practice (Cook and Brown, 1999: 387). Referring to the thought of Dewey, these authors defined knowing as 'literally something which we do, not something that we pos-sess'. For this reason, the epistemology of practice is able to show the coordinated activities of individuals and groups in doing their 'real work' as it is informed by a particular organizational or group context. The practice in this case is embedded in a particular organized context, articulated into specific practices of behaviour, socially developed through situated learning and training for the profession: 'by practice we mean, as most theorists of practice mean, undertaking or engaging fully in a task, job, or profession' (Brown and Duguid, 2001: 203).

Practice-based learning or work-based learning

The label 'practice-based learning' is used mainly by researchers who investigate the social and collective process of learning that takes place in education (Raelin, 1997; Boud and Middleton, 2003; Billett, 2004; Fenwick, 2006; Raelin, 2007); but also by those interested in organizational learning within a community (Strati, 2007), at the boundaries among different communities (Carlile, 2004) or at distance (Nicolini, 2007). Educationalists also use the label 'work-based learn-ing' to denote how learning takes place, not only in a school classroom through teaching, but also in the workplace through observing, discussing and acting in different social worlds and in rela-tionship with numerous other learners. A social learning theory was developed along the lines of pragmatism on one side and symbolic interactionism on the other (Elkjaer, 2003) in order to look at conflict perspectives and tensions within and between social worlds as a driver to learn (Elkjaer and Huysman, 2008).

Raelin (1997: 572) argues that 'this approach recognizes that practitioners in order to be profi-cient need to bridge the gap between theory and practice. Work-based learning subscribes to a form of knowing that is context-dependent. Practitioners use theories to frame their understanding of the context but simultaneously incorporate an awareness of the social processes in which organizational activity is embedded'. In this case the focus is on the theory/practice gap evidenced by studies on informal learning in workplaces (Billett, 2001; Boud and Middleton, 2003) or on the processes of adult education (Fenwick, 2006).

The idea of introducing practice into studies on teaching has been developed further by Raelin, who proposes an outright epistemological change: 'an emerging practice epistemology will view learning as a dialectical mediated process that intermingles practice with theory' (Raelin, 2007: 506). A similar concern pervades the management literature which complains about the distance between academic studies and everyday managerial practice. In this regard, the label highlights the opposition between theory and practice, but it is also employed to emphasize that practical knowledge is a process, and that learning takes place as things are done in the relationship between human and non-human elements.

The role of objects in structuring and stabilizing practical knowledge is a central theme of activity theory (see the special issue of *Organization* edited by Blackler and Engeström, 2005). In this regard, Engeström et al. (1999) introduced the term 'knotworking' to emphasize that networking does not suffice if the relationships are not then 'knotted' into enduring forms, and that objects perform this practical function. Within this theoretical framework, Macpherson and Jones (2008: 177) state that 'mediating artifacts, or boundary objects, provide an opportunity to develop new shared conceptions of activity and new modes of action'. Local and temporary events are in fact able to establish solid relations among bodies of knowledge which are neither planned nor foresighted. In these cases, unlike those in stable activity systems, the division of tasks—and therefore what each actor does in practice—changes according to the different situations made possible by the object of the activity.

Learning in work practices also occurs in virtual contexts—as evidenced by Nicolini's (2007) study on distance work, where he examines how medical practices have been spatially and temporally reconfigured by the advent of telemedicine. The latter expands medical practices in time and space. It entails much more than a simple redistribution of what already exists, because it reframes the objects and contents of activities, giving rise to new artefacts and new identities, and to changed positions among them.

Practice as 'what people do': Science as practice and strategy as practice

Another way of considering practice as an empirical object comprises the conception of practice 'as what people do', an expression often used in regard to the study of a phenomenon (science, gender, strategy, routine, leadership) 'as practice'. The theoretical referents in this case may be extreme, because they range from rigorously ethnomethodological formulations to a commonsense use of the term 'practice'.

The label of practice as 'what people do' has in recent times driven the bandwagon of strategy researchers, but it has an illustrious—if not always duly recognized—precedent in studies on science as practice. Both these strands of inquiry seek to determine what people routinely do in their particular field of practice. Whilst ethnomethodology inspires the first strand, the second has more heterogeneous theoretical sources which relate at times to activity theory, and at times to no particular theoretical tradition.

During the second half of the 1970s, studies and seminars on the 'sociology of scientific knowledge' founded a new approach to the study of science which distinguished itself first because it viewed knowledge as a social product, and second because, by discarding philosophical 'a prioris', it investigated the empirical and natural sphere (Pickering, 1990, 1992). In the 1980s, interest in these themes grew to the point that very different positions were taken up in their regard. Amid this climate of 'intellectual heterogeneity', Pickering distanced himself from traditional studies on scientific knowledge by proposing an opposition between 'science as knowledge' and 'science as practice'. He centred his analysis on scientific practice—what scientists actually do—with a correlated interest in scientific culture, meaning the set of resources on which and within which a practice operates. The practical dimension as the key to studying 'what scientists do' linked with the body of studies interested in the 'macro' social dimension of the world of science and scientific laboratories: most notably the ethnographic studies by Latour and Woolgar (1979), those on laboratory work by Knorr-Cetina (1981), the ethnomethodological studies of Lynch et al. (1983), the pragmatic and symbolic interactionist analyses of science (Fujimura et al., 1987) and the actor-network approach (Callon, 1980; Latour, 1984, 1987). As Lynch (1993) notes, during the early 1990s, philosophers, historians and sociologists of science showed great interest in the everyday practices of scientists, prompted to do so mainly by the influence of ethnomethodological studies and those on the sociology of scientific knowledge. Ethnomethodology, in particular, investigated 'ordinary practical reasoning' and made a decisive contribution to these analyses. The strength of these science-as-practice approaches was the empirical nature of their inquiry:

> they conduct case studies of actions in particular social settings; they pay attention to detail; and they try to describe or explain observable (or at least reconstructable) events. Terms of the trade like empirical observation and explanation are problematic, given their association with empiricism and positivism, but it should be clear that ethnomethodologists and sociologists of science are especially attuned to—actual—situations of language use and practical action. (Lynch, 1993: XV)

The label 'strategy-as-practice' evinces complex and composite systems of habitus, artefacts and socially-defined forms of action that constitute the flow of strategic activities (Jarzabkowski, 2003: 24). On this view, practices are defined as 'the infrastructure through which micro strategy and strategizing occurs, generating an ongoing stream of strategic activity that is practice' (Jarzabkowski, 2003: 24). Paraphrasing the shift from organization to organizing, those who study strategy propose a shift to strategizing. The 'practice perspective' (Jarzabkowski et al., 2007) seeks to identify the strategic activities reiterated in time by the diverse actors interacting in an organizational context.

The strategy-as-practice strand of analysis has been developed in particular by Whittington, Jarzabkowski, Johnson and Balogun. A first example of this 'new' perspective can be dated to 1996, the year in which Whittington published a paper entitled 'Strategy as Practice' and in which he stated that 'the practice perspective is concerned with managerial activity, how managers "do strategy"' (Whittington, 1996: 732). Starting from the theoretical framework of activity theory, Jarzabkowski (2003) argued that every system of activity can be understood by examining the ways in which management practices translate strategy into practice. The following year Jarzabkowski (2004) resumed her analysis by focusing on the concepts of 'recursiveness' and 'adaptation'. Drawing on a composite theoretical base comprising the concepts of 'structuration' (Giddens, 1984), 'habitus' (Bourdieu, 1990), 'social becoming' (Sztompka, 1991) and 'communities of practice' (Lave and Wenger, 1991), Jarzabkowski showed the existence of a system of 'practices-in-use' (Jazabkowski, 2004).

Whittington contributed decisively to the development of these reflections (Whittington, 1993, 2002, 2003; Whittington et al., 2003). He suggested that research on strategy should be founded upon a 'new' theoretical basis which combined 'strategy praxis', 'strategy practices' and 'strategy practitioners' (Whittington, 2006). In the following year, Whittington (2007) proposed the model of the '4 Ps'—'praxis', 'practices', 'practitioners' and 'profession'—to enable thorough analysis of organizational strategy by going beyond the distinctions between intra-organizational and extra-organizational levels.

The methodology to analyse the strategizing dimension prompted a study by Balogun et al. (2003). Analysing strategy-as-practice is not to consider solely the strategies of senior executives, but also those of middle managers and non-managerial personnel. The aim of research on strategy is to verify how the instructions of management are translated by actors into day-to-day practices with the purpose of creating and exchanging strategy. In this view, strategy is what is done, or otherwise, within an organizational context in regard to the strategic directions laid down by the management. The attention is here more on the substantive field than on practice, whose definition is rather heterogeneous.

Practice as a way of seeing

After 2000 the bandwagon of PBS moves toward a more explicit acknowledgement of practice as epistemology and four new labels appeared: 'practice-oriented research', 'knowing-in-practice', 'practice-based perspective' and 'practice-based approaches'.

The first two labels—'practice lens' or 'practice-oriented research' and 'knowing-in-practice'—relate to two rather homogeneous communities of scholars, the first situated in the United States and the second in Europe. Both are interested in practical knowledge, but they draw on somewhat different bodies of sociological thought: Giddens and structuration theory in the former case, ethnomethodology and actor-network theory in the latter.

Practice lens and practice-oriented research

One of the first works to propose the use of the 'practice lens' for the study of technologies has been Orlikowski (2000), which draws on Giddens' (1979, 1984) structuration theory to propose use of 'a practice lens to examine how people, as they interact with a technology in their ongoing practices, enact structures which shape their emergent and situated use of that technology. Viewing the use of technology as a process of enactment enables a deeper understanding of the constitutive role of social practices in the ongoing use and change of technologies in the workplace' (Orlikowski, 2000: 404). Starting from the assumption that technologies have two dimensions—that of the artefact and that of its use (what people do with the technological artefact in their recurrent and situated practices)—Orlikowski observes how organizational subjects activate structures pertaining to technology-in-use. These structures 'are not fixed or given, but constituted and reconstituted through the everyday, situated practice of particular users using particular technologies in particular circumstances' (Orlikowski, 2000: 425). The concept of 'technologies as social practice' or technology-in-use has also inspired the study by Suchman et al. (1999), who theorize that technology acquires different identities in relation to the circumstances and the practices in which it is embedded. The designers of a technology must therefore consider the context and the working practices in which the technological structures will be inserted (Suchman, 1987). For example within the field of information technology (Levina and Vaast, 2006) Bourdieu's practice theory has been used to show how the production of boundary-spanning practices involves varying degrees of embodiment (i.e. relying on personal relationships) and objectification (i.e. relying on the exchange of objects).

The metaphor of the 'practice lens' is associated with the label 'practice-oriented approach'. For example, Schultze and Boland (2000) stress that it is essential when designing and implementing technologies to adopt a 'practice-oriented approach' which focuses on 'what people "actually" do rather than on what they say they do or on what they ought to be doing' (Pickering, 1992, in Schultze and Boland, 2000: 194). Studying what people actually do also requires understanding the results of technological implementations, and consequently, observing the practices within the circuit of repro-duction described by Bourdieu (1973, 1998). To paraphrase Foucault (1982: 787), this means that when technologies are implemented, importance should be given not only to what people do but also to the consequences of their doing ('what doing it does') (Schultze and Boland, 2000: 195). A few years later Schultze and Orlikowski (2004: 87) argued that the practice lens 'highlights how macro level phenomena such as interfirm relations are created and recreated through the micro level actions taken by firm members'. Finally, Østerlund and Carlile (2005) illustrate, through a re-reading of three classic studies on communities of practice, how practice-oriented research is based on a relational thinking in which the practice is the locus for the production and reproduction of social relations.

Knowing-in-practice

The point of departure for reflection on the concept of knowing-in-practice is the special issue of *Organization* edited by Gherardi (2000), which seeks to explain why and how the traditions of research represented by activity theory (AT), actor-network theory (ANT), situated learning theory (SLT) and cultural perspectives on learning (CP) can be grouped under the heading of 'practice-based theorizing'. The basic idea is that knowledge is not something present in the heads of people; nor is it a strategic productive factor located in the organization's management: rather it is a 'knowledge-in-practice' constructed by practising in a context of interaction. In this view, practice is the 'figure of discourse that allows the processes of knowing at work and in organizing to be articulated as historical processes, material and indeterminate' (Gherardi, 2000: 220–21, 2006, 2008). The practice constitutes the 'topos' that ties the 'knowing' to the 'doing'. Participation in a practice is on the one hand a way to acquire knowledge in action and, on the other, a way to change/perpetuate such knowledge and to produce and reproduce society (Gherardi, 2000: 215). Studies on knowing-in-practice have spread a 'new vocabulary' in organization studies (Nicolini et al., 2003). The study of knowing-in-practice prefers action verbs able to transmit the idea of an emer-gent reality, of knowing as a material activity. Numerous studies use terms and expressions con-nected to material artefacts: sociality is related not only to human beings, but also to symbolic and cultural artefacts. The debate on practice is rich in terms linked with the space-time location of the 'doing' of actors, that is, with the 'situatedness' of practices. Finally, the debate is characterized by the use of words that denote uncertainty, conflict and incoherence, understood as features intrinsic to practices because they produce innovation, learning and change.

A few years later, Orlikowski (2002: 249) also used a 'perspective on knowing in practice'. The use of this label 'suggests that knowing is not a static embedded capability, or stable disposition of actors, but rather an ongoing social accomplishment, constituted and reconstituted as actors engage the world of practice'. The practices of the context (the author refers in particular to identity shar-ing, face-to-face interactions, the alignment of efforts, learning-by-doing and participation) pro-duce a collective 'knowing how' that is constantly activated and enables organizational subjects to operate across temporal, geographical, political and cultural boundaries (distributed organizing).

Various empirical studies have analysed knowing-in-practice. Gomez et al.(2003: 122), for example, describe the complex nature of knowing in a kitchen: 'cooking practice is a mix of personal predisposition, knowledge acquired through tough training and repetitive practice, knowledge of rules integrated and internalized by cooks, and knowledge acquired through reflexive thinking about practice'.

Knowing-in-practice links with both the sensible knowledge and the aesthetic judgment that practitioners use to appraise and transmit a practice. Strati (2003, 2007: 62) investigates the dimension of sensory knowledge and aesthetic judgement. 'Aesthetic' or sensible knowledge comprises 'what is perceived through the senses, judged through the senses, and produced through the senses. It resides in the visual, the auditory, the olfactory, the gustatory, the touchable and the sensitive-aesthetic judgment'. If we consider work routine, in all jobs—though obviously to different extents—people use their bodies and activate their senses to learn the community's practices. Strati (2007: 69–70) illustrates the relation between sensible knowledge and practice-based learning with various examples. One of them concerns a group of building labourers working on a roof without safety protection. Work on the roof involved the senses of touch, 'feeling the roof under your feet', and those of hearing and sight, 'looking with the ears' at the movements and noises of workmates and objects. The perceptive-sensory capacities were therefore crucial for performance of the roofing work, like others, because they influenced the choice of that kind of work, its teaching, its learning and the selection of those capable of performing it. More generally, they comprised every aspect of what people do when they work.

With the labels of 'practice-based perspective' and 'practice-based approach' we shall see how the reference to the conception of practice as epistemology become even more explicit.

Practice-based perspective

In the literature on practice, some authors are distinguished by their use of the expression 'practice-based perspective'. The pathfinder for this 'wagon' has assuredly been the study by Sole and Edmondson (2002), which examines the role of knowledge and learning processes in dispersed teams working on development projects. The article conducts detailed analysis on the role of knowledge situated in diverse geographically dispersed local contexts. The 'practice-based perspective' is defined as the lens able to highlight the role of 'knowledge grounded in site-specific work practice' (Sole and Edmondson, 2002: 18). In support of their theoretical contentions, Sole and Edmondson (2002: 18) furnish their own definition of the concept of 'practice' as the dimension which:

> emphasises the collective, situated and provisional nature of knowledge, in contrast to a rational-cognitive view of knowledge. Practice connotes doing and involves awareness and application of both explicit (language, tools, concepts, roles, procedures) and tacit (rules of thumb, embodied capabilities, shared worldviews) elements. Central to the practice perspective is acknowledgement of the social, historical and structural contexts in which actions take place.

The 'practice perspective' thus locates the dimension of practice in the context in which it is performed. Actors always undertake their actions within a constantly-evolving historical-cultural setting. The dimension of the 'provisional' and of the 'historically situated' are combined in the everyday 'doing' of actors.

In addition to Sole and Edmondson, the label 'practice-based perspective' has been used more recently by Swan et al. (2007), who study innovations in biomedicine. Using a theoretical approach which combines symbolic interactionism and theory of practice, these authors investigate the interactions among the various actors making up research groups for innovation in the biomedical sector. Within this framework:

> Practice-based perspectives provide important additional insights into the nature and role of objects in innovation. First, they illuminate the relationship between objects, knowledge, work practices, social groups and social context. [..] Second, where symbolic interactionist views tend to stress the essentially individual nature of knowledge, practice based perspectives make a distinctive contribution by differentiating those forms of knowledge that are acquired individually and those that are acquired collectively (Swan et al., 2007: 1813).

The practice merges the individual and collective dimensions, human and technological elements, describing and explaining the ways of doing, bodies of knowledge and situations that develop in a given work setting.

Practice-based approaches

A final label on the broad bandwagon of practice is the expression 'practice-based approach'. The author who has pioneered this part of the caravan is Carlile (2002), whose theoretical and empirical research is based on what he himself calls a 'practice-based research approach'. Every organizational context should be studied by adopting a 'pragmatic view' able to explore the dimension of knowledge 'localized, embedded and invested in practice' (Carlile, 2002: 445). Knowledge is structured in practice in its relation to 'objects'—the artefacts with which practitioners interact in their everyday work—and 'ends'—the products of the creation and manipulation of those objects by the actors. The practical approach enables exploration of how individuals solve their problems, that is, how they construct their competence in practice. Practice is the dimension able to convey the process by which an actor's know-how is built: the 'trial and error' process (Carlile, 2002: 446) whereby which a person's situated practical knowledge is constructed.

In addition to Carlile, Yanow (2004) also uses the expression 'practice-based approaches'. But unlike Carlile, Yanow uses the noun 'approach' in the plural, perhaps because in her theoretical framework this serves to indicate the existence of a plurality of 'practice-based approaches to the study of organizational learning' (Yanow, 2004: 10). The study of practice brings out the specificities of behaviour and meaning in situated contexts. Knowledge can be distinguished into two types: one definable as 'expert', the other as 'local' (Yanow, 2004: 12). The 'expert' dimension comprises the stock of explicit, theory-based, academic, professional or scientifically-based, abstract and generalizable knowledge and techniques. The 'local' dimension instead comprises the complex array of forms of knowledge and ways of doing which are tacit and practice-based, and which derive from experience and interaction in a specific context. Practice therefore affords understanding of the everyday interactions between the 'expert' and 'local' dimensions of people's knowledge. Understanding the practices of individuals enables interpretation of the situated learning processes that take place in organizations.

Where is the bandwagon heading?

To answer this question we must first ask whether or not the analogy between the cancer research bandwagon and that of PBS holds. It was said at the outset that bandwagons serve to institutionalize a field of study and that the ambiguity of its definition makes allomorphic processes possible. We may therefore state that the institutionalization process has worked successfully in organizational studies because the sequence of labels containing the word 'practice' has by now covered a time span of almost 30 years, and the polysemy of the term has indubitably favoured its use with a wide variety of meanings and within conflicting theoretical perspectives. Nevertheless, unlike the cancer research bandwagon, which has gone through a phase of the 'collective appropriation' of the label and has developed shared protocols and a 'snowball' effect, the PBS bandwagon seems bound to undergo a partition following its institutionalization.

This ambiguity has favoured the use of the term and its enlargement, and we are certainly not arguing for a univocal definition of the concept. However, although none of the definitions is wrong in itself, when they are interrelated many of them prove incompatible. First, a commonsense use in which practice means routine or 'being closer to reality' and 'being more practical' is simply pointless. If one uses a concept which has a long and ramified pedigree in both philosophy and sociology, behaving like the man in the street and inventing fanciful neologisms does not help in elaborating a more rigorous theoretical framework. As Clegg et al. (2007: 85) noted with reference to the 'strategy as practice' strand (one of the labels containing the word 'practice' but remaining within the tradition of mainstream, functional research) institutionalization comes at a price. The processes of institutionalization give rise to ceremonialism, in which a certain form of rationality and coherence is promoted while at the same time allowing for its interpretive glossing (Garfinkel, 1967; Meyer and Rowan, 1977). The ambiguity of the term practice within PBS, which is undoubtedly useful for creating a loosely coupled network of actions, ideas and people with different agendas, might, at the same time, hinder its theoretical advancement, as improbable glosses accumulate.

Acknowledging the origins and resuming the sociological tradition that has conceptualized what constitutes 'practice' enables theoretical breadth to be given to empirical research on practices. When looking behind the labels for their theoretical strands of reference, we find their cultural indebtedness to Bourdieu, Giddens, Garfinkel and Foucault, on the one hand, and to activity theory on the other. Comparison among these strands of theoretical analysis, although interesting, would be beyond the scope of this article. Reference to them serves to show that one of the greatest difficulties in the collective appropriation of the concept of practice[1] resides in the polysemy of the term itself.

We find that the concept of practice is built around three dimensions:

1. the set of interconnected activities that, if socially recognized as a way of ordering, stabilize collective action and the common orientation;
2. the sense-making process that supports the accountability of a shared way of doing things and which allows the continuous negotiation (ethical and aesthetic) of the meanings of a practice by its practitioners;
3. the social effects generated by a practice in connection with other social practices. This is the dimension of the reproduction of practice that answers the question as to what doing the practice does.

According to whether the emphasis is placed on one dimension rather than the other, we have different accounts of what a practice is; and through these accounts we have differing accesses to organizational reality. When the researcher's attention is focused on the first dimension—activity—it is very likely that his/her theoretical background concerns activity theory and the analysis of situated activities mediated by artefacts. This dimension of practice is innovative in organizational studies because it enables analysis of work to be linked with that of organizing, and because it opens the way to the study of work in its routine doing (Licoppe, 2008).

When the attention is focused on the second dimension—sense-making and account giving—it is possible that the researcher's theoretical background lies in ethnomethodology, so that the empirical object is on the one hand the negotiated order that enables collective action and, on the other, the processes of power enactment that tie it to situated knowledge. Whilst in the previous case the focus was on 'doing', in this one it shifts to the dimension of values and to the discursive practices that sustain the sense of this 'doing' for those who do it.

Finally, the third dimension—the reproduction of practices—probably concerns a theoretical background which refers to Bourdieu and the circuit of practice reproduction, and to Foucault and social effects. This third dimension considers practice not only in its 'doing' with regard to the object but also in its 'doing' of society. Two phenomena are highlighted in particular: first that practices are interconnected with each other (Swidler, 2001), and second that recursiveness (or reproduction) is the feature that distinguishes practice from action. When this conception of practice is used in organization studies, it makes it possible to show that the dynamic of the everyday reproduction of practices is not a mechanical iteration of the same activities: on the contrary, it is a process of innovation by repetition, that is, constant adaptation to changing circumstances, and innovation engendered by practice. To use an apt expression which Clot (2002) borrows from Bernstein (1996), one may speak of '*répétition sans répétition*' (repetition without repetition) as the dynamic of innovation and as a possible area of intervention for practice development (McCormack and Titchen, 2006).

When these three dimensions are taken together, construction can begin of a practice theory of organization based on a critique of rationalism, cognitivism and functionalism (Gherardi, 2009b). For the PBS bandwagon to be able collectively to appropriate the critical power of the practice lens, a partition is necessary that separates the routes pursued by those who base a commonsense notion of practice on a conception of organization like the resource-based view of the firm or dynamic capabilities, and by those who have resumed the concept of practice and are seeking a critical definition of organizing. It is in this direction that methodological reflection on PBS is now moving.

Conclusions

The bandwagon of PBS has spread through a pluralism of conceptual labels. In fact, we may consider the label 'practice-based studies' as an 'umbrella concept' which covers a plurality of similarities and differences. The various articles and contributions that have been created within this debate, far from representing a single school of thought, resemble a 'social world' composed of intertwined reflections and a broad set of interpretations of the notion of practice. Over the years, the various labels have highlighted the existence of a continuously evolving conversation. The labelling process illustrated here is an expression of a collective season of reflections by several authors who, albeit in different ways, use the practice dimension to examine organizations. Despite their differences, these 'sensibilities' support the 'practice turn' (Rouse, 2001; Schatzki et al., 2001). This turn, or re-turn, represents, in its essence, a powerful device with which to re-discuss the positivist and rationalist paradigms, which are still active in various fields of organizational studies.

The PBS bandwagon has been set in motion, and it has already achieved the aim of institutionalizing a field of studies and aggregating a community of scholars. Nevertheless, the bandwagon has been less successful in achieving the collective appropriation of the general label. In trying to guess where the bandwagon is heading, one foresees a partition set in motion by the differences in studying practice as an empirical object or as a way of seeing (an epistemology), and in conceiving practice mainly as an array of activities or as a collective knowledgeable action (a practising). Beneath this articulation of possible fields of research and ways to define practice lies an incompatibility between hosting the practice concept within the mainstream functional programme in organization studies or using it as a critical concept for defining knowledge as a practical activity and linking knowing and acting for studying working practices in different ways and in relation to the social effects produced by organizational practices. The promise of the critical appropriation of the practice concept within organization studies lies in leading towards a practice theory of organization.

Notes

1. The commonsense meaning of practice also has a plurality of senses: *practice as a learning method*—people learn by 'doing' through constant repetition of their activities, as in the proverb 'Practice makes perfect'; *practice as an occupation or field of activity*— 'practice' is a word able to express the field of activity in which an individual works, like medical or legal practice, for example—*practice as the way something is done*. Practice is a processual concept able to represent how practitioners recognize, produce and formulate the scenes and regulations of everyday affairs.
2. This article is the result of an entirely collaborative effort by the three authors. If, however, for academic reasons, individual responsibility must be assigned, Gessica Corradi wrote the section 'Practice as empirical object', Silvia Gherardi wrote the introduction, the conclusion and the sections 'The bandwagon analogy' and 'Where is the bandwagon heading?' and Luca Verzelloni wrote the section 'Practice as a way of seeing'.

References

Balogun, J., Huff, A. S. and Johnson, P. (2003) 'Three Responses to the Methodological Challenges of Studying Strategizing', *Journal of Management Studies* 40(1): 197–224.

Barley, S R. and Kunda, G. (2001) 'Bringing Work Back', *Organization Science* 12(1): 76–95.

Bernstein, N. A. (1996) 'On Dexterity and its Development', in M. L. Latash and M. T. Turvey (eds) *Dexterity and Its Development*, pp. 3–44. Mahwah, NJ: Lawrence Erlbaum.

Billett, S. (2001) 'Knowing in Practice: Re-conceptualising Vocational Expertise', *Learning and Instruction* 11(6): 431–52.

Billett, S. (2004) 'Workplace Participatory Practices: Conceptualising Workplaces as Learning Environments', *Journal of Workplace Learning* 16(5–6): 312–25.

Blackler, F. and Engeström, Y. (eds) (2005) 'Special Issue on the Rise of Objects in the Study of Organizations', *Organization* 12(3): 307–30.

Boud, D. and Middleton, H. (2003) 'Learning from Others at Work: Communities of Practice and Informal Learning', *Journal of Workplace Learning* 15(5): 194–203.

Bourdieu, P. (1972) Esquisse d'une Théorie de la Pratique Précédé de Trois Etudes de Ethnologie Kabyle. Switzerland: Librairie Droz S. A.

Bourdieu, P. (1973) 'Three Forms of Theoretical Knowledge', *Social Science Information* 12(1): 53–80.

Bourdieu, P. (1990) *The Logic of Practice*. Cambridge: Polity Press.

Bourdieu, P. (1998) *Practical Reason: On the Theory of Action*. Cambridge: Polity Press.

Brown, J. S. and Duguid, P. (1991) 'Organizational Learning and Communities of Practice: Toward a Unified View of Working, Learning and Bureaucratization', *Organization Science* 2(1): 40–57.

Brown, J. S. and Duguid, P. (2001) 'Knowledge and Organization: A Social-Practice Perspective', *Organization Science* 12(2): 198–213.

Callon, M. (1980) 'The State and Technological Innovation. A Case Study of the Electrical Vehicle in France', *Research Policy* 9(4): 358–76.

Carlile, P. R. (2002) 'A Pragmatic View of Knowledge and Boundaries: Boundary Objects in New Product Development', *Organization Science* 13(4): 442–55.

Carlile, P. R. (2004) 'Transferring, Translating and Transforming: An Integrative Framework for Managing Knowledge across Boundaries', *Organization Science* 15(5): 558–68.

Clegg, S. R., Kornberg, M. and Rhodes, C. (2007) 'Business Ethics as Practice', *British Journal of Management* 18(2): 107–22.

Clot, Y. (2002) 'Clinique de l'Activité et Répétition', *Cliniques Méditerranéennes* 66(2): 23–47.

Cohen, I. J. (1996) 'Theories of Action and Praxis', in B.S Turner (eds) *The Blackwell Companion to Social Theory*, pp. 111–42. Cambridge: Blackwell.

Contu, A. and Wilmott, H. (2003) 'Re-embedding Situatedness: The Importance of Power Relations in Learning', *Organization Science* 14(3): 283–96.

Cook, S. N. and Brown, J. S. (1999) 'Bridging Epistemologies: The Generative Dance between Organizational Knowledge and Organizational Knowing', *Organization Science* 10(4): 381–400.

Czarniaswka, B. and Joerges, B. (1995) 'Winds of Organizational Change: How Ideas Translate into Objects and Actions', in S. Bacharach, P. Gagliardi and B. Mundell (eds) *Research in the Sociology of Organizations*, pp. 171–209. Greenwich, NJ: JAI Press.

Czarniaswka, B. and Sévon, G. (2005) *Global Ideas*. Copenhagen: Copenhagen Business School Press.

Elkjaer, B. (2003) 'Social Learning Theory: Learning as Participation in Social Processes', in M. Easterby-Smith and M. Lyles (eds) *The Blackwell Handbook of Organizational Learning and Knowledge Management*, pp. 38–53. Malden and Oxford: Blackwell.

Elkjaer, B. and Huysman, M. (2008) 'Social World Theory and Organizational Learning', in D. Barry, D. and H. Hansen (eds) *Sage Handbook of New Approaches in Management and Organization*, pp. 170–77. London: Sage.

Engeström, Y., Engeström, R. and Vahaaho, T. (1999) 'When the Center does not Hold: The Importance of Knotworking', in S. Chaiklin, M. Hedegaard and U. J. Jensen (eds) *Activity Theory and Social Practice: Cultural-Historical Approaches*, pp. 345–74. Aarhus: Aarhus University Press.

Fenwick, T. J. (2006) 'Work, Learning and Adult Education in Canada', in T. J. Fenwick, T. Nesbit and B. Spencer (eds) *Contexts of Adult Education: Canadian Perspectives*, pp. 187–97. Toronto: Thompson.

Foucault, M. (1980) *Power/Knowledge: Selected Interviews and Other Writings 1972–1977*. London: Harvester.

Foucault, M. (1982) 'The Subject and Power', *Critical Inquiry* 8(4): 777–5.

Fox, S. (2006) 'Inquiries of every Imaginable Kind: Ethnomethodology, Practical Action and the New Socially Situated Learning Theory', *Sociological Review* 54(3): 426–45.

Fujimura, J. (1988) 'Molecular Biological Bandwagon in Cancer Research: Where Social Worlds Meet', *Social Problems* 35(3): 261-83.

Fujimura, J. (1995) 'Ecologies of Action: Recombining Genes, Molecularizing Cancer, and Transforming Biology', in S. L. Star (ed.) *Ecologies of Knowledge*, pp. 302–46. Albany, NY: State University of New York Press.

Fujimura, J., Star, S. and Gerson, E. (1987) 'Méthodes de Recherche en Sociologie des Sciences: Travail, Pragmatisme et Interactionnisme Symbolique', *Cahiers de Recherche Sociologique* 5(2): 65–85.

Garfinkel, H. (1967) *Studies in Ethnomethodology*. Englewood Cliffs, NJ: Prentice Hall.

Gherardi, S. (2000) 'Practice-Based Theorizing on Learning and Knowing in Organizations: An Introduction', *Organization* 7(2): 211–23.

Gherardi, S. (2006) *Organizational Knowledge: The Texture of Workplace Learning*. Oxford: Blackwell.

Gherardi, S. (2008) 'Situated Knowledge and Situated Action: What do Practice-Based Studies Promise?', in D. Barry and H. Hansen (eds) *Sage Handbook of New Approaches in Management and Organization*, pp. 516–25. London: Sage.

Gherardi, S. (2009a) 'Community of Practice or Practices of a Community?', in S. Armstrong and C. Fukami (eds) *Handbook of Management Learning, Education and Development*, pp. 514–30. London: Sage.

Gherardi, S. (2009b) 'Introduction to the Special Issue on the Critical Power of the Practice Lens', *Management Learning* 40(2): 115–28.

Gherardi, S. and Lippi, A. (2000) *Tradurre le Riforme in Pratica*. Milano: Cortina.

Gherardi, S., Nicolini, D. and Odella, F. (1998) 'Toward a Social Understanding of how People Learn in Organizations: The Notion of Situated Curriculum', *Management Learning* 29(3): 273–98.

Giddens, A. (1979) *Central Problems in Social Theory*. London: MacMillan.

Giddens, A. (1984) *The Constitution of Society*. Cambridge: Polity Press.

Gomez, M.L., Bouty, I. and Drucker-Godard, C. (2003) 'Developing Knowing in Practice: Behind the Scenes of Haute Cuisine', in D. Nicolini, S. Gherardi and D. Yanow (eds) *Knowing in Organizations: A Practice-Based Approach*, pp. 100–25. Armonk, NY: M. E. Sharpe.

Handley, K., Sturdy, A., Fincham, R. and Clark T. (2006) 'Within and Beyond Communities of Practice: Making Sense of Learning through Participation, Identity and Practice', *Journal of Management Studies* 43(3): 641–53.

Jarzabkowski, P. (2003) 'Strategic Practices: An Activity Theory Perspective on Continuity and Change', *Journal of Management Studies* 40(1): 23–55.

Jarzabkowski, P. (2004) 'Strategy as Practice: Recursiveness, Adaptation and Practices-in-Use', *Organization Studies* 25(4): 529–60.

Jarzabkowski, P., Balogun, J. and Seidl, D. (2007) 'Strategizing: The Challenges of a Practice Perspective', *Human Relations* 60(1): 5–27.

Knorr-Cetina, K. (1981) *The Manufacture of Knowledge: An Essay on the Cconstructivist and Contextual Nature of Science*. Oxford, New York: Pergamon Press.

Latour, B. (1984) *Les Microbes, Guerre et Paix*. Paris: Métailié.

Latour, B. (1987) *Science in Action: How to Follow Scientists and Engineers Through Society*. Cambridge, MA: Harvard University Press.

Latour, B. and Woolgar, S. (1979) *Laboratory Life: The Social Construction of Scientific Facts*. Los Angeles, CA: Sage.

Lave, J. and Wenger, E. (1991) *Situated Learning. Legitimate Peripheral Participation*. Cambridge: Cambridge University Press.

Levina, N. and Vaast, E. (2006) 'Turning a Community into a Market: A Practice Perspective on Information Technology Use in Boundary Spanning', *Journal of Management Information Systems* 22(4):13–37.

Licoppe, C. (2008) 'Dans le "Carré de l'Activité": Perspectives Internationales sur le Travail et l'Activité', *Sociologie du Travail* 50(3): 287–302.

Lynch, M. (1993) *Scientific Practice and Ordinary Action: Ethnomethodology and Social Studies of Science*. Cambridge: Cambridge University Press.

Lynch, M., Livingston, E. and Garfinkel, H. (1983) 'Temporal Order in Laboratory Work', in K. D. Knorr-Cetina and M. Mulkay (eds) *Science Observed: Perspectives on the Social Study of Science*, pp. 205–38. London: Sage.

Lyotard, J. F. (1979) *La Condition Postmoderne*. Paris: Les Editions de Minuit.McCormack, B. and Titchen, A. (2006) 'Critical Creativity: Melding, Exploding, Blending', *Educational Action Research: An International Journal* 14(2): 239–66.

Macpherson, A. and Jones, O. (2008) 'Object-Mediated Learning and Strategic Renewal in a Mature Organization', *Management Learning* 39(2): 177–201.

Meyer, J. W. and Rowan, B. (1977) 'Institutionalized Organizations: Formal Structure as Myth and Ceremony', *American Journal of Sociology* 83(2): 340–63.

Nicolini, D. (2007) 'Stretching out and Expanding Work Practice in Time and Space: The Case of Telemedicine', *Human Relations* 60(6): 889–920.

Nicolini, D., Gherardi S. and Yanow D. (2003) (eds) *Knowing in Organizations: A Practice-Based Approach.* Armonk, NY: M. E. Sharpe.

Orlikowski, W. J. (2000) 'Using Technology and Constructing Structures: A Practice Lens for Studying Technology in Organizations', *Organization Science* 11(4): 404–28.

Orlikowski, W. J. (2002) 'Knowing in Practice: Enacting a Collective Capability in Distributed Organizing', *Organization Science* 13(3): 249–73.

Orr, J. (1987) *Talking About Machines: Social Aspects of Expertise. Report for the Intelligent Systems Laboratory.* Palo Alto, CA: Xerox Palo Alto Research Center.

Orr, J. (1990) 'Sharing Knowledge, Celebrating Identity: War Stories and Community Memory in a Service Culture', in D. S. Middleton and E. Edwards (eds) *Collective Remembering: Memory in Society*, pp. 303–26, CA26. Beverley Hills: Sage.

Østerlund, C. and Carlile, P. (2005) 'Relations in Practice: Sorting Through Practice Theories on Knowledge Sharing in Complex Organizations', *The Information Society* 21(2): 91–107.

Pickering, A. (1990) 'Knowledge, Practice and Mere Construction', *Social Studies of Science* 20(4): 682–729.

Pickering, A. (1992) *Science as Practice and Culture.* Chicago, IL: University of Chicago Press.

Raelin, J. A. (1997) 'A Model of Work-Based Learning', *Organization Science* 8(6): 563–78.

Raelin, J. A. (2007) 'Toward An Epistemology of Practice', *Academy of Management Learning & Education Journal* 6(4): 495–519.

Roberts, J. (2006) 'Limits to Communities of Practice', *Journal of Management Studies* 43(3): 623–39.

Rouse, J. (2001) 'Two Concepts of Practices', in T. R. Schatzki, K. Knorr-Cetina and E. von Savigny (eds) *The Practice Turn in Contemporary Theory*, pp. 189–98. London: Routledge.

Schatzki, T. R. (1996) *Social Practices: A Wittgensteinian Approach to Human Activity and the Social.* Cambridge: Cambridge University Press.

Schatzki, T. R. (2001) 'Introduction. Practice theory', in T. R. Schatzki, K. Knorr-Cetina and E. von Savigny (eds) *The Practice Turn in Contemporary Theory*, pp. 1–14. London: Routledge.

Schatzki, T. R., Knorr-Cetina, K. and von Savigny, E. (2001) (eds) *The Practice Turn in Contemporary Theory.* London: Routledge.

Schultze, U. and Boland, R. (2000) 'Knowledge Management Technology and the Reproduction of Knowledge Work Practices', *Journal of Strategic Information Systems* 9(2–3): 193–212.

Schultze, U. and Orlikowski, W. (2004) 'A Practice Perspective on Technology-Mediated Network Relations: The Use of Internet-Based Self-Serve Technologies', *Information System Research* 15(1): 87–106.

Sole, D. and Edmondson, A. (2002) 'Situated Knowledge and Learning in Dispersed Teams', *British Journal of Management* 13(S2): 17–34.

Strati, A. (2003) 'Knowing in Practice: Aesthetic Understanding and Tacit Knowledge', in D. Nicolini, S. Gherardi and D. Yanow (eds) *Knowing in Organizations*, pp. 53–75. Armonk, NY: M. E. Sharpe.

Strati, A. (2007) 'Sensible Knowledge and Practice-Based Learning', *Management Learning* 38(1): 61–77.

Suchman, L. (1987) *Plans and Situated Action: The Problem of Human-Machine Communication.* Cambridge: Cambridge University Press.

Suchman, L., Blomberg, J., Orr, J. E. and Trigg, R. (1999) 'Reconstructing Technologies as Social Practice', *American Behavioural Scientist* 43(3): 392–408.

Swan, J., Scarbrough, H. and Robertson M. (2002) 'The Construction of Communities of Practice in the Management of Innovation', *Management Learning* 33(4): 477–96.

Swan, J., Bresnen, M., Newell, S. and Robertson, M. (2007) 'The Object of Knowledge: The Role of Objects in Biomedical Innovation', *Human Relations* 60(12): 1809–37.

Swidler, A. (2001) 'What Anchors Cultural Practices', in T. R. Schatzki, K. Knorr-Cetina and E. von Savigny (eds) *The Practice Turn in Contemporary Theory*, pp. 74–92. London : Routledge.

Sztompka, P. (1991) *Society in Action: The Theory of Social Becoming*. Cambridge, MA: Polity Press.

Taylor, C. (1995) *Philosophical Arguments* Cambridge, MA: Harvard University Press

Turner, S. (1994) *The Social Theory of Practices: Tradition, Tacit Knowledge, and Presuppositions*. Chicago, IL: University of Chicago Press.

Wenger, E. (2000) 'Communities of Practice and Social Learning Systems', *Organization* 7(2): 225–46.

Wenger, E. and Snyder, W. (2000) 'Communities of Practice: The Organizational Frontier', *Harvard Business Review* 78(1): 139–45.

Whittington, R. (1993) *What is Strategy and Does it Matter?* London: Routledge.

Whittington, R. (1996) 'Strategy as Practice', *Long Range Planning* 29(5): 731–35.

Whittington, R. (2002) 'Practice Perspectives on Strategy: Unifying and Developing a Field', paper presented at the Academy of Management Meeting, Denver, August 2002.

Whittington, R. (2003) 'The Work of Strategizing and Organizing for a Practice Perspective', *Strategic Organization* 1(1): 117–25.

Whittington, R. (2006) 'Completing the Practice Turn in Strategy Research', *Organization* 27(5): 613–34.

Whittington, R. (2007) 'Strategy Practice and Strategy Process: Family Differences and the Sociological Eye', *Organization Studies* 28(10): 1575–86.

Whittington, R., Jarzabkowski, P., Mayer, M., Mounoud, E., Nahapiet, J. and Rouleau, L. (2003) 'Taking Strategy Seriously: Responsibility and Reform for an Important Social Practice', *Journal of Management Inquiry* 12(4): 396–409.

Yanow, D. (2004) 'Translating Local Knowledge at Organizational Peripheries', *British Journal of Management* 15(S1): 9–25.

Yanow, D. (2006) 'Talking about Practices: On Julian Orr's Talking About Machines', *Organization Studies* 27(12): 1743–56.

PART II

KEY CONCEPTS

[6]

Management Learning
Copyright © 2007 Sage Publications
London, Los Angeles, New Delhi
and Singapore
http://mlq.sagepub.com
Vol. 38(1): 61–77
1350-5076

Article

Antonio Strati

University of Trento, Italy

Sensible Knowledge and Practice-based Learning

Abstract   *The article shows that there is a close connection between knowing and learning in practice and sensible knowledge. It does so by referring to field research conducted in a variety of workplaces: a sawmill, a roofing firm and a secretarial office. The concluding remarks argue for the re-construction of organizational discourse through aesthetic understanding, because this is an approach which brings out the 'don't-know-what' characteristic of a large part of practical experience in organizations.* **Key Words:** *aesthetics; organizational an-aesthetization; organizational learning; practice; practice-based studies; sensible knowledge*

This article stresses the relevance of sensible knowledge in practice-based theorizing on organizational knowing and management learning. It asks the following question: is it possible to study practice-based knowledge and learning in organizations without taking account of sensible knowledge? Although here the question is rhetorical, it is not so in the large majority of organizational studies, given that only in the final years of the last century did organizational scholars pay closer attention to sensible knowledge (Carr and Hancock, 2003; Dean et al., 1997; Gagliardi, 1996; Guillet de Montoux, 2004; Linstead and Höpfl, 2000; Ottensmeyer, 1996; Rafaeli and Pratt, 2005; Strati, 1999; Strati and Guillet de Montoux, 2002) and to 'practice' in organizational life (Blackler, 1995; Gherardi, 2000; Gherardi and Nicolini, 2001; Heath and Button, 2002; Lave and Wenger, 1991; Nicolini et al., 2003; Suchman et al., 1999, 2002; Whalen et al., 2002).

The article draws on the results of empirical studies to show the connection between sensible knowledge and practice-based learning in organizations. It focuses on the knowledge and learning that derive from the sensory faculties of touch and hearing—and also sight, with reference to the sociologist Georg Simmel's observations made almost a century ago. Also examined are the problematic nature of sensible knowledge and the relation between aesthetics, emotion and affectivity in organizational life.

The article is structured as follows. Its first part illustrates the notion of sensible knowledge and then reflects on the relation between this notion and practice-based

DOI: 10.1177/1350507607073023

62   **Management Learning 38(1)**

learning established by empirical research. This connection is discussed within a broader framework, the purpose being to highlight (i) the problematic nature of knowledge deriving from the senses, (ii) the relation between such knowledge and the valorization of practice in the study of knowledge-building and learning in organizations and (iii) the implications of these various aspects for styles of empirical organizational research. The article draws on three empirical studies to illustrate the importance of sensible knowledge for the practice-based study of organizational life. First, however, it is necessary to define what is meant in this article by 'sensible knowledge'.

Sensible Knowledge and the Practice in Organization

Sensible knowledge concerns what is perceived through the senses, judged through the senses, and produced and reproduced through the senses. It resides in the visual, the auditory, the olfactory, the gustatory, the touchable and in the sensitive–aesthetic judgement. It generates dialectical relations with action and close relations with the emotions of organizational actors. I must expand a little on these statements.

Sensible Knowledge

First of all, sensible knowledge is directed towards 'sensible' worlds (from the ancient Greek *tà aisthetà*). That is, it is a form of knowing—and acting—profoundly diverse from the knowledge gathered and produced through the logical and ratiocinative cognitive faculty directed towards 'intelligible' worlds (*tà noetà*). The French phenomenologist philosopher Maurice Merleau-Ponty provides us with an elegant example of sensible knowledge. He comments (Merleau-Ponty, 2002: 44) that the Other is knowable through a person's gaze, gestures and looking, that is through his/her *body*. To be stressed is that this body *acts*; it is not just the 'container' of the Other's mind. Without reducing the Other to his/her body, continues Merleau-Ponty, one cannot dissociate somebody from his/her silhouette, his/her accent, his/her gait and appearance.

Sensible knowledge, warn Carchia and D'Angelo (1999: 255), is not solely the modification induced in the subject by the actual presence of objects, that is, 'sensation' *stricto sensu*. It is also the 'sensible representations of absent objects, which are the fruit of the imaginative faculty'. In other words, sensory perception is not based on

> terminal sensors, more or less veridical, able to grasp the external world as modes, for the subject, of being sensible to the world. Nor are they instruments of a sovereign consciousness, of a subject constituent and autonomous with respect to an object; rather, they are places of the flesh where the flesh of the world becomes visible. (Prezzo, 2004: 8)

This is a crucial point in regard to sensible knowledge, for it does not restrict such knowledge to the mere direct, physical and objectively observable relation; instead, it accounts for the subject's intimate, personal and corporeal relation with the experience of the world. Moreover, Merleau-Ponty (2002) points out, even when I consider my encounter with the Other, I do not dissociate him/her from his/her corporeality. Likewise—Merleau-Ponty (1989) observes—my sensible knowledge of the Other concerns also the aspects of his/her person which I cannot see. These hidden aspects I nevertheless grasp 'perceptively' as present because I 'feel' that they are close by, and I 'feel' (beyond ratiocinative thought or my knowledge of geometry) that I can reach out and touch them—just as I 'feel' the side that I cannot see of a cube or a lamp.

Secondly, sensible knowledge reveals the continuous interactions between the knowing subject and the Other. The Other considered above was a human being with its silhouette and its allure, but also the non-human element sensed via touch, hearing, smell, sight and taste reveals its active involvement in the process of producing sensible knowledge. Merleau-Ponty (2002: 26–7), drawing on Sartre, cites the case of the 'honeyed' (*mielleux*). Honey is fluid, but has some consistency and is viscous. Whenever it is touched, it 'touches' in its turn. The non-human element—in our terms—shows an ability to be active and a certain autonomy in its relationship with the human being, since it takes the initiative of spattering his or her fingers with mud, or colouring and perfuming them, or dirtying them.

While working at my computer, I have on several occasions 'sensed' something that could be called 'honeyed': the materiality of the hardware and the immateriality of the information and telecommunication technologies with which I am working are perceived as if they are spattering me with mud, and I feel that the initiative for action is no longer mine alone. Yet this is not a form of reasoning. It is sensible knowledge of being positioned and immersed not only in physical and material reality but also in so-called 'virtual' reality. This is the 'new sensibility' described by Jean-François Lyotard in reference to the 'Les Immatériaux' (*The Immaterials*) exhibition of which he was co-curator at the Centre Pompidou in Paris in 1985 (Baumgärtel, 2005): a sensibility, that is, which is specific to the post-modern condition in contemporary society and which springs from the increasing 'semiotization' of social practices due to the pervasiveness of information and telecomunication technology—as testified, for that matter, by the Net and telecommunication art.

Thirdly, sensible knowledge highlights the diversity between one person and another, but also empathic openness towards the diverse Other generated by a specific and contingent point of view. Sensible knowledge is characterized by a twofold activity, as the sociologist Georg Simmel (1908: 356) observed:

> It is through the medium of the senses that we perceive our fellow-men [sic]. This fact has two aspects of fundamental sociological significance: (*a*) that of appreciation, and (*b*) that of comprehension.

Sensation, as said, is not the mere capacity to 'receive' the sensible qualities of people and artefacts—their presence/absence, visibility/invisibility, materiality/immateriality—but rather the capacity to enjoy them and understand them by experiencing them within ourselves (Dufour-Kowalska, 1996: 161). It is the fact that I perceive myself while I perceive the world. I perceive, writes Rosella Prezzo (2004: 11), 'my inherence to a point of view': such inherence 'makes simultaneously possible both the finiteness of my perception and its openness to the plural world'. It is the genesis of a perspective which is both mine own and intercorporeal because it is empathic openness to the dimension of the Other and renders perceptive experience paramount in knowledge because it is 'co-born', that is, born together with an Other with flesh different from my own.

People in workplaces all differ because they interpret and act according to different capabilities and abilities (Pareyson, 1954): some are 'clear-sighted', others have 'fine noses', others are 'sharp-eared', 'have taste' or 'manual dexterity', while there are others who do not possess these capacities. Yet at the same time they constantly interact with the Other because they are born corporally with the Other, albeit with their own *différance* (Derrida, 1967) and personal knowledge (Polanyi, 1962).

Hence, viewed in these terms, sensible knowledge involves what is 'got' emotionally, the affectivity connected with what is perceived, taste-based judgment, the style of action. To return to the 'honeyed', it may be unpleasant to feel the honey on one's fingers; a negative emotion that only subsides when the honey stops 'touching' the fingers, or one may feel disgust at the viscosity of the honey; alternatively one may feel pleasure at its sweetness and perfume. These as Robert Legros (2005: 158–9) puts it, are sensitive judgements 'of the senses', as if they were the body's thought (*pensée du corps*). Or one may feel nostalgia remembering the honeyed. According to Michel Henry (1963: 625–9), there is no sensory activity that is neutral and impassive; sensory activity always involves passion, and every sensation is affective.

Sensible Knowledge: A Surprisingly Recent History

Even though it extends back through philosophical, religious and political–social theory until antiquity, sensible knowledge took shape as an independent notion in the seventeenth and eighteenth centuries. It was only then, in fact, that sensible knowledge became a subject of the modern disciplines following the advent of aesthetic philosophy (Baumgarten, 1735, 1750–58; Vico, 1725), a social practice which instituted, framed, enabled and definitively qualified the social experience of art, and more generally of studies of society.

> Obviously without wishing to suggest rigid causal connections, it is quite clear that the moment when philosophical aesthetics was born was also the moment when, in culture and society, the figure of the artist was given stable and 'modern' definition as the producer of those peculiar types of objects that are works of art, and when these objects came to be conceived unitarily within the common category of 'aesthetic quality'. (Vattimo, 1977: 7)

Thus, sensibility acquired theoretical status as a form of knowledge—Baumgarten's *scientia cognitionis sensitivae*—and, with Vico's *Logica poetica*, knowledge in society came to be viewed as the fruit of the imagination, of mythic thought, of metaphorical operations, of poetic sensibility. The individual is a sensible subject which, with its sensing, expresses aesthetic judgements revealing a taste that cannot be guided by objective rules (Kant, 1790). Indeed, observes Agnès Lontrade (2004: 105–8), the aesthetic autonomy of pleasure which marked the birth of aesthetic philosophy derives from the fact that the aesthetic judgement makes its own rules.

Apparent here is a controversy on the nature of knowing, which is set in relation not to the 'divine' but to the 'mundane' corporeality of sensible knowledge, and in polemic—more markedly in Vico—with rational knowledge and Cartesianism.

This polemic on forms of knowledge has also been apparent in the history of organizational thought, and it culminated in the critique waged against the rationalist paradigm during the 1970s and 1980s. Organization studies in those years stressed the importance of the emotions, symbolic constructs, institutionalization and aesthetics. They highlighted the manner in which quotidian organizational routine is known, learned, constructed and reconstructed.

Sensible knowledge was revalued in antithesis to the 'mentalization' of organizational life, to descriptions which neglected the corporeality of human experience in organizations, to the 'dehumanizing' rationality that Weber (1922) had already identified and criticized in the ideal type of bureaucracy. In particular, sensible knowledge became a central theme of studies on the aesthetic dimension of organizational life. These studies emphasized that individuals in organizations use their bodies to feel and judge, to sense and to act, and that they exhibit their difference and personal knowledge in organizational and working practice. The knowledge that they display is, as said, the knowledge acquired through the senses of sight, hearing, smell, taste and touch; it is the *pathos* of organizational artefacts, whether material or immaterial, enduring or ephemeral; it is the 'I-don't-know-what' (Franzini, 1999) that characterizes both artistic activity and everyday work in organizations; it is taste and aesthetic judgement. It is the materiality of everyday life in organizations—although this, note, is made up of nuances, shades of emphasis, emotions, *pathos*, the materiality of organizational experience that often evades analytical–rational description and which stems from the knowledge-evoking process.

The 'materiality' of everyday life highlights quotidian social practices in organizational contexts. But what is meant by 'practice' in organization studies?

The Notion of Practice and Knowing/Learning in Organization

First to be emphasized is the polysemy of the term 'practice', which comprises:

- the knowledge 'situated' in the organization as a local phenomenon but connected with globalization;
- the expertise expressed in the performativity of organizational action and in the post-social interaction where persons and non-human elements constantly interrelate and consisting in both tacit and explicit knowledge and aesthetic understanding;
- the importance of material cultures, artefacts and the organizational space, together with discursive practices and normative codes;
- the *habitus* constituted by playfulness, personal abilities and inventiveness legitimated in the community of practice, the organization and the network of interorganizational relations;
- the organizational communication of knowledge, which highlights that processes of organizational learning—by individuals, groups and communities—are grounded on socialization to practice.

The concept of 'practice' therefore does not separate the mental from the corporeal, routine from improvisation, tradition from creativity (Bourdieu, 1980). Instead, it emphasizes social and post-social interaction, collective negotiation, the collective construction of the 'legitimacy' of the practice itself within a specific organizational setting.

The notion of 'practice' has profoundly altered the manner in which knowledge and learning in organizations are studied. At the end of the last century, these themes became of central importance to analysis, although they were obviously ones with traditions reaching back to the origins of organizational analysis until the classical school, when the managerial revolution of Taylorism institutionalized the conflict between management and workers on the knowledge basis of industrial employment. How is knowledge created in organizations? What is the subject-matter of organizational learning? In what way are knowledge and learning connected with practice? This last question marks a turning point in the organizational study of knowledge and learning. Since practice-based organizational knowledge and learning are distinguished from:

1. An organizational endeavour to bring out tacit knowledge so that it can be translated into explicit knowledge—as in cognitivist studies of organization (Gioia and
   Cameron, 1995)—all the more so if the importance of tacit knowledge for the
   organization is denied on the grounds that it cannot be explained in cognitive
   and rational terms (Sanchez, 1997). This is a theoretical position not shared, *inter
   alia*, by Nonaka and Takeuchi (1995), who do not seek a cognitive translation of
   tacit knowledge but instead propound a hypertextual model of organization
   where tacit and explicit knowledge are connected together by 'links' and 'jumps'
   in the organizational creation of knowledge.
2. The traditional cognitive theory which—Stephen Fox comments (1997)—considers
   organizational learning in terms of the individual mental process developed
   through formal and institutional education furnished by specialists and theoreticians of learning. Contrary to these cognitivist claims, Silvia Gherardi (2000) has
   argued that organizational learning does not take place in the head and that it is
   not a commodity; rather, it is a process that generates knowledge 'situated' in
   organizational practices. The latter are accessed via organizational socialization
   and they are acquired by being performed in awareness of the 'mystery' that
   distinguishes their putting-into-use.

Knowledge rooted in 'practice' and 'situated' organizational learning are distinctive features of the knowledge society characteristic of the contemporary world of indus-trial and post-industrial production. They emphasize that it is people who create, invent and enact organization, doing so not as individual yet interrelated 'minds' but through their corporeality—which enables them to acquire sensible knowledge as well as to engage in intellectual ratiocination—and always in relation to the non-human elements that make up the organizational space.

Sensible Knowledge and Organization Studies

The following examples taken from diverse empirical research studies are meant to clarify the notion of sensible knowledge, its importance for organizational study and, in particular, its centrality within practice-based learning. They exemplify the orga-nizational knowledge and learning in organizations furnished by the senses. I shall begin with the sense of touch, a perceptive-sensory faculty which does not enjoy elevated theoretical status in philosophical aesthetics or theories of art or the social sciences. Painting, sculpture, architecture, dance and music—notes Chantal Jaquet (2001: 219)—have consecrated the supremacy of sight and hearing over the other senses. The same phenomenon is apparent in organization studies, beginning with the methods of empirical research: observation, conversation and interview, questionnaire and the study of archive materials assign sight and hearing pre-eminence over the other senses. We shall now instead see the importance of the perceptive faculty of touch (and later also of hearing) in organizational life—although it should be borne in mind that sensible knowledge is yielded by all the perceptive-sensory faculties, even when attention concentrates on the knowledge-generating action of only one of them. The purpose of the examples that follow is to argue that sensible knowledge concerns these aspects of organizational life:

1. The 'practices' of knowing and learning in organizations as processes which are not only mental and logical-analytical but also corporeal and multi-sensorial.
2. The materiality of organizational life and the constant interaction between the individual and non-human elements like the technologies (beautiful or ugly) that they use, the organizational spaces (cramped, well-lit or grotesque) in which they work, and the artefacts (elegant or repellent) that they produce.
3. The aesthetic categories—the ugly, the beautiful, the comical, the tragic, the sublime, the sacred, the rhythmic—used in discursive practices on organization and for which philosophical aesthetics provides a theoretical grounding that emphasizes the plurality—rather than the univocity—of the meanings that attach to each of them.

With the Hands

Touch, as one of the five senses, is essential if a person is to be able to move and work. In the case of a doctor, for example, we immediately note the importance of sensible knowledge in organizations. A doctor uses his/her hands to 'feel', to 'know', to 'operate' and to perform other actions essential for his/her work. If we move from the doctor's surgery to a photographer's dark room, we observe the photographer moving—even groping—his/her way round it, using the perceptive faculty of touch to orient him/herself and to 'see'. Other work contexts, as well, show how essential the sense of touch is: the hands are used to take notes at a meeting, to serve food in a restaurant, to tune a car engine, to greet other people. It is instead more difficult to say when, during their routine work in organizations, people do not use their hands, and do not move their bodies to 'touch' something, to 'use' something, to 'do' something. Touch, therefore, despite the technological revolution of information systems, is still an essential human faculty with which people know, learn and act in organizations.

This observation may seem banally obvious. Yet it serves to highlight an aspect of work life that tends to be neglected, and which is sometimes merely taken for granted even by qualitative studies of work, and by the organizational ethnographies that lend themselves best to the sociological analysis of the social processes and dynamics that generate organizational routine. To illustrate this point I shall briefly refer to an ergonomic study conducted in sawmills in the northeastern Alps.

During my research, I observed that the workers in the plank stacking yards of some sawmills did not use the gloves prescribed by the regulations to protect their hands. Working in pairs, the men—all the yard workers were men—would grab planks of the same length but different thicknesses and call out a number: 'two and a half', 'three', 'four and a half', 'three', 'two and a half', and so on. Working in rapid rhythm, according to the number called, the men would lay the plank in their hands on the stack of others of the same thickness. The number indicated the thickness in centimetres of the plank, which the stackers measured 'by hand' without using a gauge or some other instrument.

Gloves would have interfered with this touch-based operation. The fear of injuring themselves with splinters, or of freezing their bare hands in the bitter winter air of the stacking yard, was not part of the men's workplace safety culture. The workers in the plank stacking yard drew on a form of knowledge and action that was based, not on intellective–analytical understanding, but on aesthetic understanding, and it was on this dimension that they performed their work.

Knowledge in this particular work practice was based on 'interpretation by touch', after which both the workers: (1) verbally formulated the number indicating the thickness of the plank—and therefore the discursive practice; (2) agreed or otherwise on the number; (3) moved towards the correct stack; and (4) placed and arranged the plank, again using their hands because it was by means of the perceptive-sensory faculty of touch that the two workers adjusted the plank's position so that the stack was stable and ready to receive further planks.

Work and organizational practice in the yard was therefore a complex matter. It depended on the ability of the senses to know and act simultaneously; it was made possible by the capacity for action furnished by speech acts; it interwove with the capacity for ratiocination. It was performed in the interaction between the two workers who coordinated themselves in sensory interpretation and then enacted their corporeality by bending over and grasping the plank. It followed the rhythm with which they formulated the number and decided whether it was the correct one, moved towards one of the stacks in the yard, synchronizing the few steps taken and assuming the correct bodily posture to lift the plank the short distance necessary to place it on the stack, and then checked the stability of the stack, which they shook and rearranged if necessary. 'Feeling' with the hands was knowledge and action at the same time; so was moving around the yard 'touching' the organizational space with the feet; so too was assuming the correct posture to perform this particular work practice at the sawmill.

What else should be noted about this work activity? That it did not involve formal, 'explicit' scientific knowledge—in the sense of the distinction drawn between explicit and tacit knowledge by the Hungarian philosopher Michael Polanyi (1962)—because the workers did not make scientific measurement using appropriate instrumentation, as instead happened when the yard foreman checked the quality of the work once the stack had been completed. Observed instead was an act of measurement learned with practice under the guidance of a more expert worker, who showed those with aptitude how to feel the thickness of a plank with their hands. For some workers this action had become habitual practice which had social legitimacy and was based on individual dexterity—that is, on an ability that not all individuals possess in equal measure and the learning of which cannot be prescribed. In other words, it was a work skill used by the organization to store planks for the purpose of seasoning and then selling them. However, it was a skill that had to be learned and transmitted in practice by drawing on the sensible knowledge possessed by the individual worker. In fact, not all the workers at the sawmill had this capacity for knowledge and action. Consequently:

- aesthetic knowledge is individual practice that marks out those with the ability to use the perceptive-sensory faculties;
- the discursive practice, like Wittgenstein's speech act (Wittgenstein and Barrett, 1966), is simultaneously assessment and action about what one is working on;
- the organization availed itself of the competences distinctive of this phase of the work process, where authority to take decisions—on stacking the planks according to their thicknesses—was based neither on formal education nor on scientific knowledge, nor on specific technologies, which were instead used by the yard foreman to check that the workers had taken the correct decisions.

The perceptive-sensory faculty of touch is not restricted to the hands. It involves touching with the rest of the body as well, and therefore movement around the work setting. It is in this way that a person explores and gains familiarity with the organizational space, learns how to use it, and how to adopt the bodily movements and postures appropriate to working within it. It is done occasionally or is made habitual by work practice. The example that follows is intended to illustrate further the complexity of organizational knowledge and learning furnished by the sense of touch.

With the Feet

I have already shown how the two workers in the stacking yard not only used their hands but adjusted their entire bodies into the postures with which to handle the planks correctly and move within their organizational space. All this had to do with sensible knowledge, but another of my empirical studies shows even more clearly that touching as a perceptive-sensory faculty does not concern the hands alone, but rather the entire body. While conducting empirical research, I observed a group of workmen as they stripped the roof from a building: an organizational event described more thoroughly elsewhere (Strati, 2003) and which I now reprise only to the extent that it enables me to show how aesthetics is a form of personal knowledge related to practice-based learning in organizations. From a second-floor window in a building opposite the roof-strippers I had a good view of them as they worked. There were three of them, and judging from his movements one of them was the foreman. In fact, he moved around the roof, helping one workmate and then the other, and he took over work from the others when they seemed unable to cope. He gave orders which I could not hear but which were apparent from his posture and gesticulations. Although very overweight, he moved with surprising agility across the steeply sloping roof, which became increasingly perilous as the work proceeded. The other two strippers worked, sometimes alone, sometimes together, on removing the section of the roof beneath their feet. As they did so, they threw the debris down into the courtyard below, with loud crashes. They worked quickly, only slowing down to deal with particular difficulties. How—I asked myself—can they avoid overbalancing and falling if they have to use their hands to work?

I put this question to the workmen during their lunch break. Their immediate response was to say generally that 'the important thing is not to be afraid', but then they began arguing among themselves because, they said, that reply was wrong. I went back to talk to them on several occasions, and also asked how I could learn to perform the work they were doing. They told me that the most important thing was 'to feel the roof with your feet', indeed 'feel that your feet are fastened to the roof', and that this feeling had to come by itself, because it could not be taught. Other important aspects to their work were 'almost leaning on the air' between the body and the roof, or 'listening' to noises and paying attention to suspicious ones, or again 'appreciating the beauty' of working up there. In short, aesthetics emerged as a form of knowledge: the roof-strippers knew by 'feeling with the feet' or by 'leaning with the body' or by 'listening to noises', and also by 'enjoying a sentiment of beauty'. This was aesthetic knowledge of vital importance to the roof-strippers:

• for their choice of work;
• for confidence in their workmates;
• for selection of new team members.

We may observe that knowledge which has not been formalized in scientific terms is difficult to teach even when an explicit desire to learn is manifested. This is because—as Polanyi (1962) has pointed out—in everyday practice we are often aware of being able to do something but unable to describe analytically how we do it, to explain it scientifically, and thereby turn it into explicit rather than implicit and entirely personal knowledge. Sensible knowledge has precisely this characteristic: it evades logical–analytical description and scientific formalization and is better expressed evocatively and metaphorically. We may also observe that desire to know how to learn interweaves with sensing and feeling able to perform the task whenever explicit knowledge fails to teach and train.

It was said in the Introduction that the importance of sensible knowledge in organizational life is not usually recognized in the organizational literature; nor indeed is it recognized in workplaces. The next example, which centres on the sense of hearing, shows that those responsible for the management of organizations are dissuaded from taking action to ensure that the organization learns from experience by the problematicity of sensible knowledge.

With the Ear

While conducting other field research (Strati, 1999), on entering the secretary's office of a manager whom I was about to interview, I turned to one of the two secretaries present and said 'Isn't that nice! You've got music here', or words to that effect. I still remember the faces pulled by the two women and their angry reply. 'Don't you dare mention the subject!', one of them told me, and then explained that for days they had been trying to interest the office manager in their problem.

The building was located in the medieval centre of a town in central-northern Italy. In the small square outside the building, for the past few days, a young busker had been playing the flute for small change from passers-by. The two secretaries had initially found the flute music as pleasant as I did. But the busker never varied his repertoire. He played the same tune again and again: he began the tune, played it for some minutes, paused briefly, and then started it all over again. Music that had initially been pleasant became a torture as the hours and days passed. At a certain point the two secretaries could stand the flute music no longer and looked for a solution to the problem. They tried closing the windows, but the summer heat soon made the room unbearable. They then tried to blot out the sound of the flute by playing music more to their liking on one of the office computers, but the manager objected, saying that the office was not a discotheque. They then resorted to headphones, but had to take them off whenever the telephone rang, the manager called, or a visitor came into the office—putting on the headphones to block out the sound of the flute, taking them off and hearing the music again, putting the headphones back on: in short, 'We got so stressed'. They asked the manager to deal with the situation and tell the busker to go somewhere else, but the office manager replied that there was nothing he could do, that the young man had every right to be where he was and to do what he was doing, even if the manager himself found the situation irksome. The secretaries thereupon concluded that the 'organization was completely uninterested in their problem' and that they would 'make their grievance heard', although they did not specify precisely how.

The two secretaries had wanted to deactivate their auditory faculty in order not to hear sounds that their ears found intolerable, but the ears cannot be switched on and off in the same way as the eyes can, for example. It was impossible for the secretaries to hear the manager and not hear the flute music at the same time; they could not speak on the telephone without also having to listen to the endlessly repeated tune; they could not deal with visitors and not be aware of the music. The sound of the flute thus crossed the organization's boundaries to provoke the problems just described. The point that I want to stress is that the two secretaries' sense of hearing passed judgement sensitively: the flute music was initially pleasant; but then the monotonous repetition of what was essentially the same pleasant music made it disagreeable. The initial beauty of the event—which I myself had been able to appreciate—had become a problem which both disturbed the workplace environment and damaged relations between the secretaries and the manager. The charm that had momentarily seduced me when I entered the office had dissipated; it was now only a memory even for me, supplanted as it had been by the aesthetic sentiment of ugliness induced in me by the two secretaries' account of the organizational event.

Once again evidenced by this example is the corporeality of a person's modes of action and knowledge in working and organizational practices. More specifically, the example highlights:

1. The ability of an artefact's 'aesthetic quality' to engender a social process within an organization, giving rise by virtue of its beauty, attractiveness or ugliness to opportunities for action.
2. By contrast, the manager's inability to learn from practice. In fact, the manager had ignored the problem until it compounded to the point that it impacted on everyday work and damaged both the quality of organizational life and work relations with his office staff. This is an organizational issue that Fred Steele (1973) stressed many years ago: managers are often confronted by organizational problems caused by the aesthetic judgements of work colleagues, but they tend not to consider these problems as organizational matters. They do not have the necessary formal training, and they seek to deal with such problems by downplaying

their importance, rather than activating learning processes based on practical experience within the organization.

3. Beauty and ugliness are not objective qualities inhering in the artefacts with which people work during their daily organizational routines. Pleasant music may become unbearable in the sensitive–aesthetic judgement of people and thus damage the quality of work in organizations.

4. The sensitive–aesthetic judgement is collectively and socially constructed in the interaction among the diverse subjects involved in the organizational negotiation process. It regards both the actual sensing—that is, hearing the music—and its sensible evocation. It judges the organizational event in itself, as well as more general organizational features of organizational life.

Discussion

In this section I shall reprise a number of points already made in order to emphasize the elements that I regard as crucial in arguing that, when studying practice and practice-based organizational knowledge and learning, the organizational analyst must take due consideration of sensible knowledge and of the research that has been conducted on the phenomenon.

The Knowledge-producing Activity of Sensible Knowledge

I wish to emphasize—doing so by citing Georg Simmel—that sensory perceptions should be examined in their specificity and as they perform their knowledge-producing activity. Firstly, aesthetic knowledge among persons gives rise to interaction and the construction of social relationships:

> The sense-impressions of any object produce in us not only emotional and aesthetic attitudes toward it but also an understanding of it. In the case of reaction to non-human objects, these two responses are, in general, widely separated ... These two diverse reactions which are independent of each other are with human beings generally integrated into a unified response. Theoretically, our sense-impressions of a person may be directed on the one hand to an appreciation of his emotional value, or on the other to an impulsive or deliberate understanding of him [sic]. Actually, these two reactions are coexistent and inextricably interwoven as the basis of our relation to him. (Simmel, 1908/1969: 357)

Secondly, the senses produce different kinds of knowledge which give rise to different social relations. Sight, for example, often involves an interaction between people.

> Of the special sense-organs, the eye has a uniquely sociological function. The union and interaction of individuals is based upon mutual glances. This is perhaps the most direct and purest reciprocity which exists anywhere ... The interaction of eye and eye dies in the moment in which the directness of the function is lost. But the totality of social relations of human beings, their self-assertion and self-abnegation, their intimacies and estrangements, would be changed in unpredictable ways if there occurred non glance of eye to eye. This mutual glance between persons, in distinction from the simple sight or observation of the other, signifies a wholly new and unique union between them ... The eye cannot take unless at the same time it gives ... What

occurs in this direct mutual glance represents the most perfect reciprocity in the entire field of human relationships. (Simmel, 1908/1969: 358)

Simmel continued his analysis of the senses and of their value for sociological knowledge. He explored other characteristics of sight as well, like its capacity immediately to create social formations which lose their specificity. These he compared with the characteristics of hearing, and then moved to smell, and so on. However, what is relevant in his analysis to this part of the article has already been said: the essential property of aesthetics is that it enhances, at the same time, knowledge-production and activity.

Ambiguity of Sensible Knowledge

I stress the ambiguity of sensible knowledge. As shown by the foregoing examples drawn from empirical analysis of various workplaces, sensible knowledge is often spurious, in the sense that it is closely connected with judgements that pertain to organizational ethics, rather than aesthetics, and to the emotions, which, as Stephen Fineman argues (1997), are an integral part of organizational competences and learning processes in organizations. I shall dwell for the moment on the latter, beginning by noting that the organizational study of the emotions, like the study of the aesthetic dimension, is a crucial part of the alternative put forward to the cognitivist and rationalist imperative in the understanding of organizational life. Also the emotions, whether they concern the ethical or aesthetic codes of working and organizational practices, are generally taken for granted. Yet they constitute a fundamental feature of everyday routine in organizations and are an important dimension of the *pathos* of organizational life: seeing, hearing, touching, smelling and tasting provoke emotions—in both the organizational actor and the researcher—which are sometimes of considerable somatic intensity. What, therefore, distinguishes sensible knowledge from emotion? It is the emphasis placed on sensory perception and the aesthetic judgement.

Sensible Knowledge and Organizational An-aesthetization

I also wish to stress that the aesthetization of work experiences and organizational practices may blunt our sensibilities and conceal, mask or disperse whatever is ugly or unpleasant in our work and participation in the construction and reconstruction of our everyday organizational lives. The phenomenon is more widespread and pervasive than might be thought, and it can be observed in many organizational practices. One is alarmed—writes Odo Marquard (1989: 11–12)—by this aesthetization of reality which, posited as man's self-redemption, continues to revolutionize reality. This is the last stage of 'an authorization of the domain of illusion' whereby the aesthetic leads not to 'aesthetic experience' but to an anaesthetic dulling of experience, that is to say, to the individual's anaesthetization.

This is a dramatic denunciation, for in certain respects it has the same value as Weber's problematization of the iron cage constituted by bureaucracy. It underlines the organizational control which operates through sensible knowledge (Hancock and Tyler, 2000). Organizational an-aesthetization, like the collective emotional repression of an unpleasant event, is the organizational practice by which disagreeable and problematic workplace experiences are muffled and silenced. Thus, dynamics and events which may be unpleasant to the point of provoking disgust are eliminated so that the work and organization process can be aestheticized. Whatever is experienced as ugly disappears; its place taken by an image of the process which, rather than comprising all its controversial features, is shining clean, with the perfection—or the desired imperfection—of a work of art. Aesthetizing work and organization practices is somewhat similar to what an artist does when s/he rids his/her work of all the flaws and impurities that have crept in during its production (Strati and Guillet de Montoux, 2002). Hence, the aesthetization of work processes and organizational phenomena may be deleterious—as Marquard acutely points out—because it blunts our capacity to acquire multiple and complex knowledge of them.

Sensible Knowledge, Practice-based Learning and Empirical Research in Organizations

The final point that I wish to make concerns the relation between sensible knowledge and practice-based learning by those who conduct empirical research in organizations. Those who study organizations, in fact, may draw upon aesthetic as well as cognitive understanding (Strati, 1992, 1999). Sensible knowledge has been long neglected by organization studies, even though—as I have sought to show—it is habitually used by people to comprehend, act and learn in organizations. As far as researchers are concerned, as soon as they conceive their research, they may experience aesthetic sentiments on which they can draw to gain nuanced, precise and subtle understanding of the organizational phenomena studied. These may be sensations of pleasure arising from the desire for knowledge and learning, or they may be sensations of disgust and boredom at the way in which the research is progressing. Once in the field, researchers see ugly and beautiful things; they smell perfumes, unpleasant odours or note the absence of odour; they hear agreeable or disagreeable noises; they are angered by the conditions in which people are forced to work, or they may be enchanted by the beauty of particular work stations. They may be seduced by a well-told story or annoyed by overblown rhetoric; they 'feel' their research, they are pleased by its progress, or they may be annoyed by it. As they process their research materials, they may be attracted by the beauty of some of them or bored or even disgusted by others. They are intrigued by certain themes and allow themselves to drift with the pleasure of ideas and discoveries, or are moved by verifications of their intuitions and working hypotheses. When they write a paper or prepare a multimedia or oral presentation—that is, the expository architecture of their research results—they use the aesthetic canons of ritual, they invent new ones and they rely on processes which evoke as well as expound knowledge. Obviously, researchers may use all, some or none of these resources, but if they do use them, they are employing the language of aesthetics to give form to the 'tacit' dimension of their organizational knowledge, for more is often learned in the course of empirical research than can be conveyed in logical–rational terms.

Conclusions

I have sought to argue in this article that sensible knowledge is an important part of working and organizational practices, and that it is impossible to study practice-based knowledge and learning in organizations without taking due consideration of the aesthetic understanding possessed by both organizational actors and the researcher him/herself. By illustrating and discussing examples of organizational life taken from various empirical research studies, I have described different configurations of the relation between sensible knowledge and practice-based learning in organizations. Sensible knowledge springs from the perceptive-sensory faculties of individuals, and from their aesthetic judgement, and this brings into sharp focus the artefacts and material culture, the bodies and the objects that take part in the everyday lives of organizations. The scholar's attention thus shifts to the specific differences among people at work. What one of them is able to feel another may not, and the 'reality' of these aesthetic sentiments is socially formed by collective negotiations which also involve the researcher. We have seen the importance of the perceptive-sensory faculty of touch for situated organizational learning in a sawmill and a roofing firm. The sense of hearing has been shown to be of importance for the learning and management of sensory knowledge in an organization. Hence, although sensible knowledge is one basis for practice-based learning in organizations, it is not a pure form of knowing and learning. Rather it is a form made spurious and complex by the emotion and affectivity distinctive of it, and by its relationship with the several features that characterize 'practice' in organizational life.

References

Baumgärtel, T. (2005) 'Immaterial Material: Physicality, Corporality, and Dematerialization in Telecommunication Artworks', in A. Chandler and N. Neumark (eds) *At a Distance: Precursors to Art and Activism on the Internet.* Cambridge, MA: The MIT Press.

Baumgarten, A. G. (1735) *Meditationes philosophicae de nonnullis ad poema pertinentibus.* Halle in Magdeburgo: Grunert. [English trans., *Reflections on Poetry*, ed. K. Ashenbrenner and W. B. Holter. Berkeley, CA: University of California Press, 1954.]

Baumgarten, A. G. (1750–58) *Aesthetica.* Kleyb: Frankfurt am Oder (photostat, Olms: Hildesheim, 1986).

Blackler, F. (1995) 'Knowledge, Knowledge Work and Organizations: An Overview and Interpretation', *Organization Studies* 16(7): 1021–46.

Bourdieu, P. (1980) *Le sens pratique.* Paris: Les Éditions de Minuit. [English trans., *The Logic of Practice.* Cambridge: Polity Press, 1990.]

Carchia, G. and D'Angelo, P. (eds) (1999) *Dizionario di estetica.* Roma-Bari: Laterza.

Carr, A. and Hancock, P. (eds) (2003) *Art and Aesthetics at Work.* Basingstoke: Palgrave Macmillan.

Dean, J. W. Jr, Ottensmeyer E. and Ramirez R. (1997) 'An Aesthetic Perspective on Organizations', in C. Cooper and S. Jackson (eds) *Creating Tomorrow's Organizations: A Handbook for Future Research in Organizational Behavior*, pp. 419–37. Chichester: Wiley.

Derrida, J. (1967) *L'écriture et la différence.* Paris: Seuil. [English trans., *Writing and Difference.* Chicago, IL: University of Chicago Press, 1978.]

Dufour-Kowalska, G. (1996) *L'art et la sensibilité. De Kant à Michel Henry.* Paris: Librairie Philosophique J. Vrin.

Fineman, S. (1997) 'Emotion and Management Learning', *Management Learning* 28(1): 13–25.

Fox, S. (1997) 'Situated Learning Theory versus Traditional Cognitive Learning Theory: Why Management Education Should Not Ignore Management Learning', *Systems Practice* 10(6): 727–47.

76   **Management Learning 38(1)**

Franzini, E. (1999) *Estetica e filosofia dell'arte*. Milano: Guerini.
Gagliardi, P. (1996) 'Exploring the Aesthetic Side of Organizational Life', in C. Hardy, S.R. Clegg and W.R. Nord (eds) *Handbook of Organization Studies*, pp. 565–80. London: Sage.
Gherardi, S. (2000) 'Practice-based Theorizing on Learning and Knowing in Organizations. Introduction to the Special Issue on Knowing in Practice', *Organization* 7(2): 211–23.
Gherardi, S. and Nicolini, D. (2001) 'The Sociological Foundations of Organizational Learning', in M. Diekers, A. B. Antal, J. Child and I. Nonaka (eds) *Handbook of Organizational Learning and Knowledge*, pp. 35–60. Oxford: Oxford University Press.
Gioia, D. and Cameron, F. (1995) 'Tacit Knowledge, Self-Communication, and Sensemaking in Organizations', in L. Thayer (ed.) *Organization-Communication 3*, pp. 77–96. Norwood, NJ: Ablex.
Guillet de Montoux, P. (2004) *The Art Firm. Aesthetic Management and Metaphysical Marketing*. Stanford, CA: Stanford University Press.
Hancock, P. and Tyler, M. (2000) ' "The Look of Love": Gender and the Organization of Aesthetics', in J. Hassard, R. Holliday and H. Willmott (eds) *Body and Organization*. London: Sage.
Heath, C. and Button, G. (eds) (2002) 'Workplace Studies', Special Issue of *British Journal of Sociology* 52(2).
Henry, M. (1963) *L'Essence de la manifestation*. Paris: PUF.
Jaquet, C. (2001) *Le corps*. Paris: PUF.
Kant, I. (1790) *Kritik der Urteilskraft*. Frankfurt am Main: Suhrkamp, 1968. [English trans., *The Critique of Judgement*. Oxford: Oxford University Press, 1952.]
Lave, J. and Wenger, E. (1991) *Situated Learning. Legitimate Peripheral Participation*. Cambridge: Cambridge University Press.
Legros, R. (2005) *La naissance de l'individu moderne*, in B. Foccroulle, R. Legros and T. Todorov (eds) *La naissance de l'individu dans l'art*, pp. 121–200. Paris: Bernard Grasset.
Linstead, S. and Höpfl, H. (eds) (2000) *The Aesthetics of Organization*. London: Sage.
Lontrade, A. (2004) *Le plaisir esthétique. Naissance d'une notion*. Paris: l'Harmattan.
Marquard, O. (1989) *Aesthetica und Anaesthetica. Philosophische Uberlegungen*. Paderborn: Schoningh.
Merleau-Ponty, M. (1989) *Le Primat de la perception et ses conséquences philosophiques*. Grenoble: Cynara (1947). [English trans., *The Primacy of Perception, and Other Essays on Phenomenological Psychology, the Philosophy of Art, History, and Politics*. Evanston, IL: Northwestern University Press, 1964.]
Merleau-Ponty, M. (2002) *Causeries 1948*. Paris: Éditions du Seuil.
Nicolini, D., Gherardi, S. and Yanow, D. (eds) (2003) *Knowing in Organizations: A Practice-Based Approach*. Armonk, NY: M. E. Sharpe.
Nonaka, I. and Takeuchi, H. (1995) *The Knowledge-Creating Company. How Japanese Companies Create the Dynamics of Innovation*. Oxford: Oxford University Press.
Ottensmeyer, E. (1996) 'Essays on Aesthetics and Organization', Special Issue of *Organization* 3(2).
Pareyson, L. (1954) *Estetica. Teoria della formatività*. Giappichelli: Torino. [Reprinted 1988, Milano: Bompiani.]
Polanyi, M. (1962) *Personal Knowledge. Towards a Post-Critical Philosophy*. London: Routledge & Kegan Paul (1958).
Prezzo, R. (2004) 'Il primato di un paradosso', in M. Merleau-Ponty (ed.) *Il primato della percezione e le sue conseguenze filosofiche*. Milano: Medusa.
Rafaeli, A. and Pratt, M. (eds) (2005) *Artifacts and Organizations*. Mahwah, NJ: Lawrence Erlbaum.
Sanchez, R. (1997) 'Managing Articulated Knowledge in Competence-based Competition', in R. Sanchez and A. Heene (eds) *Strategic Learning and Knowledge Management*, pp. 163–87. Chichester: Wiley.

Simmel, G. (1908) *Soziologie. Untersuchungen über di Formen der Vergesellschaftung.* Leipzig: Duncker & Humblot. [English partial trans., in R. E. Park and E. W. Burgess (eds) *Introduction to the Science of Sociology,* pp. 356–61. Chicago, IL: University of Chicago Press, 1969.]

Steele, F. I. (1973) *Physical Settings and Organization Development.* Reading, MA: Addison-Wesley.

Strati, A. (1992) 'Aesthetic Understanding of Organizational Life', *Academy of Management Review* 17(3): 568–81.

Strati, A. (1999) *Organization and Aesthetics.* London: Sage.

Strati, A. (2003) 'Knowing in Practice: Aesthetic Understanding and Tacit Knowledge', in D. Nicolini, S. Gherardi and D. Yanow (eds) *Knowing in Organizations: A Practice-based Approach,* pp. 53–75. Armonk, NY: M. E. Sharpe.

Strati, A. and Guillet de Montoux, P. (2002) 'Organizing Aesthetics'. Introduction to Special Issue of *Human Relations* 55(7): 755–66.

Suchman, L., Blomberg, J., Orr, J. E. and Trigg, R. (1999) 'Reconstructing Technologies as Social Practice', *American Behavioral Scientist* 43(3): 392–408.

Suchman, L., Trigg, R. and Blomberg, J. (2002) 'Working Artefacts: Ethnomethods of the Prototype', *British Journal of Sociology* 53(2): 163–79.

Vattimo, G. (1977) 'Introduzione', in G. Vattimo (ed.) *Estetica moderna.* Bologna: Il Mulino, pp. 7–46.

Vico, G. (1725) *Principi di una scienza nuova.* Naples: Mosca, 3rd edn, 1744. [Eng. trans., *The New Science of Giambattista Vico,* ed. T. G. Bergin and M. H. Fisch. Ithaca, NY: Cornell University Press, 1968.]

Weber, M. (1922) *Wirtschaft und Gesellschaft. Grundrisse der verstehenden Soziologie.* Tübingen: Mohr. [English trans., *Economy and Society: An Outline of Interpretive Sociology I–II.* Berkeley, CA: University of California Press, 1978.]

Whalen, J., Whalen, M. and Henderson, K. (2002) 'Improvisional Choreography in Teleservice Work', *British Journal of Sociology* 53(2): 239–58.

Wittgenstein, L. and Barrett, C. (1966) *Lectures and Conversations on Aesthetics, Psychology and Religious Belief.* Oxford: Blackwell.

Contact Address

Antonio Strati is in the Department of Sociology and Social Research, Faculty of Sociology, University of Trento, piazza Venezia 41, 38100 Trento, Italy. [email: antonio.strati@soc.unitn.it]

[7]

MIND, CULTURE, AND ACTIVITY, *14*(1-2), 83–102

Knowing in a System of Fragmented Knowledge

Attila Bruni, Silvia Gherardi, and Laura Lucia Parolin

Trento University

Knowing is a situated activity. Adopting a practice-based approach, this article describes a workplace characterized by technologically dense practices as a setting in which human actors and technological objects work "together." The case of remote cardiological consultation is paradigmatic of how information and communication technologies (ICT) enter workplaces and reshape them as "systems of fragmented knowledge:" that is, learning settings in which people, symbols, and technologies work jointly to construct and reconstruct understanding of social and organizational action. Working at a distance, therefore, requires the acquisition of skills relative to the mobilization of fragmented knowledge, and the latter's alignment into a fully-fledged work practice. Knowing-in-practice is accomplished by discursive practices: *Framing and postscripting*, as practices that generate a "space" of signification for the subsequent action; *footing*, as the dialectic that enables people to align themselves within a predetermined frame and disrupt its coordinates; and *delegation to the nonhuman*, as the ability of humans to delegate the performance of clinical practice to nonhuman systems, which come to be regarded as active subjects within the remote consultation

Information and communication technologies (ICT) have substantially changed work practices in recent years, requiring workers and organizations to learn different ways to work, use information, and communicate. The expertise developing around work with new technologies goes beyond the mere performance of computer-mediated work, and requires workers to learn how to deploy practical knowledge and how to translate codified knowledge into knowing-in-practice. It is therefore necessary not only to study what the new technologies "are" (in terms of design) and how to introduce them appropriately into workplaces, but also to ask what they "do" in relation to the enactment of knowledge in situated work practices.

The articles in Engeström and Middleton's (1996) book analyzed work as activity situated in practice and mediated by technological artifacts. Numerous later studies have drawn on this work. Practical knowledge has been studied as knowledge distributed among individuals and between humans and artifacts (Cole & Engeström, 1993; Conein, Dodier, & Thévenot, 1993; Hutchins, 1993; Latour, 1987). Although artifacts perform a fundamental role in mediating action, they are connected in a complex manner with work practices and the knowledge activities within them. The greater attention being paid to practice and knowing-in-practice, linking such diverse research traditions as the cultural approach to learning, situated learning theory, activity theory, and actor-network theory (Gherardi, 2000), means that practical knowledge is

Correspondence should be sent to Enrico Attila Bruni, Università degli Studi di Trento, Dipartimento di Sociologia e Ricerca Sociale, Via Verdi, 26, 38100 Trento, Italy. E-mail: anomalo@libero.it no longer viewed, in cognitivist terms, as a stable and well-defined set of tasks, but rather as a collective achievement that work groups pursue through material-discursive practices. We may say that knowing is a situated activity and—adopting a practice-based approach (Gherardi, 2006)—describe workplaces characterized by "technologically dense" practices (Bruni, 2005a) as settings in which human actors and technological objects work "together" (Heath & Button, 2002; Schmidt, 2000). These new settings consist not only of physical spaces, but also of mental and social ones, in which the same actors engage in both traditional and new practices flanking or penetrating already-existing ones. In this case the research questions that arise are the following: How do humans and nonhumans associate in performing knowing-in-practice together? How is knowledge enacted and transformed in the activity of knowing?

In the empirical case presented here, ICT furnished the infrastructure for a new type of activity in which the practices of medical examination and specialist consultation were redefined by the new opportunities for interaction offered by remote consultation. The specialists, a cardiologist and a general practitioner, interacted by transmitting ECGs online, and by discussing them by telephone, to determine the patient's state of health. The activity observed in this work setting was substantially different from conventional medical practices: It was not a cardiological examination, nor was it a general medical one, nor a specialist training initiative. Rather, it was a hybrid of these practices. Remote consultation is a new type of medical practice that obliges the two specialists to learn new forms of work and action, in the social as well as material systems in which they are embedded. The work setting produced by ICTs required the two specialists to learn how to mobilize knowledge embedded in a heterogeneous network where bodies, material artifacts, symbols, organizational procedures, and several types of expertise should be brought together and aligned in order to support interpretation of the patient's state of health.

The case of remote medical care described struck us as paradigmatic of how ICT enters workplaces and reshapes them as "systems of fragmented knowledge:" that is, learning settings in which people, symbols, and technologies work jointly to construct and reconstruct understanding of social and organizational action. Working in such settings means learning how to act at a distance in a social-material context, using discursive practices to align heterogeneous materials.

In the following sections we define what is meant by "system of fragmented knowledge" by describing the places in which knowledge resides: not only in patients and professionals, but also in rules and artifacts. We then focus on the processes by which this fragmented knowledge is mobilized and enacted by means of discursive practices that give sense to collective action, and serve to organize it.

KNOWING-IN-PRACTICE AS A COLLECTIVE ACCOMPLISHMENT

The practice-based approach to theorizing knowledge arises from multiple perspectives and streams of research which, traversing the boundaries of several disciplines, are converging on an understanding (and methodology) based on a pragmatic theory of knowing that reframes traditional research into organizational learning (Gherardi, 2001; Schatzki, Knorr Cetina, & von Savigny, 2001). The concept of practice provides a way to theorize "knowing at work" historically and culturally so as to capture the current materiality of specific forms of knowing, as well as to indicate the indeterminacy of that form of knowing (i.e., that it will, in turn, develop). The advantage of this conceptualization, when analyzing organizational life, is that it allows work, learning, innovation, communication, negotiation, conflict over goals, interpretation of goals, and history to all coexist with one another. Practice articulates the spatiality and facticity of knowing as enactment. As with Weick's (1977) enactment theory, Giddens' (1984) structuration theory, Engeström's (1987) expansive learning, and Unger's (1987) notion of formative contexts, the concept of knowing-in-practice conveys the idea of the social construction of knowledge in mundane working activities and within social structures that are both the production of human activities and the context for them.

The metaphor of knowing as enactment conveys the idea of a network that is socially woven around a domain of knowledge. This metaphor is grounded in an actor-network sensibility and in concepts such as "knowing-as-displacing" (Law, 2000), or learning in the face of mystery (Gherardi, 1999). At its heart lies the idea of enactment as "an occasion in a location, a set of actions with a series of effects" (Law, 2000, p. 349). The knowledge, the subjects, and the objects of knowledge may be understood as mutually produced within a situated practice.

The heuristic value of the concept of practice, therefore, resides in the possibility of articulating spatiality (the locus of knowledge) and facticity (the situated production of knowledge). Knowing can, hence, be conceived as a situated activity, an activity that is repeated, stabilized, and institutionalized, but that is enacted again and again as the work practice is performed repeatedly. When we conceive knowledge as substance, we see it as materialized in objects; when we conceive it as a property, we see it as owned by individuals. When we look at knowing-in-practice, we define it as the mobilization of the knowledge embedded in humans and nonhumans performing workplace practices.

A practice such as remote consultation can be defined as the mode—relatively stable in time and space, and socially recognized—of ordering heterogeneous elements into a set of activities normatively sustained by a community of practitioners. Practicing can be defined as the situated performance of a practice within the network of human and nonhumans symmetrically associated in the ongoing enactment.[1]

One of the most important directions taken by practice-based approach to research is the study of the practical organization of knowledge in the form of methods of reasoning and action in the association of human and nonhuman elements (Bruni, 2005b). In the following section we assume an *equivalence* relation between knowing and practicing, in the sense that practicing is knowing-in-practice, whether the subject is aware of it or not. Acting as a competent practitioner is synonymous with knowing how to connect successfully with the field of practices thus activated.

REMOTE CONSULTATION AS THE ENACTMENT OF A SYSTEM OF FRAGMENTED KNOWLEDGE

ICT is increasingly changing the nature of workplaces by introducing distance, thereby disconnecting time and space, which entails changes in consolidated work practices, and requires

---

[1]The notion of symmetry was first introduced in the sociology of science (Bloor, 1976). It was then developed by actor-network theory (Latour, 1987; Law, 1992) in order to analyze the creation of social, natural, and technological phenomena without distinguishing a priori between human actors, on the one hand, and natural and technological objects, on the other.

work groups to collectively learn ways to work at a distance. To analyze how this happens, and to show how working with ICT signifies knowing-in-practice how to align bits and pieces of fragmented knowledge, we consider remote consultation as a practice that enacts a *system of fragmented knowledge* (SFK).

An SFK is constituted by the relations among the heterogeneous elements that embody knowledge, which are mobilized by work practices and transformed into knowing-in-practice. It is a concept that allows us to represent the spatiality of knowing-in-practice, by tracing the boundaries around the elements that enter into reciprocal relationships when a working practice associates them. Knowing-in-practice may therefore be represented as the successful association of all the knowledge that is fragmented and embedded into an SFK, keeping in mind that the action of associating the elements creates the knowledge formed in the action itself, and by means of it.

We prefer the adjective "fragmented" over "distributed" because it distances a practice-based approach from the tradition of distributed cognition studies. We are indebted to the latter for many reasons and, in fact, they have paved the way for the shift from knowing-as-cognition (seen as a mental activity) to knowing-as-a-situated-accomplishment that is something people do together. In fact, on returning to the origins, we note that studies on so-called human-computer interaction assumed a simplified concept of cognition that undervalued the commonsense competences, which orient action in the real circumstances of everyday life. Human-computer interaction's notion of communication with machines lacked the interactive and negotiated dimension of communication and action. Suchman (1987) subsequently drew on Garfinkel's (1967) ethnomethodology to show that interpretative and cognitive work in social settings is guided by the interpretation of clues provided by the context of interaction. Almost simultaneously, the critique of the individualistic and decontextualized conception of cognition was deepened by Lave (1988), who argued that cognition is a complex social phenomenon, and that if we observe it in everyday practices, we find that it is distributed—stretched over, not divided among—culturally organized minds, bodies, activities, and settings. Lave's work highlighted the distributed character of cognition not only among individuals but also among artifacts and objects present in the setting. Extension of the notion of agency to include nonhuman actors as well, in the sense proposed by actor-network theory (Latour, 2005), has enabled analytical attention to focus directly on the social processes of associating and aligning heterogeneous elements. These are processes that can be observed directly without having to attribute a logical and ontological priority to human actors and their cognitive processes. Within the sociology of organization, the practice-centered ethnomethodological tradition lends itself better to analysis of knowledge as a mundane and social activity, and therefore within an approach that conjugates knowledge with power, and allays the suspicion that the adjective "distributed" refers to a mental representation of a harmoniously shared reality. The use of "fragmented" is also intended to emphasize that possession of the pieces of knowledge necessary for a shared practice is a collective problem regardless of the will or ability to put them together. To illustrate the heuristic potential of the concept of SFK, we describe an example of its application.

The data presented pertain to a broader research project conducted on organizational learning in virtual work settings by the Research Unit on Communication, Organizational Learning, and Aesthetics.[2] The research focused on a number of case studies in the field of remote health care (Gherardi & Strati, 2004) where the features of the setting merged a plurality of organizational, professional, and occupational memberships. The research was conducted in a remote cardiology unit in the north of Italy, the Health Telematic Network, which was set up in 1998 and is today one of the most advanced remote cardiology call centers in Italy. The unit is staffed by cardiologists who examine electrocardiograms sent to them telematically by general practitioners (GPs) in various regions. The GP records the patient's ECG with a portable apparatus. The recordings may be made at the doctor's surgery or in the patient's home, because the apparatus is able to store around 10 traces that can be transmitted at a later time. The call center coordinates the referral procedure by establishing contacts between GPs and cardiologists while handling transmission of the ECGs. The traces are sent by the doctor, downloaded using special software at the call center, and distributed among the cardiologists, who can read them on their computer screens. The traces are discussed by telephone with the GPs and then sent back to them by fax with the report attached. The GP usually sends the trace immediately after recording it and uses the remote consultation service while examining the patient. In this case, the service takes the form of a "distance cardiological examination" performed by the cardiologist with the mediation of the GP. In other cases, usually in nonurgent ones, the GP records several ECGs and them transmits them in a batch to the cardiologist.

Where Does Knowledge Reside in an SFK?

A remote consultation may be defined as the outcome of a collaborative practice that aligns all the relevant knowledge embedded in the SFK designed to carry it out. Knowledge is fragmented and resides in bodies, machines, images, evaluations, routines, laboratory techniques, and it is enacted by material-discursive practices. Mapping the elements considered to embody relevant knowledge and the relationships among them is the first step in determining who and what is involved in a "successful" remote consultation (as judged by the practitioners). The course of action will activate some elements and not others: some will be significant by their presence, others by their absence. The concept of SFK is a heuristic framework, useful for mapping in terms of knowledge repositories, the interdependent elements that, on the one hand, constitute the setting for the remote consultation, and on the other, provide the resources for performance of the practice.

Knowledge is Embedded in Patients

In the setting examined, the patients' perceptions of their bodies and feelings, and their reasons for consulting their GPs, constituted a repository of situated knowledge. In this case, relevant knowledge was the capacity to perceive an "anomaly" and to translate it into accountable elements through language and the narration of symptoms. This preliminary description and stock of knowledge was supported by the GP's own knowledge, which translated the patient's

---

[2]The research was carried out as part of the MURST project "Pratiche organizzative e tecnologie di mediazione della conoscenza nelle comunità virtuali" coordinated by Silvia Gherardi, with the participation of Rino Fasol, Attilio Masiero, Davide Nicolini, Antonio Strati, Attila Bruni, and Laura Lucia Parolin.

subjective knowledge—assumed to be strongly influenced by individual factors and therefore unreliable—into scientific knowledge couched in medical terminology.

Knowledge is Embedded in a Medical Community

As shown by Cicourel (1986), medical expertise consists in the transformation of the idiomatic and "folk" expressions of patients and their external characteristics into "objective" knowledge through the systematic use of medical vocabulary. The distinctive feature of health care is the application of expertise to common sense. Studying the interactions between doctor and patient and between an expert doctor and a novice, Cicourel found that doctors make constant reference to commonsense elements (expressions, emotions, and tactile and auditory sensations). Distinctive of medical training, in fact, is the large proportion of practical knowledge acquired from long periods of hospital internship, besides the lengthy duration of formal apprenticeship. Medical expertise also consists in the competent use of formalized and recognized rules and notions constituting a body of standardized knowledge, some of which is codified in written protocols intended to guide medical action and support decision-making.

Knowledge is Embedded in Organizational Rules and Habits

Organizations may be conceived as distributed knowledge systems (Tsoukas, 1996) and, in particular, as professional bureaucracies using skill standardizations as a form of coordination (Mintzberg, 1989). Hence, by hiring specialists, they internalize previously codified bodies of knowledge, while codifying other bodies of knowledge by institutionalizing models of behavior into norms or standard routines. The organization lays down rules that regulate medical action by prescribing the skilled behaviors and actions to be enacted in particular conditions, whose "correctness" as endorsed by the medical community signifies meaningfulness. As skill-standardization instruments, protocols are defined by the medical community: They thus traverse the boundaries of the professional bureaucracies—hospitals for instance—whose needs have generated them. Protocols are based on the segmentation of therapy and intervention into an array of microactions ordered into a correct sequence, resulting from a rationalization of medical knowledge intended to deprive individual actors of margins of discretion. The rationalization of medical knowledge (Berg, 1997) serves the purpose of limiting the margins of error caused by the human factor in rational medical reasoning. Protocols, argued Michael Lynch (2002), have been an object of interest to sociology because they are accounts of individual reasoning and social action, but in medical practice all the actors involved respecify medical knowledge through their actions in practice.[3]

According to Lynch (1997), we may argue that standard protocols must be interpreted in relation to the context, and the knowledge necessary for their definition and competent use must be identified in the context. This consideration enables us to emphasize that an SFK frames the space where the prescriptions of protocols merge with situated practices, and

---

[3] Analytic philosophers and sociologists have long entertained the hope of using protocols (and related artifacts like rules, laws, plans, maps, propositions, norms, and programmes) as stable, reproducible and adequate accounts of individual reasoning, social action, and social structure. This theoretical hope has to do with the advantages of treating orders of text as proxies for (or even privileged representations of) orders of lived activity (Lynch, 2002).

require both local rewriting, amendment, and already-consolidated competence, on the part of users.

Knowledge is Embedded in Artifacts

Knowledge resides not only in humans and rules, but also in the artifacts—tools, texts and objects—that participate in and constitute the setting. There are tools (like protocols) that perform action and interaction through the rules embedded in them. This signifies that artifacts, tools, and technologies should be conceived of as social practices, or as "collective accomplishments" (Garfinkel, 1967) of particular forms of order and action. Furthermore, according to Barnes (2001), social practices are

> accomplishments readily achieved by, and routinely to be expected of members acting together, but they nonetheless have to be generated on every occasion, by agents concerned all the time to retain coordination and alignment with each other in order to bring them about. (p. 25)

In the case examined, for example, the cardiologist had to compile a patient file card as an instrument of organizational accountability that defined the sequence and content of the questions the cardiologist usually addressed to the general practitioner. The telephone interactions between the cardiologist and the GP exhibited a very similar structure, at least in the preliminary exchanges, to that of the patient card. This set of preestablished questions not only shaped the interaction between cardiologist and GP, but also reflected the forms of knowledge deemed relevant in the situation.

Besides the patient file card, there was another tool in the setting that shaped medical knowledge through the constraints and rules that it imposed. The referral software used by the service imposed report-writing constraints on the distance consultation, thereby not only facilitating the interaction with the GP, but also shaping the rationality that reconstructed medical action *a posteriori*.

The artifacts in use within an SFK embody not only their designers' knowledge (Norman, 1990) and suggestions for use, but also potential courses of action resulting from knowledge of use. The adoption of the electrocardiograph was an implicit acknowledgment of the validity of the knowledge necessary for its design and use that enabled the artifact to transform the impulses emitted by the human body into representations of its activity. At the same time, however, the representation of the patient furnished by the ECG artifact assumed value according to the narrative of which it was part: that is, in a situated manner in accordance with the network's relations. In fact, the knowledge embedded in artifacts derives only partly from the designers' vision of the world; the meaning of the inscriptions may change as relations in the network change.

Knowledge is Embedded in a Technological Infrastructure

Teleconsultancy practices are made possible by a technological infrastructure that enables interaction. Technological apparatuses, texts, language, human actors, organizational routines, and ad hoc practices connect the GPs and the cardiologists, and mediate the interaction between them.[4]

This infrastructure is made up not only of technological apparatuses such as computers, telephones, telephone cables, and ECG recording machines, but also of the languages and codes necessary to link them together. The infrastructure is the telematic network consisting of cables and terminals, but it is also the programming and connection languages that manage the system and regulate the flows of information. The package transmission technology, the codification system, and the compression format used to transmit the ECG are elements that constitute the infrastructure mediating between the physical body (the patient's heart) and the representation of the organ's functioning (the ECG) that the cardiologist receives.

The infrastructure is invisible in the sense that it is taken for granted; it is "simply present" or just "transparent" (Star, 1999; Winograd & Flores, 1986) and it forms the background to the interaction. This background emerges only at moments of breakdown, when its malfunctioning forcefully emphasizes its existence.

Knowledge is Embedded in a Dedicated Organization

The intermediaries between patient and cardiologist are not solely technologies and the languages that represent and codify their use. There is also a dedicated organization, created ad hoc, which makes the interaction possible and conditions its form: the call center, which represents a center of coordination (Suchman, 1997) consisting of knowledgeable people, the telephone operators, with their tasks, roles and actions, and the accords and expectations among the actors who regulate the service. The practice of telecardiology is a "here and now" event whose realization requires a prior series of agreements and actions that make it possible in space and time. It is the call center that receives the telephone call and the telematic ECG, contacts the cardiologist on duty, sends him/her the trace, and puts him/her in contact with the GP waiting online. The call center service is the intermediary between the GP and the cardiologists, and thus becomes a crucial component in the new medical practice of telecardiology. Like the technological infrastructure, the ad hoc organization that manages the service and makes it possible is transparent. It is not visible when the service is being delivered properly, but becomes the main actor in the SFK when a breakdown occurs, because embedded in the service is the knowledge presupposed by the mediation activity.

This brief description of the bits and pieces of knowledge embedded in the SFK has highlighted that the knowledge necessary for remote consultation is fragmented among hetero-

---

[4]Mediation is one of the main concepts in activity theory, originally envisioned by Vygotsky (1978). Previous Vygotskian theorizing has, however, mainly focused on a single individual or a dyad of two subjects using a single, well-defined mediating tool or artifact. Language as mediator has required a more complex approach, but studies of semiotic mediation have commonly excluded material instruments and tools. In interventionist studies of expansive learning, the mediational setup is complex and multilayered both semiotically and instrumentally (Engeström, 2001). Actor-network theorists prefer to talk of "intermediaries," (sometimes called translation "agents" or "interessement mechanisms"), defined simply as what passes from one agent to another and gives rise to a network of relations. The notion of intermediary covers diverse and heterogeneous materials like objects, artifacts, individuals, and groups, with their skills and capabilities, money, texts, and symbolic inscriptions. The two concepts are very similar even if they are inscribed in different disciplinary traditions. For a comparison between them, see Koschmann, Kuutti, and Hickman (1998); Miettinen (1999, 2001); and Latour (1994).

geneous material and symbolic entities, and that their enactment can be seen as a situated practice. In order to perform "a remote consultation," all the relevant elements must be aligned.

An SFK can therefore be defined as the heterogeneous network of elements associated with knowledge, power, and ordering processes, which must be translated into an adequately aligned set of sociotechnical elements so that they become stable and able to support the movement of things and persons through time and space. Although the SFK represents the spatiality of an ongoing practice, alignment represents the facticity of that practice. In the next section, we illustrate how, in remote consultation, alignment is performed through material-discursive practices.

DISCURSIVE PRACTICES AS THE ALIGNMENT OF A HETEROGENEOUS NETWORK

We now describe how knowledge is mobilized and aligned in an SFK through material-discursive practices. The data analyzed were collected by listening to all the recorded telephone calls made to the center in one month (November 2002) for a total of just over 1,000 calls.[5]

The average duration of a conversation was around $2^1/_2$ minutes. From a methodological point of view, the phone calls provided an excellent opportunity to analyze a practice from its beginning to its end. The form of the interaction was highly standardized, both because of the protocols used in cardiology (which homogenize the data and criteria to which the two doctors refer) and because the cardiologists had to compile a patient file card for each ECG consultancy and therefore asked the GPs standard questions, almost always in the same order.

The outcomes of the teleconsultations were divided into five categories: only 5.8% of consultations concluded with the patient's dispatch to Accident and Emergency; 20.4% concluded with the prescription of further tests; 60.3% resulted in no particular action being taken; 1.1% led to assessment of the patient's state of health being postponed; and in 1.6% of the cases no technical consultation was made (the trace was unreadable or the consultation was declared invalid). We analyze not so much the content of the questions and/or answers that characterize a teleconsultation as the discursive practices of alignment within the SFK used by the actors.

The telephone calls followed an invariant pattern: The cardiologist opened the conversation, the GP explained the reason for the call and described the case, the cardiologist asked for further information, and the GP replied.

20021102–103643 (1:34)[6]

			Times
	C:	pronto?	5"
Opening	GP:	Ciao, this is …	
	C:	This is … , Ciao, tell me …	
	GP:	I've done this electrocardiogram mostly as a control. This male patient has just been with me …	

---

[5]Selected from 1,137 telephone calls were 1,052 deemed "valid" because the consultation process was completed. Most of the other calls were cases of infrastructure breakdown and made up 8% of the total.

[6]The codes for the telephone calls denote the day, month, year, and time of the call (in this case, therefore, at 10:36 on November 2, 2002). They are followed by the duration of the call.

Patient description		I found an initial hypertension ... he's dyspneic ... dyspneic, slightly, especially ... when stressed ... he's overweight and a heavy smoker. It's a check more than anything else ...	5"–23"
	C:	Is he on medication, this man?	
Request for further	GP:	No, no.	
Information	C:	Wait till I get the rest of the trace, so tell me ... have you put him on something for the pressure, or ...	23"–38"
GP's reply with further information	GP:	... no, no, it's a check now, because I've done ... I've started, ... I've also had him take haemotochemical tests ... to see whether, you know, whether there are ...	38"–53"
Interruption when ECG is received	C:	... I understand. Listen, he's got a sinus rhythm, arterioventricular delivery within the norm. He's got an incomplete right branch block. The rest of the trace is perfectly normal. There's nothing else as far as I can see.	53"–1'24"
	GP:	I agree	
Closure	C:	I'll send you the trace, then ... ciao.	1'24"–1'34'
	GP:	Right ... yes ⋯ yes, thanks ... ciao.	

As shown by the transcript, the conversation structure is affected by the fact that, when the consultation begins, the cardiologist has usually not yet received the ECG (which takes around 50 seconds to transmit/receive). While waiting, the cardiologist asks the GP about the patient and then interrupts (more or less brusquely) when the trace is received. The activity of interpretation seems to be unproblematic, and the telephone call lasts as long as is necessary to close the conversation. Consequently, the presence of a telematic ECG, and the time required to wait for it, give the two doctors a chance to "teleconsult;" the ECG is an active element that is read, but also has its own "voice" in the interaction. Although the ECG is indeed an important element, it is not the only object present in the consultation. The discourse of the two doctors usually calls into play and activates a network of elements (objective assessments, references to other examinations, risk factors, pharmacological therapy), the alignment of which contributes to determining the result of the remote consultation and, in consequence, the patient's "trajectory." The technological infrastructure, the work done by the call operators, and the habits and rules embedded in the organizational setting remain invisible as long as the consultation works. All other repositories of knowledge remain silent and invisible when they have been unproblematically aligned with the doctors, the patient (who sometimes takes part in the discursive practices), and the call center. Otherwise they need alignment work to be performed.

This is particularly evident in those (frequent) situations where there is no automatic correspondence between the patient's state of health as shown by clinical assessment and the ECG trace, so that the two doctors are obliged to construct a discourse that follows other paths and redefines the meaning of the situation by involving other objects.

20021106–125929 (2:57)
(Greetings.)

GP: I've had this ECG done on a patient already affected with chronic ischemic cardiopathy, because he felt ill while he was eating, he felt faint and a weight on his stomach (…)

C: Mah … the trace doesn't seem … how is he now?

GP: He's lying down now … He feels weak … he hasn't got dyspnoea, absolutely not … He still feels this weight … I think it's indigestion. I mean, he needs to vomit … but, you know … I preferred to do the ECG …

CP: I'd say … there aren't any evident alterations … of course, then you have to look at the clinical [assessment] … because these things sometimes … these things are a bit tricky … For the moment I'd keep an eye on him … There's a left axial deviation … (…) There's … some ventricular extrasystole … (…) Is he taking Cardioaspirin?

GP: No, in fact I wanted to give it to him …

C: … He has a history of ischemic cardiopathy … but he hasn't had acute episodes?

GP: No, no. Perhaps … 5 years ago, there was something … when the chronic ischemia diagnosis was made …

C: … I'd wait a bit longer … how old is he?

GP: 85.

C: The risks are clearly there. If the thing doesn't sort itself out, I'd have him looked at, just to be on the safe side … (…) but, at the moment the trace doesn't show anything …

GP: … out of the ordinary …

C: … although traces can sometimes be negative … (…)

GP: … right … in fact … That's true, you can't always rely on the trace …

C: … No, no there's a good percentage of heart attacks with normal traces … except that this … well … I mean … at 80 years old, of course, some problem always comes out!

GP: Yes, I'll give him an antacid and then we'll see …
    (Salutations.)

The telephone call just reported shows that, when the ECG and the patient do not align (for example, the ECG is normal but the patient feels ill), various elements are discursively mobilized, and the trace moves into the background, losing its status as a privileged object. To paraphrase Latour (2002), it is as if the trace has become a "labyrinth" through which the two doctors must find their way. Thus, previous ECGs, reports on other examinations, medications, and family histories, become elements that must be discursively activated and aligned in order to restore meaning to the situation. The cardiologist and the GP seem almost to be suggesting interpretations to each other, as in a dance where two actors must lean on each other to find a point of balance that permits their movement. The action of the cardiologist and the GP, in fact, does not take place in an empty space but internally to a broader medical practice. It is consequently to the latter that they turn in the absence of points of contact between patient and ECG.

In the previous transcript, for example, the doctors collaborate to discredit discursively the predictive capacity and reliability of an ECG, mobilizing elements which, though contrasting, are meaningful in everyday medical practice. The cardiologist deploys a discursive practice typical of medicine (Cicourel, 1986), showing that there is a scientific basis for his disparagement of the value of the trace ("there's a good percentage of heart attacks with normal traces …") and then substantiates his assertion with a common-sense observation ("at 80 years old, of course, some problem always comes out!"). The GP, for his part, adheres to the same practice, agreeing that an ECG (on its own) is unable to ensure the stability of the elements ("that's true, you can't always rely on the trace ..."), and identifying a commonsense remedy (an antacid) as able (momentarily) to "align" the patient's case.

Framing and Postscripting

During the teleconsultation, it is essential for the doctors to deploy discourses that make the trace and the patient compatible. For this to occur, it may happen (as in the case just seen) that GP and cardiologist align themselves around a discourse whose task is to belittle the significance of the ECG in order to foreground everyday medical practice, but the reverse may happen as well: The doctors instead discredit the patient's symptoms, activating from the first exchange onward—as in the following case—complicity on the latter's unreliability.

20021111–182817 (2:22)
(Greetings.)

GP: Ciao. She's a girl who's always got these pains here ... She's already been examined by a cardiologist but ... (Laughs.)

C: ... (Laughing.) There's nothing you can do ... She's convinced she's going to die tomorrow ...

GP: ... Right ... but I can't die for her ...
(They laugh.)

C: It seems that everything's fine here, a sinusoidal rhythm, normal atrioventricular delivery ... There's a slight delay in right branch conduction. There's an incomplete right branch block ... That's almost normal, especially in women, and anyway there's no ischemic alteration, and there are no significant alterations in the repolarization.

GP: OK ...

C: ... I'd say that everything's fine ...

GP: ... At least we've made her happy ...

C: ... We've made her happy ... I don't think so ... According to me, she'd be happier if we told her she had something ...

GP: All right, so let's tell her ...
(Salutations with laughter.)

As he begins to describe the patient, the GP already introduces elements that point to a nonproblematic reading of the trace. At first, the GP does not describe the patient's pain but gives a generic interpretation, suggesting that the nature of the pain is almost a characteristic of the patient ("she's a girl who's always got these pains here ..."), to the point that other specialists have not been able to resolve her "problem" ("she's already been examined by a cardiologist but ..."). The ECG is therefore invoked as an element of accountability (Garfinkel, 1967; Heath & Luff, 2000; Timmermans & Berg, 1997) that furnishes her GP with "objective" and "scientific" arguments for transforming the patient's problem into a problem manageable in terms of everyday routines ("I can't die for her ..."). Moreover, it is made explicit that it is the performance of the consultation itself (regardless of the outcome of the reading of the trace) which resolves the patient's problem in the final exchange, when the cardiologist's ironic suggestion ("according to me, she'd be happier if we told her she had something …") is promptly taken up by the GP ("All right, so let's tell her …").

But it is above all the initial framing activity that produces the discursive alignment of the actors. Pollner and McDonald-Wikler (1985) used the terms "framing" and "postscripting" to denote those situations in which the actors construct a set, before or after the action, in which the action is then interpreted. As in the case just seen, characteristics of the situation (such as the unreliability of the patient), activated before the event occurs (the referral of the ECG) then return to within the event itself and delineate its meaning boundaries so that an "incomplete right branch block" may become "almost normal." That the entire consultation is marked by a framing activity is once again evident in the final moves of the conversation, when the cardiologist shares and reinforces the GP's framing by suggesting to him a response coherent more with the setting than with the ECG trace itself.

Thus, although framing is used *ex ante* to generate a "space" of signification for the (subsequent) action, postscripting corresponds to "commanding the already done" (Pollner & McDonald-Wikler, 1985, p. 245) and therefore to the retrospective reproduction of meaning for the event. Examples of this activation mechanism are easily found in cases (like the one that follows) where, although the ECG does not signal any problems, the patient's symptoms acquire meaning in relation to their importance within the medical practice.

20021122–121225 (2:07)
(Greetings.)

> GP: The patient was born in '62 … A couple of hours ago he had a lipothymic episode accompanied by sweating. Now he's got sternocostal pain but in correspondence with the joints … irradiates when palpating … He has a pain in the right subscapular region …
>
> C: … But is he cardiopathic?
>
> GP: No … This episode lasted 5 minutes, I think …
>
> C: … He's not cardiopathic? Did he lose consciousness?
>
> GP: Yes, he had this lipthymic episode and was attended to, then he recovered.
>
> C: But did he lose consciousness?
>
> GP: Yes, for 5 minutes.
>
> C: So he had a syncope … ?
>
> GP: … A syncopal event, sure …
>
> C: Mah, here the trace is normal … but someone who's had a syncope should be kept under observation …
>
> GP: Right, so the trace is normal …
>
> C: … The trace is fine … but does he suffer from any disease?
>
> GP: No, now he's only overweight … He doesn't take medication …
>
> C: Do you think he should be hospitalized?
>
> GP: Yes, I reckon so … What do you advise?
>
> C: Syncope is by definition something rather important …
>
> GP: Right, so I'll have the checks made … thanks.
> (Salutations.)

In this case, the cardiologist and the GP find it difficult to construct a meaningful context for the event, to the point where they exchange roles for a moment, with the cardiologist asking the GP for advice on what should be done ("Do you think he should be hospitalized?"). The way out results from a postscripting practice: The cardiologist responds to the GP's "advice" by shifting the attention from the meaning of the ECG to the meaning of a syncope within medical practice, and therefore, "by definition," offers a solution to the problem.

Footing

Framing and postscripting are often accompanied by another discursive practice: footing (Goffman, 1974, 1980), or the dialectic that enables people to align themselves within a predetermined frame and disrupt its coordinates; once "in step with it" they are able to disturb its rhythm and deviate its path.

20021112–185537 (2:11)
(Salutations.)

GP: The girl's always been in good condition, her grandmother's recently died ... She has a familiarity with quite severe diabetes (...) and her father's had a stroke. She said that she's had nighttime episodes when she felt her heart racing ... and that it was missing beats. I advised her to have some thyroid tests ... but there shouldn't be anything serious.

C: The trace is absolutely normal ...

GP: ... Right!

C: Exactly, the electrocardiogram is absolutely normal ... There are no tachycardias, there are no extrasystoles ... Also because she's young, this woman ...

GP: ... But in fact it was she who asked me for it ... I realized she was going through a particular time ... (...) and I did what she wanted ... but I reckon it was more to do with the thyroid than a cardiac problem ...

C: ... Also because a woman of this age ... thinking about a cardiopathy ...

GP: ... I would never have thought of it. It was she who asked me (laughs) ...

C: ... Exactly ...

GP: ... More at the psychological level ... to reassure her ...

C: ... so reassure her ...
(Salutations.)

In this conversation, the discursive alignment between the GP, the cardiologist, and the ECG seems to be the emergent result of the interaction itself between the two doctors. The cardiologist interjects in the GP's discourse by aligning himself on the normality of the trace, but he introduces a change of "rhythm" by referring to the age of the patient, which should already have induced the GP to rule out cardiological problems ("the electrocardiogram is absolutely normal ... Also because she's young"). At this point the GP has to tune in with the cardiologist's discourse, an operation performed through the distinction made by the GP between cardiological medical practices, to which the specialist alludes, and those of a general practitioner, who knows his patients and understands their needs ("I realized she was going through a particular time ... and I did what she wanted"). This last change of rhythm in the conversation allows the GP, again, to deviate the course of the discourse, and the entire conversation between doctor and cardiologist thus reacquires meaning as a medical (discursive) practice intended to reassure the patient ("so reassure her").

Delegating to the Nonhumans

The final discursive practice deployed by the doctors to have trace and patient coincide centers on the ability of the two actors to delegate the performance of the clinical practice to nonhumans, which they construct as active subjects within the teleconsultation.

20021122–124650 (3:12)

> GP: The patient has already had two ECGs done with other doctors, but she says they couldn't read the V1. She's got to have surgery and she must have an ECG. Let's try with mine ...
>   C: ... The trace is not very good, in fact, but the V1 is clear and it has an incomplete right branch block. It has low voltages in the precordials ... Is she robust?
> GP: No.
>   C: This here is certainly due to the position of the electrodes ...
> GP: ... Eh ... I know ... except that ... where shall I put them? I mean, if it put them ...
>   C: ... I don't know ...
> GP: ... They probably go too low in the sense that ...
>   C: ... No, no, it's certainly not that. The reason is this ... probably ... so, anyway the position is weird because this type of rotation with the ... from V1 to V5, there's an extremely low R, and this you get with clockwise rotations, for example in a broncopneumopathy patient. If she isn't one, or if she's thin, perhaps with a drip-shaped heart, we should have a normal rotation. Here, probably it's either the position of the electrodes or she's so thin that you get a rib ... and a rib is disastrous.
> GP: Ehm ... that's what I suspect.
>   C: Yes, it sometimes happens, and it's probably the position of the electrodes ... It's as if all the recordings were made from the front ... It's probably either that the electrical axle is rotated askew or there's an adhesion problem with the electrodes. Anyway, from a practical point of view, the trace is compatible with the woman's young age ... It has a frequency of 65 and an incomplete right branch block ... (...) I report a slow progression of the R wave, but with no pathological significance ...
> GP: ... Right ...
>   (Salutations.)

That nonhumans play an active role in medical practice, and more generally in organizational settings, is well-established in the literature (Berg & Mol, 1998; Knorr-Cetina, 1997; Law, 1994), and it was already apparent in the previous telephone calls, where (for example) medicines were sometimes attributed the capacity to substitute for and/or substantiate clinical action. The previous transcript, however, shows a more radical delegation, and moreover, a delegation involving an object not typically part of medical practice, but without which teleconsultancy would not be possible: the apparatus that records the ECG traces.

The framing work with which the GP depicts the patient as nonproblematic (she needs the trace for surgery, not for cardiological problems) enables the cardiologist to recognize the anomalies in the trace as due not to pathological factors but to errors in the positioning of the apparatus, which thus becomes the focus of the discourse. The two doctors discuss the height at which the apparatus should be placed, the adherence of the electrodes to the patient's body, her thin thorax, the interference caused by the ribs, the shape of the heart—as if all these things could influence the recording of the electrocardiogram. From a certain point of view, it is as if the doctors' discourse constructs the patient's body parallel with the "body" of the apparatus, in an endeavor to align human and nonhuman bits and pieces (ribs, electrodes, heart, R wave, and so on). It is interesting that this parallel construction of "bodies" manifests the blending of tacit and aesthetic knowledge that forms the background to medical practice (Polanyi, 1958; Strati, 2003). The patient's physique (thin/robust), the "weird" rotation of the electrical axle, the ribs that are "disastrous," the recordings that seem to have all been "made from the front": These are all expressions that do not impede the advancement of the conversation; indeed, they seem to facilitate it.

Constructing a narrative able to align all these various elements thus permits the cardiologist to conclude that the trace is "compatible" with the patient's age, and to report to the GP in neutral and almost off-handed tones (at the end of the conversation) a "slow progression of the R wave, but with no pathological significance." Bearing in mind that a slow progression of the R wave can be easily associated with infarct, one realizes that the cardiologist's entire discourse makes sense as a discursive translation of the meaning possessed by the various elements and their relations "from a practical point of view" (as the cardiologist emphasizes)—that is, from within professional medical knowledge and action. These latter no longer concern human bodies alone, but technical apparatuses as well, and they no longer consist of material practices alone, but of discursive ones as well.

CONCLUSIONS

What is it that ICTs "do" when they modify an already-existing work practice? In the case of the remote cardiological examinations analyzed, modification of the medical practice involved

- Distance between the patient and the cardiologist.
- A human being, the GP, as intermediary for the reconstruction of the patient's "absent body."
- A specific technology, the electrocardiograph, as intermediary for the representation of the "absent body."
- A technological infrastructure formed by a telephone, a fax machine and a computer, and integrated ICTs.
- A call center—a dedicated organization—that delivers a service and coordinates patients, cardiologists, GPs, and ECGs through protocols, file cards, referral software, and organizational rules and habits.

If all these interdependent elements, whose reciprocal relations constitute an SFK, are to become recognizable expertise (and if the cardiologist is to attribute meaning to the ECG on his/her computer screen and be able to say that she/he has mastered a new practice—remote cardiological consultation), they must be aligned and held together: That is, performed within the SFK. This requires that all the heterogeneous elements that make up the system and embody fragments of the necessary knowledge must be mobilized and transformed from "known" into "knowing." This activity does not require conscious and intentional production; rather, it arises from emergent coconstruction that aligns the heterogeneous elements of the SFK by means of situated material-discursive practices. Our analysis has foregrounded the discursive practices between the two doctors, suggesting that the materiality of their practice is invisible in the context of consultation (the patient file card, the software, the professional, tacit knowledge, and the intermediary work of getting connected) as long as their reciprocal relations hold. When for any reason, these relations do not hold, those among the elements of the SFK must be realigned. This means that, in the SFK considered, some interdependencies are critical and constitute the core of the practice—the ECG that represents the patient, the professional expertise, and the electrocardiogram standing for itself as a medical artifact—whereas the other elements remain invisible, as long as their reciprocal relations hold. In the materiality of work practices, objects can be defined as "affiliative objects" (Suchman, 2005, p. 379), in the sense that they are able to hold relations together because "objects are not innocent, but fraught with significance for the relations that they materialize" (Suchman, 2005, p. 379). Not only do they "work together" with each other, they also work together with humans, and in so doing, help stabilize the network. In other words, affiliated objects embody a set of relations that give durability to the SFK and thus constitute not only the setting of the practice but also the material resources for its performance.

As a theoretical concept, the SFK may usefully shift the focus to the network of inter-dependent elements in which the knowledge necessary for the performance of a practice is embedded. The SFK, as an empirical map of situated relations, represents the spatiality of knowledge (where knowledge resides). As an interpretative device, it enables the researcher to investigate the modes ordering elements and their interdependencies, associations, or nonasso-ciations, and the work that should be performed by humans and nonhumans in order to put knowledge in practice. We have proposed a theoretical framework for analysis of a virtual workplace based on knowing as a collective accomplishment. A work practice, as a situated activity normatively sustained by a community of practitioners, takes place in time and space (i.e., within the boundaries of an SFK), and unfolds through the mobilization of knowledge-in-practice.

We describe a variety of ways in which the mobilization of knowledge (i.e., alignment of elements in an SFK) is accomplished by discursive practices:

- *Framing and postscripting*, as practices that generate a "space" of signification for the subsequent action, or for the retrospective reproduction of meaning.
- *Footing*, as the dialectic that enables people to align themselves within a predetermined frame and disrupt its coordinates.
- *Delegation to the nonhuman*, as the ability of humans to delegate the performance of clinical practice to nonhumans, which they construct as active subjects within the remote consultation.

The case described prompts more general reflection on how ICTs modify work practices and workplaces, especially as remote communication technologies alter the time and space of the traditional workplace. The principal effect of ICTs consists in a redrawing of the work space as a system of fragmented knowledge embedded in people, artifacts, organizational rules, and habits, supported by an infrastructure. Working at a distance, therefore, requires the acquisition of skills relative to the mobilization of fragmented knowledge, and the latter's alignment into a full-fledged work practice. The resources used for this purpose are commonsense resources.

Of these, the actors have little awareness, and they activate them by gradual approximation: They transform the potential knowledge into a knowing.

The aim of this study on remote consultation in cardiology has been to contribute to the body of inquiry into telemedicine (Aanestad & Hanseth, 2000; Berg, 1997; Rajani & Perry, 1999) that analyzes how technology and its users constantly modify each other as they seek to establish a durable alignment and constitute, as Aanestad and Hanseth (2000) put it, a "hybrid collectif." Managing a telemedicine system resembles cultivating a "collective," the members of which (like the collective itself) can learn to improve its performance. Telemedicine can be considered a technological process based on the practical negotiation of its use consequent upon its still precarious technological stability, and its incomplete translation into a "normal" set of practices. Our contribution to the debate, we submit, consists in proposing a theoretical and methodological framework grounded on firsthand data that can be used to delineate the place and practices of such negotiation, a framework that can also be employed when the operators of a telemedicine system are being trained.

ACKNOWLEDGMENTS

This article is the result of an entirely collaborative effort by the three authors. If, however, for academic reasons, individual responsibility must be assigned, Silvia Gherardi wrote the introduction, the first section, and the conclusion; Laura Lucia Parolin wrote sections 2 and 3; and Attila Bruni wrote section 4.

REFERENCES

Aanestad, M., & Hanseth, O. (2000). Implementing open network technologies in complex work practices: A case from telemedicine. In R. Baskerville, J. Stage, & J. I. DeGross (Eds.), *Proceedings of the Conference on the Social and Organizational Perspective on Research and Practice in Information Technology* (pp. 255–69). Norwell, MA: Kluwer Academic.

Barnes, B. (2001). Practice as collective action. In T. R. Schatzki, K. Knorr Cetina , & E. von Savigny (Eds.), *The practice turn in contemporary theory* (pp. 17–29). London: Routledge.

Berg, M. (1997). *Rationalizing medical work*. Cambridge, MA: MIT Press.

Berg, M., & Mol, A. (Eds.). (1998). *Differences in medicine: Unravelling practices, techniques and bodies*. Durham, NC: Duke University Press.

Bloor, D. (1976). *Knowledge and social imagery*. London: Routledge & Kegan Paul.

Bruni, A. (2005a). Shadowing software and clinical records: On the ethnography of non-humans. *Organization, 12*(3), 357–378.

Bruni, A. (2005b). Practicing organizational objects: Learning and knowing as "flirting" with material heterogeneity. In Gherardi, S. and Nicolini, D. (Eds.), *The passion for learning and knowing. Proceedings of the 6th Annual Conference on Organizational Learning and Knowledge*. Trento, Italy: University of Trento e-books.

Cicourel, A. V. (1986). The reproduction of objective knowledge: Common sense reasoning in medical decision making. In G. Bohme & N. Stehr (Eds.), *The knowledge society* (pp. 87–122). Dordrecht, The Netherlands: Reidel Publishing.

Cole, M., & Engeström, Y. (1993). A cultural-historical approach to distributed cognition. In G. Salomon (Ed.), *Distributed cognitions. Psychological and educational considerations* (pp. 1–46). New York: Cambridge University Press.

Conein, B., Dodier, N., & Thévenot, L. (Eds.). (1993). *Les objets dans l'action*. Paris: Edition de l'Ecole des Hautes Etudes en Sciences Sociales.

Engeström, Y. (1987). *Learning by expanding: An activity theoretical approach to developmental research.* Helsinki, Finland: Orienta-Consultit.

Engeström, Y. (2001). Activity theory as a framework for the study of organizational transformations. Paper presented at the conference *Knowing in Practice,* Trento, Italy, February 28.

Engeström, Y., & Middleton, D. (Eds.). (1996). *Cognition and communication at work.* Cambridge, England: Cambridge University Press.

Garfinkel, H. (1967). *Studies in ethnomethodology.* Englewood Cliffs, NJ: Prentice Hall.

Gherardi, S. (1999). Learning as problem-driven or learning in the face of mystery? *Organization Studies, 20,* 101–124.

Gherardi, S. (2000). Practice-based theorizing on learning and knowing in organizations: An introduction. *Organization, 7,* 211–223.

Gherardi, S. (2001). From organizational learning to practice-based knowing. *Human Relations: Studies Towards the Integration of the Social Sciences, 54,* 131–139.

Gherardi, S. (2006). *Organizational knowledge: The texture of workplace learning.* Oxford, England: Blackwell.

Gherardi, S., & Strati, A. (2004). *La telemedicina: Tra tecnologia e organizzazione.* Rome: Carocci.

Giddens, A. (1984). *The constitution of society: Outline of a theory of structuration.* Cambridge, England: Polity Press.

Goffman, E. (1974). *Frame analysis: An essay on the organization of experience.* New York: Harper & Row.

Goffman, E. (1980). *Forms of talk.* Oxford, England: Basil Blackwell.

Heath, C., & Button, G. (2002). Editorial introduction [Special issue on workplace studies]. *The British Journal of Sociology, 53,* 157–161.

Heath, C., & Luff, P. (2000). *Technology in action.* Cambridge, England: Cambridge University Press.

Hutchins, E. (1993). Learning to navigate. In S. Chaiklin & J. Lave (Eds.), *Understanding practice: Perspectives on activity and context* (pp. 35–63). Cambridge, England: Cambridge University Press.

Knorr Cetina, K. (1997). Sociality with objects. *Theory, Culture and Society, 14*(4), 1–30.

Koschmann, T., Kuutti, K., & Hickman, L. (1998). The concept of breakdown in Heidegger, Leont'ev, and Dewey and its implications for education. *Mind, Culture, and Activity, 5,* 25–41.

Latour, B. (1987). *Science in action.* Milton Keynes, England: Open University Press.

Latour, B. (1994). On technical mediation. Philosophy, sociology, genealogy. *Common Knowledge, 3*(2), 29–64.

Latour, B. (2002). Morality and technology. The end of the means. *Theory, Culture, and Society, 19*(5/6), 247–260.

Latour, B. (2005). *Reassembling the social. An introduction to actor-network-theory.* Oxford, England: Oxford University Press.

Lave, J. (1988). *Cognition in practice.* Cambridge, England: Cambridge University Press.

Law, J. (1992). Notes on the theory of the Actor-Network: Ordering, strategy and heterogeneity. *System/Practice, 5,* 379–393.

Law, J. (1994). *Organizing modernity.* Oxford, England: Blackwell.

Law, J. (2000). Comment on Suchman, and Gherardi and Nicolini: Knowing as displacing. *Organization, 7,* 349–354.

Lynch, M. (1997). *Scientific practice and ordinary action: Ethnomethodology and social studies of science.* Cambridge, England: Cambridge University Press.

Lynch, M. (2002). Protocols, practices and the reproduction of techniques in molecular biology. *The British Journal of Sociology, 53,* 203–220.

Miettinen, R. (1999). The riddle of things: Activity theory and actor-network theory as approaches to studying innovations. *Mind, Culture and Activity, 6,* 170–195.

Miettinen, R. (2001). Artifact mediation in Dewey and in cultural-historical activity theory. *Mind, Culture, and Activity, 8,* 297–308.

Mintzberg, H. (1989). *Mintzberg on management: Inside our strange world of organizations.* New York: The Free Press.

Norman, D. (1990). *The design of everyday things.* New York: Doubleday/Currency.

Polanyi, M. (1958). *Personal knowledge. Towards a post-critical philosophy.* London: Routledge & Kegan Paul.

Pollner, M., & McDonald-Wikler, L. (1985). The social construction of unreality: A case study of a family's attribution of competence to a severely retarded child. *Family Process, 24,* 241–254.

Rajani, R., & Perry, M. (1999). The reality of medical work: The case for a new perspective on telemedicine. *Virtual Reality, 4,* 243–249.

Schatzki, T. R., Knorr Cetina, K., & von Savigny, E. (Eds.). (2001). *The practice turn in contemporary theory.* London: Routledge.

Schmidt, K. (2000). The critical role of workplace studies in CSCW. In P. Luff, J. Hindmarsh, & C. Heath (Eds.), *Workplace studies* (pp. 141–149). Cambridge, England: Cambridge University Press.

Star, S. L. (1999). The ethnography of infrastructure. *American Behavioral Scientist, 43,* 377–391.

Strati, A. (2003). Knowing in practice: Aesthetic understanding and tacit knowledge. In D. Nicolini, S. Gherardi, & D. Yanow (Eds.), *Knowing in organizations: A practice-based approach* (pp. 53–75). Armonk, NY: Sharpe.

Suchman, L. (1987). *Plans and situated action: The problem of human-machine communication.* Cambridge, England: Cambridge University Press.

Suchman, L. (1997). Centres of coordination. A case and some themes. In L. Resnick, L. Saljo, C. Pontecorvo, & B. Burge (Eds.), *Discourse, tools and reasoning. Essays on situated cognition* (pp. 41–62). Berlin: Springer Verlag.

Suchman, L. (2005). Affiliative objects. *Organization, 12,* 379–399.

Timmermans, S., & Berg, M. (1997). Standardization in action: Achieving local universality through medical protocols. *Social Studies of Science, 27,* 273–305.

Tsoukas, H. (1996). The firm as a distributed knowledge system: A constructionist approach. *Strategic Management Journal, 17,* 11–25.

Unger, R. (1987). *False necessity: Anti-necessitarian social theory in the service of radical democracy.* Cambridge, England: Cambridge University Press.

Vygotsky, L. S. (1978). *Mind in society: The development of higher psychological processes.* Cambridge, MA: Harvard University Press.

Weick, K. E. (1977). *The social psychology of organizing.* Reading MA: Addison Wesley.

Winograd, T., & Flores, F. (1986). *Understanding computers and cognition: A new foundation for design.* Norwood, NJ: Ablex.

[8]

Journal of Management Studies 39:4 June 2002
0022-2380

LEARNING IN A CONSTELLATION OF INTERCONNECTED
PRACTICES: CANON OR DISSONANCE?*

Silvia Gherardi

Davide Nicolini

Università di Trento

ABSTRACT

In this paper we argue that the learning of safety in a constellation of communities of practice is mediated by comparison among the perspectives of the world embraced by the co-participants in the production of this practice. Our discussion is based on two empirical research projects in which we investigated the accounts of the causes of accidents provided by the members of three different communities of practice (engineers, site foremen and main contractors), in a medium sized building firm. In the paper we suggest that comparison among perspectives is made possible by a discursive practice targeted on the alignment of elements both mental and material, within mutually accountable discursive positions. These alignments are provisional and unstable, they produce tensions, discontinuities and incoherence (cacophony) just as much as they produce order and negotiated meanings (consonance).

INTRODUCTION

> Practice is where nature and society and the space between them are continually made, un-made, and remade. (Pickering, 1992, p. 21)

Learning in a community of practice is described in the literature as a process of progressive 'engagement' in the practices of that community. Yet there are practices that traverse the boundaries of several communities and which – as in stellar formations – create a network of relations within a constellation of communities of practices tied together by interconnected practices. How do people learn to cope with the knowledge embedded in their community, and the knowing nested in a constellation of practices? A construction site will provide the setting for an answer to the question.

A 'site' is the concrete aggregation of whatever abstract systems have been imposed upon it. And planners or users of a site become involved in a multiplicity of systems, at once designed and unpredictable (Turner and Pidgeon, 1997,

Address for reprints: Silvia Gherardi, via Verdi 26, 38100 Trento, Italy (silvia.gherardi@soc.unitn.it).

p. 57). Difficulties in organizing derive precisely from this 'on-site' situatedness, which is characteristic of all constellations of interconnected practices.

How, then, is co-ordination and learning achieved within a constellation? How do the continuities and discontinuities among communities of practices help or hinder the circulation of knowledge?

The most accredited answers in the literature describe the process in terms of negotiated order (Strauss, 1978), the negotiation of meanings (Wenger, 1998), alignment effects (Law, 1994; Suchman, 2000), or processes of collective sense-making (Weick, 1995). These descriptions emphasize the consensual and pre-dominantly harmonious aspect of the process and, in our view, they more appropriately describe the production of knowledge within a single community. But in their effort to explain the work of mutual understanding, they tend to obscure the residual dimension of discontinuity among interconnected practices, and they fail to describe how knowledge remains isolated and not communicated from one community to another. The 'dark side' of the effort to understand across boundaries – what remains not understood, what is misrepresented or ignored – tends to be removed and forgotten.

Our argument is that, in a constellation of interconnected practices, discourse among communities is a specific practice whose aim is not only to reach under-standing and/or to produce collective action, but also to foster learning by com-parison with the perspectives of all the co-participants in a practice. Nevertheless, comparing among different perspectives does not necessarily involve the merging of diversity into some sort of synthesis – harmonizing individual voices and instruments into consonance or unison – but rather contemplation of the har-mon*ies and* dissonance, consonance *and* cacophony, that may coexist within the same performance.[1]

We shall therefore seek to show that discursive practice in a constellation of interconnected practices is fundamentally and necessarily also a dissonance and a cacophony. To do so we shall refer to empirical research conducted on a building site, which we consider as a constellation of interconnected practices among its principal communities of practice: the engineers, the site foremen, and the main contractors, all of whom belonged to the same building firm, and other, secondary communities of practice.

LEARNING IN PRACTICE, LEARNING A PRACTICE

Recent practice-based theorizing has reconceptualized the term 'organizational learning', detaching it from the original psychological domain of learning theo-ries in order to examine the metaphorical operation (Gherardi, 2000a) which, by juxtaposing two unrelated terms, constructs a representation of an organization as if it were engaged in practices concerned with knowledge and knowing.

Amid the diversity of the schools of thought, the specific contribution of practice-based theorizing to analysis of the knowledge intrinsic in practice can be summed up as follows:

• Learning is acquired through participation in communities of practice (Brown and Duguid, 1991; Lave and Wenger, 1991; Wenger, 1998).

- Organizing can be seen as an 'activity system' which reveals the tentative nature of knowledge and action (Blackler, 1993, 1995; Blackler et al., 2000). Incoherences, inconsistencies, paradoxes and tensions are integral parts of every practice.
- Knowledge and action are located in ecologies of social–material relations (Fujimura, 1995; Star, 1995).
- Knowing is enacted (Weick, 1979), situated (Suchman, 1987), resilient but provisional (Unger, 1987), public and rhetorical (Vattimo, 1985).
- Practice involves the accomplishment of alignments across human and non-human elements (Latour, 1986; Law, 1994) from a particular positioning at a particular time within a network of relations (Suchman, 2000).

Emphasis on practice focuses the research on knowledge on the 'doing' and on the materiality of social relations, thereby detaching it from the idealist tradition and the cognitive approaches. In practice-based theorizing the Marxist, materialist and anti-functionalist approaches join forces.

Learning a practice involves active participation in a set of activities with concrete individuals who recognize this participation as competence. Learning in practice involves the ability of behaving as a competent member in a discursive community. In this paper we shall focus on practices of communication among communities of practice, where this involves explaining why accidents happen, or how to prevent them, or how to attribute responsibility for them. The concept of 'discursive community' (Vaux, 1999) is used to convey the idea that, in a constellation of interconnected practices, the boundaries of the speaking community, the character of the audience and the identity of the object under discussion – safety in our case – are all, in principle, up for negotiation.

Becoming a competent member of a community of practice, developing the ability to join the conversations on practice, is a process that takes place with others and in relation to others. Accordingly, when we join a community, when we are enabled to develop a new identity with reference to others engaged in the same activity, we also necessarily become accountable to them and to the other communities with which they interact. Learning is therefore both belonging and positioning oneself in a discourse. The idea of several communities of practice forming a discursive community presupposes not that a unified object or a shared set of values or beliefs exists, but that the identity of the community is maintained through the negotiated performance of community (Vaux, 1999), where each community mantains its own voice while listening to the voice of the Other, and where communication is both negotiated order and disorder.

For example, as site foremen learn building site practices, they also learn how to be site foremen. They develop an identity as site foremen belonging to a particular firm, and they acquire or refine their 'builder's' vocabulary so that, when they deal with practical problems, they are able to talk about their practices with other foremen, as well as with non-foremen. So too do the engineers, main contractors and all the industry and trade members. Their engagement in a joint enterprise also gives rise to relations of mutual accountability among those involved. The sense of what they do must be made accountable both to themselves and to the persons around them. Competence in doing something must be recognized and appreciated within the community. And it is transmitted with linguistic codes and aesthetics (Polanyi, 1958, 1967; Cook and Yanow, 1993; Strati, 1999) in order to develop a sensibility and an aesthetic and moral judgement on appropriacy codes. When learning is conceived as the taking up of a new identity (Lave and Wenger, 1991), it entails developing a sensitivity to boundaries, the capacity to perceiving who is 'in' and 'out', to whom one is accountable and in what way, as well as the capacity to recognize and talk about differences and commonalties. In so far as identity is both a way of being ourselves and of narrating ourselves, discursive practice enters the practice twice: as a way of acting in the world and as a way of describing our location in the discourse we help to create.

Mutual accountability is therefore a process which consolidates learning mediated by the differences of perspectives, thereby shaping identity and specific cultural forms. This in turn sets communities of practice as processes which depend at the same time on self – reference *and* interdependence.

How then does conversation come about between two or more communities of practice, given that they are both independent and interdependent?

Wenger (1998, p. 129) answers the question by pointing to two elements: styles (which spread as people in a community of practice borrow, imitate, import, adapt and reinterpret ways of behaving) and discourses (which travel across boundaries and combine to form broader discourses as people coordinate their enterprises, convince each other, reconcile their perspectives, and form alliances). However, Wenger writes, 'styles and discourses are not practices in themselves. They are available material – resources that can be used in the context of various practices'.

We dispute Wenger on the latter point: discursive practice is a practice in itself which is not performed only to produce negotiation over meanings, or to convince, or to form alliances, or to coordinate, even though these outcomes may arise and be visible. Discursive practice in a constellation of interconnected practices is also a way of accommodating a plurality of discourses and legitimating their co-existence. It is a way of working knowledges together while keeping them distinct. Accordingly, we may say that a constellation of communities of practice constitutes a discursive community which makes co-ordination possible: competent participation in discourse in practice and on practice both construct the practice and shapes each of the communities involved (Vaux, 1999).

Our argument is grounded on the assumption that the practice which ties a community, or several communities, together is what 'performs' the community or the constellation of communities. The performance of a community is achieved mainly through material and discursive means which put the community on stage, on the basis of the things it is good at doing. In a recent study we tested this idea empirically, investigating whether the members of a community of practice do in fact share a common discourse that varies across communities. For this purpose, we chose a relevant topic – safety – and concentrated our field research on both the causal accounts provided by the three communities of practices as to why on-site accidents happen and their conversations in practice.

THE RESEARCH SETTING

In the building industry, dangerous situations frequently arise in both work activity and the work environment. Consequently, building workers and managers view safety as an issue of crucial importance. Moreover, at least three distinct but inter-

dependent (in terms of skills and hierarchical position) communities of practice
share responsibility for safety on a building site. Can we assume that they share a
common safety culture? And, if they do not, how do different safety cultures dialogue in an interdependent practice? Our aim was to answer these questions, and
in order to do so we chose to investigate the accounts of the causes of accidents
provided by the members of three different communities of practice (engineers,
site foremen and main contractors) within a medium-sized cooperative building
firm located in Modena, northern Italy. Their causal accounts in explanation,
justification or criticism of accidents constitute a communicative practice which
makes the organizational phenomena 'accountable' to one's community and to
others as well.

Causal accounts define a semantic space in which facts (what happened) and
beliefs (why it happened and the meanings of what happened) are interchange-
ably mixed and made accountable to the speaker as well as to the listener (Antaki
and Fielding, 1981). This is especially true of beliefs concerning events that the
organization views as problematic: namely accidents. The causal accounts of why
workplace accidents happen were collected by means of interviews (recorded and
transcribed) conducted with the members of the three communities (six engineers,
three main contractors and six site foremen). Only causal accounts couched in
ordinary language were examined.

As regards methodology we first analysed the causal accounts used by the three
communities in order to prove that each has a distinctive safety culture. Subsequently, in order to gain a broader picture of how the three discursive positions
dialogue in practice, we conducted an ethnographic study of a building site and
integrated the transcripts from the interviews with our field notes.[2] Detailed analysis of the models of causal explanations used in the three communities would be
beyond the scope of this article (see Gherardi et al., 1998b for an extended discussion). We refer to these models here only in support of our hypothesis that each
community has a distinctive safety culture, and that a building site, understood as
a temporary organization, always requires the interdependence of a plurality of
communities with their own safety cultures. As such, it entails the construction
of a discursive community of speakers on safety which produces knowledge and
modes of ordering located in, and accountable to, their particular historical,
discursive and material circumstances of production.

In the following section we shall briefly illustrate our findings, showing how,
despite being part of the same organization, the three communities have their own
culture of safety. We then discuss how mutual accountability is achieved in their
daily practice and how they form a discursive community.

BEING ON-SITE: DISSONANT CULTURES OF SAFETY

Our argument is that, in a constellation of interconnected practices, discourse
among communities is a specific practice intended to achieve not so much understanding and/or the production of collective action as learning mediated by comparison among the perspectives of all the co-participants in a practice. Comparing
among different perspectives (among different safety cultures) does not necessarily involve the merging of diversity into some sort of synthesis – harmonizing individual voices and instruments into a symphony (or a canon) – but rather

the contemplation of harmonies and dissonances that may coexist within the same performance.[3]

The Site Foreman's Experience

The site foreman is responsible for the day-to-day running of small building sites. He is aware of being the node at which numerous practices intersect. Indeed in our research, a site foreman described himself as:

> a traffic warden supervising the pieceworkers, the crane-drivers, the carpenters, and those with lorries to unload. I act as the warden and give urgency to the work as I want. (Interview 3/2)

This image of the 'warden' shows how the site foreman's explanations of the causes of accidents relate to the simultaneity of events. A building site is a relatively confined physical space which becomes the theatre for action by numerous groups of actors who are both independent and closely interdependent. This is why the site foreman describes accidents in terms of:

(1) Temporal interdependence. One team goes further ahead with the work, and those that follow are put in danger. The pieceworkers do not bother to keep the site tidy, and those that come after them work in dangerous conditions.

(2) Spatial interdependence. Everything happens at the same time. The work is never perfectly synchronized, and management of the physical space should be a collective task.

(3) Cultural models. Specific working conditions like piecework or black market work create a lack of concern with personal safety which jeopardizes the safety of others. Conversely, the 'trusties' personify control delegated by the site manager.

In explaining the causes of accidents and how to prevent them, the site foreman expresses a vision of the world which is not shared by all the site foremen working for the firm, nor by all the persons who do that particular job. Yet a shared perspective can be identified, and it is constructed by participation in shared practices, by experience of similar situations, and above all by taking active part in discursive practices centred on the practice itself. For example, the site foremen shape their community by constructing their view of safety around the theme of the simultaneity of events:

> When it's a scattered site, I have to be everywhere at once. So there are five or six people working, and it may happen that one of them does something that endangers someone else who comes later and doesn't know about it. There has to be a bit of cooperation. (Interview 1/5)

> The site's in order the evening before, but when the men start working the problems begin. If they need a piece of wood, they take it from the scaffolding and don't think about the consequences. When they're plastering and the scaffolding gets in the way, they remove it. They always act as if they were in the jungle. (Interview 3/13)

When the site foremen talked about their safety practices, they produced a 'situational' vision of safety. They exemplified it by narrating actual episodes or dangers averted. These situations were inhabited by numerous actors who coordinated, or otherwise, their actions. They therefore also produced an occupational identity centred on the image of the traffic warden and the analogy between road traffic and the danger-generating intersection of specific practices – each with its own 'safety' criteria – in the same physical space. Unlike a traffic warden, who possesses a highly codified gestural vocabulary, the site foreman constantly wandered around the site, looking for danger and pointing it out to the others. To do so he used discourse, persuasion and the linking-up of non-communicating practices.

This activity has been termed 'brokering' (Eckert, 1989; Wenger, 1998), given that the broker personifies the ability to transfer and translate certain elements of one practice to another, to understand and appreciate the differences in perspective between one community and another, and authorization to influence the practices of one or more communities. Brokering is often associated with innovativeness, or the creative copying that results from exporting elements of a practice developed in one particular community to another. This may be the case, for example, of a site foreman who moves to another firm and persuades his new community to adopt elements of his former community's practice. But brokering is also what the site manager does in his day-to-day work, when he acts as a living intermediary to synchronize the practices of a plurality of actors, each with a specific body of knowledge. His own knowledge consists in an ability to understand the others' knowledge to the extent necessary to get them to communicate, and it involves translation, mobilization, and alignment (Latour, 1986; Law, 1992) among perspectives. His brokering practice constructs a social structure that reflects shared learning and which, although it may utilize non-human intermediaries in the form of technological artifacts (or boundary objects), is prevalently a discursive practice based on the ability to translate from one language to another.

The Engineers' Knowledgeability
Communities of practice are self-referential cultural systems which prevent their members from comparing their implicit beliefs. Conflict or simple differences of view are therefore a given additional to the complexity generated by space and by a multiplicity of events in the same space. As we have seen, the site foremen viewed and narrated the accountability of on-site safety on the basis of their practical experience, by citing examples, entering into detail, interrogating themselves on what else they could have done – in other words, locating safety at the level of relations among practices. The engineers, by contrast, recounted safety in terms of events that should not have happened, of failures of foresight or regulation. For the site foremen, accidents were part of 'the order of things' and whether or not they happened depended on circumstances; for the engineers, accidents symbolized the disorder that interferes with and upsets an ideal order. In the community of engineers:

> You study the site plan on paper, which means deciding where to put the equipment, the junction boxes, the crane . . . When you prepare the cement mixers you already know that they've got to have safety protection . . . so you're aware of a set of regulations. At the planning stage you're in control of what the safety

requirements should be so that the various work phases can go ahead. (Interview 2/2)

The basic problems of safety are always the same, and the rules to obey are always the same. But then it's easier to enforce them on one site than another, for objective reasons . . . Some things you can generalize, others you have to look at case by case. (Interview 1/3)

Good information management on a scientific rather than a voluntary basis [makes] the information available to everyone, and then it's information not interpretations. (Interview 3/6)

Formalizing means clarifying what the objective is, and how corporate resources can be deployed to achieve the declared objective, rather than everyone acting according to what they think is right or most important. (Interview 3/6)

Safety is therefore accountable by virtue of norms of technical rationality and managerial rationality. The reverse case is constituted by rules which are inadequate and disobeyed. This is the perspective expressed by 'check-list logic', where the check-list symbolizes the practice that made the engineers accountable to their community.

Although they declared that they had learnt safety not at university but on-site, their professional knowledge enjoyed a social legitimacy – and therefore an authority and authoritativeness – that the site foremen's knowledge did not. The former was abstract knowledge and it bestowed qualities like generalizability, codifiability or transferability; the latter was practical knowledge, and it was contingent, situated, implicit, and did not confer social authoritativeness. The former informed the technical rules and legal practices of ascribing responsibility, as well as scientific 'risk analysis'; the latter was good practical 'housekeeping', and it was codified only as a practice code. The former belonged to the symbolic universe of the male; the latter to the female.

The Main Contractor's Economic Rationale
The main contractor as a professional, full-time manager and employer – as opposed, for example, to the traditional figure of a tradesman who was both an expert practitioner and the owner of the business – is a relatively new figure in the Italian SME building industry. The main contractor embodies the economic rationality which now flanks, and/or conflicts with, the technical rationality of the engineers and the relational rationality of the site foremen. The main contractor's point of view is overtly biased towards the economic aspects of safety:

If you're sorted [with the law], things go better, then you avoid fines and also accidents, because accidents cost you. The insurance companies make you pay more if you've had a certain frequency of accidents. (Interview 2/3)

I have to immediately work out what my difficulties are going to be in running the building site. But it's not that I can alter the project; I must only decide how to get it done well and in the least time possible, and safety. Time is money, and I always have a keep an eye on accident prevention. (Interview 1/6)

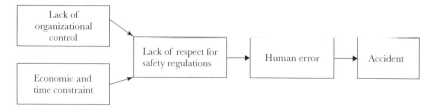

Figure 1. The engineers' explanation – plotting of a causal scheme

As to be expected, the main contractor's discourse concentrates on economic considerations. And yet it 'enters into conversation' with the discursive positions of others, acknowledging their situated legitimacy:

> Usually most sensitive to safety are the persons legally responsible for it, who in certain cases are our in-house engineers. (Interview 2/6)

> I've got fifteen building sites and not all the site foremen are equally safety-aware. Even we technicians, we're not all the same, we don't see things in the same way. (Interview 2/4)

> As a group it's the carpenters who make on-site safety. (Interview 1/4)

The results of the quantitative analysis of the causal accounts in the three main communities suggested that the causal schemes plotted from the interview transcripts fitted into three ideal-typical models of causal explanation: a linear model, a co-occurrence model, and a ramified or factorial model. Starting with the same set of possible causes of an event, the linear model takes the form of a sequential chain of causes; the co-occurrence model assumes the synchronous action of several causes; and the ramified model explains the event in terms of a single factor (or latent cause) which encapsulates other antecedent causes.

Statistical analysis suggested the existence of a relationship between community membership and use of one of the various accident explanation models.[4] The ramified model was associated with membership of the community of the engineers (the significance of this association for a sample of 12 cases was 5% (Fisher exact test) and the value of the coefficient of association chosen (Goodman and Kruskal Tau) was 0.466 with 10% significance); the co-occurrence model was associated with membership of the occupational community of the site managers (the significance of this association for a sample of 12 cases was 13% (Fisher exact test) and the value of the coefficient of association chosen (Goodman and Kruskal Tau) was −0.800 with 0.8% significance); the linear model was not significantly associated with either of the three communities of practice. Figure 1 gives a typical example of a causal scheme used in the community of the engineers, and Figure 2 contrasts it with the causal scheme used in the foremen's community.

For the sake of simplicity, we have restricted participation in the conversation about safety to the three communities comprising the engineers, site foremen and main contractors. But, of course, other communities with different positioning could have taken part in the same conversation. Firstly, the three communities

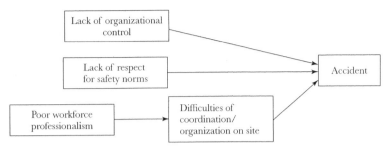

Figure 2. The site-managers' explanation – plotting of a causal scheme

analysed were those with most authority and responsibility *vis-à-vis* safety, but also present on-site was the community of workers from the subcontractor firms:

> [Compliance with the law] doesn't concern only our workers, who are under control, but also the other people who work on the site for us . . . who are outside the company's jurisdiction, external and distant from company headquarters. (Interview 3/7)

> The employment relationship discriminated participation in a discursive community on safety between the workers employed by the firm and the piece-workers from the subcontracting firm – even though they participated in the same practice.

In summary, we have described three of the main voices that contribute to the discourse on safety in a building site. We have also suggested that other, distant and yet present voices are also continuously referred to (e.g., the institutional voice). Participating in a community of practice means being able to understand the boundaries of the speaker's community and, at the same time, the discourses on practice of other communities. In explaining these communication dynamics, Boland and Tenkasi (1995) use the concepts of 'perspective making' with reference to communication which strengthens the unique knowledge of a community, and 'perspective taking' with reference to communication which improves the community's ability to take account of the knowledge of other communities. While their approach is of great practical usefulness in, for example, designing communication systems to support perspective making and perspective taking, in our opinion it undervalues the symbolic and expressive role performed by discursive practice in identity building and in positioning identity within a discursive community.

As we shall show in the next section, discursive practice on practice enables the speakers to position themselves and their community of practice within the network of power/knowledge relations, and to legitimize that positioning.

DISCURSIVE PRACTICE AS POSITIONING

The concept of positionality originated in gender studies (Alcoff, 1988; Davies and Harré, 1990; Gherardi, 1995), and it is used mainly to examine the problem of the production of subjectivity. For Davies and Harré, the concept of positioning belongs to social psychology, and their use of the term 'positioning' contrasts with the concept of human agency as role player. It is therefore useful for analysis of the production of self as a linguistic practice within the dynamic occasions of encounters. A discourse is an institutionalized use of language and of other similar sign systems, and it is within a particular discourse that a subject (the position of a subject) is constructed as a compound of knowledge and power into a more or less coercive structure which ties it to an identity.

A subject position incorporates both a conceptual repertoire and a location for persons within the structure of the rights pertaining to those who use the repertoire. A position is what is created in and through conversations as speakers and hearers construct themselves as persons: it creates a location in which social relations and actions are mediated by symbolic forms and modes of being.

As people assume a discursive position for themselves, they also attribute – explicitly or implicitly – discursive positions to possible audiences.

> The engineer and the site foreman conduct an internal site review with a view to an imminent inspection by safety enforcement officials:
>
> 'How about the way the scaffolding is anchored . . .'
>
> 'I think it's all right . . . it's safe, I checked, it is not moving and the anchors are really solid'
>
> 'Yeah, but if the inspector were here he'd say that the law states that . . .'
>
> 'Yes, but the law also states that we should build that special scaffolding under the roof . . . for three days of work . . . it would cost us a fortune . . .'
>
> '. . . The old man at the office [the main contractor-entrepreneur owner of the firm] would have an heart attack if we spent all that money . . . you know him . . . he's happy for us to take the risk, otherwise how are we going to make any money . . .'. (Reconstructed from field notes)

Through practices of mutual accountability, speaking subjects not only make the world more intelligible but choose a discursive position for themselves and for others. Learning in constellations of interconnected practices is mediated by comparison among all these different perspectives. As in some of our examples, these perspectives, however, do not necessarily blend to produce a single and harmonious safety culture. On the contrary, the fact that they are situated in material and social relations means that they assume discursive positions that may equally well be unintelligible and antagonistic, so that their simultaneity produces dissonance rather than a canon, as in the following exchange between a safety consultant (an engineer) and a (trade) site foreman:

> 'According to the law you'll have to fence off that area while you take the beam down . . . safety regulations, you know . . .'
>
> 'But that doesn't make sense . . . that's not how we usually do it . . . it'll get in the way . . . We'll have to walk all around it . . . doesn't make sense . . .'

'Yeah, I know, but you'll have to do it anyway . . .'

'OK, but it will be a mess . . . this is stupid'. (Reconstructed from field notes)

Our findings here are similar to those of Betchky (1999), who studied the (mis)communication across occupational communities in an electronic firm. Betchky noted that engineers and assemblers manifest their different ways of understanding things in their use of different languages (the former, as in our case, have an abstract understanding of things, the latter a concrete one). Because they live in different 'linguistic games' (Wittgenstein, 1953), members of the two communities use homonyms (same signifier but reference to different material objects) and decontextualization (different terms for the same item). As a result, they can successfully talk about something without understanding each other.

Discursive practice among interconnected communities of practice comes about in the form of both discourse-in-practice and discourse-on-practice. When the engineer and the site manager were deciding how to set up the site or to solve a problem, they were united in a shared practice: doing and saying were the same things.

The engineer and the site foreman continue their tour of the site, double-checking installations. The engineer looks up at the scaffolding:

'We'll have to move that rail there, it is not compliant . . . it's too low'

'That's fine . . . I'll tell C. to do it . . . We should also move some of these brick piles over here . . . but then the men will have quite a bit of walking to do . . .'

'Yes, but they give a bad impression . . . officials in this area are pernickety . . . also move that piece of machinery there, I am not sure we have all the paper work . . . better if it's out of sight'. (Reconstructed from field notes)

Words were just as instrumental as drawings or any other artifact. The two practitioners were *de facto* setting up the site by means of words.

Instead, when they were talking about practice – for instance, trying to understand why an accident had happened, or at any rate working out the reasons for some or other on-site episode – this was a reflexive discourse which interrupted the flow of the practice to make space for the social activity of mutual accountability.

A group of operatives gather around a long steel beam that should support the new ceiling. The beam is too short, it doesn't fit. People sit on other beams with their legs hanging, or stand on the ground floor below with their noses in the air. A bottle of water appears from someone's lunchbag and is passed around. The site foreman is called in. He too stands and takes a drink of water. He is the first to break the silence, speaking in a soft voice, as if talking to himself at first:

'We'll have to notify the engineer, he's going to get mad . . . Can I know who in the world measured this thing . . .'

'We followed the drawings . . .'

'But can't you see that the room is crooked . . . don't you know you always have to measure things again!? The architect just draws straight lines, he doesn't know what this old building is really like . . . (Reconstructed from field notes)

Situated practices are both pre-reflexive (depending on unstated assumptions and shared knowledge for the mutual achievement of sense) and reflexively constitutive of the situated members' contexts from which they arise. Reflexivity is the outcome of the separation or breakdown between subject and object and, for ethnomethodologists, the need for 'accountability' – by which is meant making the world comprehensible to oneself and to the other members of a collectivity (Flynn, 1991). Reflexivity is used to create a sense of orderliness for action but it reflexively creates that selfsame context (Garfinkel, 1967). Reflexion on practice makes the world comprehensible both to oneself and to others. It may modify the practice or may leave it untouched, but in both cases the function of talk about practices is principally symbolic. It symbolizes membership and competence in discursive practice among different communities (apart from one's own), and it celebrates identity. Discursive practice about practice puts the community on-stage, producing it culturally and symbolically. Consequently, participating in a discursive community means being able to *relate to* the discourses on practice of other communities.

To summarize, using Boland and Tenkasi's concepts, we may say that perspective making and perspective taking are mediated by boundary objects, artifacts or tangible definitions and by discursive practices within each specific community and among a constellation of communities. But discursive practices are not only instrumental to understanding and negotiating; they are also the expression and the means for positioning a community identity within a subject position in a discourse. Between perspective making and perspective taking there is positionality, i.e. the social construction of the subject position and its location within the structure of the rights pertaining to that position. Voice, knowledge and power legitimate a subject position within a discursive community and, while consonance is necessary for understanding each other positioning, dissonance is necessary for asserting identity.

DISCUSSION

We have described discourse on safety as a practice which engenders conversation in a discursive community, internally to which various communities of practice assume their positioning.

It is widely acknowledged that different communities of practice have different explanations of how an organization works. Schein (1996), for example, identifies three different types of extremely common management culture: (i) an operator culture, or a line organization which views work as involving interconnected systems and cooperation among people; (ii) an engineering subculture which values technical, error-free solutions; and (iii) an executive subculture which focuses on the financial bottom line. Our site foremen, engineers and main contractors can be easily related to Schein's three occupational subcultures. If we consider the set of ideas that they express, their beliefs indubitably induce coherent predispositions towards action (safety prevention). That thought precedes action is a belief widely held in Western culture, with its profound faith in rationality, although one could equally well argue the opposite, and also maintain that the linkage between thought and action is almost non-existent, as in hypocrisy (Brunsson, 1982, 1989; March and Olsen, 1976).

The theoretical problem that Schein's model does not address is how coordinated action in the presence of an incoherent thought system is possible. Schein's definition of culture, in fact, emphasizes the ideational elements that come to be shared. Consequently, everything that is not harmonized or sedimented inevitably ends up in a residual category which we may call 'noise'.

A further example – one very close to our research experience in that it concerns an incident review programme in a nuclear plant, and a root cause analysis at a chemical process plant from a learning perspective – is provided by Carroll (1998). The article begins by quoting the words of a station manager at a nuclear plant with an excellent safety record: 'What we do around here doesn't always make sense'. The question that Carroll asks, therefore, is why should effective behaviours and activities not be explicable and perhaps not discussible? The answer is that the difficulty lies in the available 'mental models' (Senge, 1990) or understandings of organizations, people and technologies.

Carroll explains the difficulty in terms of four categories of logic obtained by cross-referencing two dimensions: anticipation versus resilience (or fixing orientation versus learning orientation) and concrete versus abstract. He finds that design engineers work with logics that help them anticipate and therefore defend against problems in concrete objects. Their world is visual, and their natural reaction is to fix the problem and restore everything to its original state. Also executives are focused on anticipation, models and strategic plans, but their world is numerical rather than visual. By contrast, operators and craftspeople, who have their hands on equipment, are concerned with resilience, and their world is manual or tactile. Finally, there are the social scientists, management consultants and human factor experts, with their long-term view of experimentation and learning in the abstract. Theirs is a verbal world of ideas, written publications and persuasive conversations (Carroll, 1998, p. 711).

Carroll's article is very convincing in its description of two research projects in which groups of people from different communities of practice come together to produce knowledge on the theme of safety. Carroll's argument is that learning in groups is actuated by a feedback cycle (observing, reflecting, creating, acting), and that 'mental models' create difficulties for both learning and organization. His interpretation presupposes a conception of learning as a mainly cognitive activity, and an idealist conception of knowledge and knowing.

This is a legitimate representation of learning, knowledge and knowing in organizations, but it is antithetical to our system of representation, which conceives learning as intrinsic to every form of practice and which emphasizes the material character of knowledge and the social character of knowing.

Our interpretation of what happens in groups of people with various organizational and cultural backgrounds, who meet for a period of time in order to analyse a problem or to draw up a project (Gherardi, 2000b), is that they create a discursive community and activate a situated discursive identity which enables them to compare among different perspectives, but which also makes them realize that they may remain isolated, juxtaposed, non-communicating, and even conflictual. Comparing among perspectives means both comprehending and not comprehending, accepting diversity as well as rejecting it, understanding and misunderstanding. To assume a discursive position is a political move, it equates to positioning oneself in a network of social relations structured by power, interestedness and the mobilization of interests.

When we look at the practices that weave other practices together, the image of 'heterogeneous engineering' (Law, 1992) 'in which bits and pieces from the social, the technical, the conceptual, and the textual are fitted together' may prove useful. However, 'heterogeneous engineering' also refers to the fact that this alignment is by definition precarious and incomplete. It is the contingent and unstable result of the work performed by the local discursive practices. Change in one or more of the constellations of interconnected practices is a likely outcome of this working of knowledges together through language and communication. However, the change in question amounts to subtle shifting, 'rubbing', pollution, contamination, drawing and re-drawing boundaries, translation and misunderstanding between knowledges – all figures that are substantially different from those used in the rhetoric of, say, 'knowledge management' which uses a message transmitting framework.

Discursive practice is central to organizational knowing and acting because it accomplishes the ephemeral and unstable alignment that preserves the arrangement of materials, persons, technologies and knowledges in a form recognizable as a practice. In this sense one may argue that discourse is a practice generative of other practices, a mode of ordering distinguished by its capacity to handle both coherence and incoherence, harmonies *and* dissonances, consonance *and* cacophony.

CONCLUSIONS

Safety is an organizational competence which arises from a constellation of interconnected practices. A practice-based approach has been used to show that the learning of safety in a constellation of communities of practice is mediated by comparison among the perspectives of the world embraced by the co-participants in the production of this practice.

Comparison among perspectives is made possible by a discursive practice undertaken to align elements, mental and material, within mutually accountable discursive positions. These alignments are provisional and unstable because the practices of each of the communities are situated within specific views of the world (and of safety) and power relations *vis-à-vis* the other communities. They therefore produce tensions, discontinuities and incoherences just as much as they produce order and negotiated meanings.

Discursive practice among interconnected communities of practice is a mode of ordering which produces a body of knowledge shared by the communities involved, but not only in the form of stable, cumulative knowledge institutionalized in routines. Indeed, the distinctive feature of a building site is that it is a temporal organization which is usually born and dies within a year and cannot rely on structuring processes akin to organizational memory. The discursive practice that we have described does not rule out the processes of harmonization, negotiation of meanings, and the integration of local forms of knowledge; nor does it rule out the complementary ones of competition, conflict, dominance and exclusion, although it should be stressed that all these processes take place through discourse and in the materiality of talk: understanding is less necessary to be able to talk than recognition of the discursive position and discourse legitimacy of the Other.

We have proposed a metaphor for discursive practice in a constellation of interconnected practices: those who listen to it will not recognize the harmony of a canon, nor the orchestra rehearsals conducted to produce a symphony; rather, they will learn to distinguish the dissonance of practice and the places in which the cacophonies are produced, thereby perceiving a form and a mode of ordering in what at first seemed only to be noise or music.

Communities of practice – in our case, the engineers, site foremen and main contractors – assume their respective positionings within the situated discourse on safety. The engineers conduct conversation in order to accredit a technical and error-free conception; the site foremen emphasize the contingency and impermanence of concomitant events, and the main contractors highlight the compatibility/incompatibility of safety costs with other parameters. In their shared discursive practice they compare their perspectives both during discourse *in* practice (i.e. in the course of collective action) and during discourse *on* practice (i.e. when the narrative concerns accountable action).

Whilst it is relatively easy to conceive a constellation of interconnected communities of practices performing a practice, it is more difficult to see how that practice 'performs' the community. And yet the two concepts define each other, and it is through discursive practice that the constellation acquires shape for those looking at it.

Just as learning in a community of practice can be described by the concepts of legitimate peripheral participation (Lave and Wenger, 1991; Wenger, 1998) and of situated curriculum (Gherardi et al., 1998a), so learning in a constellation of interconnected practices can be described as a brokering activity situated in a discursive practice which relates situated bodies of knowledge to the minimum extent necessary to 'perform' the discursive community.

NOTES

*The present article is based on research into organizational learning as part of a project for the Kolleg 'Organizational Learning in Various Environmental Conditions', financed by the Daimler-Benz Foundation. It is the outcome of joint and indivisible work by the authors; however if individual authorship is to be assigned, Silvia Gherardi wrote the introduction, the conclusion and the first and second sections, and Davide Nicolini the third and fourth sections.

[1] We are indebted to Attila Bruni and Katrin Gilbert for their comments on musical metaphors.

[2] The research study described in this paper results from the two interrelated projects – an ethnography and a discourse analysis – that have been partially presented in previous works concerning the situated curriculum of a novice site manager (Gherardi et al., 1998a) and his engagement in a community of practice (Gherardi and Nicolini, 2002), but it has never been integrated into the same interpretative frame.

[3] A dissonance is a combination of discordant tones producing a harsh effect; it is also a note which in combination with others produces this effect. A canon is a sort of musical composition in which the different parts take up the same subject one after another, either at the same or a different pitch, in strict imitation. We use the musical metaphor to convey the image of positioning one's voice while listening to others without necessarily joining them, as in a canon.

[4] In performing the analysis we encountered a problem of significance due to the extremely small size of the sample. However, in these cases it is possible to draw on the very specialized field of statistics (StatXact) usually applied by biometrics and epidemiological studies and performed through combinatory calculus exact statistical tests. We were informed of this possibility by Prof. Hans M. Schadee, to whom we are greatly indebted for his advice and help. We also wish to thank our colleague Francesca Odella for her assistance in the statistical processing of the data.

REFERENCES

ALCOFF, L. (1988). 'Cultural feminism versus post-structuralism: the identity crisis in feminist theory'. *Signs*, **13**, 3, 405–36.

ANTAKI, C. and FIELDING, G. (1981). 'Research on ordinary explanations'. In Antaki, C. (Ed.), *The Psychology of Ordinary Explanations of Social Behaviour, European Monographs in Social Psychology*. London: Academic Press.

BETCHKY, B. (1999). 'Creating Shared Meaning Across Occupational Communities: An Ethnographic Study of a Production Floor'. Paper presented at the 1999 Academy of Management Meeting, Chicago, August.

BLACKLER, F. (1993). 'Knowledge and the theory of organizations: organizations as activity systems and the reframing of management'. *Journal of Management Studies*, **30**, 863–84.

BLACKLER, F. (1995). 'Knowledge, knowledge work and organizations: an overview and interpretation'. *Organization Studies*, **16**, 1021–46.

BLACKLER, F., CRUMP, N. and MCDONALD, S. (2000). 'Organizing processes in complex activity networks'. *Organization*, **7**, 2, 277–300.

BOLAND, R. and TENKASI, R. (1995). 'Perspective making and perspective taking in communities of knowing'. *Organization Science*, **6**, 4, 350–72.

BROWN, J. and DUGUID, P. (1991). 'Organizational learning and communities-of-practice: toward a unified view of working, learning and innovation'. *Organization Science*, **2**, 40–57.

BRUNSSON, N. (1982). 'The irrationality of action and action rationality: decision, ideologies and organizational actions'. *Journal of Management Studies*, **19**, 29–44.

BRUNSSON, N. (1989). *The Organization of Hypocrisy*. Chichester: Wiley.

CARROLL, J. (1998). 'Organizational learning activities in high-hazard industries: the logics underlying self-analysis'. *Journal of Management Studies*, **35**, 699–717.

COOK, S. and YANOW, D. (1993). 'Culture and organizational learning'. *Journal of Management Inquiry*, **2**, 373–90.

DAVIES, B. and HARRÉ, R. (1990). 'Positioning: the discursive production of selves'. *Journal of the Theory of Social Behaviour*, **1**, 43–63.

ECKERT, P. (1989). *Jocks and Bourouts: Social Categories and Identity in the High School*. New York: Teachers College Press.

FLYNN, P. (1991). *The Ethnomethodological Movement*. New York: Mouton de Gruyter.

FUJIMURA, J. (1995). 'Ecologies of action: recombining genes, molecularizing cancer, and transforming biology'. In Star, S. L. (Ed.), *Ecologies of Knowledge*. Albany: State University of New York Press.

GARFINKEL, H. (1967). *Studies in Ethnomethodology*. Englewood Cliffs: Prentice Hall.

GHERARDI, S. (1995). *Gender, Symbolism and Organizational Culture*. London: Sage.

436   S. GHERARDI AND D. NICOLINI

GHERARDI, S. (1999). 'Learning as problem-driven or learning in the face of mystery?'. *Organization Studies*, **20**, 101–24.
GHERARDI, S. (2000a). 'Practice-based theorizing on learning and knowing in organizations: an introduction'. *Organization*, **7**, 2, 211–23.
GHERARDI, S. (2000b). 'Where learning is: metaphors and situated learning in a planning group'. *Human Relations*, **53**, 8, 1057–80.
GHERARDI, S. and NICOLINI, D. (2002). 'Learning the trade. A culture of safety in practice'. *Organization*, **9**, 2, 191–223.
GHERARDI, S., NICOLINI, D. and ODELLA, F. (1998a). 'Toward a social understanding of how people learn in organizations: the notion of situated curriculum'. *Management Learning*, **29**, 3, 273–98.
GHERARDI, S., NICOLINI, D. and ODELLA, F. (1998b). 'What do you mean by safety? Conflicting perspectives on accident causation and safety management inside a construction firm". *Journal of Contingencies and Crisis Management*, **7**, 4, 202–13.
LATOUR, B. (1986). 'The power of association'. In Law, J. (Ed.), *Power, Action and Belief: A New Sociology of Knowledge?* London: Routledge and Kegan Paul.
LAVE, J. and WENGER, E. (1991). *Situated Learning: Legitimate Peripheral Participation*. New York: Cambridge University Press.
LAW, J. (1992). 'Notes on the theory of the actor network: ordering, strategy, and heterogeneity'. *System Practice*, **5**, 4, 379–93.
LAW, J. (1994). *Organizing Modernity*. Oxford: Blackwell.
MARCH, J. and OLSEN, J. (Eds) (1976). *Ambiguity and Choice in Organizations*. Universitetforlage Bergen.
PICKERING, A. (1992). *Science as Practice and Culture*. Chicago: University of Chicago Press.
POLANYI, M. (1958). *Personal Knowledge*. London: Routledge.
POLANYI, M. (1967). *The Tacit Dimension*. New York: Anchor Books.
SCHEIN, E. (1996). 'The three cultures of management: implications for organizational learning'. *Sloan Management Review*, **38**, 9–20.
SENGE, P. (1990). *The Fifth Discipline. The Art and Practice of the Learning Organization*. New York: Doubleday Currency.
STAR, S. L. (1995). *Ecologies of Knowledge*. Albany: State University of New York Press.
STRATI, A. (1998). *Organization and Aesthetics*. London: Sage.
STRAUSS, A. (1978). *Negotiations*. San Francisco: Jossey-Bass.
SUCHMAN, L. (1987). *Plans and Situated Action*. Cambridge: Cambridge University Press.
SUCHMAN, L. (2000). 'Organizing alignment: a case of bridge-building'. *Organization*, **7**, 2, 311–27.
TURNER, B. A. and PIDGEON, N. (1997). *Man-Made Disasters*. Oxford: Butterworth-Heinemann.
UNGER, R. (1987). *False Necessity*. Cambridge: Cambridge University Press.
VATTIMO, G. (1985). *Fine della modernità* (End of Modernity). Milano: Garzanti.
VAUX, J. (1999). Social Groups and Discursive Communities: Context and Audience in the Explanatory Practices of the Artificial Intelligence (AI) Community'. Paper presented at The Transformation of Knowledge conference, University of Surrey, 12–13 January.
WEICK, K. (1979). *The Social Psychology of Organizing*, 2nd ed. Reading, MA: Addison Wesley.
WEICK, K. (1995). *Sensemaking in Organizations*. Beverly Hills: Sage.
WENGER, E. (1998). *Communities of Practice. Learning, Meaning and Identity*. Cambridge: Cambridge University Press.
WITTGENSTEIN, L. (1953). *Philosophical Investigations*. Oxford: Blackwell.

[9]
Aesthetics in the Study of Organizational Life

Antonio Strati

INTRODUCTION

The strand of inquiry which concerns itself with organization and aesthetics is rooted in the culturalist turn in organization studies that came about during the 1980s, and in particular in those studies which analysed the organization in terms of every-day life experience and symbolic and aesthetic construction. These two aspects have mainly distinguished the aesthetic approach to organizations (Strati, 1992) among the various styles of inquiry into the aesthetic dimension of organizations developed since the early 1990s (Benghozi, 1987; Carr and Hancock, 2003; Gagliardi, 1990; Linstead and Höpfl, 2000; Guillet de Monthoux, 2004; Jones et al., 1988; Ottensmeyer, 1996; Rafaeli and Pratt, 2005; Ramírez, 1991; Schroeder, 2006; Strati, 1999; Strati and Guillet de Monthoux, 2002; Watkins et al., 2006). But what is the significance of this strand of organization studies for empirical research and organizational theory? What are its implications for the future of organizational analysis?

Answering these two questions requires us first to look at the origin of this strand of inquiry. This I shall do in the first part of the chapter, where I describe how my study on the aesthetic dimension of organizational life took shape, and then frame it in the context of other studies which, together with mine, gave life and social legitimacy to the study of the aesthetic dimension of organization. This was largely academic research which began and developed within the mainstream of symbolic-cultural studies on organizations. It addressed a wide range of classic topics in organization studies but shifted them to unexplored and experimental terrain where they were theoretically and methodologically renewed. The second part of the chapter consists of five 'fragments of organizational discourse' which I feel are crucial for re-invigorating the desire for knowledge and the passion for organizational research.

AESTHETICS AS 'ART OF ORGANIZATIONAL SIN'

My reflections on the aesthetic dimension of organizational life began to take shape during research conducted in the departments of mathematics, education, and visual arts of one of the oldest universities in Europe. This research brought me to realize that aesthetics pervades everyday life in workplaces; that it is a component of organizational cultures; and that it does not always 'act' in the same way in different organizations. These findings prompted my first work on organizational aesthetics (1990) and formed the basis for the reflections put forward shortly afterwards in my publications (1992, 1999) proposing an aesthetic approach to organization study.

It should be borne in mind that the same period saw other works on organizational aesthetics. Indeed, never since has there been a collective scientific endeavour, neither organized, nor even less coordinated, on this topic with such impact and importance. Art and aesthetics and the notions of beauty and *pathos* became part of the vocabulary of organizational discourse in:

- works which argued that the management of organizational processes should be grasped in its nature as an aesthetic phenomenon, because its participants are 'craftpersons and aesthetes' (Jones et al., 1988: 160), and that the organizational metaphor of the 'manager as artist' can be used to make sense of the plurality of organizational forms (Dégot, 1987);
- works which addressed the theoretical-methodological issue of how empirical research can grasp the beauty of the organization as a whole (Ramirez, 1991; Strati, 1990) for the actors involved in organizational dynamics;
- works which stressed the *pathos* of the artifacts (Gagliardi, 1990) that constitute the organization's symbolic landscape by virtue of their influence on the basic assumptions of people at work, and which are consequently a form of organizational control exercised at the emotional and aesthetic level rather than the normative and cognitive one.

Art and aesthetics became *constitutive items in the definition of both 'organizational*

actor' and 'organization'. They connoted as much the materiality of everyday organizational life – asserting the corporeality of people's knowledge and interactions, and the physicality of non-human objects – as the immateriality of fantasizing with organizational metaphors (the manager as artist) and aesthetic sentiments on theoretical abstractions like the organization *tout court*.

This was akin to a Copernican revolution in organizational theories, although it did not have the same impact. The dispute with positivist and rationalist studies centred on a *theoretical proposal which questioned the definitional bases of what was meant by not only 'human being' and 'organization' but also 'organizational study'*, because aesthetics, sentiment, and pathos restored theoretical value and scientific significance to the knowledge-evoking process – then overshadowed by the predominant logical-analytical procedures – and art acquired theoretical-methodological legitimacy rather than delimiting one type of social world.

What was the outcome of studying the aesthetic dimension of the three university departments mentioned above? That *aesthetic difference is a distinctive feature of organizations*.

Aesthetics, as we know, affirms that individuals differ in their sensory perceptions, and in the judgements that they make using their taste and senses. If we have to choose a perfume or an aftershave, we do not usually just read the chemical ingredients listed on the label – that is, the scientific definition of the product's ontology; nor do we rely solely on the corporate *ethos* symbolized by the brand. What we do is sprinkle some drops on our skin and sniff them: 'it's too sweet; it's too spicy; it doesn't suit me; it's good (in the aesthetic, not ethical, sense); it's right for an evening at a discotheque or at the theatre; it's different, so I can change my image'.

Hence we rely on our taste, as constructed by our social interactions, and on our sense of smell, which though absolutely personal, has likewise undergone social processes that have refined or blunted it: for example, the possible choices provided by the number of the varieties of the product. However large this number may be, it signals to us that among users of perfumes and aftershaves, there are many who make the same choices as ours, even if they may not smell exactly as we do because perfumes or aftershaves merge and react with other skin odours. But what essences are we able to identify in the perfume or aftershave which we are examining with our sense of smell? Theoretically, a human being is able to distinguish ten thousand different odours. How many can our own sense of smell identify? What happens if the person with us says: 'Oh no, don't tell me you like this one! Can't you feel that it's not right for you?' Does there not now begin the negotiating dynamic whereby, overwhelmed by a medley of perfumes, we eventually settle for a particular product, only to find that it smells differently when we put it on at home? This example from everyday life serves two purposes. First, it highlights an organizational phenomenon which consists of perfume houses, perfume shops, and the organized social settings in which perfumes are used. Second, it gives us an experiential (albeit imaginary) answer to the following question: how does the 'nose' – the term for the in-company expert who invents new perfumes – avoid the anaesthetizing of his perceptive-sensory faculties, and create products that may or may not be to the taste of customers only imagined or potential until the perfume or aftershave is placed on the market?

Aesthetics therefore highlights the individual differences due to our perceptive-sensory faculties and sensitive-aesthetic judgement. What my study on the three university departments showed was that aesthetic difference pertains to collectives and organizations as well. Each of the three departments – visual arts, education, and mathematics – had its own relation between aesthetics and organization. This I shall now illustrate, beginning with the department institutionally most concerned with aesthetics, and concluding with the one least so concerned.

The department of visual arts

In the department of visual arts, the aesthetic dimension of organizational practices was deep and pervasive; but it related more to the beauty, allure, and sacredness of materials and workplaces than it did to the manner in which research, documentation and teaching was conducted. The beauty of work in the department was constituted above all by materials, and the appreciation of such beauty was both the motive and meaning of the work choices of the teaching staff, research staff and, in many respects, the technical staff as well. The study of beautiful materials and frequent contact with 'art' works constituted the fundamental aesthetic dimension of working and organizational practices in the department, where the aesthetics of materials and places influenced various of its organizational features.

The question 'Do you make beautiful things?' further highlighted this feature. All replies to it stressed that the department's academic and technical-administrative staff produced not beautiful things but 'useful' ones. One interviewee commented that the department produced things which were:

> beautiful in the sense of good. But, you know, all those words ... beautiful, good, valid ... if by beautiful you mean valid then yes, I believe in what I say, in the method that I propose, and so I believe it is valid, positive, 'beautiful' if you want to use – though very improperly – the adjective 'beautiful', but beautiful means valid, efficient ... Yes, it gratifies me ... there's also gratification ... but, I mean to say, I'm not a creator, I'm a scholar, I don't do art, I study the art done by others, so let's leave beauty to those who actually produce it.

The department's members were able to spend their working lives producing a *'beauty'which belongs to ethics rather than to the aesthetics.* Ethical beauty characterized their symbolic construction of the organizational life of the visual arts department, within a setting – or an organizational landscape (Gagliardi, 1990) – largely made up of artifacts with considerable beauty, yet also of artifacts that were ugly, repellent and kitsch. This organizational landscape, of course, did not coincide with the department's front desk and the sheets of paper, books, slides and photocopies temporarily placed upon it. Rather, it was an 'imaginary workplace' constructed on the basis of both the departmental work settings and the other places where the department members were conducting their study and research, such as an art gallery, a library, a sacristy, or a private house where family portraits were collected and eventually displayed.

The education department

In the education department, by contrast, the aesthetic resided neither in the materials on which research was conducted nor in the imaginary workplace described above. Instead, the aesthetic dimension emerged in relation to (a) academic teaching and (b) university management. This is apparent from the following remarks by a researcher and a lecturer in the department:

> We'd been working here for a year and we did something really beautiful, all the researchers … and I think it was extremely important. We held a seminar and all the students for all three years of Education could attend […] We organized everything, we got everything ready … and it was really beautiful … it all went well, with the exams, everything. But it was never repeated. And every so often when we get together for a chat, etcetera, we feel nostalgic for that time, because I believe it was a beautiful event. The university really came alive.
> I believe that these people should have a minimum of aesthetic taste […] if you teach education you have to enjoy yourself, otherwise you do it very badly! So I said that, according to me, the character of the staff is very important. I must say that when I was dean, I got into loads of shouting matches, and in the end I had a heart attack […] but I enjoyed myself, how I enjoyed teaching!

Besides the enjoyment of teaching or organizing a seminar described as 'beautiful', these interview extracts also highlight the aesthetic taste for 'managing these things', the 'taste for power' of those who assumed official responsibilities as the head of a department, of a master programme, or the dean of a faculty. The above comments show that the aesthetic dimension of the education department became manifest when it interwove with an organizational culture inspired by

civic commitment and social utility. Once again, *aesthetics was linked to ethics*, almost depending upon the latter, which provided the frame for its organizational approval. Otherwise, aesthetics was an organizational 'sin' and remained hidden, seen and unseen, and inexpressible, as in the case of the relation between aesthetics and research stressed by one of the lecturers:

> Instinctively, I'd say no, because ethically I've come to consider the presence of aesthetics … as sin! It must be accomplished with time, but in an underhanded way, in the sense that it is camouflaged … sometimes the scientific dimension is not evidently aesthetic but I know that it is aesthetic … a beautiful table [of statistics] has every reason to be aesthetic, but the others don't know it.

One notes *the conflict between ethics and aesthetics* here, and also the fact that this conflict characterized the symbols and culture of the education department. Indeed, as the following extract illustrates, its members were confronted by contrasts:

> … then, I like doing research … I mean, working regardless of social utility. This is one of the jobs that allow you to do that … I mean, the self-directedness of the work … independently of external ends …

Here the aesthetic dimension of knowledge creation and learning management lay concealed behind a veil of modesty. It thus constituted *an organizational paradox: aesthetics as civic and social commitment, and aesthetics as liberation* from the constraint that work in the department should be socially useful.

The mathematics department

Matters were different in the mathematics department. There, it was the mathematicians themselves who made beautiful things by creating knowledge; who produced mathematics as an artifact with aesthetic appeal; who constructed a research practice symbolically connected to aesthetics:

> the most beautiful result is one where the author has been able to identify fundamental ideas, after which he works out his theory following a line of reasoning and a generally geometric intuition, and the thing acquires a particular significance, it

becomes clearer, it's easier to understand ... A beautiful result is often one in which the author demonstrates more than he says.

Another member of the department clarified the organizational character of engaging directly in a discourse carried forward at both the mathematical and the aesthetic levels. He recounted how an eminent Italian mathematician had decided to publish a theorem even though its proof did not work because 'it was beautiful all the same':

> ... he could do that because it was at such a level that it was acceptable even without a proof. He'd done a great deal in any case, because he'd made [...] you feel that the thing held together. After which, proving it was another matter.

This account also highlights the beauty of the eminent mathematician's gesture, namely his organizational practice of creating an idea to appreciate, an intuition upon which to reflect, a problem to study, and which was available to other scholars. Here, as often happens in organizations, aesthetics and ethics interwove so that it was often very difficult to determine whether or not 'beautiful' was being used as a synonym for 'good'. In this case, however, one is struck by how closely a beautiful idea was bound up with the values that inspire the beauty of the organizational practices of mathematicians in creating both knowledge and learning – as the following comment by another member of the department illustrates:

> The wonder you feel at this type of proof is like having a sensation of the beautiful ... you understand that it's a mathematical, logical, philosophical type of beauty which perhaps can't be compared with the artistically beautiful, but the fact that simple propositions have been proved with profound ideas is something whose beauty even a non-specialist is able to understand.

In the mathematics department, we may therefore conclude *aesthetics was collective life*: it underpinned the intellectual production and transmission of scientific knowledge, and it was one of the central pillars for the work identity of the organization's members. Seen from afar, mathematicians resemble scientists. But they describe themselves as

if the cleavage between art and science, and the dominance of scientific discourse in the organization of academic knowledge, had never happened. Compared with their colleagues in the other two departments, they seemed obsolete in the age of modernity, where science has very little to do with art.

To recapitulate

What was the result of this study on organizational aesthetics? On the one hand it brought out distinctive features of the organizational cultures studied, and demonstrated that the aesthetic is socially constructed in organizations on the other. These are two closely interconnected organizational themes, but in certain respects they are very distinct. The former finds in the aesthetic dimension *a way to study organizations*; the latter finds in organizational experiences the *negotiative processes that give shape to the aesthetic* and to its relations with the classic issues of ethics and truth.

Beauty was truth in itself – organizational truth, we would say – in the mathematics department: the mathematicians invented, described, cooperated and organized by weaving the aesthetic, the ethical, and the truth dimensions together. But this was not so in the other two departments, where ethics was socially instituted as the theoretical framework within which the meanings and organizational valences of aesthetics were determined. The visual arts scholars sharply separated their historical/scientific output from the aesthetic dimension underpinning their choice of work, the network of scholars with whom they collaborated, and the organization that they had decided to join. Although those who worked in the education department appreciated the aesthetic dimension of teaching and of running the university, they tended to downplay it and keep it under control, emphasizing the ethic of social utility instead. Consequently, in both these departments the aesthetic dimension did not possess organizational truth in and of itself; rather, it depended on the ethical dimension. Aesthetics was the *art of organizational sin*, and although it was intrinsic to the organization's practices, it lay at a lower level than ethics and was regulated by the latter. Thus aesthetics was sterilized by the organization's ethics: the aesthetics were silenced and concealed, seen and not seen, while ethics dictated the content of organizational discourse.

Such were the beginnings of my aesthetic approach to the study of organizational life. The next section discusses the issues raised for future research by current developments in the aesthetic strand of organization studies.

FRAGMENTS FOR A DIALOGUE IN ORGANIZATION STUDIES

It seems that the empirical and theoretical analysis of the relations between aesthetics and organization is now well-established: witness the several texts that seek to systematize the organizational literature on aesthetics (Dean et al., 1997; Gagliardi, 1996; Ramírez, 2005; Strati, 1999, 2007; Taylor and Hansen, 2005), the work of virtual communities – in particular, the Art, Aesthetics, Creativity, and Organisations Research Network (AACORN), and the increasingly frequent discussions on the topic at conferences, conference sections, and workshops. Recent years have seen mounting intellectual interest in organizational aesthetics, a flourishing of cultural initiatives in its regard, and a fierce polemic against the organizational theories that still divide art from science so that the logical-analytical dimension of intellectual inquiry may maintain its dominance.

All this has happened amidst a severe crisis of faith in scientific beliefs and the myth of rationality which, during the last century, presided over the social construction of organizational discourse until the culturalist turn in the social sciences at the end of the 1980s. A turn, moreover, which occurred in aesthetics as well (Jimenez, 1997: 397–432), both in philosophical debate and in art production and art criticism.

What are the implications of these developments for organizational theory in general, and management studies in particular? Certainly not the likelihood of any predominance of aesthetic understanding in organization studies; but rather, a new register somewhat like a new musical note used as the benchmark to tune a musical instrument. Consequently, instead of conducting systematic treatment, I shall use 'fragments' from the aesthetic discourse on organizations to develop a dialogue – also based on conflict and controversy – with other approaches.

Why fragments? Because I find fragments particularly appealing, as will be apparent from the following image based on a story about Gaudì's architecture. The story which I am about to recount – its authenticity is of little relevance here – describes the interactions among Gaudì, a master crafts-man, the great sheet of glass produced by the craftsman for the main door of Gaudì's building, and the ground. When Gaudì was shown the beautifully prepared sheet of glass, he said to the craftsman something like: 'It's perfect. Now drop it on the ground!' And when the glass had shattered into pieces of various sizes, he said, accompanying his words with hand gestures, 'Right, now assemble these fragments with wrought iron and make the building's front door'.

A fragment has (intuitively) very little to do with the systematic information yielded by an excerpt made *ad hoc*. The fragment from the story about Gaudì acquires form in the interaction between different competences, and between humans and artifacts. 'How' the glass shattered is just as important as 'how' the craftsman dropped it or 'how' the latter obeyed the architect's instructions. Conflict between feelings and aesthetic judgement, hierarchical power and expert knowledge, processes of organizational destruction and construction connote this organizational inter-action performed on the aesthetic dimension, and in which the glass fragments demonstrate 'that the situation of creative invention is that of striving to an end that, even if it is impossible to specify and plan, is in a sense directing the process' (Menger, 2006: 63). There are some fragments of aesthetic discourse on organizations that strike me as especially significant, viz.:

1 Embedding the study of organizational aesthetics in the context of *paradigmatic controversies* in organizational theory. The latter has rarely concerned itself with aesthetic-sensory knowledge, taste, the aesthetic judgement, or art; in short, it has neglected numerous dimensions of 'practice' in organizations (Nicolini et al., 2003). By contrast, study of the aesthetic dimension emphasizes the practical knowledge, passion, and taste – all socially constructed – which give difference and specificity to every individual and every collectivity (community of practices, occupational or professional community, organizational culture). An organization is therefore an artifact configured within post-social relations. It does not exist independently of the symbolic interactions between humans and artifacts. It is these features that distinguish the interpretative theoretical paradigm in organization studies from the functionalist paradigm. Within the former, the study of organizational aesthetics privileges critical analysis of the factors impeding organizational actors from full self-realization through their creativity and difference. Principal among these factors is the social aesthetization which anaesthetizes (Marquard, 1989) rather than activates their aesthetic-sensory sensibilities.

2 The qualitative methodology used by empirical research on the aesthetic dimension in organizations. This methodology draws on research styles which conventionally distinguish between qualitative and quantitative analysis: ethnography, non-structured methods of empirical inquiry, and techniques which let the theory emerge from the data, as in constructionist and phenomenological grounded theory. It explores other avenues as well, drawing on visual anthropology and interactionist visual anthropology to do so, as well as on artistic experience (Barry, 1996; Brearley, 2001; Guillet de Monthoux, 2004; Steyaert and Hjorth, 2002; Strati, 2005; Taylor, 2004; Warren, 2002). The *methodological novelty of this mixing and hybridization of art and science is primarily theoretical*, in that it conducts an epistemological critique of the cleavage that has logical-analytical understanding predominate over empathic-evocative understanding. It is also innovative in regard to everyday research practice – its styles and rituals – because it mixes and merges actions with different time frames (consider

the ephemerality of artistic performance and the open-ended time horizon of research) and distinct professional competences, namely those of the art world and academe. Third, it is innovative by virtue of the *ethos* – 'comprehension-cum-action' – that inspires research, given that this requires activation of the sensory faculties, the aesthetic judgement, and the cognitive and ratiocinative capacities of both the researcher and the participants in the research.

3 *Organizational power for the emancipation* of actors – individual and collective – *and also for their subjection* to organizational cultures. Aesthetics is individual difference first and foremost; but it is also what aggregates or disperses collectives in organizational settings through both personal commitment and organizational manipulation of individual feelings. Tastes, professional lifestyles, missions, talents, inventiveness, and ability are all sources of aesthetics-based organizational power, although they are seldom examined together with those based on norms, economic, or technological position and investigated relative to their emancipatory or subjugatory ambivalence. Aesthetics is organizational power that operates both reactively, as testified by the expression 'I/we don't like it', and proactively through the assertion of an operational style, a product design, or a sense of humour. This can be well understood if one considers the control over the organization's zones of uncertainty (Crozier and Friedberg, 1977) exercised by complex organizational actors consisting of inter-related people and artifacts. These are areas of interaction that the organization regards as important, if not crucial: for example, the area controlled by someone with a good sense of smell, the 'nose', in a perfume house, or someone with a good eye who directs an international photography collection, or again, someone with a passion for writing software programs and who creates a virtual community. The power of aesthetics therefore has its main root in the tacit dimension of knowledge (Polanyi, 1958) essential for organizational practices and the formation of communities of practice in organizations. In other words, it is rooted in that form of organizational knowledge whereby actors know how to do things and are able to describe their ability in the evocative terms of the metaphorical language pertaining to aesthetic understanding, but not in logical-analytical terms. It has another root as well: the organizational control exerted through the *pathos* of the organizational artifacts making up the organization's symbolic landscape

(Gagliardi, 1990), and through the disciplining of corporeality (Hancock and Tyler, 2000) and the anaesthetizing aesthetization (Marquard, 1989) mentioned above.

4 The *dynamic between the semiotization of working and organizational practices and sensible knowledge*. The semiotization of activities in organizational settings followed the advent of mass education and the diffusion of written texts in the industrialized societies. Now supported by information and telecommunications technologies, it has allegedly reduced the range of the sensory perceptions and aesthetic judgements activated as people work in organizations. But this is not the case, for if one observes software programmers at work, one notes their evident private relationship with the code being written, a relationship based on personal taste and affect which gives rise to 'quarrels about which are the most beautiful programs, which are the best programming languages and who is entitled to have a say in those discussions' (Piñeiro, 2004). In this case, too, art is valuable because it reminds us that reading a poem 'is equivalent to entering into *contact*: experiencing its sense as inseparable from its verbality. Reading a poem is to verify it tactilely; it is a sensual experience. It involves a *physics of sense*' (Cortellessa, 2006: XXII). Awareness is particularly significant for the aesthetics of the organizational discourse, since the semiotization is dominant in the practices of organizational research and its representation.

5 *Challenging logico-analytical knowledge* in order to create metaphorical spaces for dialogue. Aesthetic understanding and logical-analytical understanding alternate with each other: they overlap, they merge, they cancel each other out. They exist, not in spite of each other, but in a reciprocal challenge in which aesthetic understanding has numerous strengths. I shall dwell on two of them in particular. The first highlights areas where aesthetic understanding is particularly appropriate but analytical understanding is not. The second is the case in which aesthetic inquiry reveals organizational phenomena of particular importance for organizational theory – phenomena which analytical inquiry also appropriately investigates in its own fashion. The former case is exemplified by the forms of organizational knowledge that aesthetics equips with language for their expression, as happens apropos the tacit dimension of knowledge in organizations: by virtue of the evocative process of which it is capable, aesthetic understanding

does not violate the tacitness of such knowledge, while logical-analytical understanding instead does. The second case can be exemplified by the materiality of organizations and by the post-social relations that weave their everyday lives together. This is the study of the 'symbolic artifacts' (Gagliardi, 1990; Rafaeli and Pratt, 2005) to which aesthetic understanding attributes a capacity for action in many respects like that ascribed to 'non-human elements' in logical-analytical understanding (Latour, 2005). Of course, organizational discourse operates at several levels; but it is remarkable that in these very same years the 'object' has changed theoretical status in both analytical and aesthetic studies, becoming in the former an actant, or an intermediary able to activate courses of organizational action, and in the latter, the symbolic artifact whose *pathos* activates organizational knowledge.

CONCLUSIONS

In this chapter, I have sought to illustrate the rationale for studying the relations between organization and aesthetics. In these conclusions I would add a final consideration prompted by the following theoretical-methodological question: Why should we continue to study aesthetics in the everyday lives of organizations? My answer is not scientific but aesthetic: 'because it is pleasurable'. As long as it is so, and as long as aesthetic and emotional pleasure is the principal purpose of this strand of organization studies, analysis of the relationships among art, aesthetics and everyday life in organizations will maintain its roots in, and derive its features from, aesthetics. Studying organizational aesthetics *for the pleasure of doing so* is not to attribute such inquiry with the teleological purpose of determining which form of organizational understanding is better, more profound, more complete or more useful – that pertains to endeavours with knowledge objectives inspired by the principles of the good and the true, but not the beautiful.

The chapter has proposed some 'fragments' of the aesthetic organizational discourse in order to develop dialogical knowledge and learning in organization studies. They are not intended to provide the basis for a systematic, exhaustive and complete discourse furnishing emotional reassurance and scientific support for organizational scholars and students of organizational life. They are only fragments, and to grasp them fully we must rely on art and on what we have learnt from studies on art. The organizational discourse on art and aesthetics in the everyday lives of organizations is a collective symbolic construct accomplished socially by moving 'towards an unspecified end' (Menger, 2006: 62), but doing so purposefully, selecting among the many opportunities that we see and those that we intuit without really understanding them.

REFERENCES

Barry, Daved (1996) 'Artful inquiry: A symbolic constructivist approach to social science research', *Qualitative Inquiry*, 2 (4): 411–438.

Benghozi, Pierre-Jean (ed.) (1987) 'Art and organization', Special Issue of *Dragon*, 2 (4).

Brearley, Linda (2001) 'Exploring creative forms within phenomenological research', in R. Barnacle (ed.), *Phenomenology*. Melbourne: RMIT University Press. pp. 74–87.

Carr, Adrian and Philip Hancock (eds) (2003) *Art and Aesthetics at Work*. Basingstoke: Palgrave Macmillan.

Cortellessa, Andrea (2006) *La fisica del senso. Saggi e interventi su poeti italiani dal 1940 a oggi (The Physics of Sense: Essays on Italian Poets since 1940)*. Rome: Fazi.

Crozier, Michel and Erhard Friedberg (1977) *L'acteur et le système. Les contraintes de l'action collective*. Paris: Seuil. (Eng. trans.: *Actors and Systems: The Politics of Collective Action*. Chicago: University of Chicago Press, 1980.)

Dean, James W. Jr, Ottensmeyer, Edward and Rafael Ramírez (1997) 'An aesthetic perspective on organizations', in C. Cooper and S. Jackson (eds), *Creating Tomorrow's Organizations: A Handbook for Future Research in Organizational Behavior*. Chichester: Wiley. pp. 419–437.

Dégot, Vincent (1987) 'Portrait of the manager as an artist', *Dragon*, 2 (4): 13–50.

Gagliardi, Pasquale (ed.) (1990) *Symbols and Artifacts: Views of the Corporate Landscape*. Berlin: de Gruyter.

Gagliardi, Pasquale (1996) 'Exploring the aesthetic side of organizational life', in S.R. Clegg, C. Hardy and

W.R. Nord (eds), *Handbook of Organization Studies*. London: Sage. pp. 565–580.

Guillet de Monthoux, Pierre (2004) *The Art Firm. Aesthetic Management and Metaphysical Marketing*. Stanford: Stanford University Press.

Hancock, Philip and Melissa (2000) '"The look of love": Gender and the organization of aesthetics', in J. Hassard, R. Holliday and H. Willmott (eds), *Body and Organization*. London: Sage. pp. 108–129.

Jimenez, Marc (1997) *Qu'est-ce que l'esthétique*. Paris: Gallimard.

Jones, Michael Owen, Moore, Michael D. and Richard C. Snyder (eds) (1988) *Inside Organizations. Understanding the Human Dimension*. Newbury Park, CA: Sage.

Latour, Bruno (2005) *Reassembling the Social. An Introduction to Actor-Network-Theory*. Oxford: Oxford University Press.

Linstead, Stephen and Heather Höpfl (eds) (2000) *The Aesthetic of Organization*. London: Sage.

Marquard, Odo (1989) *Aesthetica und Anaesthetica. Philosophische Uberlegungen*. Paderborn: Schoningh.

Menger, Pierre-Michel (2006) 'Profiles of the unfinished: Rodin's work and the varieties of incompleteness', in H.S. Becker, R.R. Faulkner and B. Kirshenblatt-Gimblett (eds), *Art from Start to Finish. Jazz, Painting, Writing, and Other Improvisations*. Chicago: The University of Chicago Press. pp. 31–68.

Nicolini, Davide, Gherardi, Silvia and Dvora Yanow (eds) (2003) *Knowing in Organizations: A Practice-Based Approach*. Armonk, New York: M.E. Sharpe.

Ottensmeyer, Edward (ed.) (1996) 'Essays on aesthetics and organization', *Organization*, 3 (2).

Piñeiro, Erik (2004) *The Aesthetics of Code. On Excellence in Instrumental Action*. Stockholm: Fields of Flow Series.

Polanyi, Michael (1958) *Personal Knowledge*. London: Routledge & Kegan Paul.

Rafaeli, Anat and Michael G. Pratt (eds) (2005) *Artifacts and Organizations: Beyond Mere Symbolism*. Mahwah, NJ: Lawrence Erlbaum Associates Inc.

Ramírez, Rafael (1991) *The Beauty of Social Organization*. Munich: Accedo.

Ramírez, Rafael (2005) 'The aesthetics of cooperation', *European Management Review*, 2: 28–35.

Schroeder, Jonathan (ed.) (2006) 'Aesthetics, images and vision', Special Issue of *Marketing Theory*, 6 (1).

Steyaert, Chris and Daniel Hjorth (2002) '"Thou art a scholar, speak to it …" – on spaces of speech: A script', *Human Relations*, 55 (7): 767–797.

Strati, Antonio (1990) 'Aesthetics and organizational skill', in B.A. Turner (ed.), *Organizational Symbolism*. Berlin: De Gruyter. pp. 207–222.

Strati, Antonio (1992) 'Aesthetic understanding of organizational life', *Academy of Management Review*,
17 (3): 568–581.

Strati, Antonio (1999) *Organization and Aesthetics*.
London: Sage.

Strati, Antonio (2005) 'Organizational artifacts and the
aesthetic approach', in A. Rafaeli and M. Pratt (eds),
Artifacts and Organizations. Mahwah, NJ: Lawrence
Erlbaum Associates Inc. pp. 23–39.

Strati, Antonio (2007) 'Sensations, impressions and
reflections on the configuring of the aesthetic
discourse in organizations', *Aesthesis. International
Journal of Art and Aesthetics in Management and
Organizational Life*, 1 (1): 14–22.

Strati, Antonio and Pierre, Guillet de Monthoux (eds)
(2002) 'Organizing aesthetics', Special Issue of
Human Relations, 55 (7).

Taylor, Steven (2004) 'Presentational form in first person
research: Off-line collaborative reflection using art',
Action Research, 2 (1): 71–88.

Taylor, Steven and Hans Hansen (2005) 'Finding
form: Looking at the field of organizational
aesthetics', *Journal of Management Studies*, 42 (6):
1210–1231.

Warren, Samantha (2002) 'Show me how it feels to
work here': Using photography to research organizational aesthetics', *Ephemera. Critical Dialogues on
Organization*, 2 (3): 224–245.

Watkins, Ceri, King, Ian and Stephen, Linstead (eds)
(2006) 'Art of Management and Organization
Conference series', Special Issue of *Culture and
Organization*, 12 (1).

[10]

Volume 14(3): 315–329
ISSN 1350–5084
Copyright © 2007 SAGE
(Los Angeles, London, New Delhi
and Singapore)

The Passion for Knowing

Silvia Gherardi
University of Trento, Italy

Davide Nicolini
IKON, Warwick Business School, University of Warwick, UK

Antonio Strati
University of Trento, Italy and University of Siena, Italy

What are we talking about when we merge knowledge, organizations and passion together? Although this may seem a somewhat eccentric question, it in fact highlights a very simple and everyday relation. We are talking about the importance of the expressive relation and attachment to the world and the limit of a purely instrumental and economic view of human activity: the idea that people do what they do for the love of what they do and not for the money.

This relation requires brief historical contextualization. The oppositional and hierarchical relationship between emotion and rationality, with the latter term predominating over the former, is a relatively recent phenomenon. As noted by Elias (1994), the individual control and the public regulation of emotions are a central part of the process of modernization. The removal or deferral of emotions and passions from the public and organizational sphere can thus be fully identified as one of the main features of the project of modernity.

Things, however, used to be different. Many of the 17th-century writers were concerned with the passions as a source of self-knowledge, self-control, and power over others; and they were moving away from the treatment of passions embedded in discussion of vice and virtue. Most of these works are not well-known today, even if they contributed to an early philosophy of mind (James, 1997). The 17th century was marked by a growing spirit of inquiry 'that moved from experience to generalization,

DOI: 10.1177/1350508407076146

Organization 14(3)
Introduction

not only concerning experience in the physical world but also the mental world of psychological and socio-economic relations' (Barbalet, 2005: 186). This was a historical period of growing market exchanges and efforts to understand market practices in theoretical and practical terms. This intellectual development was expressed by Adam Smith in *The Theory of Moral Sentiments* (1759). Market exchanges at that time relied mainly on informal credit, and it was consequently important to understand the uses of emotions and how to build trust relations. It was only subsequently, with the growth of institutions regulating the market, that the orientation shifted to the commodity alone. Utilitarianism was a modern project based on trust and the myth of rationality. 'Formal and rational' organizations epitomized the spirit of modernity, and the ways in which they were studied, described and theorized relegated the passions to the private sphere of individual emotions while simultaneously connoting them as irrational.

The removal of passion, however, was never fully accomplished. Like a river in the desert which runs for long stretches underground only to emerge occasionally on the surface, the idea that emotion and passion play a central role in individual and social conducts has remained alive during the last two centuries.

Haliwell (1999), for example, suggests that common threads connect apparently distant authors such as James, Binswanger, Luria, and Sacks. All these psychologists rejected the 'normal science' of their times and argued that excluding experience, emotion and mystery from the explanation of conduct means excluding what can be called fundamentally human. This common framework, which Luria attributed to the legacy of 'romantic science' (Haliwell, 1999), is especially visible in the pragmatist treatment of the relationship between emotion and knowledge. Take sensation, embodied desire, and the aesthetic experience out of the act out of human activity, say authors such as James, Dewey, and Mead, and what you are left with is a pale representation of both how people know and what it means to be human.

Sensitivity to the constitutive role of emotion and passion, however, goes well beyond the individual sphere. Knorr Cetina (1997), for example, has convincingly argued that the passion of knowledge fuelled by the inherent incompleteness of epistemic objects is a primary source of sociality, both for scientists and, increasingly, for members of society at large. To the extent that objects in everyday life become high tech devices which warrant a continuous process of refinement and development, they trigger emotional affiliation, common search processes, and collective obligations which all become power sources for post communitarian relationships and organization.

Knorr Cetina is just one of the many authors who in recent years have resumed the idea that pathos should be considered a primary explanatory cause of social phenomena.

This applies to the sphere of work and production as well. Arendt (1959), argues that the exclusion of passion from the sphere of sociality

The Passion for Knowing
Silvia Gherardi et al.

and production is a consequence of the historical conflation (or confusion) between what she calls labour and work. While labour is a function of biological and economic necessity, work is intrinsically creative rather than merely reproductive. As such, work and passion cannot be thought of in complete opposition.

Schwalbe (1986), addresses the unexamined affective dimension of Marx's analysis of labour. He argues that a pivotal dimension of work is its aesthetic and passionate character. All activities have an aesthetic dimension to the extent that the actor experiences 'an appreciation of the end value of the act as the act is being carried out' (Schwalbe, 1986: 64). Such dimension is strategically underplayed in the capitalist mode of production. By concealing the aesthetic experience derived from the manipulatory phase, and focussing exclusively on the consummation phase, capitalism promises to repair alienation through material consumption, thus fuelling an endless circuit of domination through consumerism. Passion, in the neutral sense of pathos, although often invisible, hidden or repressed, is thus a key ingredient of what Schwalbe (1986) calls 'natural' (as opposed to alienated) work. Such passion can be found in almost all human activities, and it is not relegated to such specific spheres as those of art or leisure. Accordingly, passion is an inherent trait which is not limited to the increasingly common type of work that Freidson (1990) would define 'labor of love', e.g. working for a charity or for an 'alternative' organization. Passion, unrecognized and unexplored, is an ingredient of most human activities—such as Spinoza argued against Hobbes (Bodei, 1991)—provided we are ready to critically interrogate the conventional attachment of work, or labour to economy and exchange.

This Special Issue begins with an invited essay[1] by Pasquale Gagliardi which reflects on these topics and on the development of intellectual debate in organization studies over the past 30 years. His point of departure is the observation that while considered legitimate today, passion as a topic was previously censored within the spirit of the discipline. How has this happened, and what does it teach us?

Within the modernist knowledge project, organizational discourse was constructed and intellectually organized on the basis of the dualism between utility and gratuitousness, and of the hierarchical order between these two terms, where the former prevailed over and dominated the latter. Consequently, the literature, and also, the awareness itself of organization scholars, privileged interpretative categories which, on the basis of the value ascribed to utility, engendered a socially constructed blindness to all experience that could not be related to instrumentality, rationality, and utilitarianism. Thus, as modern scientific knowledge was formed, the dimension of pathos gave way to those of logos and ethos. But the return of pathos—which Gagliardi explains in light of the spread of qualitative and ethnographic methods and the greater sophistication of theoretical concepts—has expanded our understanding of what constitutes 'knowledge'.

Organization 14(3)
Introduction

One contribution that this Special Issue intends to make to the study of organization is consequently to broaden the concept of organizational knowledge so that it encompasses intellectual and sensory knowledge as well. Organizational knowledge is not solely mental. It is not situated in the brain of the human body or the organization; nor do the body or the organization serve as its instruments. Valorizing pathos in organization studies is giving salience to the corporeality of sensitive-aesthetic knowledge and to organizational action undertaken through the senses (Strati, 2007). It emphasizes the ability to express judgements based on taste, and to live the social practices performed in organizations with emotion, affect and attachment. Pathos in understanding organizational life requires due scholarly attention to be paid to the intimate, confused, and ambiguous relations among feeling, thinking and acting in the world of experience. This world is material and social even when it reveals its impalpability in, for example, the work and organizational practices concerned with the virtual domain of information and telecommunication technologies.

If we consider organizational knowledge no longer in terms of 'one-dimensional knowledge' (to paraphrase Marcuse)—and therefore not as cognitive and mental knowledge based on thought, or indeed restricted to only the rational thought capable of causally modelling social and post-social relations (Knorr-Cetina, 2006) in organizational settings—then much of the organizational literature will leave us disappointed and dissatisfied. For a large part of the organizational discourse, as regards both representations of organizational lives and the methods and epistemologies of the social research which produces them, is a censorial narrative that seeks to 'rationalize', 'sterilize' and 'moralize' everyday organizational life. Such disclosure is consequently able to recount neither the plurality of the experiential forms of organizational knowledge and action, nor the human richness embedded in them.

Reflecting upon, deconstructing, and destabilizing the interpretative categories of a discipline comprising such a large body of theoretical and empirical analysis as organization studies requires interrogation of the politics of knowledge and the effects thereon of the dominant discourses. In this regard, it is of interest to include other disciplinary areas, so that forms of organizational knowledge can interact with other approaches to the study of contemporary society. Thus possible will be a view of organizational life obtained through the eyes of other disciplines concerned with the issue of the politics of knowledge. This is the purpose of the second invited essay in this Special Issue. Written by the feminist philosopher Carla Locatelli, it examines the complex social phenomena bound up with the everyday nature of social and post-social relations in organizations.

The ambiguity of the categories used to interpret attachment to the world, or love, is paradigmatic for interpretation of value and power relations. 'Love', writes Locatelli (p. 339), is the 'stereotype of passive care-giving ascribed to women's "natural" loving attitude' which often justifies

318

The Passion for Knowing
Silvia Gherardi et al.

'women's exploitation in the most diverse social situations', and which implies that 'the domain of women's knowledge is just "emotional", "emphatic", "timic"'—although, in truth, it generally signifies that 'women's knowledge is illogical, non-objective, and engrossed'. We again find here the effects of representation in binary terms explored by Gagliardi. Rationality is inscribed in the domain of instrumentality, utilitarianism, logos and the male, while emotionality is inscribed in pathos, gratuitousness and the female. But just as art suffers from being segregated in museums and in the sphere of leisure-time entertainment, so love suffers from being segregated in the sphere of femaleness. Locatelli's essay suggests that love should be conceived not (only) as emotion, but also as action, and that we should consequently interrogate the politics of desire. The politics of knowledge and desire are the core themes of this Special Issue, and they induce examination of the knowing subject and the type of knowledge that it produces. The theme of passion foregrounds relationality, proximity and attachment. These, in their turn, display empathy with the world but also the potential destructiveness and self-destructiveness of that bond. By contrast, the image of dispassionate, objective and rational knowledge is constructed on the spatial metaphor of distance, uninvolvement and estrangement. As we shall see, this theoretical register traverses all the articles in this Special Issue. Indeed, almost all the authors examine, each in his/her own way, the social responsibility of creating, proposing, representing and communicating organizational knowledge. They assign this responsibility to the education system, as well as to 'experts' like ourselves as intellectual workers. But Locatelli's article does so even more forcefully by giving voice to the feminist reflection on gender as politics of knowledge (whose knowledge is considered legitimate knowledge?) and quoting Luce Irigaray (1996): 'Can the "I" separated from the "she" count (or even figure), as an agent of knowledge?'. We shall address this question by translating it as follows: can an organizational knowledge purged of pathos be considered knowledge?

The theme of passion for knowledge and in knowledge prompts further reflection regarding organization studies. Such reflection concerns:

• How a non-instrumental conception of knowledge activates unconventional styles of research, and leads to the identification, invention and communication of forms of organizational understanding based on the revision of analytical and interpretative categories or the construction of new ones
• How the sociology of attachment reveals unusual aspects of the connections among those who work, the objects of their work, and the subjective and objective meanings of work and of organizing work relations
• The results of valorizing forms of sensible knowledge in terms of the theory on organizations and organizing.

319

Organization 14(3)
Introduction

This approach has antecedents and corollaries that are apparent in the essays collected. They include: the strand of studies concerned with aesthetic knowledge about and within organizations (Strati, 1999); the potential role of the humanities in refounding managerial knowledge and in promoting an extended notion of knowledge that also comprises character formation (Gagliardi, 2006); and the 'mystery-driven' knowledge (Gherardi, 1999) related to non-knowledge and practical knowledge (Nicolini et al., 2003).

Before proceeding, we would specify that the term 'passion' does not denote some univocal and easily definable phenomenon. Rather, it is a polysemous term able, in certain respects, to comprise meanings that may even be contradictory: for instance the simultaneous feeling of pleasure and pain. In this regard, passion has a feature in common with the aesthetic category of the sublime as comprising beauty both intense and painful.

Passion in Knowledge and for Knowledge and the Study of Organizations

How can it be argued that knowing is a mundane activity which mobilizes emotions and desires, creates bonds and attachments, and produces pleasure and pain? This task is undertaken by Steve Linstead and Joanne Brewis, who converse with the two invited essays preceding their own.

Whilst Gagliardi and Locatelli deal with the dualisms of utility versus gratuitousness, and rationality versus emotionality, Linstead and Brewis argue that the heuristic and emancipating value of the idea of a passionate knowing is strictly dependent on a non-domesticated reading of the idea of passion, a reading which does not reduce the latter to something else—be it need, aspirant desire as the fulfilment of a lack, or motivation.

Linstead and Brewis recall the etymology of the terms 'passion' and 'desire' to highlight the duplicity and ambiguity of their roots. In Latin, passion conveyed a sense of pain and suffering, and also of passivity. For passion, like love, may be destructive and anything but pleasurable. Those prey to their own passions or those of others are passive: they have lost or relinquished control over themselves. Constructed on the myth of control over oneself and the situation is the image of the volitive and volitional actor: the self-made man (sic!) master of his destiny in the world of organizations created by industrial capitalism. By contrast, being prey to one's passions is indicative not only of intensity of feeling but also of dubious morality and a weakness of will. Moreover, passion binds a person to his/her body, because it is the latter which desires. When the mind is discursively separated from the body, it becomes the seat of knowledge uncontaminated by physical urges and a desiring body. It becomes, for our purposes here, the non-material locus of the sociology of organizations, of organization theories, and management studies—the non-corporeal intermediary of organizational life.

Here, we may again intermingle organizational analysis with other disciplines. In the history of Western philosophy. 'Aristotle', write Linstead

The Passion for Knowing
Silvia Gherardi et al.

and Brewis (p. 355), used the general term *orexis* 'to indicate the natural human desire to know'. This desire calls for practical reason because 'it causes humans to reach out for something or someone'. In fact, someone who 'does not reach out, or has no desire, is *anorexic*'. The desire to know is therefore intrinsic to human nature and, as suggested by the etymology of the Latin term *desiderium* (*de* + *sidu* mening 'toward a celestial object'), it is the force that drives outwards and upwards towards the Other as if it were a 'heavenly body'.

Linstead and Brewis's interpretation of desire as flow—in light of the philosophical reflections of George Bataille and Alexandre Kojève—is set in opposition to interpretations of desire as 'lack of'. The intransitive use of the verb 'desire' enables desire to be viewed as a desiring state: as an amorphous urge—the authors contend (p. 356)—which 'lies beneath our basic curiosity about and willingness to engage with the world'. It is in this sense that the Special Issue proposes a reading of 'knowing as desiring',[2] or in other words, of desire as an epistemological mode to know about the world through the relation that ties the knowing subject to it. Desire constitutes this basic curiosity about the world and willingness to engage with it. As Linstead and Brewis well illustrate (p. 356), the 'reconceptualization of desire as flow allows for "non-knowledge", "the passion for not knowing" (Bataille, 2001: 196), whereby we are drawn to things around us even when they seem at best ambivalent or counterproductive, and at worst threaten to overwhelm or imperil us'.

But Linstead and Brewis's intention is not only to specify a philosophical conception of desire. They also use the conception as the basis for two 'cautionary tales' on how organization studies have appropriated the notion of desire for knowledge and tamed it within a discourse of control. Two constructs in particular have anaesthetized desire in organization studies: its routinization and reduction to motivation, which evinces an endeavour to tame desire; and the discourse of knowledge management that constructs knowledge as something that can be managed/tamed and bent to the organization's will.

Is this to operationalize the concepts of desire and knowledge for practical purposes, or is it to enfeeble the concept of desire for knowledge? The three articles that follow the one by Linstead and Brewis reflect on the topic in light of empirical research. They provide a detailed description of how passion is expressed in desire and through the desire for knowledge in work and organizational settings.

Landscapes of Organizational Knowledge and Passion

The connection among work, the workplace and the object of work is a subjective relation made up of love and hate, obsession and pleasure, exploration and passionate knowledge. In the words of one of the sailors interviewed by Kathy Mack, it is 'feeling alive there'. Consequently, there is a bond of passion with what we do that makes us 'present' when doing

321

Organization 14(3)
Introduction

it, and also with the place where we do it. The aesthetic knowledge that springs from the senses and from the corporeality present in situation is a way of being in-relation with ourselves and with the world. At the same time it is to relate and communicate with those who have the same passion as ourselves by sharing stories, memories and a 'state of mind'.

The first of the three articles which explore the relationship between passion and work describes the passion felt by sailors for the sea and for seascapes. The sea is the workplace of sailors, and the sense of place and the aesthetics of the natural environment are parts of their occupation. Being a competent member of the 'blue water workforce' means knowing what a passion for the sea signifies, recognizing the relation between certain odours and the memories that they evoke, sensing that places have histories and stories, and that these histories and stories form part of individual and collective biography. Mack explores the aesthetic (but also unaesthetic) relationship between the seafaring occupation and the sense of the place in which it is performed. She argues that, because the sea always exceeds the limits of the frame, it becomes both a source of the sublime and an obsession. The sea is to sailor what the object of research work is to Knorr Cetina's scientists: an endless source of attraction and pathos that becomes an inexhaustible and incontrollable lure. In this sense, her analysis can be extended to other occupations as well. And in fact, the aesthetic bond between individual, workplace, object of work and the community of workers is again apparent among the mathematicians studied by Paolo Landri, or in the community of Weblog producers described by Kaiser and colleagues.

What Kathy Mack's article highlights is the materiality of the passional bond. The passion for knowledge is anchored in the corporeality and physicality of the work setting. The 'sense of place' constitutes the symbiotic connection between aesthetic knowledge and the multisensorial experiences of people at work. Workplaces are not abstract containers of equally abstract activities. Rather, they are actively appropriated and interiorized by:

- The body and its perceptive faculties (feeling, seeing, smelling, hearing and tasting): intrinsic to all of these faculties is the sensitive-aesthetic judgement
- The community of workers, which develops a vocabulary to communicate those sensations, learn and distinguish them, to enjoy them (or be repelled by them), and to transmit them to new members
- The discursive practices that give shape to the negotiative processes which give rise to the aesthetic categories used in organizational action, which develop and stabilize an aesthetic knowledge conserved in the community's work practices, and which pass aesthetic judgement on the beauty or ugliness of one practice compared to another.

Aesthetic knowledge is passionate knowledge; just as passion is the aesthetic relationship with the world, both because it passes through

The Passion for Knowing
Silvia Gherardi et al.

the senses, and because it underpins the aesthetic judgements with which a community relates to the work practices that distinguish it. Aesthetic judgements about the workplace, its natural environment, and the persons who perform it, socially sustain work practices.

Paolo Landri's study of a school of mathematicians theorizes passion as 'active conditioning', where the explicit reference is to a sociology of attachments (Hennion, 1993). Whether studied in a community of enthusiasts (for music, drugs, wine) or in a community of practitioners, passion is considered to be an activity which weaves together the individual, the community, the knowledge object, and the environment in which these relations arise. As an activity, passion creates continuity between what are apparently opposites: in the words of Gomart and Hennion (1999: 227) between 'passivity and activity, determining and determined, collective and individual, and intention as against causality'.

The mathematicians of the Naples school demonstrate how passion for the knowledge object is a force which creates community and identity. It drives the discussion within the epistemic community on what constitutes good and elegant mathematical practice, and thus enables the practice itself to be innovated. Landri's article depicts passion not just as an emotion or an individual relationship, but as a situated practice of knowledge transmission, and as a historically situated cultural practice of meaning creation, belonging, community, and organization. Hence, the passion for the knowledge object which underpins an occupation or a skill is also an 'organizing' practice: it creates organizations, and organized groups within organizations. Passion therefore socially sustains work practices, and the continuing practise of the latter requires constant discussion among the practitioners on what constitutes a good practice.

Weber (1919) wrote that there is a vocation (*Beruf*), or calling, in professions. Does not being 'called', in the secular sense, represent the intimate and passionate relationship with what one does? Landri adds a pragmatic dimension to this view by showing that the maintenance and transmission of passion is a social practice within work practices. The mathematicians of Naples, whom Landri studies by historically reconstructing the life of their charismatic leader, formed a school within the mathematics before World War II and created a school of thought which was able to survive through the routinization of passion.

Passion can be seen as the situated mobilization of feelings, understandings, identities, practices and organizations, which unfolds on appropriate occasions. Passion is therefore socially produced and reproduced, and it sustains both the object of mathematicians' work and their identity, as well as the material organization of doing mathematics at a particular time.

The passion-mobilizing practices described by Landri—and which can be found in other professional communities which work with knowledge—are celebrating talent, arguing about work practices with other communities of practitioners, socially constructing the beauty of the knowledge object, founding the division of labour on competence, extolling the community, and keeping its memories alive.

Organization 14(3)
Introduction

Passion as the attachment of people in knowledge-related practices is also described as technologically-mediated passion in the article by Stephan Kaiser, Gordon Müller-Seitz, Miguel Lopes and Miguel Pina e Cunha. Their contribution leads us through the landscape of the Blogoshere,[3] and prompts us to ask whether there is a difference between looking at the sea with passion and gazing at a computer screen. These are two different panoramas which can be taken to be paradigmatic of a love for nature and a love for technology. It is possible to lose oneself in both the sea and the computer screen: we may surrender to both of them in an act of love; both can make us suffer. Technoscapes are today's new ecosystems, and they are also a new source of metaphors for knowledge and the collective imagination.

The term 'Blogoshere' denotes the set of Weblogs interconnected by various means of interlinking on the internet and constituting a distinctive IT-instantiated media ecosystem. As a metaphor it evokes a lifestyle, a post-capitalist ethic (Himanen, 2001), the cultural movement of open source development, and practices of freedom and communality. The Blogoshere is therefore a technological medium of high symbolic value embedded in strongly ideologized interpretative frames. In a certain sense, it is an ideal setting in which to study knowledge production and circulation practices, and it well represents passion for knowledge for its own sake. Open source embodies a community which voluntarily devotes time and energy to producing a knowledge-intensive good developed collaboratively. In this case, technology is the environment of the cooperation as well as its medium and purpose. The gratuitousness of this collaboration generally resists instrumental explanation, and is therefore construed in terms of 'passion'. But in what does this passion consist, and what drives the practice of Weblogging?

The authors use the standard terms of motivation theory, distinguishing between intrinsic and extrinsic motives. Within this framework they show that technological mediation gives rise to new discursive practices, and therefore to diverse forms of participation in discourses on practices. Their reasoning on the passion for knowledge proceeds as follows. They begin by arguing that Weblogging mingles pleasure with suffering, and that passion as the experience of pain and suffering arises during flow states (Csikszentmihalyi, 1997) which occur while reading, commenting upon, and writing Weblog entries.

According to Kaiser and colleagues (p. 405), flow states are self-motivating experiences 'that can be characterized roughly as an intense and focused concentration whereby action and awareness are merged so that temporal awareness is distorted'. Pleasure resides in flow, in the fit between the difficulty of the task and the competence of the person, while anxiety or boredom characterizes the misfit.

Desire for this kind of pleasure can be described as passion for an activity as an end in itself, or as a state of grace in which the distinction between the

324

The Passion for Knowing
Silvia Gherardi et al.

self and the world disappears and pleasure is experienced as the plenitude of self and absence of desire. Domination over technology is the moment when the latter becomes incorporated into the subject and the activity, so that there is only 'presence' or flow.

Can cyberspace as rarefaction of space and time more easily produce the pleasure of flow? The experience of Weblog practitioners shows that it can, even when the flow is accompanied by suffering and comprises passion's two semantic referents: suffering and attraction.

However, Kaiser and colleagues are less interested in the subjective dimension of attachment to work for its pleasure's sake than they are in the collective dimension of Weblogging as a social practice which creates its community of practitioners. In this latter context, the authors argue, the motives of Webloggers are extrinsic and based on social recognition and the reputation acquired as an expert practitioner. This interpretation echoes the findings in the literature on communities of practices, but the authors add a further dimension: that where the Blogosphere is a specific context of practices. In what sense is now explained.

We have seen in the cases of seamen and mathematicians that passion for knowledge and in knowing are mediated by and anchored in corporeality and materiality, and also in conversations both direct and indirect. Web-loggers evidence that technological mediation heightens the pleasure intrinsic to work by intensifying and 'densifying' the discursive practices that sustain work practices. If we base our interpretation on the distinction between talking *in* practice and talking *about* practice (Gherardi, 2006), we find that the Weblog is a large discursive ecosystem in which practitioners develop knowledge through discourse both about practice and in practice. We have seen the aesthetic dimension of talk about practice in the case of the Naples mathematicians who disputed on proofs, doing so at a time when they could only do so at a distance with published papers. Talk about practices keeps those practices alive, gains them accreditation in the community, and institutionalizes them. The Blogoshere has become a technological environment in which discursive practices determine participation in the community and anchor the passion for Weblogging itself. In regard to how the practices enabling participation in the discourse on practice come about, Kaiser and colleagues cite the following factors:

- Freedom to decide upon one's own involvement regarding the use of the Weblog (a practice of freedom);
- The ability to have an impact in improving the software (a practice of direct participation);
- The social bonds among Webloggers (a practice of social linking).

The passion for the object of knowing is therefore anchored in, and develops through, participation in the conversations that create and maintain the community. And technologies are important media for developing and maintaining attachment to the activity.

Organization 14(3)
Introduction

Bringing Passion and Invention Back on the Agenda

The Special Issue closes with an article by Pascal Dey and Chris Stayaert which reflects critically on management education in business schools and furnishes an image—the troubadouresque—with which to explore and configure alternative knowledge-production based on the passion for knowledge: the love for wisdom and aesthetic understanding. This article completes the trajectory that began with the invited essays by making explicit the reflexive and metatheoretical concern with organizational knowledge-creation that traverses all the articles and inspires them in various ways. In other words, Dey and Steyaert's article directs our attention not only to teaching practices in management schools—in which many of the contributors to this Special Issue work—but also, and especially, to knowledge-production practices. It thus explicitly expresses a concern and a reflexive attitude regarding the passion for developing and communicating organizational knowledge of a more general kind.

We may say, in fact, that two lines of argument traverse all reflection on the connection between passion and knowledge in and about organizations:

- The first concerns passionate attachment to knowledge for its own sake. This argument comprises a radical critique of the instrumentality of knowing, the commodification of knowledge, and the view of knowledge as a new production factor—what Lyotard (1984) has called the 'performativity' of knowledge;
- The second concerns a reflexive attitude in 'academic' writing—that is, personal and collective practices to 'produce knowledge' and the 'knowledge object'—which more or less openly questions its position in doing so, and the effects that these practices produce.

Consequently, reflection on education can be viewed as reflection on the work practices that unite organizational scholars as authors producing and reproducing institutionalized knowledge. This reflection therefore concerns the crux of the debate on 'knowledge productive' practices: how can the McDonaldized dystopia of the educational institutions be subverted? The search for an answer proceeds by degrees, but it centres crucially on the image of an 'affirmative invention'.

Dey and Steyaert describe a 'reflective practice' based on Derrida's notion of deconstruction 'as a counter-force to the restrictive influence of end-orientation' (p. 11), on a 'culture of questioning' as defined by Giroux (2005), and all the pedagogies in which knowledge and knowing are propelled by passion and mystery. The authors resume the critique against 'problem-driven' knowledge and explore the image of knowledge as relation with the unknown, the mysterious, the Other (Gherardi, 1999). The concept proposed is that of unconditionality (and of the unconditional university): a sort of utopia 'which capitalizes on the tension between dream and reality, and which invites passion, dedication and play and seeks transformation without enforcing it' (p. 17). While Derrida's pedagogy combines passion and knowledge, Serres' combines critique and invention.

The Passion for Knowing
Silvia Gherardi et al.

Hence the troubadour of knowledge, or better the troubadouresque as 'an index of personal style and sensibility' (p. 25), is finally proposed to represent a utopia consisting of passionate knowledge, Whitehead's 'atmosphere of excitement', and the spirit of the 'epicurean learners that combine adeptness with passion' (p. 25).

This relates to the desire and the passion that have inspired this Special Issue: the endeavour to explore the research styles and practices that communicate the open road where the humanities are rediscovered and passionate knowledge about the life of organizations is formed. In the awareness that, just as every dystopia contains a fragment of utopia, so the performativity of knowledge denounced by Lyotard as one of the main features of the post-modern condition contains a utopian antidote in the passion for knowledge.

Notes

1 The Special Issue comprises two invited papers (Gagliardi and Locatelli) whose authors have been key-note speakers at the conference 'The Passion for Learning and Knowing' that took place in Trento (9–11 July 2005) organized by the three editors of the special issue.
2 At the 17th EGOS Colloqium, (Lyon, 5–7 July 2001) there was a subgroup on 'Knowing as Desiring', convened by Silvia Gherardi, Hervé Laroche and Elena Antonacoupolou, in which the theme of knowledge and desire in organizations was proposed and which gave birth to the Standing Working Group on Practice-based Studies that continues reflection on sensible knowledge and working practices.
3 Blogoshere or Blogsphere is the collective term encompassing all Weblogs or blogs; or bloggers as a community.

References

Arendt, Anna (1959) *The Human Condition*. New York, NY: Doubleday.
Barbalet, Jack (2005) 'Smith's *Sentiments* (1759) and Wright's *Passions* (1601): The Beginnings of Sociology', *The British Journal of Sociology* 56(2): 171–89.
Bataille, Georges (2001) *The Unfinished System of Nonknowledge*. Minneapolis, MN: University of Minnesota Press.
Bodei, Remo (1991) *Geometria delle passioni. Paura, speranza, felicità: filosofia e uso politico*. Milano: Feltrinelli.
Csikszentmihalyi, Mihaly (1997) *Finding Flow: The Psychology of Engagement with Everyday Life*. New York, NY: Basic Books.
Elias, Norbert (1994) *The Civilizing Process*. Oxford: Blackwell (originally published in 1936).
Freidson, Eliot (1990) 'Labors of Love in Theory and Practice: A Prospectus', in K. Erikson and S.Vallas (eds) *The Nature of Work*. Yale, CT: University Press.
Gagliardi, Pasquale (2006) 'A Role for Humanities in the Formation of Managers', in P. Gagliardi and B. Czarniawska (eds) *Management Education and Humanities*. Northampton: Edward Elgar Publishing, Inc.
Gherardi, Silvia (1999) 'Learning as Problem-driven or Learning in the Face of Mystery?', *Organization Studies* 20(1): 101–24.

Organization 14(3)
Introduction

Gherardi, S. (2006), *Organizational Knowledge: The Texture of Workplace Learning.* Oxford: Blackwell Publishers.

Giroux, Henry A. (2005) 'Higher Education and Democracy's Promise: Jacques Derrida's Pedagogy of Uncertainty', in Peter P. Trifonas and Michael A. Peters (eds) *Deconstructing Derrida: Tasks for the New Humanities,* pp. 53–81. New York, NY: Palgrave MacMillan.

Gomart, Emilie and Hennion, Antoine (1999) 'A Sociology of Attachment: Music, Amateurs, Drug Users', in J. Law and J. Hassard (eds) *Actor Network and After,* pp. 220–47. Oxford: Blackwell Publishers.

Halliwell, Martin. (1999) *Romantic Science and the Experience of the Self: Transatlantic Crosscurrents from William James to Oliver Sacks.* Aldershot: Ashgate.

Hennion, Antoine (1993) *La passion musicale. Une sociologie de la médiation.* Paris: Métailié.

Himanen, Pekka (2001) *The Hacker Ethic and the Spirit of Information Age.* New York, NY: Random House Inc.

Irigaray, Luce (1996) 'The Other: Woman', in *I Love to You: Sketch for a Felicità Within History.* London: Routledge

James, Susan (1997) *Passions and Action: The Emotions in Seventeenth-Century Philosophy.* Oxford: Oxford University Press.

Knorr-Cetina, Karin (1997) 'Sociality with Objects', *Theory, Culture, and Society,* 14(4): 1–30.

Knorr-Cetina, Karin (2006) 'Post-humanist Challenges to the Human and Social Sciences', in P. Gagliardi and B. Czarniawska (eds) *Management Education and Humanities.* Northampton: Edward Elgar Publishing, Inc.

Lyotard, Jean François (1984) *The Postmodern Condition,* Manchester: Manchester University Press.

Nicolini, D., Gherardi, S., Yanow, D., eds (2003) *Knowing in Organizations: A Practice-based Approach.* Armonk, NY: ME Sharpe.

Smith, Adam (1759) *The Theory of Moral Sentiments.* Oxford: Oxford University Press (1976 edition).

Strati, Antonio (1999) *Organization and Aesthetics.* London: Sage.

Strati, Antonio (2007) 'Sensible Knowledge and Practice-based Learning', *Management Learning* 38(1): 61–77.

Schawlbe, Michael. (1986) *The Psychosocial Consequences of Natural and Alienated Work.* New York, NY: SUNY Press.

Weber, M. (1919) *Politik als Beruf, Wissenschaft als Beruf.* Berlin: Duncker & Humblot.

Silvia Gherardi is Professor of Sociology of Work at the University of Trento, Italy, where she is responsible for the Research Unit on Communication, Organizational Learning, and Aesthetics (RUCOLA). Her research activities focus on workplace learning and knowing. Her theorethical background is in qualitative sociology and organizational symbolism. **Address:** Dipartimento di Sociologia e Ricerca Sociale, piazza Venezia 41, I-38100 Trento, Italy. [email: silvia.gherardi@soc.unitn.it]

Davide Nicolini is Assistant Professor and RCUK Fellow at the Research Unit on Innovation Knowledge and Organizational Networks (IKON) of Warwick Business School. His recent work focuses on the development of a practice-based approach to the study

The Passion for Knowing
Silvia Gherardi et al.

of organizations and its application tho understanding of knowing, learning, and change in organizations. **Address:** IKON, Warwick Business School, University of Warwick, Coventry, CV4 7AL, UK. [email: davide.nicolini@wbs.ac.uk]

Antonio Strati is Professor of Sociology of Organization and lectures at the Universities of Trento and Siena, Italy. He is a founder-member of the Standing Conference on Organizational Symbolism (SCOS-EGOS), and of the Research Unit on Communication, Organizational Learning and Aesthetics (www.unitn.it/rucola). His research interests focus on aesthetics and the qualitative study of organizational life. **Address:** Dipartimento di Sociologia e Ricerca Sociale, piazza Venezia 41, I-38100 Trento, Italy. [email: antonio.strati@soc.unitn.it]

[11]

Management Learning
Copyright © The Author(s), 2009.
Reprints and permissions:
http://www.sagepub.co.uk/journalsPermissions.nav
http://mlq.sagepub.com
Vol. 40(5): 535–550
1350-5076

Article

Silvia Gherardi
University of Trento, Italy

Practice? It's a Matter of Taste!

Abstract *This article aims to enhance our understanding of how practice is socially sustained, learnt and constantly refined by arguing that practice is much more than a set of activities—it involves, beside instrumental and ethical judgements, taste and appraisal. Taste is a sense of what is aesthetically fitting within a community of practitioners—a preference for 'the way we do things together'. Taste is based on subjective attachment to the object of practice and is learnt and taught as part of becoming a practitioner; it is performed as a collective, situated activity within a practice. The elaboration of taste and the refining of practice within a community involves taste-making, which is based on 'sensible knowledge' and the continual negotiation of aesthetic categories. The article examines how in a variety of practices, taste-making occurs through three processes: sharing a vocabulary for appraisal; crafting identities within epistemic communities; and refining performances. **Key Words:** attachment; normative accountability; practice-based studies; sensible knowledge; taste-making*

Introduction

Practice theories have attracted a great deal of attention from organizational and management scholars in recent years (Brown and Duguid, 1991, 2001; Orr, 1996; Gherardi, 2000; Orlikowski, 2000; Yanow, 2004) and a new label—Practice-based Studies—has been coined to denote an heterogeneous ensemble of empirical studies with no common definition of the term 'practice'. As the collected book edited by Schatzki, Knorr-Cetina and Von Savigny (2001) exemplifies, practice-based studies represent 'a practice turn', despite their internal differences.

The reasons in favour of naming yet another turn in organization studies reside in the critical lens used to criticize the rational-cognitivist view of knowledge and to reject the conventional distinction between micro and macro levels of explanations. What many studies of practice have in common is an interest in the collective, situated and provisional nature of knowledge and a sense of shared materiality in such diverse fields of practices as technological innovation (Orlikowski, 2000), photocopier repairing (Orr, 1996), bridge building (Suchman, 2000), strategy development (Blackler et al., 2000; Samra-Fredericks, 2005), *haute*

DOI: 10.1177/1350507609340812

cuisine (Gomez et al., 2003), to name just a few. At the same time, disagreements persist on central issues such as the conception of practice itself.

The greater spread and acceptance of practice-based studies have been accompanied by concerns over their loss of critical power when the term 'practice' is assumed to be synonymous with 'routine', 'competitive advantage', 'embodied skills', or taken to be a generic equivalent of 'what people do', without theoretical foundations illuminating the nature of the object of study and its original and distinctive contribution to understanding the social order. With reference to scientific practices, Rouse (2002: 161) argues that there is confusion in the field owing to two ways of understanding practice: 1) practices identified with regularities or commonalities among the activities of social groups; 2) practices characterized in terms of normative accountability of various performances.

The first definition leads to the domestication of practice-based studies, in that practices become equated with activities and their productive endeavour. The second definition, to which this article intends to contribute, makes it possible to signify both our production of the world and the result of the production process. Practices are not only recurrent patterns of action (level of production) but also recurrent patterns of *socially* sustained action (production and reproduction). What people produce in their situated practices is not only work, but also the (re)production of society. In this sense, practice is an analytic concept that enables interpretation of how people achieve active being-in-the-world. A practice is not recognizable outside its intersubjectively created meaning, and what makes possible the competent reproduction of a practice over and over again and its refinement while being practised (or its abandonment) is the constant negotiation of what is thought to be a correct or incorrect way of practising within the community of its practitioners.

The topic of how the reproduction of practices contributes to the production of social order within working practices has been neglected by practice-based studies. Its under-evaluation prevents us from studying how practices are socially sustained through situated ways of learning the criteria for appraising and situated ways of transmitting them. The present article intends to illustrate how the passionate attachment of a community of practitioners to the object of their practice is the basis of taste-making, i.e. a collective achievement that allows practitioners to appraise the various performances of their working practices that, in being appraised and contested, are constantly refined.

In the following sections I shall first describe how a sociology of attachments can contribute to framing the relationship between a community and the object of its practice in terms of aesthetic judgements that socially sustain the meaning of the practice for its practitioners. Then I shall argue that the elaboration of a vocabulary for appraising the nuances of a competent practice performance and for transmitting (and contesting) these constitutes the core of the activity of taste-making. I define taste-making as a collective, emergent discursive process that constantly refines practices, and which is done by saying, and which is said by doing. I therefore distinguish analytically three processes internal to taste-making and present them in separate sections: sharing a vocabulary for appraisal; crafting identities within epistemic communities; and refining performances. In the concluding section I shall discuss how taste-making sustains working practices, their skilled reproduction, and competent refinement.

Situating Taste and Aesthetic Judgment within Practices: A Sociology of Attachment

There has developed within the sociology of translation (or Actor-Network Theory, ANT) an interesting theory of the subjective attachment to action that problematizes the way in which the subject is conceived and how it relates to the object and the context. Just as in ANT studies 'objects have been turned into networks and thereby radically re-defined. An analogous project is now starting to take shape: the study of subject-networks' (Gomart and Hennion, 1999: 220). This is a project that centres its theoretical and empirical inquiry on the attachment of subjects to the objects of their passion, and asks how practitioners are able to put their passions into practice (Gherardi et al., 2007) and how practising their passions may contribute to the development of a field of practices and the elaboration of an aesthetics of practice.

Attachment is defined as the reflexive result of a corporeal, collective and orchestrated practice regulated by methods that, in their turn, are ceaselessly discussed (Gomart and Hennion, 1999) within the community of practitioners. While psychology has traditionally framed attachment (and attachment theory) in terms of relationship with other humans (caregivers or beloved ones), a sociology of attachment also sees it in relation to non-material and non-human objects. The attachment to the object of practice—be it of love or hate, or of love and hate—is what makes practices socially sustained by judgments related not only to utility, but to ethics and aesthetics as well.

Taste and amateur practices, like those of music buffs, food or wine tasters, or even drug addicts, constitute the empirical basis on which a sociology of attachments has developed (Hennion, 1993, 2001; Teil, 1998; Gomart and Hennion, 1999; Hennion and Maisonneuve, 2000; Hennion and Teil, 2004; Hennion, 2007). The relationship with the object—food, music, drug—exemplifies a relation in which the amateur is indeed active, that is, she or he deploys a set of situated practices in order to use and enjoy the object of his/her passion individually and collectively, but she or he is also passive, in that she or he deliberately, and in a 'cultivated' manner, abandons him/herself to the effect of the object in so far as she or he predisposes the material conditions for the enjoyment of music, food or drugs and socially shares this passion within a community of amateurs. The relationship may be developed with a physical object but also with an abstract one—mathematics, accounting, a brand of car—or more generally, all the objects of a working practice.

The word 'amateur' has a Latin root: *amare*, which literally means 'to love'. An amateur is somebody who practices as a dabbler (i.e. non-professional, not for duty) and somebody who practices for the love of what she or he does. An amateur of classical music is therefore not a professional, but common sense holds that a soprano is a lover of classical music. I therefore propose to analyse practitioners as 'amateurs', in order to explore the collective dimension of the attachment to the work object that sustains working practices and makes them change over time. Talking of practitioners as 'amateurs' may seem a contradiction in terms, yet this signals that work has been stripped of the passionate element and subjected to a predominantly instrumental logic.

The attachment that ties the practitioner to his/her practice and its object, as well as to his/her identity as a practitioner and to other practitioners, is a problem of a passionate and pleasurable or painful relation both shared and collectively elaborated. Attachment is not only the relation with the object of practice and the associated feelings—it is also the effect of the collective formation of taste at the moment when the aesthetic judgments supporting the practice are formed. Taste may therefore be conceived in terms of taste-making, i.e. a situated activity that rests on learning and knowing how to appraise specific performances of a practice.

Belonging to a choir and gaining pleasure from music, and belonging to a scientific community and gaining pleasure from a particularly brilliant article, are forms of attachment socially supported by the respective communities, which have developed vocabularies and specific criteria of taste in order to communicate, share and refine the ways in which such practices are enacted. Practitioners in both fields can be termed 'amateurs', in the sense that they 'dwell' in a practice and experience an intellectual pleasure that they share with others.

When I say that practitioners 'dwell' in their practice, I am referring to Heidegger's concept of dwelling as feeling at home and finding shelter; in opposing building to dwelling he is even more explicit:

> Usually we take production to be an activity whose performance has a result, the finished structure, as its consequence. It is possible to conceive of making in that way; we thereby grasp something that is correct, and yet never touch its nature, which is a producing that brings something forth. (Heidegger, 1971: 113)

To define practice as activity is like looking at 'building', while the stress on practices as accountability is like 'dwelling'.

The relationship between building and dwelling was used by Heidegger (1971) to question the relation between means and ends. One of his famous dictums is that 'dwelling comes before building', and we see in this phrase the idea that a social practice comes together with the tools that enable it. He writes: 'to dwell means merely that we take shelter in them [the buildings]' (p. 145). And Polanyi (1958/1962: 195) uses the expression 'dwelling in a practice' in order to emphasize that it is both intimate acquaintance with, and mastery of, a practice that generates the pleasure of practising it: 'astronomic observations are made by dwelling in astronomic theory, and it is this internal enjoyment of astronomy which make the astronomer interested in the stars. This is how scientific value is contemplated "from within".'

When work practices are viewed 'from within', what is of interest to the researcher is the intellectual, passionate, ethical and aesthetic attachment that ties subjects to objects, technologies, the places of practices and other practitioners. In particular, I shall pay attention to the elaboration of taste 'from within' a community of practitioners and to the deployment of discursive practices for expressing aesthetic judgements, since taste is learned and taught as part of becoming a practitioner and it is performed as a collective, situated activity—taste-making—within a practice.

The sociology of attachment furnishes a theoretical framework (and a methodology) particularly suited to the study of practices as collectively supported by the constant refinement of taste within a community of practitioners, because it is based on a set of 'shifts' which propose a different conception of action (Gomart and Hennion, 1999):

- From *action* to *passion*. Instead of focusing on the subjects, the researcher asks: through what mechanisms is this kind of 'active passion' performed?
- From '*who acts*' to '*what occurs*'. Instead of focusing on action, the researcher turns to events and asks: what occurs, how is the effect produced, which mediators are present?
- From *making* to *feeling*. The researcher asks: how can certain people tentatively help events to occur? How is feeling actively accomplished?

With these questions in mind, we can regard the normative accountability of practices as pragmatics, i.e. in terms of a reflexive activity mediated by language (Hennion, 2001). In the next section we shall thus see emerging in the practitioner-amateur the figure (and the lexicon) of the critic—she or he who formulates aesthetic judgements on practice.

Learning Practices and Taste as a Collective Achievement

The sociology of attachment proposes a conception of taste at odds with the sociological tradition, which since Veblen (1899/1970), Simmel (1905/1981) and Bourdieu (1979) has set taste in relation to a process of social distinction and has analysed the aesthetic judgment in relation to cultural consumptions, and the influence of elites in spreading fashions as imposition and imitation. This sociological literature on taste bases itself on a strategic theory of taste formation that gives a pre-eminent explanatory role to socio-economic status and the refinement process, meaning increasing sophistication of taste according to social distinction and systems of domination. We may therefore argue that while classic sociological theories on taste assumed a macrosociological framework, by contrast, it was first Blumer (1969) and then Douglas (1996) and DiMaggio (1997) who set taste in relation to a process of 'collective selection' and the local negotiation of taste within distinct institutional settings. More or less at the same time, an interest in aesthetics was born within organization studies (Strati, 1992) and flourished in the following years.

Within philosophy, Gadamer (1960) saw taste as the point of contact between analytic and continental philosophers, between historical and aesthetic culture, and between logical and scientific culture. For Gadamer, therefore, taste is the ability to discriminate and to criticize, but without recourse to absolute principles. This 'relative' dimension enables us to understand that the aesthetic judgment supports local and situated modes of practising, and while it sustains a normative accountability of practice it constantly refines its modalities, nourishing the passion of the practitioners for what they do.

In organization studies in particular, interest in aesthetics has produced an impressive body of literature (Strati, 2009) exploring the non-rational dimension of organizational life, where taste is analysed within the micro-politics of everyday aesthetic judgements and in relation to knowing through the senses. Sensible knowledge 'is a form of knowing and acting directed towards "sensible" worlds; it concerns what is perceived through the senses and is judged, produced and reproduced through them. It is profoundly different from the knowledge produced through the ratiocinative faculty directed towards "intelligible" worlds' (Strati, 2007: 62). Sensible knowledge, feeling as a modality of relating with the world, underpins the aesthetic judgment that expresses our feelings of pleasure or displeasure. But 'beauty or ugliness are confused phenomena, so that it is on the judgement of the senses that we must rely' (Strati, 1999: 109). And, following Kant, the judgement of the senses is the confused judgement that applies to the perfection or imperfection of a particular thing and has the nature of sentiment or taste.

Therefore, I frame taste as 'a problematic modality of attachment to the world' (Hennion, 2004: 10), and in order to move from the relationship with the object of practice to the formation of an aesthetic judgment I have to introduce the role of language. This requires reference to pragmatics, a discipline of linguistics which analyses language as a discursive, communicative and social phenomenon (Jacques, 1979).

There are several strands within pragmatics, but the one closest to the sociological sensibility considers the origin of signification in the practical use made of it, and therefore studies the ability of natural language speakers to communicate more than what they explicitly state. The pragmatic competence developed within a community of practitioners—as in the case that I am about to describe of participants on a course on odours—consists not only of the appropriation of an expert vocabulary and its competent use during interactions, but also in knowing how to understand what others are saying, in regard to its implications for action and as the expression of the aesthetic judgement. The pragmatics of communication among practitioners, within their community, develops and refines the taste for the practice through talk *about* the practice and its evaluation according to aesthetic categories that are not necessarily made explicit. Moreover, empirically analysing the pragmatics of communication among practitioners enables us to describe how practices are taught and learned within a community.

To give an example, I refer to an article by Geneviève Teil (1998), which describes how she learned to develop taste during a course to train the sense of smell. This sense and the professional skills associated with it constitute a field of expertise in demand by both the food and perfume industries. This ability can be learned in the surprisingly short period of five days, but its maintenance requires constant practice. In order to study the transmission of this knowledge, Teil attended the course and conducted self-ethnography as well as participant observation. How, therefore, does one become a taster? Teil describes how learning produced changes in tastes and in olfactory practices during the training course, and how this brought about a change in the relationship between the novice and the object through:

• learning how to manage one's body and brain, so that the 'olfactory tool' is circumscribed within the body;

Learning and Knowing in Practice-Based Studies   *163*

Gherardi: Practice? It's a Matter of Taste!   541

- learning how to use the tool in accordance with collective norms; and above all
- learning how to check its operation in a suitable way.

The trajectory of learning therefore proceeds through: (a) feeling (perception of sensory impressions which delimit a context and an olfactory measure, and control over the brain's interpretations); (b) describing (development of a classificatory language with which to categorize sensations and to communicate, abandonment of the hedonism of feeling oneself naive, acquisition of an expert aesthetic to judge sensations), (c) using (to stabilize the link between the odour and its olfactory descriptor, gaining control over application of the metrological criteria that enable measurement of the relationship between describer and odour, and relying on the network of practitioners in order to heighten the performance of the olfactory tool).

From Teil's theoretical analysis we ascertain not only that the learning of sensory knowledge develops through stages, extending from the mundane knowledge of the novice to the mastery of expert knowledge within a professional community, but also how participation in the community is contextual to the learning of an expert language with which to express aesthetic judgments. As this process unfolds, the novice changes into an expert, and the expert into a critic of taste, and each of these figures has a different relationship with the object because it engages in practices specific to each community: simple amateurs, experts or critics.

I have illustrated how taste starts from sensible experience to become an aesthetic judgment and finally a professional competence. My purpose has been to show that 'with taste the faculty to judge is freed from every logical function (...), taste is a reflexive or evaluative judgement that enables the discovery of the subjective conditions of knowledge' (Brugère, 2000: 5). Moreover, this modality allows me to direct attention to:

- the body as the instrument and primary source of the relationship with the world, as well as the source of sensible knowledge;
- language as a means to interpret and describe sensible knowledge, and
- the collective dimension of the elaboration of situated discursive practices.

In the sections that follow, I shall analyse how taste-making is a collective achievement realized through three processes: the collective development of a lexicon of taste; the formation of a sense of belonging to an epistemic community; and the refining of performances through the negotiation of aesthetic judgements.

Sharing a Vocabulary for Appraisal

Gaining pleasure from the object of a practice and sharing this pleasure with other practitioners is something that is learned and taught to newcomers through the collective elaboration of a shared lexicon for communicating about sensible feelings.

One of the best-known examples in this regard is provided by Cook and Yanow (1993). It concerns flutemakers and how apprentices are trained to learn whether a flute sounds right. In this production process, each flute is worked on by several flutemakers in succession and each craftsman is skilled in only a few aspects of the process. A flute goes down the production line but also back up it, until it is ready. In describing how this takes place, Cook and Yanow (1993: 380) note that:

> a flutemaker would typically make only cryptic remarks, such as 'it does not feel right' or 'This bit doesn't look quite right'. The first flutemaker would then rework the piece until both were in agreement that it had 'the right feel' or 'the right look'.

When the apprentice became a judge of his own work, this marked of the end of the apprenticeship, and

> in this way, at one and at the same time, an apprentice would both acquire a set of skills in flutemaking and become a member of the informal quality control system that has unfalteringly maintained the style and quality of these instruments. (p. 380)

In this example, taste-making is performed through (few) words, gestures and the tacit negotiation surrounding the development of sensible knowledge. The material and discursive practices that allow the negotiation of sensible know-ledge simultaneously construct the normative accountability of the practice and the taste for 'the right sound'. But how is taste routinized, stabilized, but also innovated within a community to become an organizational element, as in the style of a restaurant? The example that follows shows that repetition and innovation are not antithetical.

I shall refer to a study (Gomez et al., 2003) of French *haute cuisine* restaurants that describes the creation, routinization and innovation of taste among the chefs. The authors report that when a chef has an idea for a new course, he draws a technical card which is distributed to members of the team. His technical cards are handwritten. They describe the courses, their style, their own world and their tone. They are not recipes; they do not codify quantities or cooking times. As Chef A puts it:

> There is a technical card [...] which gives them [the cooks] the general outline and we discuss it before they implement it. [...] I give them a framework within which they do whatever they want [...] They do what they want but the framework is precise [...] They are not automatons.
>
> [...]
>
> Starting with the technical card cooks give life to Chef A's ideas. The result (what is on the plate) is then tasted by Chef A and discussed with the team to adjust it by 95%. This is where 'innovations' by cooks can enrich the course. (Gomez et al., 2003: 114)

This example shows how taste-making is collective and incremental, and uses sensible knowledge and a vocabulary for appraisal that allows for very practical material goals—producing flutes or dishes—and at the same time allows for identities and pleasures or disgust, as in the following examples.

In fact aesthetics is also about the ugly and the painful, because workplaces, as sources of sensible knowledge and aesthetic judgement, are often unpleasant and malodorous, and the vocabulary to express the disgust is distasteful. For example, Patricia Martin (2002: 867), in an ethnography on old people's homes, describes how:

> I saw OPH [old people's home] staff socially constructing residents' bodies through talk and practice. They enacted a conception of bodies – as strong or weak, able or disabled, touchable or untouchable, clean or dirty, fair or foul smelling – in ways that shaped residents' perceptions, experiences, and feelings.

The effect of the staff's pragmatics of taste on residents' self-conception is reported also by Gubrium (1975), in a study of US nursing homes. In such organizations, staff members are routinely required to perform tasks that they view as repugnant and even disgusting. He describes the removal of impacted faeces from extremely constipated residents; staff don plastic gloves and reach inside the resident's rectum to 'gouge' out hardened, dried faeces, bit by bit. Staff hate this task relative to the sights, smells and touch it entails, and their distaste often transfers to the residents, diminishing their show of respect and attentiveness.

Patricia Martin introduces the term 'spirit of a place' in order to focus on a form of organizational knowledge that reflects a facility's culture and *emotional climate* relative to social relations, practices, routines and tacit understandings. The spirit of a place is an efficacious expression to convey the type of emotional attachment, sensible knowledge and aesthetic judgement that a collectivity expresses through the situated activity of taste-making.

Other researchers, like Kathy Mack (2007), who studied sailors' attachment to the sea, suggest that workplaces are sensed through multi-sensory experiences (sight, sound, taste, smell and touch) that bring forth the 'senses of place' and make them more accessible. For example, seascapes are *sensed* through the stories accumulated in the nooks and crannies of sailors' steel mobile homes that form a structure upon which sailors may build a sense of seascapes. For seafarers, these stories carry the tacit knowledge of seafaring and at the same time construct and express it.

The elaboration of an appraisal vocabulary (be it cryptic expressions, indexical accounts or full narratives) allows practitioners to communicate aesthetic judgements and express their passion for the object of practice and their sense of place.

Crafting Identities and Epistemic Communities

The attachment to the object of the practice sustains identity, but the object may be contested, and within larger communities of practice different ways of relating to it may give rise to different identities and different tastes. For example, we can see how epistemic communities elaborate their objects and their subjectivities in the field of the academy.

Scientific disciplines consist of bodies of knowledge that are situationally practised within competing 'schools of thought'. Mathematics, for example, can be 'done' in many different ways. What is it that sustains the practice of a particular school and the identity of its practitioners?

A historical study by Paolo Landri (2007) on the 'School of Naples', which formed around the charismatic figure of Caccioppoli at the end of the Second World War, shows how passion for an innovative development in functional analysis mobilized an epistemic community around its founder. In those years, doing mathematics in the School of Naples was a practice clearly identifiable by the international academic community, and for the mathematicians belonging to the school it meant producing a distinctive 'epistemic community'.

Landri (2007: 410) writes that 'the fabric of mathematics develops within an epistemic community; it unfolds through the differentiation of schools of mathematics implying differences in terms of practice, and reflects diversities in aesthetic judgments on the objects of knowledge'. Objects of knowledge are the focus of ongoing collective aesthetic judgments that put an end to controversies within the epistemic community and mobilize passion for knowledge.

The mobilization of passion for the object of one's own practice contributes to the emergence of a distinctive epistemic community, as illustrated in Caccioppoli's own words. His discourse developed through hints at reasoning in the making and through the use of metaphors, without using formulae or writing on the blackboard. At the end of the conference, he himself identified what he had presented:

> Not a method, but a general direction. A point of view, if you like; a skeptic will call it a taste; a politician would call it a plan, probably, and why not?; a poet can call it a state of mind. Anouilh used to refer to the landscape as a state of mind; in the end, a set of theories could be a state of mind. (Landri, 2007: 418–9)

The importance of beauty for defining mathematical objects has been confirmed by other researchers as well. Strati (2008: 232–3), in a study on a mathematics department, reports how a mathematician defined the object of knowledge in ethical/aesthetic terms:

> the most beautiful result is one where the author has been able to identify fundamental ideas, after which he works out his theory following a line of reasoning and a generally geometric intuition, and the thing acquires a particular significance, it becomes clearer, it's easier to understand ... A beautiful result is often one in which the author demonstrates more than he says.

The author comments that here, as often happens in organizations, aesthetics and ethics interweave, so that it is often very difficult to determine whether or not 'beautiful' is being used as a synonym for 'good', or vice versa. Ethics and aesthetics are often intertwined in language, and judgements on correct or incorrect practices take into account not only criteria of instrumental rationality, but also of style, elegance, skill, innovativeness and so on.

I have referred to these studies in order to show that the attachment of practitioners to the object of practice is constructed in the moment and in the space of the practising, in intuitive knowledge, and that judgements on the correctness or otherwise of the practice are not external to its practising but are formed

Learning and Knowing in Practice-Based Studies   *167*

Gherardi: Practice? It's a Matter of Taste!   545

within the action, and are not only *sustained* by practice but *constitute* it. Internal appraisal of performances, done from 'within' the community, elaborates the vocabulary of taste necessary to refine practices while skilfully repeating them. And within repetition, the sharing of the pleasure of doing is also the sharing of the pleasure of being. Attachment is linked to individuation. Without denying the relationship with the audience of the practice, be it customers of restaurants, of flutes, other mathematicians, etc., the internal accounting of practices creates identity while putting in motion a process of innovation through incremental repetition and stabilization of a social and material world, as we shall see in the next section.

Refining Performances

Taste shapes work practices and refines them through negotiation and reflectivity, which suspend the flow of the action in order to intervene and savour the practice and express an aesthetic judgement of it. We may say that practices are constantly refined through the taste-making process, which works both on a sentiment of the perfectible and on repetition as tension toward a never-achieved perfection. Artistic practices easily illustrate this dynamic.

In recent years, jazz has been widely used (and misused) in organizational studies (Kamoche et al., 2003), because it introduces a way of viewing organization as improvisation and as an emerging phenomenon. Collective performances, both in the arts and in the workplace, offer an excellent example of how practices are realized thanks to the tacit coordinating ability at the core of action, and through the ability of all participants to maintain a shared stance towards the object of the practice, and, I would add, through the dynamic of taste-making.

I shall now discuss the discursive modes through which this ability to grasp the taste of a practice is transmitted. The following excerpt recounts a episode concerning the Duke Ellington orchestra (Crow, 1990, cited in Weick, 1999: 550):

Duke came to me and said: 'Clark [Terry], I want you to play Buddy Bolden for me on this album'.

I said: 'Maestro, I don't know who the hell Buddy Bolden is!'

Duke said: 'Oh sure, you know Buddy Bolden. Buddy Bolden was suave, handsome, and a debonair cat who the ladies loved. Aw, he was so fantastic! He was fabulous! He was always sought after. He had the biggest, fattest trumpet sound in town. He bent notes to the *n*th degree. He used to tune up in New Orleans and break glasses in Algiers! He was great with diminished. When he played a diminished, he bent those notes, man, like you've never heard them before!'

By this time Duke had me psyched out! He finished by saying: 'As a matter of fact you are Buddy Bolden!' So I thought I was Buddy Bolden.

On conclusion of the session Duke went to him and said, 'That was Buddy Bolden'.

This example prompts reflection on the non-rational but emotional way in which knowledge is transmitted through evocative, expressive modalities which recall a state of mind by assonance. At the same time, they construct a vocabulary with which to speak about taste, to share an experience, and to refine the taste of the practice intersubjectively. Thus, playing like Buddy Bolden becomes a shared code, a way to perpetuate a practice beyond the community of practitioners that originally produced it. Similarly, cooking like Chef A, doing mathematics in the vein of Caccioppoli, or adopting an OPH's style all express that taste is teachable and learnable.

A second reflection prompted by this example concerns what Weick (1999: 548) has called 'retrospect as form', in order to introduce a contrast between forms developed by the blueprint method and forms developed by the retrospective method. While the former are based on prior planning in the form of a blueprint, the latter are based on improvisation sustained and supported by what has already been done. For example, a painter develops his/her work from preliminary sketches, just as for the novelist the final form is contained in outlines and rough drafts.

Retrospective rationality explains how practices emerge through the constant improvisation that changes their execution but maintains their form. The repetition of practices is not mechanical, just as every execution of the same piece of jazz is not identical to the previous one. This consideration brings us to a last analogy between jazz and non-artistic work practices.

Jazz has been called 'an imperfect art' (Gioia, 1988), and this definition enables Weick, and us, to talk of the aesthetics of imperfection. Just as jazz is partly about false starts, failures and flawed execution in search of excellence and continuous innovation, so a group of practitioners may be genuinely committed to innovation and will constantly reflect on the quality of its performance and draw shared pleasure from the way in which it reproduces the same practice while constantly innovating around it.

Taste-making: Crafting and Sustaining the Attachment to the Object of Practice

This article has been born from a desire to contribute to resumption of the concepts of practice as normative accountability and practical knowledge that identify the salient feature of practice in its being 'teachable and learnable'. Knowing-in-practice as a situated collective activity is a research topic distinctive of practice-based studies, but it is still little explored from the point of view of the attachment of practitioners to the object of their practices.

Starting from a distinction between a definition of practice as regularity in activities and a definition of practice as normative accountability of its performances, I have argued that although the former conception is useful, it is restrictive, while a conception that views practice as a *socially sustained* activity yields a more composite interpretation because it problematizes not what is done, but what socially sustains 'a way of doing things together'. Practitioners' aesthetic judgements not only sustain practices socially, but contribute both to the practitioners' attachment to what they do and to the dynamic of the incessant change in practices as they are practised.

Learning and Knowing in Practice-Based Studies   *169*

Gherardi: Practice? It's a Matter of Taste!   547

Following Bauman (1995), we may say that the conception of practice in terms of 'arrays of activities' denotes a 'handling' relationship with the world: that is, a modernist one of wanting to dominate the world by taming it with practices of calculation and consumption. The conception of practices 'as ways of doing things together' denotes a 'tasting' relationship: that is, a postmodern one that sustains a different morality. In Bauman's words:

> As far as the moral engagement goes, 'tasting' the world seems to offer a considerable advance on 'handling' it. S/he who handles is oblivious to, often angered by, the shapes of things as they are – as s/he knows what shape (or shapelessness) s/he wants them to have. S/he who tastes wants thing to have flavour, and an original flavour, and a flavour of their own. (Bauman, 1995: 125)

Therefore, in order to illustrate the dynamic of taste-making, I proposed to look at practitioners as 'amateurs'. This analogy enabled me to explore the competence of the practitioner not as an 'expert', nor as a 'connoisseur', but as a 'lover' of something. Taste-making has been defined as the process of giving voice to passion and negotiating aesthetic criteria that support what constitutes 'a good practice' or 'a sloppy one' and 'a beautiful practice' or 'an ugly one' within a community of practitioners. It is formed within situated discursive practices. The aesthetic judgement is made by being said—and therefore it presupposes the collective elaboration and mastery of a vocabulary for saying—and it is said by being made.

Taste-making is therefore the process that socially sustains the formation of taste and the sophistication of practices through:

- the mobilization of sensible knowledge (the bodily ability to perceive and to taste), the sharing of a vocabulary for appraising the object and the object in place. Developing a vocabulary of appraisal enables the community of practitioners to communicate about sensible experiences, to draw distinctions of taste and to spread them through the community;
- the mutual constitution of the subject and the object within practice. Taste-making crafts identities and epistemic communities at the same time, and sharing an aesthetics provides the feeling of belonging to a specific community within a community;
- the aesthetics of imperfection accounts for the constant refinement of practices and their historicity in relation to past practices and continuation in future ones. If we use Kant's definition of aesthetic judgement as a judgement on perfection/imperfection, we can see in the formation of taste both its dependence on aesthetic judgments made in the past and embedded in current practice, and the aesthetics of imperfection that through repeated attempts and the inner dynamics of the critical aesthetics constantly refines the practice.

Finally to be stressed are the limitations of the analogy between amateur and practitioner. Being an amateur—in the sense of having a passion for a specific doing, and the associated knowledge about, a specific form of consumption (food or music)—presupposes voluntary adherence to a field of practices and a certain freedom in abandoning such practices or practising them in more sporadic form. The amateur freely associates with those who share a certain taste for a

548   **Management Learning 40(5)**

practice and relatively freely dissociates him/herself from tastes that she or he does not share. Amateurs are practitioners of a certain amatory practice that thereby differs from professional practice. Whilst all amateurs are practitioners, not all practitioners are amateurs of what they do, both in terms of the normative structuring of the field of their practices that responds to an occupational or organizational accountability, and in terms of attachment to the object of the practice. Within a community of practitioners-professionals, attachment to the object of the practice may take the ideal-typical form of 'sine ira et studio' as much as that of the profession: '*beruf*', that is, vocation. The negotiation of collective attachment to the object of the practice can then be viewed as a gradated system of amateurship. This realization opens the way for analysis of the forms of attachment, their temporal and situated dimension, the negotiation of aesthetics, and their contextualization in relation to the dynamics of power. This way forward is feasible, I believe, if practice-based studies more decisively address the problematic of what sustains practices and their situated reproduction.

References

Bauman, Z. (1995) *Life in Fragments: Essays in Postmodern Morality*. Oxford: Blackwell.
Blackler, F., Crump, N. and McDonald, S. (2000) 'Organizing Processes in Complex Activity Networks', *Organization* 7(2): 277–300.
Blumer, H. (1969) 'Fashion: From Class Differentiation to Collective Selection', *Sociological Quarterly* 10: 275–91.
Bourdieu, P. (1979) *La distinction. Critique sociale du jugement de goût*. Paris: Minuit.
Brown, J. S. and Duguid, P. (1991) 'Organizational Learning and Communities of Practice: Toward a Unified View of Working, Learning and Bureaucratization', *Organization Science* 2: 40–57.
Brown, J. S. and Duguid, P. (2001) 'Knowledge and Organization: A Social-practice Perspective', *Organization Science* 12(2): 198–213.
Brugère, F. (2000) *Le goût: Art, passions et société*. Paris: Presses Universitaires de France.
Cook, S. and Yanow, D. (1993) 'Culture and Organizational Learning', *Journal of Management Inquiry* 2(4): 373–90.
Crow, B. (1990) *Jazz Anecdotes*. New York: Oxford.
DiMaggio, P. (1997) 'Culture and Cognition', *Annual Review of Sociology* 23: 263–87.
Douglas, M. (1996) *Thought Styles: Critical Essays on Good Taste*. London: Sage.
Gadamer, H. G. (1960) *Wahrheit und Methode*. Tübingen: Mohr.
Gherardi, S. (2000) 'Practice-based Theorizing on Learning and Knowing in Organizations: An Introduction', *Organization* 7(2): 211–23.
Gherardi, S., Nicolini, D. and Strati, A. (2007) 'The Passion for Knowing', *Organization* 14(3): 309–23.
Gioia, T. (1988) *The Imperfect Art*. New York: Oxford.
Gomart, E. and Hennion, A. (1999) 'A Sociology of Attachment: Music, Amateurs, Drug Users', in J. Law and J. Hassard (eds) *Actor Network and After*, pp. 220–47. Oxford: Blackwell.
Gomez, M. L., Bouty, I. and Drucker-Godard, C. (2003) 'Developing Knowing in Practice: Behind the Scenes of Haute Cuisine', in D. Nicolini, S. Gherardi and D. Yanow (eds) *Knowing in Organizations: A Practice-based Approach*, pp. 100–25. Armonk, NY: M. E. Sharpe.

Learning and Knowing in Practice-Based Studies *171*

Gherardi: Practice? It's a Matter of Taste! 549

Gubrium, J. F. (1975) *Living and Dying at Murray Manor.* New York: St. Martin's Press.

Heidegger, M. (1971) *Poetry, Language, Thought,* trans. Albert Hofstadter. New York: Harper Colophon Books.

Hennion, A. (1993) *La passion musicale: Une sociologie de la mediation.* Paris: Métailié.

Hennion, A. (2001) 'Music Lovers: Taste as Performance', *Theory, Culture & Society* 18(5): 1–22.

Hennion, A. (2004) 'Une sociologie des attachments. D'une sociologie de la culture à une pragmatique de l'amateur', *Sociètès* 85(3): 9–24.

Hennion, A. (2007) 'Those Things that Hold us Together: Taste and Sociology', *Cultural Sociology* 1(1): 97–114.

Hennion, A. and Maisonneuve, S. (2000) *Figure de l'amateur: Formes, objets et pratiques de l'amour de la musique aujourd'hui.* Paris: La Documentation Française.

Hennion, A. and Teil, G. (2004) 'Le goût du vin: Pour une sociologie de l'attention', in V. Nahoum-Grappe and O. Vincent (eds) *Le goût des belles choses,* pp. 111–26. Paris: Editions de la MSH.

Jacques, F. (1979) *Dialogiques: Recherches logiques sur le dialogue.* Paris: PUF.

Kamoche, K., Pina e Cunha, M., Viera da Cunha, J. (2003) 'Towards a Theory of Organizational Improvisation: Looking Beyond the Jazz Metaphor', *Journal of Management Studies* 40: 2023–51.

Landri, P. (2007) 'The Pragmatics of Passion: A Sociology of Attachment to Mathematics', *Organization* 14(3): 407–29.

Mack, K. (2007) 'Senses of Seascapes: Aesthetics and the Passion for Knowledge', *Organization* 14(3): 367–84.

Martin, P. (2002) 'Sensations, Bodies, & the "Spirit of a Place": Aesthetics in Residential Organizations for the Elderly', *Human Relations* 55(7): 861–85.

Orlikowski, W. J. (2000) 'Using Technology and Constituting Structures: A Practice Lens for Studying Technology in Organizations', *Organization Science* 11(4): 404–28.

Orlikowski, W. J. (2002) 'Knowing in Practice: Enacting a Collective Capability in Distributed Organizing', *Organization Science* 13: 249–73.

Orr, J. (1996) *Talking About Machines: An Ethnography of a Modern Job.* Ithaca, NY: Cornell University Press.

Polanyi, M. (1958/1962) *Personal Knowledge.* London: Routledge and Kegan Paul.

Rouse, J. (2002) *How Scientific Practices Matter.* Chicago, IL: University of Chicago Press.

Samra-Fredericks, D. (2005) 'Strategic Practice, "Discourse" and the Everyday Interactional Constitution of "Power Effects"', *Organization* 12(6): 803–41.

Schatzki, T. R., Knorr-Cetina, K. and Von Savigny, E. (eds) (2001) *The Practice Turn in Contemporary Theory.* London and New York: Routledge.

Simmel, G. (1905/1981) *Philosophie der Mode.* Frankfurt: Suhrkamp.

Strati, A. (1992) 'Aesthetic Understanding of Organizational Life', *Academy of Management Review* 17(3): 568–81.

Strati, A. (1999) *Organization and Aesthetics.* London: Sage.

Strati, A. (2007) 'Sensible Knowledge and Practice-based Learning', *Management Learning* 38(1): 61–77.

Strati, A. (2008) 'Aesthetics in the Study of Organizational Life', in D. Barry and H. Hansen (eds) *The Sage Handbook of New Approaches in Management and Organization,* pp. 229–38. London: Sage.

Strati, A. (2009) '"Do You Do Beautiful Things?": Aesthetics and Art in Qualitative Methods of Organization Studies', in D. Buchanan and A. Bryman (eds) *The Sage Handbook of Organizational Research Methods,* pp. 230–45. London: Sage.

Suchman, L. (2000) 'Organizing Alignment: A Case of Bridge Building', *Organization* 7(2): 311–27.

Teil, G. (1998) 'Devenir expert aromaticien: Y a-t-il une place pour le goût dans les goûts alimentaires?', *Sociologie du Travail* 4: 503–22.

Veblen, T. (1899/1970) *The Theory of the Leisure Class: An Economic Study of Institutions.* London: Unwin.

Weick, K. (1999) 'The Aesthetic of Imperfection in Orchestras and Organizations', in M. Pina e Cuhna and C. Alves Marques (eds) *Readings in Organization Science,* pp. 541–64. Lisbon: Instituto Superior de Psicologia Aplicada.

Yanow, D. (2004) 'Translating Local Knowledge at Organizational Peripheries', *British Journal of Management* 15(S1): 9–25.

Contact Address

Silvia Gherardi is in the Research Unit on Communication, Organizational Learning and Aesthetics, Department of Sociology and Social Research, University of Trento, Via Verdi, 26, I-38122, Italy.
[email: silvia.gherardi@soc.unitn.it]

PART III

METHODOLOGICAL INSIGHTS FOR A PRACTICE-BASED APPROACH

[12]

Studies in Cults., Orgs. and Socs., 1995 Vol. 1, pp. 9–27
Reprints available directly from the publisher
Photocopy permitted by license only

When Will He Say: "Today the Plates are Soft"? The Management of Ambiguity and Situated Decision-Making

Silvia Gherardi

Department of Sociology and Social Research, University of Trento

The article proposes a method for ethnographic studies based on "interview with the double". This approach suggests interpreting the cognitive process of collective decision-making as a situated activity, and provides an interpretive description of "quota restriction" as management of ambiguity. The linguistic construct "today the plates are soft" emphasises the social function of this symbolic phrase, internally to Signor Rossi's occupational community as a symbol producing collective identity and social bonding, and externally as a menas to control power relations with management. For the action "quota restriction" to occur (or not) full agreement on values and meanings is not necessary: an unstable minimal accord may be sufficient in so far as it stems from a negotiating process which manages: a) the ambiguity inherent in the social process of interpreting; b) the ambiguity of the implicature from one interpretation to others; c) the ambiguity of implementing the action.

Introduction

One of the foundations of the modern age is the myth of univocality: the exact sciences, sociology, and politics invariably insist on rigorous language, on unambiguous terminology, on standard and universally comprehensible discourse. The heroes of the struggle against ambiguity were Galileo, Descartes and Newton, who founded modern science on univocal discourse, on the scientific definition of categories and on the formalization of theories. Indirect, metaphorical and allegorical expressions were regarded as provisional, as subordinate, as embellishments; or else they were dismissed as expressive forms which belong to the realms of poetry, literature, philosophy – to the humanities in general – and which only enfeebled scientific enquiry.

Intrinsic to the history of ideas in the modern West is what Morin (1974) has called the "morbid rationalism" made manifest in the endeavour to have the real coincide with the rational, to discard the event because it represents the unknown, and to reject rich, polysemous and polyphonic language because it is uncertain: 'the stuff of literati' not of 'the hard-headed men (*sic!*) of science'. Yet this has not always been so in the history of human thought. Indeed the "flight from ambiguity", as Levine (1985) has termed it, is a modern process which received its major impetus from the rise of Western bureaucracy.

Recently, however, the concept of ambiguity has been of considerable benefit to organizational studies, and especially for decision theory, because it sheds light on new aspects of old problems. In this regard the works of Cohen *et al.* (1972), March and Olsen (1976), Weick (1979, 1985), Starbuck (1987), and Daft and Weick (1984) are classics that in various ways reveal the sources of organizational ambiguity in the decision process: the ambiguity of preferences, of relevance, of history, of interpretations. They identify as sources of organizational ambiguity various phenomena such as high mobility of people, the lowering of standards of acceptable performance, sudden changes in authority or job descriptions, or other poorly defined or definable characteristics of work.

However, it is in cultural studies that the concept of ambiguity has acquired particular status (with the "linguistic turn") and where it is conceptualized as an epistemological problem rather than as a property inhering in phenomena which occur in the outside world. Ambiguity arises in the relationship that subjects establish with the world and with other subjects; in the relationship between the subject, his/her language and cultural forms; and in the relationship between the subject, his/her actions, reactions and collective actions. Added to this is the fact that the production of knowledge by any scholar entails the symbolic mediation of ambiguity between the interpretation of the social world studied and the representation of these interpretations within a specialist interpretative system.

Despite their wide variety, cultural studies share the common recognition that organizational phenomena do not have univocal meaning. They are constituted by and through multiple interpretations made as much by organizational actors as by researchers and the academic community. Multiple interpretations pose a wide range of problems for knowledge because they contradict the assumptions of positivism and challenge empiricist methodology. Ethnographic studies constitute a tradition in this sense, but here too the problems of how to gather data, how to handle multiple interpretative levels, and how to represent the knowledge produced are both methodological and theoretical (Norris, 1985; Rosen, 1991; Linstead, 1994).

Cultural research that sets ambiguity in relation to culture and considers it a source of richness has proceeded in a variety of directions. Rosen (1985) analyses informal behaviour at parties and reports the emotions generated by ambiguity. Levitt and Nass (1989) study textbook publishing and consider ambiguity to be a feature of this industry (and perhaps of other cultural industries as well). Meyerson (1991), Feldman (1991), and Lanzara (1993) have studied, respectively, social workers, policy analysts, and mental health workers in order to show the pervasiveness of ambiguity in these occupations, and how metaphor is used to communicate ambiguity. Martin (1990), and Hatch and Ehrlich (1993) analyze stories or expressions of spontaneous humour in order to evidence the co-presence of contradictions, incongruences and incoherences that sustains a variety of cultural forms.

Meyerson and Martin (1988) and Martin (1992) very tellingly single out three perspectives in culture research: the integration, differentiation and fragmentation views, each of which is characterized by a specific attitude towards ambiguity. The integration approach considers culture to be a system of shared meanings and ignores or excludes ambiguity. The differentiation approach describes culture as something that is internally inconsistent, while subcultures constitute islands of inner coherence that emerge from the sea of ambiguity; thus ambiguity is cut away from the subculture by limited consensus.

Finally under the fragmentation approach, ambiguity is the essence of organizational culture, and consensus and dissent are issue-specific and constantly fluctuate (even within subcultures).

In terms of Martin's scheme, my conception of organizational culture belongs within the fragmentation approach. I have used this approach to study eight occupational communities and cultures (Gherardi, 1990): two blue-collar communities working on a battery assembly-line, five white-collar communities (one in a commercial office and four in technical offices) in a printing factory working on various types of product and production lines. Finally, I applied the fragmentation approach to the community of secretaries in the above offices. Within each occupational subculture I studied the system of operational discretionality, my basic idea being that discretion was whatever the subjects defined as such. I described the occupational culture of each community in terms of the decision premises that an outsider had to assume in order to understand and adapt to the framework of "being at work" in that community.

I was interested in examining the local knowledge developed and jealously guarded by each community, particular knowledge about the technical aspects of jobs, strategic interactions with significant others, and their ethical and aesthetic assessment of work. My research methodology relied on various techniques. The technique of projective interviewing was used for data collection; cognitive mapping allowed me to re-construe a collective text, and grounded theory was the basis for data analysis and the elaboration of a more general theory. My interest in the management of ambiguity grew. As participant observer I was struck by how collective action or inaction was triggered by ambiguous expressions such as: "today the plates are soft", "the customer's here" or "the boss is uptight today".

I define ambiguity in terms of the indeterminacy identifiable in linguistic ambiguity. This involves the more or less univocal meaning of words, vagueness, obscurity, polysemy, metaphor, the creation of cryptic meanings or idiosyncratic vocabularies. The ambiguity of life has to do with the fact that a situation may have two or more meanings, or it may simply be unclear or confused, people hold contradictory expectations, consequences are vague, opinions are muddled and coloured by contrasting feelings. There are a variety of facets to the ambiguity of life: empirical ambiguity as ambivalence, ambiguity as the indeterminacy or the contradictoriness of information, its inexactness, scarcity and high uncertainty, as the psychological resource which increases cognitive flexibility and enhances innovative insight (Levine, 1985). Emotion, cognition and action are interconnected and activated by ambiguity, at both individual and collective levels.

This article is not, however, a summary of all my research. Instead, I will suggest a method for ethnographic studies and an interpretation of the cognitive process of decision-making as a situated activity, and provide an interpretative description of "quota restriction" – to illustrate the process of managing ambiguity. My example is a blue-collar community working in the assembly shop of a company producing batteries. The occupational culture of this community is represented by the instructions given by Signor Rossi to a researcher acting as his double. The researcher in turn represents a system of micro-decisions necessary to describe and interpret the processes of the collective action of "making the number" and what happens when this is not the case.

Making the Number

Imagine you are Signor Rossi's double and you must take his place at work tomorrow without anyone discovering the switch. Now Signor Rossi tells you how to behave:

[1] You are a worker in the fitting shop of a firm producing batteries. You must report for work at 6:00 in the morning and work non-stop until 9:15.

[2] When you enter to take my place, the first thing to do is to check on the large board at the end of shop to find out what type of battery is being assembled that day and the quota. Then you go and meet your workmate. You'll be taking turns with him to weld the terminals onto the batteries and beat the plates.

[3] When you are the beater, lay the separators on the bench, put the negative plates on the left, the positive plates in the centre, and the separators on the right. Then put the separators on top of the negative plates and then the positive plates on top of them. Repeat the action several times to build up the units. Then put the units on the bench for your mate to pick up and weld the terminals.

[4] As the beater or the welder you will notice that the quality of the materials is highly variable; for example, the plates can be stiff or too soft:

[5] if they are too soft, you have to speak to the foreman.

[6] Any separator with more than three squashed elements you have to throw out.

[7] If you find a defective separator box you have to call the quality controller.

[8] If you find terminals set too low, try to lever them up with pliers, but if the terminals are too short, throw them out. Most important, only use a little lead when you are welding, because the weld should look nice too.

[9] Serious problems must be reported to the management; but only when you really have to, when you realize that you've got a major problem that's going to cause hold-ups and stop you from "making the number" (i.e. fulfilling your quota of finished batteries).

[10] However, it is better to solve problems by asking your mates to help,

[11] not by calling in the bosses because that wastes time.

[12] If you call the boss you have to take your gloves off, go and phone him and then hang around because either he can't be found, he is busy, or he takes too long to come.

[13] And then it depends on who's available. Signor X is on the ball, Signor Y is incompetent, and Signor Z gets his finger out.

[14] You should get the boss only in two cases: when something breaks down and the mechanic has to be called in, and when you haven't done your quota and the boss has to be told.

[16] Any reduction in output you decide with your workmates; the word goes around, you ask the others how much they can produce and then you decide to do a bit less.

[17] Then you call in the boss to show him what the materials are like,

[18] but he never sorts the problem out; he just says you have to keep on working, even though quality will suffer.

[19] You should remember that it's quantity that counts; it's only the daily production figures that matter to the bosses. The rule is: so much output in so much time, even if quality is affected.

[20] You have to put your back into it, so that you can keep the last hour free: in the first few hours you keep up a good work-rate, taking turns at beating and welding with your workmate every four batches.

[21] It's the older one of the pair who fixes the work-rate when both agree.

[22] When you have done three hours' hard work and the daily quota is in the bag, you can slow down, take a ten-minute break every hour and go out for a cigarette, a coffee or a chat.

[23] After the lunch break you don't work like you did in the morning: you finish your quota, you catch up a bit if you've fallen behind, and you try to finish earlier so you can clean your work station and take a well-earned rest. It's important to work fast in the morning so that you don't have to worry about your daily quota and you can relax in the afternoon.

[24] If you lose more than half an hour, you agree among yourselves and reduce output.

[25] To do this, it's vital to get on well with your workmates and

|26| most of all to have a partner who works in the same way as you do. It's better if you always work with the same person because you develop a good understanding and you don't argue.

|27| If tomorrow you've got Mario, there's no problem because you'll both have the same system; but if it's Antonio there's going to be trouble.

|28| There are some people who take it easy, they always want to work at the same speed.

|29| In here a good guy is someone who meets his quota; at least the bosses think so!

|30| In here you learn how to curse. The disorganization gets on your nerves, the materials are poor, the problems are always the same, and you still have to make up your quota. The foreman who was here before used to fix things that didn't work and keep the workers happy.

|31| If you're not happy then don't do anything extra; you just meet your quota, and that's it.

|32| If you've got poor materials you work badly, you get irritated, you stop more often and your workmanship is bad.

|33| Then the assembly line workers start bitching. There's friction between us and the line workers because they have to keep up with the machinery and they have to work the whole time instead of the six hours that we do. So they are envious of our breaks and easy last hour.

|34| I'm not interested in changing jobs because I've learned my trade by now and I don't want to move to a higher category.

|35| To get on you have to keep moving, learn several jobs, make yourself visible and show the bosses that you're not a layabout.

As Signor Rossi's double you must also know something about what happened years ago and has been inherited from the older workers as a working-class myth. Only thus will you understand why Signor Rossi wants to meet his quota, but only works six hours out of seven, and saves the last hour for relaxation. In fact, the "free time zone" is a legacy from the battle waged by the workers in the shop against lead pollution ten years ago. The management restructured the fitting shop and the workers emerged victorious from bargaining over productivity standards. The symbol of their resistance was the free hour at the end of the day, when they flaunted their independence. Subsequently, however, other workers were taken on, the management changed strategies and consultants were called in.

Data-Gathering, Interpreting and Representing

Signor Rossi is not a person in flesh and blood who describes his work-world in an interview for the benefit of the interviewer, and through the transcript, for the reader. He is a figment, an artefact created by the researcher who, after a process of analytical dissection, returns to natural language to recompose the situated speaking of part of an occupational community and to communicate the analysis to the reader, giving him or her the sensation of being present. Signor Rossi is a 'composite' worker constructed from interviews with the twenty workers in the shop. He is representative of the group of workers with cultural hegemony in the shop, but, as he tells us, there is a second group that wants "to take it easy" and who have a different view of work. They are the younger workers who did not take part in the factory occupation, and who are more sympathetic to the management's concern to improve productivity. The "free time zone" is unimportant to them. Since they are a dissenting minority – or a counterculture within a subculture – I have preferred to describe them indirectly through the images ascribed to them by the majority. This, in turn, was mirrored by the group of dissenters. This process

– which I have elsewhere called "the game of mirrors" (Gherardi and Strati 1990) – is of great help to the researcher in lifting the veil of secrecy over what the interviewees want to keep hidden. In fact, the secrecy that conceals local knowledge has always been one of the major obstacles against both the ethnographer seeking to become an "insider" and the management endeavouring to exert control. And it is in this regard that I now describe the techniques that I used to create the artefact Signor Rossi, for I believe that they can serve as useful tools for ethnographers, who frequently do not specify the techniques they use to gather data, nor those they use to analyze them (Gherardi and Turner 1988).

I developed a technique of projective interviewing – "the interview with the double" – to gather my data, drawing on previous experience (Oddone, Re and Briante 1977) acquired by psychologists of work, who administered a series of interviews in a training context. My interviews with the double lasted 30–45 minutes on average, according to the linguistic competence of the interviewees (the office workers talked longer than the shop-floor workers) and to their ability to cope psychologically with a setting which required them to produce a monologue. The interviewee was asked to perform what some described as a "bizarre" task:

"Now that I have analyzed your job, I want to understand it even better. I want to imagine what it would be like to do it myself. I want to imagine myself as your double, completely the same as you, and that tomorrow morning I shall be going to work in your place. How should I behave, what should I do so that no one discovers the switch?"

In my role as interviewer I then checked that the interviewee had understood the situation. To do this we exchanged roles and I gave the interviewee the example of the job she was going to perform as my double. I would begin more or less as follows:

"Tomorrow you'll go into the university, but not before 9:30 because everyone will be surprised to see you, since I'm not a morning person. Instead, I tend to stay on in the evenings, sometimes till 8 o'clock. Say good morning to everyone but don't stop and talk, because I'm crotchety in the mornings".

The example contained an implicit invitation to focus upon the minutiae of everyday life, upon relationships and feelings, rather than upon the technical aspects of the job since these had already been analyzed. The interviewee was given all the time that he or she needed, and was told that the interviewer would not intervene "so as not to interrupt your train of thought". At the end of the interview, the interviewee was asked for a list of instructions arranged in order of importance.

From a theoretical point of view, this technique rests on a number of assumptions. First it assumes reciprocal knowledge between interviewee and interviewer (the in-the-field work lasted on average two years) which should encourage a trust relationship and therefore increase the implication of accountability in the interview (Antaki 1985). The fact that the interview is a social interaction, and not an "objective" collection of data, implies three premises: social *construction* of the topic of discourse, of the speaking subject, and of the interaction; *contextuality* of both the interlocutory situation and the broader context in which the interview takes place; and *language* as the medium of interaction. Language, in fact, does not describe an objective reality to which it corresponds; rather, it organizes a discourse on truth in a partial and partisan manner. Also the theory of attribution gives importance to social and contextual factors, and the attributions made by individuals are seen as an expression of their accountability to their peers and other interactants in their social world (Semin and Manstead 1983). The descriptions yielded by the interviews with the double depend on the interactive context, and these accounts are the result of complex negotiation conducted within the conversation, both the actual conversation with the interviewer and the potential one with significant others.

A second assumption is that the interviewee is willing to accept the projective technique. This term subsumes a variety of procedures which share the common feature of a highly ambiguous, novel and sometimes even bizarre task, the meaning or interpretation of which is determined by the respondent who must structure it and render it meaningful (Branthwaite and Lunn 1985). The main advantage of projective techniques is that they yield interpretations which reflect the respondent's interests and preoccupations and overcome the barriers of self-consciousness and rationality, of social influences, and of unconscious repression, eliciting instead imaginative and unusual associations and hypothetical ("as if") conjectures. Projective techniques give the researcher access to the interviewees' modes of imposing order on reality. They render ambiguity into something that the interviewees can grasp while simultaneously preserving it in order to conceal contradictions and secrets should they be unable or unwilling to disambiguate.

The researcher refrained from interrupting the interviewee in order to observe the narrative structure used to organize his or her account. Under the hypothesis of the ethnography of speaking (Bauman and Sherzer 1989), speaking praxis is a performance, in the sense that the situated use of language communicatively constitutes social and cultural life. Moreover, the kind of task assigned (to explain what to do and how to behave in order to...) elicited a particular "performative" use of language: instructing, recommending, suggesting, and giving reasons. As one interview followed another, the interviewer gradually began to see the factory shop from the vantage point of the insider and began to reason like a detective following leads and piecing together verbal clues. Finally, the interviewer conducted a feedback session with the group, not in order to validate the results but to gain further knowledge through feedback analysis (Bloor 1983).

If the researcher is not content to transform qualitative into quantitative data, then s/he must use content analysis to face the problem of conducting qualitative analysis of qualitative data. The subjectivity of analysis is a feature inherent to the interpretation of qualitative data, and will be influenced by the researcher's interests and prejudices (Gherardi and Turner 1988). Consequently, "the proper perspective for evaluating projective tasks is as a tool for the researcher to increase his/her contact and insight into the problem at hand" (Branthwaite and Lunn 1985: p. 114).

To produce such a qualitative analysis of qualitative data, I processed the transcript of each interview in two ways. First, I graphically represented each interview on a large sheet of paper using the cognitive mapping technique (Jones 1985) in order to consider the whole interview as a unit, to respect the coherence between language and concepts, and to distinguish more clearly between what I regarded as important and as secondary, respectively. I then drew on grounded theory methodology (Glaser and Strauss 1967;

Turner 1981, 1983; Strauss 1987) to construct the categories with which to analyze the discretionality of "being at work".

My use of cognitive mapping does not follow from what has become the mainstream technique, instead it continues the tradition begun by the Bath group (Eden *et al.* 1983) and used more recently by Eden (1992). Rather than depicting thought as mainstream approaches attempt to do, in the Bath tradition cognitive maps elicit expression and reflection by subjects on what they say they think. From my point of view, cognitive mapping was a tool for analyzing the interviews, a graphic support which enabled me to compare interviews and to isolate recurrent, contradictory, central, or peripheral thought patterns, because in data analysis both common and odd responses can illuminate underlying mechanisms. Subsequently, I returned to natural language, seeking to re-utilize the terms of the community studied and to recreate a "simulated" interview with the typical worker in that community, Signor Rossi, who embodied its most common opinions and encapsulated its most frequently made suggestions.

Data collected in this manner can be processed in a variety of ways. My interest, however, was in micro-decision-making and the discretionality of individuals and occupational communities in elaborating the local meaning of "being at work". Accordingly I constructed a set of decision-making categories. To accomplish this progressive abstraction from first-order to second-order concepts in constructing a theory grounded on the data, I put the interviews from all the communities studied together (90 in total). In the next section I present Signor Rossi's micro-decisions. The numbering used to break down the interview allows the reader to trace the correspondence between first-order concepts (of the interviewees) and second-order concepts (those of the interviewer).

Being at Work as a Frame of Situated Decision-Making

Now imagine that you are a researcher trying to understand how Signor Rossi constructs a meaningful world jointly with the other members of his occupational community. That is to say, you want to see how he deals with ambiguity in his daily life. You are a researcher who has taken Glaser and Strauss and Barry Turner on board and after diligently applying the methodology of "grounded theory" you suddenly find yourself on a "drugless trip" to which Signor Rossi's micro-decisions are the key to understanding. On your drugless trip you have a vision: Signor Rossi does not want to drown in the blue existential sea of undecidability (since he is unaware of Derrida). He builds his coherence rafts and jumps from one to another without presuming that he has eliminated ambiguity or that he has a coherent philosophical theory of the world. He is quite content with meeting his quota and getting through the day.

What is Signor Rossi's secret? The researcher glimpses a pattern of micro-decisions in the way that Signor Rossi cognitively detaches figures from their background and chooses the people, things and relationships most meaningful to him, while he relegates everything of lesser significance to a remoter reality. Within the so-called organization where he works, Signor Rossi creates his own relational space and gives the view of it depicted below and in Figure 1 (numbers in brackets refer to points made by Signor Rossi in the interview with the double described earlier).

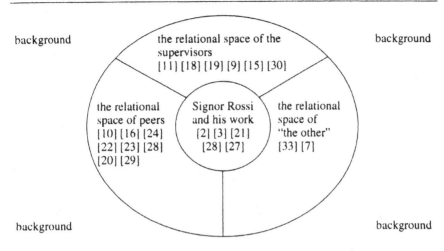

Figure 1 Signor Rossi's relational space.

• Signor Rossi's closest relationship is his reciprocal interdependence [3] with his work partner [2] within a normative framework (so much output in so much time [19]) shared by workers and bosses and which confers command by seniority [21]. This normative framework is regularly violated and delegitimated [27] by those who have a different view of the world [28].

• The relational space of Signor Rossi's peers is plotted by his relations with other workmates in asking for help [10], in collectively deciding to reduce output [16, 24], in keeping up a high work rate [20], in ensuring that production targets are met [22], and in relaxing [23]. But Signor Rossi's community of peers comprises at least two kinds of individuals, according to the typification that he uses: there are those who work fast [20], and those who take it easy [28]. At any rate, the rule for being "OK" is fulfilling your quota at the end of the day [29].

• The relational space of Signor Rossi's overseers is plotted by his characterization of relationships with "the bosses". Whoever they are [11], these individuals are to be avoided because they waste time, do not solve problems [18], and they are only interested in quantity [19]. However, the typology of bosses ranges along [18] a continuum of competence. A boss is "OK" when he is able to keep his workers happy [30]. The rules for calling in the bosses are well-defined [9, 15] and there is a clear specification of their function: ratifying the impossibility of "making the number" and formally communicating with the maintenance staff.

• Signor Rossi's relational space with "others" is more restricted and comprises his relationship with the workers in the department downstream [33]. These are conflict relations, both because of the quality of the semi-finished products that Signor Rossi and his mates send downstream and because of the envy that he imputes to these assembly-line workers. Signor Rossi's work also brings him into contact with the quality control supervisor [7], but he describes this relationship only in neutral terms.

As the researcher, you are aware of the fact that Signor Rossi is displaying his world for your benefit, and that this text can be read in terms of what it says overtly, of what it implies, and of what it leaves unsaid. The difference between you/researcher and Signor

Rossi is that you see the background, how the figures are detached from it, and how the stage is set for you as a spectator, whereas Signor Rossi no longer sees the background, he takes it for granted. Signor Rossi is largely unaware of his active role in constructing his relational space and of the micro-decisions he has taken in order to live within a chosen reality. What he describes is a "given" world – a world in which you as a researcher map the largest area of discretionality around a pattern of micro-decisions defined as a "relational space" and a "contract *with* work". The contract with work is both individually and collectively created by the occupational community. We shall first examine it as a collective undertaking.

Signor Rossi spelled out his preferred strategy to his double: Keep up a high rate of work at the beginning of the shift so that you can be sure of "making the number", then gradually slow down, clean up your work station and relax for the last hour or so. He said [33] that the assembly line workers had to work the whole shift, and you know that this lasts around seven and a half hours "instead of the six hours that we do". Signor Rossi also mentioned [20] "keeping the last hour free" and also that he takes a ten-minute break every hour. This "free time zone" can only be created and defended collectively. If it were not collective (being mostly spent playing cards), a symbol of collectively institutionalized resistance, it would be meaningless. The researcher will discover later that those who "take it easy" [28] belong to a younger generation and that the old guard will complain if there are only twenty free minutes left over at the end of the shift. There are, therefore, two models of the contract with work that are competing latently and which could soon give rise to cultural conflict.

To gain a better understanding of Signor Rossi's work, you focus on the process by which the relationship between Signor Rossi and his job models Signor Rossi himself:

If you are dissatisfied, then get your own back by doing nothing: just fill your quota and nothing more [31]. And if you've got poor materials, you work badly, you get irritated, you stop more often and your workmanship is bad [32].

Signor Rossi adjusts his relationship with his job by taking a variety of decisions (see Figure 2):

• *The image of his working self.* Has he been given a chance to work well? Signor Rossi has an idea of himself at work as "one of those who work fast" [20] and his evaluation parameters are the quality of materials [32], satisfaction of the ratio 'boss/problem-solving/his own contribution' [30], working in partnership with a "cultural brother" or not [27].

• *The boundaries of his job.* Signor Rossi conceptualizes the boundaries of what "he is duty-bound to do" in terms of "making the number"; what is "negotiated" is the amount of effort he is willing to put into reducing the number of discards [6] [7] [8]. Unlike his workmates, Signor Rossi does not have an area of "availability", i.e. a further area into which he is willing to extend the boundaries of his work in order to cope with exceptional events or well-justified requests by his bosses.

• *The commensurateness of performance with an idea of justice.* Signor Rossi is certainly not the kind of person who wants to "do more" than the quota posted on the notice board [2]. What Signor Rossi does not tell his double is that this quota is the minimum output that the management wants, while for him it is the maximum. But neither does Signor Rossi back off and "do less". Doing what is right means "making the number", perhaps reducing output but only because poor quality materials waste his time [24]. The social accounting of justice has its own units of measurement

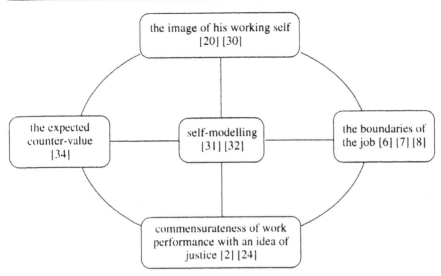

Figure 2 Signor Rossi's contract with his work.

• *The expected counter-value.* Signor Rossi's expectations reflect the way he arrives at a global evaluation "of how things stand in here" [30] and "who is OK" [29]. He is therefore uninterested in changing jobs, or in a career [34]. Hence he does not implement the appropriate strategies [35] but restricts himself to fulfilling his quota.

Discussion

Now that the reader has learned what being at work means for Signor Rossi, we may pass to the more general conclusions to be drawn from the analysis of this occupational community; conclusions which could be applied to others.

A projective ethnographic technique has enabled us to focus on a cognitive framework "being at work" which may change from one community to another, or within the same one, but which as a complex structure of meanings can be considered a central construct in the occupational culture of that community. How are these meanings created? Basically, I argue that they are produced via cognitive decision-making, both individual and collective, centred on two areas of discretionality: the mapping of relational space, and the stipulation of the contract with work. Each area consists of a set of micro-decisions which may either be independent of each other (as in the case of relational space where meaningful subjects and objects are produced according to relevance rules) or interrelated (as in the case of the contract with work which shapes the relation between activity and subject according to a series of interdependent decisions).

Every occupational community develops its own local knowledge, both tacit and explicit, technical, relational, ethical and aesthetic, which enables its members to take micro-decisions on the base of situated knowledge of the social situation, of the actors involved, and of the goals of their action. The researcher gains access to this local knowledge through understanding the local meaning of "being at work". This may not be a complete description of the occupational culture, but it nevertheless provides a serviceable key to it, especially for those wishing to conduct an ethnographic study.

However, before we can be entirely satisfied with the methodology described here, there is a further theoretical and methodological problem to deal with: how does one pass from analysis of the individual dimension of thought, of decision-making, of action to the collective dimension? Obviously, we cannot be satisfied with more or less sophisticated collage techniques, or with other summaries or accounts of collective action. Participant observation, by an observer who already possesses a certain amount of local knowledge is also needed. In this case a particular type of symbolic ambiguity, namely the symbolic statement "today the plates are soft" as a regulator or inhibitor of collective action was involved. This type of ambiguity is central to qualitative assessment made by Senior Rossi's work group because it establishes the border between soft and not-soft as a matter of "connoisseurship" (Turner 1988). However, as we shall see in the next section, the expression "today the plates are soft" is a local symbol, a cryptic label (Bougon 1992), which permits collective action or inaction according to how ambiguity is locally managed.

Having received a set of rules from Signor Rossi on how to pass unobserved, and having reduced his/her cognitive distance from Signor Rossi's world, the researcher now begins his/her participant observation.

Coping with Ambiguity as a Negotiative Process

Having learned some of this occupational community's codes, the researcher watches the social negotiation process as it unfolds in ritual form. After some time the researcher uses his/her tacit knowledge to detect the signals of irritation, increasing noise, and the electricity in the air that leads up to the explosive announcement "today the plates are soft". Sometimes the announcement is a revealed truth which is self-evident to everybody; sometimes there is a chorus of denials; sometimes the on/off button is pressed several times before the ritual begins.

The researcher learns that not all voices speak with the same authority in saying "today the plates are soft", or that the softness of the plates depends on the voice of the announcer. The researcher realizes that s/he has been given a direct answer to the question "how soft are the soft plates?", and that the ambiguity of the problem has been dealt with by the network of pre-existing power relations and by negotiation over what is "soft" and "not soft". But what does all this mean? The pragmatic meaning is that the term "soft plates" symbolizes "reduction of quota", and the researcher watches as the output reduction phase gets underway.

Someone goes to fetch the foreman, persuades him to look at the material, agrees with him that it is impossible to meet the quota, negotiates the reduction and orchestrates the chorus of support. The bosses also know this ritual and perform their roles: they try to make themselves invisible, to involve the head of quality control, to play down the event and give in with dignity.

It may seem that the announcement "today the plates are soft" is simply a device to reduce the quota and to exercise social control over those who might exceed it, and simultaneously over the managers and supervisors. This is a correct but reductive interpretation, however. Consider the power dynamics that pivot on the degree of softness of the plates:

a. individual reputation, the esteem of workmates, the workers' competence, the celebration of personal skill are at stake;
b. such interpersonal relations as status difference between young/old workers, must be maintained and reproduced;
c. the safeguarding of the work group as a collective actor must be maintained and reproduced. In fact, within the group, the conflict between the world-vision of those who want the free time zone and those who want to take it easy (or work at what they define as a steady pace) is legitimate, but it has its limits in that both groups of workers recognize that the group is a resource and a collective good;
d. the counter-power against the supervisors and management must be maintained and balanced as the right to co-determine the quota and, when this has been accomplished, the right to treat the remaining work-time as free time, workers' time, time appropriated from the boss.

Thus, when the signal is given but the above-described ritual does not take place, the inaction can have various meanings. First of all, unless the raw material is obviously impossible to work, in which case anyone is entitled to define the situation (and it is usually the first worker to lose his temper and is willing to fetch the boss), or unless the announcement is made by the one or two undisputed leaders of the workers, prior to the "official" announcement, there is a muted operation of testing the ground to see who agrees and whether the operation can start. When the signal fails to start up with the script, the atmosphere may be one of horseplay and teasing, with dirty jokes and puns on the term "soft". Or else the atmosphere may be tense because the two groups are assessing which of them is entitled to define the situation, or because they are calculating how many times that week the quota has been met, or not met, and therefore negotiating whether to reduce the quota or to give up their free time.

When the group has decided that "today the plates are soft", then the outside interlocutor is called in (an outside interlocutor does not necessarily appear along the line of the hierarchical order). The supervisor is sometimes called because he is the spokesman for the group, sometimes he is considered an opponent, and sometimes the "hierarchy leap" occurs. The rationale for the choice of the interlocutor lies in the "objective" conditions of the material (the less ambiguous the task of establishing the degree of hardness/softness, the more the supervisor is an ally), in the person of the supervisor (as more or less a class ally), and in the personal relationship between the shift supervisor and whoever goes to fetch him.

The choice of which manager to call follows a similar logic, but interestingly the group does not always take the soft option but decides to pick a quarrel. Picking a quarrel – expressing hostility, and flexing collective muscles – is one of the non-explicit goals of the negotiation over reducing the quota. Regardless of whether agreement that the quota cannot be reached is achieved, and whatever reduction is decided, the collective argument, the heated disagreement, the expression of hostility, is cathartic. It leaves the group feeling satisfied whether it wins or loses. This, in fact, is a ritual within a ritual which reproduces the group's identity on a routine basis. It is what Durkheim (1912) called a positive ritual that confirms a value and facilitates its expression.

The managers' interpretation of the situation confirms that the group reinforces its collective identity through the ritual of picking a quarrel. The managers react with boredom and apathy; for them it is "the same old story". They report, in fact, that they constantly "have to find the energy to argue", while the workers emerge refreshed from the encounter. The researcher suspects that it may sometimes be a game for its own sake, played purely for pleasure.

The dynamics of power and negotiation implicit in discussions over quota reduction form a recurrent theme in the sociology of work and organization (Whyte et al. 1955; Roy 1969; Turner 1971; Burawoy 1979) where they have frequently been studied as a cultural phenomenon. The present research largely confirms what has already been found in terms of the production of a negotiated order, although it highlights the less evident aspect of the role performed by ambiguity in making production games possible, and to illustrate the series of ambiguity-resolving micro-decisions required to produce and coordinate collective action.

It is crucial for Signor Rossi's occupational community to maintain the ambiguity of the relationship between the quality of the material and the fulfilment or non-fulfilment of the quota. At the same time, however, no decision on "reducing the quota" can be taken in conditions of ambiguity, disambiguation of this relationship is necessary for action. However, ambiguity enhances the flexibility of action, enabling one course of action to be chosen depending on whether the definition of the situation resolves its ambiguity by replacing a polysemic term with a univocal one. When a course of action is chosen, ambiguity has been reduced but does not necessarily disappear. Just as a culture requires a minimal sharing of values and meanings, so collective action requires the sharing of a minimum set of univocal meaning relations.

Observation of how Signor Rossi's community resolves semantic ambiguity in order to initiate action (and vice-versa) provides a decision model of more general applicability. Analysis of micro-decisions that enable his occupational community to handle the ambiguity of the soft plates reveals a three-stage process of negotiation:

a. *Coping with the ambiguity of interpretations:* the decision to call the plates "soft" is taken individually and collectively.
b. *Coping with the ambiguity of implication:* the utterance "today the plates are soft" may have many meanings. It may be a way to start conversation, to express tiredness or boredom, a statement of fact, an ironic joke, a secret code, and so on. But when Signor Rossi makes the announcement, his workmates know the relation between "soft plates" and "reduce output" and decide that the one implicates the other.
c. *Coping with the ambiguity of implementation.* Who initiates the script "reducing output" and how? It may be the worker who made the announcement, or it may be a chorus of two or three people. Alternatively the process may involve some kind of turn taking. In any case, rapid tacit coordination takes place and action rather than inaction is chosen.

Signor Rossi's occupational community follows a script that relates the quantity of output to the quality of materials, and that directs individual and collective behaviour. This script – which is interwoven with other cognitive schemata and strategies of action, such as "you work calmly and steadily all day" or "you step up the work rate at the beginning, you slow down towards the end, and the last hour is sacrosanct" – is not necessarily shared by everyone, and not always. It is not the sharing of a cognitive schema that triggers the action, but the decision-making process which dissolves the ambiguity that suspends will and selects a course of action.

Implications and Conclusion

An attempt to interpret another's culture is, as Geertz (1973) puts it, an exercise in hermeneutics, and the ethnographic text is thus always a fiction where truth is fully partial (Clifford 1986). An ethnographic explanation is always partial, and it is meaningful only if it appears plausible against our own set of explicit or implicit assumptions about the social process (Douglas 1975).

Plausibility is the validity criterion for the ethnographic research but, because the authority of an interpretation is always relative, it is the author's responsibility to bring the significance of his/her data and methods to the forefront of research activity. However, unless we consider language to be transparent, every meaning derives from interpretation, and every interpretative act is an act which suspends the intrinsic ambiguity of language by assigning a univocal significance to the substantial undecidability of meaning (Derrida 1967). All languages are basically metaphorical, and all meanings are undecidable, but there are limits to interpretation (Eco 1990). As Norris (1990) argues, the fact that in certain circumstances meaning is undecidable is not synonymous with the fact that meaning is always indeterminate. Producing meanings and translating meanings into action signifies living and coping with the ambiguity of language and life.

I chose to construct the example of Signor Rossi in order to talk about the ambiguity of language and life because there is apparently little or nothing ambiguous in Signor Rossi's work. The knowledge required of him is apparently entirely unsophisticated, nor does he belong to a complex communicative or technological system. He confronts purely "normal" ambiguity in his interpretations, interactions and presentation of self. Like all of us, Signor Rossi sometimes confronts the problem of using language univocally, sometimes enjoys the pleasure of ambiguous discourse, and sometimes hides himself behind ambiguity.

In presenting my data I have in part sacrificed the rich ambiguity of natural language for language used to organize action. The non-transparency of language, and the awareness that the accounts recorded by the researcher result from complex negotiation within and through conversation, induced me to flank the traditional method of participant observation with a projective technique. This proved extremely useful because various descriptions and interpretations of the same event could be combined within a specific context, which enabled me to treat the accounts expressed as negotiations of meaning and not as individual responses to a cognitive problem. I was therefore able to read the interview as a rhetorical account intended to persuade the interlocutor of the reasonableness of certain constructs, to discredit others, and to conceal yet others.

The cognitive mapping method subsequently used in initial analysis of the interviews was intended to deepen the researcher's understanding of the interviewees' accounts. It was here that the rhetorical use of ambiguous language proved crucial in creating a virtual conversation on themes deemed important by each interviewee, the interviewer, and those who were cited as allies or opponents. A community of persons and discourses was evoked in the rhetorical elaboration of self and of one's world by the double. Ambiguous, indirect, polysemic language is deliberately obscure because the interlocutor is not completely trusted, given that s/he is external to the community and in contact with other communities, like the workers downstream, the managers and other groups who may be internal to the community but "who think differently". Ambiguous language is used to communicate in psychologically ambivalent interactions characterized socially by a conflict of interests.

In discussion of the construct "today the plates are soft" I sought to emphasise the social functions of this symbolic phrase. The phrase functions internally within the community as a symbol producing collective identity and social bonding, and externally to control power relations with management. The indeterminacy of the symbol protects it and conveys its intrinsic polysemy. But it also and equally permits univocal interpretation which triggers collective action (and inaction) stemming from a social process that defines the situation. For action or inaction to occur, full agreement on values and meanings is not necessary; an unstable minimal accord may be sufficient insofar as it stems from a negotiative process which manages:

(a) the ambiguity inherent in the social process of interpreting;
(b) the ambiguity of the implication of one interpretation for others;
(c) the ambiguity of implementing the action.

According to its etymological meaning, decision-making is an interpretative frame which leads from indeterminacy to determinacy. It closes off a province of meaning and makes a commitment to action. I conceive decision-making activity not as an optimization problem or as a choice among alternatives, but as the discursive production of topics for discussion and of decision structures which enable one world (among those possible) to be realized, while others remain potential (Gherardi 1985). Deciding means thinking, negotiating, willing, choosing a "state of affairs".

In the ambiguity of interpretations of "shared" life, a number of areas of discretionality can be identified whose decision premises provide satisfactory descriptive indicators of the culture of an occupational community and which, in my experience, can be used to compare different communities. An interpretative scheme of occupational culture can be proposed which understands culture in a narrow and partial sense as a "set of decision premises" which fill the following areas of discretionality with meaning and local knowledge:

a. the social construction of the relational space in which the community in question locates itself within the organization, identifies significant others and subjectively relevant themes;
b. the process-based, contextual and contingent elaboration of a contract with work which individually and collectively regulates the relationship between the individual, the community, work, and expectations of reciprocity and justice;
c. the strategies that the community individually and collectively develops in order to cope with the rationality of the organization. Whether this is the worker "making out", the practised inefficiency of the bureaucrat, or other less universally known forms of resistance to the logic of exploitation, of evasion of the language of duty, or the elaboration of cultural forms of self-assertion, every community invents its own subterfuges and seeks to conceal them in the intimate conviction of being the first or the only ones to have thought of them.

The paradox of uniqueness (Martin *et al.* 1983) is what essentially allows ethnographers to do their work: while organizational subjects are engaged in describing the uniqueness of their point of view or the distinctive competence of their organization, and parade it in order to convince themselves and to impress the researcher, the latter, in turn, is intent on deconstructing their claim to uniqueness while exploring their praxis. The difference between researcher and organizational subjects resides in the rhetoric used to understand, explain and represent the culture that both of them help to define (Czarniawska-Joerges 1991).

References

Antaki, Charles (1985) Ordinary Explanation in Conversation: Causal Structures and Their Defence. *European Journal of Social Psychology,* 15, 213–230.

Bauman, Robert and Joel Sherzer (eds) (1989) *Explorations in the Ethnography of Speaking.* Cambridge: Cambridge University Press.

Bloor, Michael (1983) Notes on Member Validation. In Robert Emerson (ed) *Contemporary Field Research.* Boston: Little Brown: 156–172.

Bougon, Michel (1992) Congregate Cognitive Maps. *Journal of Management Studies,* 29(3), 369–389.

Branthwaite, Alan and Tony Lunn (1985) Projective Techniques in Social and Market Research. In Robert Walker (ed) *Applied Qualitative Research.* Aldershot: Gower: 101–129.

Burawoy, Michel (1979) *Manufacturing Consent.* Chicago: University of Chicago Press.

Clifford, James (1986) Introduction: Partial Truths. In James Clifford and George Marcus (eds) *Writing Cultures.* Berkeley: University of California Press: 1–26.

Cohen, Michael, James March and Johan Olsen (1972) A Garbage Can Model of Organizational Choice. *Administrative Science Quarterly,* 17, 1–25.

Czarniawska-Joerges, Barbara (1991) Culture Is the Medium of Life. In Peter Frost, Larry Moore, Maryl Reis Louis, Craig Lundberg, and Joanne Martin (eds) *Reframing Organizational Culture.* Newbury Park: Sage: 285–297.

Daft, Richard and Karl Weick (1984) Toward a Model of Organizations as Interpretation Systems. *Academy of Management Review,* 9, 284–295.

Derrida, Jacques (1967) *De la Grammatologie.* Paris: Le Seuil.

Douglas, Mary (1975) *Implicit Meanings.* London: Routledge & Kegan.

Durkheim, Emile (1912) *Les Formes Elementaires de la Vie Religieuse: le Systeme Totemique en Australie.* Paris: Alcan.

Eco, Umberto (1990) *I Limiti dell'Interpretazione.* Milano: Bompiani.

Eden, Colin, Sue Jones and David Sims (1983) *Messing About in Problems.* Oxford: Pergamon.

Eden, Colin (ed) (1992) On the Nature of Cognitive Maps (special issue). *Journal of Management Studies,* 29(3).

Feldman, Martha (1991) The Meanings of Ambiguity: Learning from Stories and Metaphors. In P. Frost *et al.* (eds) *Reframing Organizational Culture.* Newbury Park: Sage: 145-156.

Geertz, Clifford (1973) *Interpretation of Cultures.* New York: Basic Books.

Gherardi, Silvia (1985) *Sociologia delle Decisioni Organizzative.* Bologna: Il Mulino.

Gherardi, Silvia (1990) *Le Microdecisioni nelle Organizzazioni.* Bologna: Il Mulino.

Gherardi, Silvia and Barry Turner (1988) *Real Men Don't Collect Soft Data.* Trento: Quaderni del Dipartimento di Politica Sociale 13.

Gherardi, Silvia and Antonio Strati (1990) The Texture of Organizing an Italian Academic Department. *Journal of Management Studies*, 27(6), 605-618.

Glaser, Barney and Anselm Strauss (1967) *The Discovery of Grounded Theory.* Chicago: Aldine.

Hatch, Mary Jo and S. Erlich (1993) Spontaneous Humour as an Indicator of Paradox and Ambiguity in Organizations. *Organization Studies*, 14(4), 505-526.

Jones, Sue (1985) The Analysis of Depth Interviews. In R. Walker (ed) *Applied Qualitative Research.* Aldershot: Gower: 74-93.

Lanzara, GianFrancesco (1993) *Capacità Negativa.* Bologna: Il Mulino.

Levine, Donald (1985) *The Flight from Ambiguity.* Chicago: The University of Chicago Press.

Levitt, Barbara and James March (1988) Organizational Learning. *Annual Review of Sociology* 14, 319-340.

Levitt, Barbara and Clifford Nass (1989) The Lid on the Garbage Can: Institutional Constraints on Decision-Making in the Technical Core of College Text Publishers *Administrative Science Quarterly*, 34, 190-207.

Linstead, Stephen (1994) The Responsibilities of Betrayal: Deconstruction and Ethnographic Praxis. *Blurring Genres*, 6, 1-27.

Linstead, Stephen and Robert Grafton-Small (1990) Theory as Artefact: Artefact as Theory. In Pasquale Gagliardi (ed) Symbols and Artifacts: *Views of the Corporate Landscape.* Berlin: de Gruyter: 387-420.

March, James and Johan Olsen (eds) (1976) *Ambiguity and Choice in Organizations.* Bergen: Universitetforlaget.

Martin, Joanne (1990) Deconstructing Organizational Taboos: The Suppression of Gender Conflict in Organizations. *Organization Science*, 1, 334-359.

Martin, Joanne (1992) *Cultures in Organizations*, New York: Oxford University Press.

Martin, Joanne, Martha Feldman, Mary Jo Hatch and Sim Sitkin (1983) The Uniqueness Paradox in Organizational Stories. *Administrative Science Quarterly*, 28, 438-453.

Meyerson, Debra (1991) "Normal" Ambiguity?: A Glimpse of an Occupational Culture. In P. Frost *et al.* (eds) Reframing Organizational Culture, Newbury Park: Sage: 131-144.

Morin, Edgar (1974) La Complexité. *Revue International des Sciences Sociales*, 4, 6-32.

Norris, Cristopher (1985) *The Contest of Faculties: Philosophy and Theory after Deconstruction.* London: Methuen.

Oddone, Ivan, Alessandra Re and Gianni Briante (1977) *Esperienza Operaia, Coscienza di Classe e Psicologia del Lavoro.* Torino: Einaudi.

Rosen, Michael (1985) Breakfast at Spiro's: Dramaturgy and Dominance. *Journal of Management Studies*, 11(2), 31-84.

Rosen, Michael (1991) Coming to Terms with the Field: Understanding and Doing Organizational Ethnography. *Journal of Management Studies*, 28(1), 1-24.

Roy, Donald (1969) Making Out: A Counter-System of Worker Control of Work Situation and Relationships. In Tom Burns (ed) *Industrial Man.* Harmondsworth: Penguin: 359-379.

Schutz, Alfred (1971) *Collected Papers.* The Hague: Nijhoff.

Semin, Gun and Alfred Manstead (1983) *The Accountability of Conduct: A Social-Psychological Analysis.* London: Academic Press.

Starbuck, William (1987) Surmounting our Human Limitations. In R. Quinn, K. Cameron (eds) *Paradox and Transformation: Toward a Theory of Change in Organization and Management.* Cambridge: Ballinger: 65–80.

Strauss, Anselm (1987) *Qualitative Analysis for Social Scientists.* Cambridge: Cambridge University Press.

Turner, Barry (1971) *Exploring the Industrial Subculture.* London: Macmillan.

Turner, Barry (1981) Some Practical Aspects of Qualitative Data Analysis: One Way of Organizing Some of the Cognitive Processes Associated with the Generation of Grounded Theory. *Quality and Quantity,* 15, 225–247.

Turner, Barry (1983) The Use of Grounded Theory for the Qualitative Analysis of Organizational Behaviour. *Journal of Management Studies,* 20, 225–247.

Turner, Barry (1988) Connoisseurship in the Study of Organizational Cultures. In A. Bryman (ed) *Doing Research in Organization.* London: Routledge: 108–122.

Weick, Karl (1979) *The Social Psychology of Organizing.* Reading MA: Addison-Wesley.

Weick, Karl (1985) Sources of Order in Underorganized Systems: Themes in Recent Organization Theory. In Yvonne Lincoln (ed) *Organizational Theory and Inquiry: The Paradigm Revolution.* Beverly Hill: Sage: 106–136.

Whyte, William Foote, *et al.* (1955) *Money and Motivation.* Westport: Greenwood.

[13]
'Do You Do Beautiful Things?': Aesthetics and Art in Qualitative Methods of Organization Studies

Antonio Strati

INTRODUCTION

Studies and research on the aesthetic dimension of organizational life first appeared with the 'cultural turn' in organizational studies that occurred during the 1980s. These analyses concern themselves with a range of subjects, from the internal and external architectures of organizations to the discipline imposed on the bodies of the people working in them or on their behalf. They exhibit a distinctive feature: whilst they study the aesthetic dimension of the organization concerned, they develop aesthetic awareness of organizational phenomena. Put otherwise, research on organizational aesthetics is grounded at the same time on an 'aesthetic style' in the research methods used to study organizations. This chapter describes the aesthetic quality of such study in terms of a new methodological awareness comprised in the critical analysis of work and management practices in organizations. Such analysis is conducted using four approaches – archaeological, empathic-logical, aesthetic, and artistic – and it is traversed by two main themes: that of aesthetics (understood as sensible knowledge and aesthetic judgment) and organizational life; and that of art and management.

Aesthetic understanding as new methodological awareness in the study of organizational life

Awareness has only recently come about that use can be made of aesthetic as well as cognitive understanding in the empirical analysis and theoretical study of organizations. This concerns the methodologies of organizational analysis; and therefore also, in many respects, both their privileged object of study, and the research epistemology and theoretical paradigms in which this new methodological awareness finds the taste for study mixed variously with base assumptions and value premises.

A recent Europe-centred methodological awareness

For around ten years – the most recent in the century-long history of organizational theories and management studies – field studies and theoretical reflections on the aesthetic dimension of organizations, the methods used to study it, and the 'aesthetic' nature of approaches to organizational study, have been discussed at international conventions and seminars, and they appear with increasing frequency in prestigious international journals and publications. This has been observed by several scholars (Minahan and Cox, 2007) and, amongst them, by Pasquale Gagliardi in his chapter on organization aesthetics in the *Handbook of Organization Studies*, revised for its second edition. During the ten years since that handbook's first edition, studies on the topic had proliferated, and organizational aesthetics were no longer a neglected area of organization studies. There is, on the contrary:

> a growing body of literature on aesthetic themes, one in which systematic reflection is conducted on the relationships between these and organization (Dean et al.,1997; Strati,1999) and between art and management (Guillet de Monthoux, 2004); there are research anthologies as well as special journal issues (*Organization* 3/2, 1996; Linstead and Höpfl, 2000; *Human Relations* 55/7, 2002), which have resulted from seminars and conferences expressly devoted to analysis of the methodological implications of taking an aesthetic approach to the study of organizations. The aesthetics of organization is therefore taking shape as a distinct field of inquiry within organizational studies [...]. (2006: 702)

I consider organizational aesthetics research to be not merely a series of theories and methodological treatments, but rather a postsocial collective phenomenon in which organizational scholars investigate the capacities for action of people and artefacts in organization at the level of the *pathos*

of sensible knowledge and aesthetic judgement. It is a strand of organizational analysis with its 'barycentre' in Europe – as Ramirez (2005: 31) notes – because the 'main writings on this matter have been done by European scholars; in particular from Italy, Scandinavia, and France'. Thus, the main characteristics of this 'new methodological awareness', may be summarized as follows:

- It has not been subject to the strong influence of North American organizational scholars on organization theory and management studies.
- It is critical of the normative and prescriptivist stance apparent in organizational theories and management studies, and thus reprises the methodologies of organizational analysis that arose with the 'cultural turn' of the 1980s (Gherardi and Turner, 1987).
- It wages a polemic against the positivist and neopositivist methodologies of organization analysis and disputes the sharp separation among science, art and mythical thinking, thus displaying continuity with symbolist studies of organizations, as well as its own theoretical-methodological specificity.
- It also strongly controverts the interpretationist methodologies that privilege causal explanations of organizational life – such as the causal cognitive maps used by the cognitivist approach to the study of organizations (Strati, 1998) – although it shares their underlying interpretative paradigm.
- It endeavours to bring out the new humanism in organizations that opposes alienating and manipulative processes.

Methodological choices and paradigmatic controversy

If proper account is to be given of aesthetic methodological awareness in organizational theories and management studies, one must relate methodological choices – from empirical research methods to theory-building, to communication of research results – to epistemological issues and paradigmatic controversies. Striking in this regard is what I have called elsewhere (Strati, 2007) 'the maturity of the beginnings' of the aesthetic discourse on organizations: namely the collective phenomenon which, at the end of the 1980s:

- Laid the bases for definition of what is meant by 'organizational study'. Art and aesthetics, and the notions of beauty and *pathos*, gave theoretical value and scientific meaning to the evocative knowledge-creation process – obscured by the dominance of the logical-analytical process – and art acquired theoretical-methodological legitimacy, rather than circumscribing one type of social world.
- Redefined the organization by emphasising 'materiality' as its distinctive feature. The corporeality of people at work, the physicality and/or aesthetic impalpability of organizational artefacts, feelings, and emotions give materiality to organizations.
- Raised the methodological issue of how empirical research can grasp the aesthetic dimension of an organization as a whole, as well as the aesthetics of the work and organizational practices performed within it.
- Brought to light the aesthetic phenomenon constituted by organizational management, given that the members of organizations are people, not concepts or instruments, and consequently know and act through their senses, formulating aesthetic judgments.
- Stressed personal knowledge and differences among organizational actors in opposition to the organizational manipulation intended to standardize them aesthetically by means of art and taste.
- Highlighted the collective dynamics of aggregation with others and/or distinction from others via the aesthetics of both the content and form of work.
- Recast the status of objects, showing their capacity for subtle and intense action in socializing people into work cultures and organizational cultures, and also in regard to the sensible, aesthetic, and emotional control exercised by dominant organizational cultures. In those same years, at the end of the 1980s, but in very different theoretical frameworks, this capacity for action was attributed to objects by other studies which re-examined the status itself of the organizational actor, notably Workplace Studies (Hindmarsh and Heath, 2007; Nicolini et al., 2003) and those inspired by Actor Network Theory (Latour, 2005).

However, this is not to imply that the new methodological awareness is grounded on a univocal definition of aesthetics, that is, a 'single lens' through which organizations can be examined. Although the concept of aesthetics dates back only to the mid-1700s – when the term was first used to denote a relatively unitary discipline comprising the aesthetics of the sensible, the aesthetics of the sentiment of the beautiful, and the space of the apparition of art works of and reflection on art (Escoubas, 2004: 5–6) – poetry and art, the beautiful and the sublime, have been debated for millennia, and in diverse cultures and civilizations. But even if one goes no further back than the aesthetic philosophy developed approximately three centuries ago, one already finds debates and controversies on what constitutes aesthetics. What, therefore, is the aesthetic philosophy that underpins aesthetic studies on organizational life? It is the body of thought produced from Aristotle to Immanuel Kant, from Plotinus to Susanne Langer, or from Dewey to Luigi Pareyson. It is, therefore, a doctrine to which numerous philosophers have contributed; but pre-eminent among them are Giambattista Vico (1725) and Alexander Gottlieb Baumgarten (1750–8):

- The former because of his antagonism against the Cartesian rationalist tradition, and his proposal of 'a new science' founded on a 'poetic logic', where reasoning by metaphors, the imagination, evocative knowledge, and mythical thinking are legitimate ways to understand the world and social life,
- The latter because of his emphasis on sensible knowledge and the sensible-aesthetic judgement yielded by the perceptive faculties of sight, hearing, smell, taste, and touch which produce an art of the analogy of reason (*ars analogi rationis*) ancillary to the latter but independent from it.

These two aesthetic philosophies focus on forms of knowing and acting which are not rooted in methods of analysis embedded in cognition or analytic rationality, although they are always in dialogue – and often in dispute – with them.

Methodological awareness in the plural

The aesthetic philosophies of Vico and Baumgarten stress that aesthetics has not been confused with art in the debate on the theoretical and epistemological foundations of organizational aesthetics research in any of the methodological frameworks developed. These exhibit a variety of methodological and substantive nuances and details, which give sense to the aesthetic understanding of organizations as qualitative inquiry. They are now briefly described – and shaped – in terms of the four main aesthetic approaches to study of organizational life: archaeological, empathic-logical, aesthetic, and artistic.

The archaeological approach

The *archaeological approach* (Berg, 1987) is the first of them, both in time and in its capacity for action and persuasion. The reference to archaeology denotes the metaphorical operation by which, on adopting this approach, the scholar assumes the guise of an archaeologist and/or historian of art and observes organizational aesthetics in regard to the organizational cultures and symbologies that they bring to light.

For example, the aesthetics of the architectures of organizational buildings – argue Per Olof Berg and Kristian Kreiner (1990) – constitute the 'traces' used by researchers to show the predominant values of the managerial philosophy, owing to their ability to evoke individual and collective memories. By observing the aesthetics of the buildings and constructions that house organizations, as well as their internal architectures, researchers are able to demonstrate the symbolic conditioning exerted by those aesthetics on organizational action, insofar as they set value on creativeness, transparency, connectedness and openness, or conversely, on standardization, hierarchy, formal power, and prestige due to status. Moreover, the aesthetics of architectural features are able to signal, via the building, its facade, a meeting room or a workplace, the organization's institutional value as a 'totem'; that is, as a unifying symbol which stands as a central organizational referent for organizational symbols and cultures.

The approach has developed within the mainstream of symbolist studies on organizational cultures (Turner, 1990) and still

forms a bridge between aesthetic study and organizational symbolism. It has been widely adopted and adapted to the requirements of field research, in many cases implicitly rather than explicitly. It does not address the issue of methodology except in the conventional terms of research design (Bryman, 1989: 28–30) in qualitative research.

The empathic-logical approach

The *empathic-logical* approach (Gagliardi, 1990; 2006) has had wide impact, because it highlights the organizational control exercised at the level of aesthetics, beginning with the *pathos* of the organizational artefacts constituting the symbolic landscape of the tangible organization. This approach has studied 'the objects that are used in managing – premises [...], their furnishing [...], office equipment [...], public relations materials [...], and products of all type' – writes Ramirez (2005: 31) – observing 'that considerable effort was spent on rendering them attractive [...] that the physical manifestations work were systematically utilized as means to render the aesthetic appeal of cooperation'.

The attention paid by the researcher to the aesthetics of organizational architectures, however, does not focus directly and almost exclusively on organizational symbols, and in this it differs from the archaeological approach. Witkin's (1990) study of the aesthetics of a large multinational's conference rooms illustrates how the physical arrangement induced a two-dimensional understanding of reality and instead blunted the three-dimensional understanding of it. Put otherwise, the *pathos* of that organizational artifact exerted an influence at the level of the aesthetic understanding of the organization's members: on the level, that is, of what is sensorially perceivable before symbolic-valorial systems. By their nature – writes Gagliardi (2006: 714) – perceptive premises evade control by the mind, while at the same time they constitute a further level of organizational control which adds to and combines with those of (i) the directly imparted order, (ii) programmes and procedures and

(iii) the ideological premises of organizational action identified by Charles Perrow (1972).

Unlike the archaeological approach, this one divides the research into three main phases:

(a) In the first, the researcher immerses him/herself empathetically in organizational life and interrogates the feelings aroused in him or her by organizational artefacts and gives them names. Thus, immersion in organizational interaction and examination of the aesthetic sense of the experience concludes this research phase of observing organizational phenomena.

(b) The second phase involves interpretation of what has been observed, giving names to the experiences acquired, and balancing the passive 'intuition' deriving from immersion in the texture of organizational interactions with the 'active' analysis prompted by detachment from them. However, this phase should not be seen as clearly distinct from the other two, given the qualitative nature of this approach that – contrary to what happens in quantitative study – does not separate one phase from the others, but rather is in search of continuous dialogues between them.

(c) In the third phase, empathy gives way to the logical-analytical rigour with which the research is 'eloquently' reported, writes Gagliardi (2006: 720), 'without any pretence to the production of literary artifacts aimed at communicating only or mainly on the aesthetic plane'.

The aesthetic approach

Also the *aesthetic approach* (Strati, 1992, 1999) has been influential in shaping the aesthetic discourse on organizations. The aesthetic approach shows how the aesthetics from which the organization acquires its form are negotiated. It emphasizes the quotidian construction, reconstruction and destruction of the aesthetics specific to the organizational context studied. It focuses on the organizing of aesthetics, and it studies how the aesthetic categories – from the ugly to the sublime, from the comic to the sacred, from the picturesque to the *prestissimo* or *adagio* of the agogic categories – mark out the organizational specificities of the social practices examined.

For example, the aesthetic judgements on beauty expressed by the employees and collaborators of a prestigious Italian photography firm (Strati, 1999) brought into focus numerous aspects and organizational dimensions through which the beauty of their organization acquired its form: (i) the firm's nature as a flowing and interweaving microcosm of beautiful relations in everyday work, (ii) its 'opening of doors' to external interlocutors and other organizations, making the people with which it interacted 'smile', (iii) improving, with its production and promotion of a photographic style, the life-quality of people in external society, (iv) being one of the beautiful Italian things, (v) showing a renewed vitality in comparison to the past, (vi) becoming a myth if it closed. Here it was the category of beautiful that gave this specific form to the organization. Nevertheless, it is not always thus. Indeed, the aesthetic category of ugly, grotesque, or disgusting often emerges from empirical research. Its organizational meaning has been shown, for instance, by Patricia Martin (2002), who illustrates how aesthetic feelings, even those aroused by the unpleasant odours of persons and rooms in residential homes for the elderly, organized – though not unequivocally – organizational life, and that this depended on the style of organizing aesthetics in use in the old people's home.

Unlike the archaeological approach, the aesthetic approach does not consider aesthetics as ancillary to the symbolic understanding of organizational cultures, but rather as a distinctive characteristic of a specific and free-standing form of organizational understanding. And unlike the empathic-logical approach, it does not proceed through three main phases – observation/immersion, interpretation, and the 'eloquent' report – nor does it shift from empathic understanding of the observation to the analytical understanding that arises from interpretation and then characterizes the description of results. It grasps the dynamics of organizational power in the negotiation of organizational aesthetics and highlights how the researcher 'does' aesthetics.

The research process critically directs the attention of organization scholars to the fact that often, though not always, the researcher:

(a) Chooses a topic, style, and subject of analysis according to his/her taste and personal preferences for method and theory.

(b) Activates his/her sensory faculties and aesthetic judgment upon immersing him/herself in the texture of organizational interactions and empathizing with the organizational actors as they act and interact.

(c) Observes the interactions among the organizational actors and, when appropriate, also assumes the role of an imaginary participant observer, that is, using the empathic knowledge-creation process (Weber, 1922) which involves 'putting oneself in the place of' and experiencing sensorially, but always imaginarily, fragments of the organizational life under consideration.

(d) Listens for emphases and overtones in the sense constructions of the organizational actors and critically reflects on the power which accompanies their attractiveness.

(e) When the materials collected and processed – which is not a specific and freestanding phase of research but is instead confused with other aspects of the aesthetic study – lets the experiences gathered in the course of the research re-emerge so that they can be relived sensorially and rejudged aesthetically.

(f) When communicating the research results uses the evocative knowledge process, drawing on art and aesthetic philosophy, employing metaphors, leaving contradictions and ambiguities unresolved, resorting to vivid accounts of the organizational dynamics, and processes studied. So that those who read and/or listen to the results must activate their own perceptive-sensory faculties and sensible-aesthetic judgement in order to interpret and make sense of those results.

The artistic approach

The *artistic approach* (Guillet de Monthoux, 2004) has been influential in proposing views of the organization through the eyes – disenchanted – of the artist and/or the art promoter, gallery owner, museum director, or orchestra conductor. More than the other three, this approach critically focuses on the experience of art in organizing. It comprises the sensible-aesthetic experience of the empathic-logical and aesthetic approaches, and the symbolic-cultural experience that characterizes all the three other approaches – the archaeological one especially. Artistic performance is its central concern, as highlighted by its close attention to styles of leadership in organizations, their merging beyond the dualisms that separate art and science, their transmuting into styles of 'liedership' – from lieder in classical music – evocative of the crucial importance of having 'voice' in organizational communication (Putnam et al., 1996). It is, however, an approach critical of the 'popular American notion of "the experience economy" (Pine and Gilmore, 1999) (where companies attempt to produce emotionally intensive offerings to increase profits), arguing that all too often this notion ignores, and even denies, the deeper creative potential which the tension between the rational and the artistic offers' (Ramirez, 2005: 32).

If the aesthetic approach asks the interviewee 'Do you do beautiful things?', or 'What is beautiful in your organization?' – and therefore investigates how social practices within the organization and the organization itself are interpreted and enacted on the basis of the aesthetic judgment – the artistic approach instead asks: 'What is art to you?', 'Who is the artist, then?', 'How did you conceive the "art firm" you founded?' Pierre Guillet de Monthoux (2004: 352–3) asks these questions in awareness of their exploratory-colloquial character in his section on the 'Cittadellarte' (Artcity), an art foundation created by Michelangelo Pistoletto – an artist of international renown and proponent of *Arte Povera* – and his partner Maria Pioppi. ' "But what is art to you, Michelangelo?" I asked stupidly, and I heard John Dewey laugh at me in the back of my head', writes Guillet de Monthoux (p. 352), and by means of these questions gathered information on the entrepreneurial style of Cittadellarte; a style that constitutes this art firm as 'concrete action for a new kind of socially responsive-responsible art' and sees it as 'a modern version of the studios of Renaissance artists where science, production and economy were inextricably bound up with imagination, philosophy, and spirituality' (Guillet de Monthoux, p. 353). On the other hand, a study may examine research on the role of the straight line in perspectival art to deduce its influence on early writings in the theory of organization and management. 'It may seem unusual to some to discuss paintings as a means of understanding studies of management and organizations but frequently they offer us a view that is somehow more vivid', Ian King maintains (2007: 226). It is the exploration of new forms of scholarly inquiry and framing able to configure themselves by drawing upon – Daved Barry argues (2008, p. 40) – both the underlying assumptions and the 'lively qualities' of contemporary art, so as to make the working and organizational practice of research 'work done in delightful, imaginative ways'. When aesthetic issues are examined, the aesthetic form is a means both to use 'artistic methods to explore sensory experiences' – write Steven Taylor and Hans Hansen (2005: 1223–4) – and to communicate the research results by representing them in forms which draw on the wide range of genres and styles of artistic expression, i.e. the artistic performance (Scalfi, 2007; Steyaert and Hjorth, 2002). The aesthetic object of study for artistic methods consists in the artistic forms 'used to present the direct sensory day-to-day experience in organizations', continue Taylor and Hansen. These are highly promising in that they capture the feeling of the event or the organizational process being examined and, at the same time, 'work with traditional intellectual analysis to give to richer, fuller, more-embodied understanding', specify Taylor and Hansen (2005: 1224), as in the case of Laura Brearley's work (2001) 'on the experience of transition in organizational life. She tracked the experiences of managers as they went through a difficult merger. Part of her research process is creating poems, songs, and multimedia tracks from interview data and images that the managers created'.

This approach, like the archaeological approach and unlike the empathic-logical one, does not proceed through research phases; nor does it articulate the research process into several interweaving activities, as does the aesthetic approach. On the contrary, this approach envisages the hybridization of artistic creative energy and ratiocinative capacity in the performative conduct of both research and organization. It draws indiscriminately on methods of artistic understanding and those used by the social sciences. It is not, in fact, particularly concerned with the issue of the qualitative methodology of organizational analysis, unlike the empathic-logical and aesthetic approaches. Instead, it 'pragmatically overcomes' the issue of the methodology most appropriate to the aesthetic study of organizations by mixing artistic sensibility and cognitive rationality. It projects the scholar into the playfulness, improvisation, and sensuality of the research experience, and the performance distinctive of the research process until dissemination of the results.

Issues of method traversing organizational aesthetics research

All four approaches take a critical stance towards the traditional distinction between the usefulness of research and the pleasure of doing it, as well as the taste for transgressing the traditions of study accredited in organizational theories and management studies. Also shared by all four approaches is criticism of assuming a managerial standpoint. Rejection of the corporate standpoint, indeed, constitutes the specificity of European research on the aesthetic dimension of organizational life. This concern with emancipation is particularly marked in the European debate because of the aestheticizing effects (Hancock and Tyler, 2000; Pelzer, 2002; Marquard, 1989) that art and aesthetics exert on the sensibility, and on the ability to activate the perceptive-sensory faculties and aesthetic judgment that distinguish the personal knowledge of organizational actors. Moreover, all four approaches conduct an epistemological polemic against absolute belief in rationality and against the predominance of cognitivism and positivism in organizational theories and management studies. 'Much of the early work in organizational aesthetics' – write Steven Taylor and Hans Hansen (2005: 1219) – 'primarily draws on the epistemological conceptualization of aesthetics to make an argument for the importance and reasonableness of an aesthetic approach to organizations'. The methodological question is internal to the epistemological one, and it has been expressly addressed in various works. But it has been treated in diverse ways, so that studies which reflect on the qualitative methods employed – notes Samantha Warren (2008: 564) – alternate with others which 'remain strangely silent on the complexities of the methodologies employed to do this – subsuming them under the banner of "case study" or "ethnography"'.

Table 14.1 shows the distinctive features of each approach, its differences in research style, and what constitutes its emphasis, strengths, and limitations. Brief discussion is required of these latter, whilst the other points have already been treated. Each of the four approaches has limitations, which concern different areas of the methodological discourse.

The limitation of the archaeological approach resides in the symbolic and culturalist studies of organizations (Turner, 1990). Within this theoretical and methodological domain that constituted its original humus, it continues to produce studies and research. The archaeological approach is not the only one to extend its roots into the organizational symbolism approach to the study of organizations. So too do both the empathic-logical and aesthetic approaches – but less so to the artistic one, because, unlike the other three approaches, it gives equal importance to debates on how to do, promote, manage, and teach art. However, both these two approaches envisage aesthetic understanding as an autonomous branch of the qualitative study of organizational life. The methodological choice of pursuing logical-analytical rigour already in the second phase of analysis, and then especially in the third, is the limitation set on the empathic-logical approach. In this way, the aesthetic understanding of organizational life is not freed from the supremacy of the rational reasoning, but is instead constrained

Table 14.1 The four approaches of aesthetic organizational research

Research approach	Researcher's style	Emphasis on	Strengths	Limitations
Archaeological	Guise of an archaeologist and/or an historian of art using qualitative research design and methods	The symbolism of art and aesthetics in organizational life	The aesthetic side of organizational cultures and of the symbolic management of organizations	Aesthetics are ancillary to symbolism
Empathic-logical	Empathic immersion followed by emphatic and logical interpretation, and by a logical-analytical illustration of the outcomes	The *pathos* of organizational artefacts	Precognitive knowledge of organizations and the organizational control based on the *pathos* of artefacts	Aesthetics are translated into logical-analytical descriptions
Aesthetic	Empathic understanding, imaginary participant observation, aesthetic judgement, evocative process of knowing, 'open text' for communicating the outcomes	The collective everyday negotiation of organizational aesthetics	The materiality of quotidian organizational life and also of the researcher's interactions with both organizational actors and organizational scholars	Aesthetics are grounded on connoisseurship
Artistic	Hybridization of artistic creative energy and ratiocinative capacity	The creativity and playfulness of organizational interactions	The artistic performance in managing organization processes	Aesthetics are 'art-bounded'

by the latter. Connoisseurship is the limitation of the aesthetic approach, because aesthetic expertise is its object of study and so too, at the same time, are the skills required to study it. This gives elusiveness both to aesthetic experience in organizations and to research practices in use. Finally, the shortcoming of the artistic approach is its use of art as a stimulus and inspiration for the understanding of organizational life and for communicating such understanding.

These four approaches raise issues of method which to some extent traverse organizational aesthetics research in its entirety:

- The issue of method has 'a modernist musty taste' more in the artistic approach to organizations than in the others. This issue is discussed with transgressive intent and theoretical provocation in the aesthetic approach; with exploratory intent and to understand organizational life in the empathic-logical one; and taking the form of a question that traverses the entire body of analysis of organizations as cultures and symbolic constructs in the archaeological approach.
- The distinction between the construction of aesthetic knowledge about organizations and the study of organizational aesthetics with a view to intervening in organizational contexts and in organizational management is simply a 'nonsense' in the artistic approach, while it gives pre-eminence to understanding in the aesthetic approach, and has the sense of 'intervene only if it has been understood' in the empathic-logical one, and of 'symbolic management' in the archaeological one.

These are the main features of organizational aesthetics research. There now follows more detailed discussion of certain of its aspects, beginning with one shared by all four approaches to the aesthetic study of organizations: the epistemological controversy centred on the object that these approaches study.

Object of study, point of view, and sensible-aesthetic judgement

This part of the chapter illustrates and discusses the relations that connect the 'aesthetic' connotation of the four approaches outlined above with the object of study privileged by empirical and theoretical research, and with the researcher's point of view in the aesthetic study of organizations.

The polemic inherent in the object of study of aesthetic approaches

Enquiring as to what constitutes the object studied by a theoretical-methodological system is almost routine practice in the social sciences and organization theory. However, it has the merit of highlighting the specific characteristics of the theorizations generated by study of that object. Of course, this does not mean that the study object 'determines' both the research methodology and the organizational theory. It only implies that, by reflecting on the object of study, it is possible to characterize and, in part, describe important aspects of the methodological contribution made by aesthetic approaches to organizational analysis.

The object studied by organizational aesthetics research is the aesthetic dimension of organizational life. Nevertheless, what is this 'aesthetic dimension' exactly? Moreover, why does it provoke epistemological controversy among organization scholars?

If we address these two questions together, we are forced *to exclude* that 'aesthetic dimension' means *solely* what is beautiful in an organization. Beauty is certainly essential to the aesthetic dimension; but why should it give rise to epistemological controversy? Studying the beauty of the design of an organization's product – for example, the design for an Alfa Romeo automobile produced by the Pininfarina agency, or the architecture of the building at Cleveland University designed by Frank Gehry – does not in itself involve epistemological controversy, but instead a choice between competing methodologies.

But, if beauty is linked to aesthetics, and if one grasps its reflections in philosophy, art history, and semiotics, as well as in sociology, anthropology, psychology, and economics, then the epistemological controversy does emerge. This is evidenced by the etymology of the word 'aesthetic', which stems from the Ancient Greek root *aisth* and the verb *aisthánomai*. Thus emphasized is sensible knowledge as 'action' performed through the senses of sight, hearing, smell, taste, and touch, and which – stresses Baldine Saint Girons (2008: 22) – is synonymous with neither 'artistic' nor beautiful. These are perceptive-sensory faculties, not the mere terminal sensors of some sovereign conscience; they are 'places of the flesh where the flesh of the world becomes visible', writes Rosella Prezzo (2004: 8), when commenting on the work of the French phenomenologist philosopher Maurice Merleau-Ponty. That is to say, they are ways for individuals to be sensitive to the world amid their social and postsocial interactions in organizational settings. Knowing is thus sensible action, as argued – from the point of view of Deweyan pragmatic philosophy by Shusterman (2008) with his proposal of a philosophy of somaesthetics. Note, though, that it too is subject to the evocative knowledge-creation process activated by the imagination. Conceptual art forcefully reminds us of this, both with its artistic production, and with its theoretical contention that if it is legitimate to display an ordinary object – one thinks of Duchamp's ready-mades – as a work of art, it is equally legitimate to present an abstract idea, preferably drawn from daily life, as the source and content of an artistic experience (Lenain, 2006–7). This is what makes us feel an emotion, or presense it, as when we imagine the scrape of chalk on a blackboard. It immerses us, through the imagination, in the already-felt experience, not merely on the cognitive level but also on the experiential one, so that we rehear the screech of the chalk on the blackboard and our body sensorially relives the jarring sensation. It is the way in which – as Rancière (2003) puts it – certain configurations of the perceivable and the imaginable, or particular forms of experiencing and inhabiting the sensible world, come to define themselves. To conclude, the object of study constituted by the corporeality of feeling through the senses,

and by the ensuing judgement, calls into question, on the one hand, the predominance of mental processes, rational-legal norms and analytic logic, and on the other, the instrumental view of corporeality whereby people and artefacts are means to attain organizational ends.

Impalpable corporeality of aesthetics

Now examined will be the salient characteristics of the object of study in organizational aesthetics research, while bearing in mind the epistemological controversy that it provokes. Organizations have their own specific materiality made of the corporeality of persons and artefacts, but which also comprises something impalpable and invisible that can be emblematically denoted here as 'the atmosphere of the organization' – as suggested by such commonplace expressions in organizations as 'there's something in the air', 'a heavy atmosphere', 'there's an ill wind blowing', 'see which way the wind blows' or 'let in some fresh air'. The atmosphere of an organization is a study object, which:

- Is mundane, is 'everyone's' – except in person-less organizations – and pervades organizational life. It constitutes the latter and belongs, in principle, to those who participate in organizational life. It does not characterize particular organizational processes, tasks, levels, or roles, but is distinctive of everyday work and organizational practices in organizations.
- Is felt and judged by being experienced. Not, that is, through the cognitive or rational knowledge process, but through the feeling of being immersed in the air being breathed, with all the senses and the capacity for sensible-aesthetic judgment that enable identification of beauty, ugliness, and grotesqueness through the aesthetic categories of the language in-use in the organization.
- Has corporeality, even when it is evoked by the organization's language with images, metaphors, or judgements like 'there was a heavy atmosphere at the meeting'.
- Is never identical, because the air breathed in organizations is never the same, not even when it is 'stale'. It is constantly changed by being breathed, or when a window is opened, a computer is switched on, or a machine or a car is started up. In fact, if we consider the moment

when the two corporealities – that of a person's sensory abilities and that of the air – meet, there emerges a connection-in-action between them that takes the form of an interactive change process. For, as we change the air by breathing and rebreathing it, we are changed by what the air brings with it: pleasure at its freshness, distaste at its smells, and the bad humours of its tension.

• Is a hybrid object of study, rather than a pure one. We emit organizational artifacts into the organizational air that we breathe. Our breath mixes our scents, the odours of the fabrics that we are wearing, the leather of our shoes and handbags, the paint on the walls, the materials and the work instruments we are using – in a meeting room, for instance, the wood of the tables, the metal of the chairs, warm OHP projectors, the ink of board markers, printed paper, and photocopies.

The air breathed in organizations is an object of study that acquires and changes sense, meaning and value in the course of organizational interaction: it is not objectively beautiful or ugly, and it is not always subjectively so for those who breathe it. Nor is there a mechanical, deterministic unidirectional relation whereby the beauty or ugliness of the air breathed in organizations affects all their members in the same way and in the same terms. It all depends on the sensibility – and therefore again on the corporeality of the sensory faculties – of those who breathe the air, who may feel its aesthetic qualities more or less intensely. The corporeality of personal knowledge also gives rise to the paradoxical situation where the freshness of springtime air gives hay fever sufferers the sensation of suffocating rather than breathing: they open a window, take a lungful of air, and begin to weep and cough. An attractive organizational setting may be equally suffocating for those who are particularly sensitive: it bores them to death with its tedium; it is so beautiful that 'it takes your breath away'. Just as 'we can't catch our breath' when we are overwhelmed with work and cannot 'take a breather'.

Hence, if the object studied by organizational aesthetics research is the atmosphere of organizations, it is a 'common' object of study that highlights the subjective conditions of the organizational knowledge process. The air breathed in organizations is judged sensorially and aesthetically. It is judged in terms of the taste of those who breathe it and their sensibility; or in other words, by the sensible action of the knowing subject in the postsocial interactions that characterize the organization. Moreover, this knowing subject is both the organizational actor and the researcher, which shifts our attention to the point of view assumed in aesthetic research in organizations, and the communication of its results.

Point of view and aesthetic understanding

As we have seen, the object studied by organizational aesthetics research is the connection-in-action between the personal knowledge of individuals – acquired, forged, and performed in the organizational interactions that immerse them in the sociality of collective action and in a multitude of relations with artefacts – and the action of artefacts at the level of *pathos*. This connection gives salience to the taste of the researcher, doing so in the material determination of aesthetic feeling. Taste, taste judgement, or aesthetic judgement on aesthetic experiences in organizations direct the organization scholar's attention to the subjective conditions of organizational theory-building, in that they involve 'personal knowledge' (Polanyi, 1958) activated by the researcher as s/he engages in aesthetic study of the organization at hand.

Sensorial and aesthetic forming

The issue of the point of view – that is, of position in the complex of postsocial relations among organizational actors, and between them and the organizational scholar – therefore does not concern one's place in an ongoing process as if it were a road; but rather the construction of that road, not alone but collectively in postsocial organizational interaction. It is a sensorial and aesthetic 'forming' amid the postsocial interactions of organizational life. The Italian existentialist philosopher Luigi Pareyson (1954: 23) wrote that every 'human operation is always for-mative, and even a thought process and a practical undertaking demand the exercise of formativity'. Every interaction comprises invention of how to proceed: 'one cannot think or act without forming' and every action 'cannot be itself without forming'. Those who conduct empirical research in organizations are acquainted with the *formativity* described by Pareyson in his essay on aesthetics: they observe what can be observed, they jump from one organizational phenomenon to another, and they switch from examin-ing an organizational event from beginning to end to watching snatches of another event. There are also research situations in which communication with the actors of the process under investigation abruptly ceases. If one considers field research, it more frequently proceeds in fits and starts than in a linear progression yielding the sensation of completeness. However, the researcher constantly 'gives form' through doing what as it is being done invents the method to do it:

> Productive force and inventive capacity are there-fore required by thought and action, because speculative and practical operations consist of a formative activity which, in a specific field, does things at the same time as it invents how they should be done. (Pareyson, 1954: 23)

Form and 'giving form' have been treated by the sociologist Georg Simmel in his reflec-tions on art (1916; Eng. trans. 2005: 155): he writes that 'there is no human work, beyond pure imitation, that is not simultaneously fashioning and creating'. This has also been stressed by Rafael Ramirez, drawing on the aesthetic philosophy of Susanne Langer:

> It is in fact very hard to think of organizations without thinking of form – people in organizations perform; managers reform and transform organiza-tions; are concerned about subordinates informally deforming their views; so they form their personnel and ensure they wear uniforms that manifest their formal selves to others, who become informed. (2005: 32)

Imaginary shadowing

Let us now imagine that we have an opportunity to conduct 'shadowing' in an organization; that is, observe organizational life as the shadow of some organizational actor. In order to show further how the point of view can be sensorially grounded, let us imagine – also for the sake of controversy and transgression – that we have decided to observe the aesthetic understanding and action of the organization's cleaning staff. This point of view shows a general stance, since cleaning is work probably common to all organizations; but it is also very specifically situated and ambiguous, given that it concerns the experiential and not solely cognitive activ-ity performed by most of us – organizational scholars and otherwise – of cleaning the house and tidying the workplace. This ambiguity may be heightened by aesthetic feelings due to previous experiences in other organizational contexts. There will in fact be researchers who have worked as cleaners when they were students. Even the mere idea of shadowing a cleaner in the organization considered will evoke these previous experiences, so that the researcher relives and re-experiences the work and organizational practice done previously with all his/her sensible-aesthetic senses and judgements. On the other hand, there will be those who, like me, did not work as cleaners when they were students, but experienced something similar when they did military service. Thus re-emergent in their memories is the experience of being on fatigue – cleaning kitchens, barracks, latrines, parade grounds, and guard posts – which is only in certain respects similar to that of the cleaning staff in the organization where the shadowing is to take place but whose mere imagining is able to evoke the latter. Latent feelings return to the surface on contact with the smells, shapes and materiality of soaps, waters, brushes, rags, dirt, and dust. As they re-emerge, they are 'affectively' marked because – as the French phenomenologist Henry (1963) reminds us – there is no feeling which is impassive, nor any aesthetic feeling that is not affective. Moreover, feelings are relived experientially, yet not exactly, as they were but marked by the mythical thinking evoked by the memory of gestures, fatigue and disgust felt on cleaning, and on submitting to the command of military organizational life.

This command distinguishes and separates two social practices: doing the cleaning in the organization/being on fatigue and cleaning the barracks. It gives them different flavours in the experiential episode that 'forms' the researcher's point of view as s/he does the shadowing, although, in many other respects, they are similar in terms of sensible knowledge and sensible action in organizations. They cannot be made equal by the materiality of sensory contact in both situations with the smells and colours of the soiled, dilapidated organizational spaces more exposed to the ravages of people or the weather, ugliness and filth, alternated with aestheticizing embellishments, repulsive or gracious styles of organizational life. Choice, though constrained within the limits of work opportunities, gives a different flavour to cleaning, as opposed to the absence of choice when on army fatigue – a flavour, not the product of analytical thought, but which derives from reliving prior organizational experience with all the senses.

The choice vividly illustrates the aesthetic dimension of social practice in organizations, for we can ask, while 'forming' our point of view, if we would like to do cleaning work and if it would appeal to us to the extent that we could envisage it as our life's work; or if, conversely, it is work that does not appeal to us and that we would never contemplate doing, even less devoting the rest of our life to it. These are mundane issues, but they sometimes elicit responses felt 'with all one's being', 'with all one's body'.

Giving form to the point of view

We now 'know' a great deal about this work practice in the organization. We know the practice insofar as it is 'felt' experientially and in the interaction between cleaning work in the organization and the point of view being formed for the empirical research. Formativity takes place in the imagination and in sensible experience: we

have assumed a point of view and formed it sensorially before the shadowing begins. This is the 'imaginary participant observation' performed by projecting oneself into the situation through empathic understanding, and studying it by means of the evocative knowledge-creation process (Strati, 1999). As a method of organizational analysis to prefigure the future development of research, 'imaginary participant observation' activates all the senses, with their capacities for aesthetic judgment, rather than operating at the level of cognition and analytical-rational logic, and it constitutes the 'felt' personal knowledge which Michael Polanyi (1958) called the tacit dimension of knowledge.

What we now know about the work and organizational practice of cleaning predicates our point of view on the issue of whether its purpose is to improve quality and conditions through aesthetics and by operating on the aesthetic dimension. The issue arises at the level of sensible knowledge and aesthetic understanding, less on that of ethical or logical-analytical reflection, owing to the aesthetic feelings aroused by the questions concerning whether the cleaning work would appeal to us, perhaps for a lifetime. The issue is not a new one, and it has been framed in terms of concern about the deterioration in the quality of the organizational life due to both managements' failure to develop organizational aesthetics (Ackoff, 1981) and business consultants' failure to do so. Some decades ago, Fred Steele (1973) suggested in fact that consultants, by seeking the collaboration of designers, broke down the resistance of business managements and introduced organizational learning and training schemes to develop employees' abilities to make appropriate changes to the organization's aesthetic dimension. In Human Resources Development the aesthetic is precious, asserts Stephen Gibb (2006: 164), since it is 'a source of making sense of conduct' in organizations, even though science and technology render it precarious by claiming that it has little economic and political value.

Again, what we know about evoked and relived prior sensible-aesthetic knowledge of cleaning work in organizations raises the issue of choosing a paradigm. 'Forming' the researcher's point of view in this respect recalls Thomas Kuhn's (1962: 154) observation concerning aesthetic considerations which, although 'rarely made entirely explicit', have a sometimes decisive importance for the choice of theoretical paradigm for the research.

If we reprise the sociological paradigms of organization studies identified by Burrell and Morgan (1979) – 'radical humanist', 'radical structuralist', 'interpretative' and 'functionalist' – we can only base the aesthetic understanding of organizational life on those for which the organization is an artefact, inexplicable apart from the symbolic interactions among the subjects involved: the interpretative and radical humanist paradigms. This latter paradigm, in particular, enables one to reaffirm that examining the materiality of organizational life and rooting the methodologies of organizational aesthetics research in sensible experience is also to lay the epistemological bases for critical analysis of what prevents people from fulfilling themselves in organizational routine, beginning with their aesthetic-sensory sensibility, the subjective differences that they enact in interactions, and their creativity. Moreover, the aesthetic understanding of organizations shares with the radical humanism paradigm its privileging of intuition rather than analytical logic, and the evocative knowledge-creation process rather than the one based on causal explanation.

The foregoing discussion has shown that 'giving form' to the aesthetic point of view in the study of the organizational life is rooted in the corporeality and materiality of postsocial interactions, and not only in the ratiocination of cognitive processes. Moreover, it leaves nothing as it was before, as illustrated by the words to this Neapolitan song written by Pino Daniele (2007):

Il ricordo di un amore	*The memory of a love*
viaggia nella testa	*journeys in the mind*
e non c'e' una ragione	*and there is no reason*
quando cerchiamo quel	*when we look for what*
che resta	*remains*

e' come un vento di	*it is like a wind of*
passione o una	*passion or a*
rosa rossa	*red rose*
il ricordo di un amore	*the memory of a love*
ci cambia e non ci lascia	*changes us and does*
	not leave us

Love, the feminist philosopher Carla Locatelli (2007) maintains, is also an important component of organizational life: love for what one is doing; doing things 'with love'. Love is also apparent in the social practices of conducting organizational search, as revealed by the different and multifaceted passions of knowledge, learning, and invention (Gherardi et al., 2007). This may give the impression that aesthetic analysis romanticizes the understanding of organizational life (Hancock, 2005). However, it is not so much this, I believe, that is done with the aesthetic discourse on organization; rather, it is understanding of organizational life in terms of a new humanism that is achieved.

CONCLUSIONS

This chapter has illustrated organizational aesthetics research in terms of a new methodological awareness in the qualitative study of organization. The four aesthetic approaches to the study of organizations described – 'archaeological', 'empathic-logical', 'aesthetic', and 'artistic' – have illustrated the diverse features that methods of analysis – from those more consolidated in the social sciences in general (the 'intellectual' ones) to the more innovative methods rooted in the arts (the 'artistic' ones) – have assumed and may assume in the methodological debate. Their principal feature in common is that researchers immerse themselves in the life of the organization studied, activating their perceptive-sensory faculties and then detaching themselves from the context in order to judge it aesthetically and sensorially. The understanding of organizational life thus obtained is rooted in sensible knowledge constantly in dialogue and/or controversy with cognitive knowledge, and which is primarily characterized as the researcher's personal knowledge. This is a distinctive theoretical node in the aesthetic understanding of organizational life. I believe it to be of considerable importance for the study of organizations for the following reasons:

- It gives due prominence to the fact that researchers learn much more from organizational research than they are able to express and communicate in logical-analytical terms.
- It shows that aesthetics furnishes the language – metaphorical and nuanced; based on intuition and imagination; that develops between poetic logic, art, semiotics and aesthetic philosophy; and constituted by the evocative process of knowledge creation – able to 'give form' to the tacit dimension of the understanding of organizational life by both the organizational actor and the researcher.
- Rebalances relations between researcher and organizational actor, thereby giving full citizenship to researchers in the organizational interactions through which the research process is configured. The researcher is thus not obscured by the light shone on the organizational actors, and the collective and postsocial construction of organizational knowledge and organizational discourse is not subordinated to that of organizational life. This rebalance is unstable, however, because it is achieved through a sequence of everyday imbalances in research, primarily the power asymmetries which the aesthetic approach brings to the fore.
- It drives the epistemological polemic against the dominance of cognitivism, of causal explanation, the myth of rationality, and the belief in the corporate management of the aesthetic dimension of organizational life.

REFERENCES

Ackoff, R. (1981) *Creating the Corporate Future: Plan or be Planned For*, New York: Wiley.

Barry, D. (2008) 'The art of . . .', in D. Barry and H. Hansen (eds), *The Sage Handbook of New Approaches in Management and Organization*, London: Sage, pp. 31–41.

Baumgarten, A.G. (1750–8) *Aesthetica I-II*. Frankfurt am Oder: Kleyb (Photostat: Olms: Hildesheim, 1986).

Berg, P.O. (1987) 'Some notes on corporate artifacts', *Scos Note-Work*, 6(1): 24–8.

Berg, P.O. and Kreiner, K. (1990) 'Corporate architecture: turning physical settings into symbolic resources', in P. Gagliardi (ed.), *Symbols and Artifacts: Views of the Corporate Landscape*. Berlin: de Gruyter, pp. 41–67.

Brearley, L. (2001) 'Foot in the air: an exploration of the experience of transition in organizational life', in C. Boucher and R. Holian (eds), *Emerging Forms of Representing Qualitative Data*, Melbourne: RMIT University Press, pp. 151–84.

Bryman, A. (1989) *Research Methods and Organization Studies*, Boston: Unwin Hyman.

Burrell, G. and Morgan, G. (1979) *Sociological Paradigms and Organizational Analysis*, Aldershot: Gower.

Daniele, P. (2007) 'Vento di passione', in *Il mio nome è Pino Daniele e vivo qui*. CD Music Aim, Sony BMG Music Entertainment.

Dean, J.W., Ramirez, R. and Edward O. (1997), 'An aesthetic perspective on organizations', in C. Cooper and S. Jackson (eds), *Creating Tomorrow's Organizations: A Handbook for Future Research in Organizational Behavior*, Chichester: Wiley, pp. 419–37.

Escoubas, É. (2004) *L'Esthétique*, Paris: Ellipses.

Gagliardi, P. (ed.) (1990) *Symbols and Artifacts: Views of the Corporate Landscape*, Berlin: de Gruyter.

Gagliardi, P. (2006) 'Exploring the aesthetic side of organizational life', in Clegg, S.R., Hardy, C., Lawrence, T.B. and W.R. Nord (eds), *The Sage Handbook of Organization Studies* (second edn.), Sage: London, pp. 701–24.

Gherardi, S. and Turner, B.A. (1987, partial reprint 1999) *Real Men Don't Collect Soft Data*, Trent: Dipartimento di Politica Sociale, Quaderno 13. Reprint 1999 in A. Bryman and R. Burgess (eds), *Qualitative Research I-IV*, London: Sage, pp. 103–8.

Gherardi, S., Nicolini, D. and Strati, A. (eds) (2007) Special issue on 'the passion for knowing and learning', *Organization*, 14 (3).

Gibb, S. (2006) *Aesthetics and Human Resource Development*, London: Routledge.

Guillet de Monthoux, P. (2004) *The Art Firm: Aesthetic Management and Metaphysical Marketing from Wagner to Wilson*, Stanford: Stanford Business Books.

Hancock, P. (2005) 'Uncovering the semiotic in organizational aesthetics', *Organization*, 12(1): 29–50.

Hancock, P. and Tyler, M. (2000) ' "The look of love": gender and the organization of aesthetics', in J. Hassard, R. Holliday and H. Willmott (eds), *Body and organization*, London: Sage, pp. 108–29.

Henry, M. (1963) *L'Essence de la Manifestation*, Paris: PUF.

Human Relations (2002) 55/7. Special Issue on 'Organizing aesthetics', A. Strati and P. Guillet de Monthoux (eds).

Hindmarsh, J. and Heath, C. (2007) 'Video-based studies of work practice', *Sociology Compass*, 1: 1–17.

King, I.W. (2007) 'Straightening our perspective: the logos of the line', *Organization*, 14(2): 225–41.

Kuhn, T. (1962) *The Structure of Scientific Revolutions*, Chicago: University of Chicago Press.

Latour, B. (2005) *Reassembling the Social. An Introduction to Actor-Network-Theory*, Oxford: Oxford University Press.

Lenain, T. (2006–2007) 'Du mode d'existence de l'oeuvre dans l'art conceptuel', *La Part de l'Oeil*, Special Issue on Esthétique et phénoménologie en mutation, 21–22: 53–69.

Linstead, S. and Höpfl, H. (eds) (2000) *The Aesthetics of Organization*, London: Sage.

Locatelli, C. (2007) 'Women's Way of Knowing: It Is All About Love!', *Organization*, 14(3): 339–50.

Marquard, O. (1989) *Aesthetica und Anaesthetica. Philosophische Uberlegungen*, Paderborn: Schoningh.

Martin, P.Y. (2002) 'Sensations, bodies, and the "Spirit of the Place": aesthetics in residential organizations for the elderly', *Human Relations*, 55(7): 861–85.

Minahan, S. and Wolfram Cox, J. (eds) (2007) *The Aesthetic Turn in Management*, Ashgate: Gower.

Nicolini, D., Gherardi, S. and Dvora Y. (eds) (2003) *Knowing in Organizations: A Practice-Based Approach*, New York: M.E. Sharpe Armonk.

Organization (1996) 3/2. Special Issue on 'Aesthetics and Organization', E. Ottensmeyer (ed.).

Pareyson, L. (1954) *Estetica. Teoria della formatività*, Turin: Giappichelli. Reprinted 1988, Milan: Bompiani.

Pelzer, P. (2002) 'Disgust and organization', *Human Relations*, 55(7): 841–60.

Perrow, C. (1972) *Complex Organizations: A Critical Essay*, Glenview, IL: Scott, Foresman.

Pine, J.B. and Gilmore, J.H. (1999) *The Experience Economy*, Cambridge, MA : Harvard Business School Press.

Polanyi, M. (1958) *Personal Knowledge. Towards a Post-Critical Philosophy*, London: Routledge & Kegan Paul.

Prezzo, R. (2004) 'Il primato di un paradosso', in M. Merleau-Ponty, *Il primato della percezione e le sue conseguenze filosofiche*, Milan: Medusa, pp. 5–14.

Putnam, L., Phillips, N. and Pamela C. (1996) 'Metaphors of communication and organization', in S. R. Clegg, C. Hardy and W. R. Nord (eds), *Handbook of Organization Studies*, London: Sage, pp. 375–408.

Ramirez, R. (2005) 'The aesthetics of cooperation', *European Management Review*, 2: 28–35.

Rancière, J. (2003) *Le destin des images*. Paris: La fabrique éditions (Eng. transl. *The Future of the Image*, London: Verso, 2007).

Saint Girons, B. (2008) *L'acte Esthétique*, Paris: Klincksieck.

Scalfi, A. (2007) 'Untitled 2004 # Paris', *Aesthesis. International Journal of Art and Aesthetics in Management and Organizational Life*, 1(1): DVD, 20' 38".

Shusterman, R. (2008) *Body Consciousness. A Philosophy of Mindfulness and Somaesthetics*, Cambridge: Cambridge University Press.

Simmel, G. (1916) *Rembrandt, Ein kunstphilosophischer Versuch*, Leipzig: Kurt Wolff Verlag (Eng. trans.: *Rembrandt. An Essay in the Philosophy of Art*. Translated and edited by A. Scott and H. Staubmann. New York: Routledge).

Steele, F.I. (1973) *Physical Settings and Organization Development*, Reading, MA: Addison-Wesley.

Steyaert, C. and Hjorth, D. (2002) "'Thou art a scholar, speak to it …" – on spaces of speech: A script', *Human Relations*, 55(7): 767–97.

Strati, A. (1992) 'Aesthetic understanding of organizational life', *Academy of Management Review*, 17(3): 568–81.

Strati, A. (1998) '(Mis)understanding cognition in organization studies', *Scandinavian Journal of Management*, 14(4): 309–29.

Strati, A. (1999) *Organization and Aesthetics*, London: Sage.

Strati, A. (2007) 'Sensations, impressions and reflections on the configuring of the aesthetic discourse in organizations', *Aesthesis. International Journal of Art and Aesthetics in Management and Organizational Life*, 1(1): 14–22.

Taylor, S. and Hansen, H. (2005) 'Finding form: looking at the field of organizational aesthetics', *Journal of Management Studies*, 42(6): 1210–31.

Turner, B.A. (ed.) (1990) *Organizational Symbolism*, Berlin: de Gruyter.

Vico, G. (1725) *Principi di una scienza nuova*, Naples: Mosca (third edn.), (1744), (Eng. trans.: *The New Science of Giambattista Vico*, ed. T.G. Bergin and M.H. Fisch. Ithaca, NY: Cornell University Press, 1968).

Warren, S. (2008) 'Empirical challenges in organizational aesthetics research: towards a sensual methodology', *Organization Studies*, 29(4): 559–80.

Weber, M. (1922) *Wirtschaft und Gesellschaft. Grundriß der verstehenden Soziologie*. Tübingen: Mohr. (Eng. trans.: *Economy and Society: An Outline of Interpretive Sociology. I-II.* Berkeley: University of California Press, 1978).

Witkin, R.W. (1990) 'The aesthetic imperative of a rational-technical machinery: a study in organizational control through the design of artifacts', in P. Gagliardi (ed.), *Symbols and Artifacts: Views of the Corporate Landscape*. Berlin: de Gruyter, pp. 325–38.

[14]

Organizational Artifacts and the Aesthetic Approach

Antonio Strati
University of Trento, Trento, Italy

There is by now a substantial body of organizational literature on artifacts, and it has gained accreditation among organizational theories as the crisis of the rationalist and positivist paradigm has deepened (Hatch, 1997b; Strati, 2000). And since the pioneering works of Fred Steele (1973) and Franklin Becker (1981), it has also developed in relation to aesthetics (Gagliardi, 1990; Ramirez, 1991; Strati, 1992; Turner, 1990). Toward the end of the last century, the *pathos* of organizational artifacts highlighted by study of aesthetics and organizations was flanked by Michel Callon's (1980) sociology of translation—thereafter termed "actor network theory" (Law & Hassard, 1999)—and in particular by Bruno Latour's study (1992), which treated artifacts as "missing masses" from socio-technical analyses of organizational phenomena. The status of the artifact has also been changed from that of a tool to an actor in organizational dynamics by the analyses conducted within "workplace studies" (Heath & Button, 2002), as well as those on "cooperative learning" and "participatory design" applied to information systems (Ciborra, 1996; Ehn, 1988).

Organizational artifacts, even when they are physical and tangible objects, are not static, immutable, and determinable once and for all; on the contrary, constructionist, phenomenological, and interactionist analyses have shown the extent to which they are mutable and constantly self-innovative—all the more so in the case of information technology artifacts (Suchman, Trigg, & Blomberg, 2002). In short, at the beginning of this new millennium, organizational artifacts depict contemporary Western societies as some sort of *"postsocial* environment" (Knorr Cetina, 2003) in which they mediate the social relations among people to an ever-increasing extent, and in which they themselves transmogrify into transmutational objects.

The aesthetic approach, actor network theory, and the three strands of inquiry comprising workplace studies, cooperative learning, and participatory design, therefore, all emphasize the importance of the organizational artifact in the everyday lives of organizations. They stress symbolic interaction and the social and collective construction of reality. They pay close attention to socio-technical detail and to the micro dimension, conducting qualitative analysis of organizational phenomena, the constant changeableness of organizational artifacts, and the time span in which they arise and spread. By contrast, these approaches differ in the extent to which they attribute to nonhuman objects a capacity for action on a par with that of humans—actor network theory in fact theorizes the capacity for action of the organizational artifact and the scaling back of exclusively human action—and also in their conceptions of the centrality of knowledge and aesthetic experience. Nor do actor network theory or the workplace studies, cooperative learning, and participatory design approaches view the organizational artifact necessarily in terms of pathos—although some attention is paid to this aspect (Whalen, Whalen, & K. Henderson, 2002).

In order to illustrate the importance of aesthetics in the understanding of the organizational artifacts, I deal in this chapter with the production of an artifact that was particularly evanescent and equivocal because of its ephemerality and its nature as action-in-being. The artifact in question was a "performance" (Guillet de Monthoux, 2000, 2004; Hamilton, 2001; Höpfl & Linstead, 1993; Mangham, 1996; Nissley, Taylor, & Houden, 2004) produced for a female student's degree. Its antecedents were her work for two courses during which "by accident" recordings of discursive practices in work routine and study of Weber's bureaucracy coincided with "discovery" of an art installation in the civic gallery of contemporary art. The student's desire to do something different therefore arose in an extrauniversity context—the gallery—and was prompted by the mingling of various kinds of experience: her experience of academic study acquired while recording the conversations in the organizations, that of classroom learning, and her artistic experience in the art gallery.

The "Iron Cage" performance described in this chapter was therefore "situated" within a set of complex organizational dynamics where it was the pathos of the artifact-performance that set them in relation—due to the pleasure that the performance provoked, the enthusiasm that it aroused, the desire that it stimulated, and the imagery that it evoked—to the "différance" (Derrida, 1967) that distinguishes every individual, the heterogeneity of material artifacts, the multiformity of organizational processes. Indeed:

- It was the aesthetic dimension of the artifact, initially imagined but not yet existent, that stimulated the senses and the taste of the students and teachers on the two courses in sociology of organization and sociology of work, and the creative process that was thereby "improvised" (Montuori, 2003).
- It was aesthetics that connoted the organizational interaction when the artifact-performance was enacted in the faculty.
- It was aesthetic pleasure that translated the ephemeral organizational act of the performance into the collective construction of what I call, following Baudrillard, the artifact-simulacrum of the performance: to wit, the multimedia product that ensued from it and that constituted the material artifact of further organizational interactions (university lectures and conferences).
- It was aesthetics that distinguished the organizational communication (L. Putnam, Phillips, & Chapman, 1996) brought into being by the performance.

AESTHETIC APPROACH AND PERFORMANCE

The aesthetic approach (Strati, 1992, 1999) examines the artifact in its "being-in-use" in organizational settings, emphasizing material knowledge and "practice" in the study of organizations (Nicolini, Gherardi, & Yanow, 2003). The approach concerns itself with tacit knowledge (Polanyi, 1962), as well as with the being-in-use of artifacts and the aesthetic and artistic pleasure that they arouse (Jauss, 1982). Art and aesthetics furnish a language with which awareness of "knowing how"—and at the same time awareness that one's knowledge is impossible to explain scientifically—can be both expressed and studied without violating the character of tacit knowledge by having perforce to translate it (Serres, 1974) into explicit knowledge. For the aesthetic approach, the organizational artifact has pathos (it is "art" and not just "fact") just as organizational life is not only *logos* (which concerns its ontological definition, its essence, its "nature") but also *ethos* (which comprises its unwritten principles, its moral codes, its deontologies, and the constant regulation of its legitimacy) and pathos, that is, its dimension of feeling, perceiving through the senses, judging aesthetically.

Hence, everyday organizational routine comprises artifacts that are beautiful to use, graceful to the eye, or grotesque, kitsch, or repellent—and to which the language-in-use of organizational discursive practices attaches labels evocative of the aesthetic categories of beautiful, ugly, sublime, gracious, and so on (Strati, 1999). There are artifacts that are desirable or repulsive, artifacts born from our desire for knowledge, and artifacts that spring from our desire to "give form"—in that every human "forms" something (Pareyson, 1954)—and that is thus "formative." There are artifacts that arouse aesthetics feelings (and obviously emotions as well) these being not independent effects, separate and distinct from the artifact itself, but rather qualities expressive of the style that characterizes it. And there are artifacts that constantly transmute because they are observed in organizational and work practices—that is, observed in their being-in-use within organizations.

A chair, for example, acquires multiple forms and meanings in an organization (Strati, 1996): It may be a power symbol or an artifact on which to sit, a decorative item or an improvised table, a stepping-stool or a jacket hanger. The artifact "chair" does not have a well-defined ontological status that determines its organizational action; rather, its identity changes according to the interaction in which it is involved, and it sometimes assumes more than one identity. But the aesthetic approach maintains that the interaction is based on the perceptive-sensory faculties and on the sensitive-aesthetic judgment: The chair can be touched with the body and the hands; it can be smelled (albeit not deliberately); it can be heard as it creaks; it can be appreciated for its shape and style, or even for the sense of the sacred that it evokes by virtue of its workmanship and history.

It is therefore sensory knowledge and the sensitive-aesthetic judgment, and not solely ratiocination, that sets the artifact in organizational dynamics and processes. And just as the artifact has multiform and transmutational identities, so the human body, as well, is never the same from one moment to the next—as we know from medicine and biology—and never from one social interaction to the next, as we know from the social sciences, and also from art: Consider the portraits by Francis Bacon or Pablo Picasso, or the three-dimensional transformations of the human body in computer art.

The artifact discussed in this chapter is very different in nature from a chair. Nonetheless, evident are its heterogeneity and its aesthetic construal as a dialogue for noncausal knowledge (Cairns, 2002; Strati, 1999). Aesthetic knowledge of the chair springs from practice: that is, observing, imagining, or using a chair when it is in-use or in dis-use. The performance-as-artifact further enhances practice in organizations: It exists when it is in action, to the point that the opposite, its nonbeing in action, necessarily entails its nonexistence. Artifact and action are closely intertwined in performance, in the sense that the latter exists in the moment when it is enacted, when it is social, work, and organizational *practice*. In other words, whereas when the chair-artifact is not in-use it is still the outcome of organizational interaction and work, this is not the case of the performance-artifact, which is an artifact-in-action and for this reason ephemeral, evanescent, elusive, and also— as in the case of the "Iron Cage" performance described shortly—hybrid: A human being and heterogeneous materials are con-fused in it, highlighting the complexity of experiencing as well as simultaneously aesthetically understanding an organizational artifact. A performance "evokes" by means of complex action in which corporeality goes beyond the logical-rational intelligibility of the semantic content of the heard sound, of the observed gesture, and of the artifacts that interact with the body—beginning with the organizational space in which the process takes place. Sounds, body movements, and heterogeneous artifacts "evoke" and stir the emotions by their beauty, ugliness, rhythm, style, and artistic language.

It has been pointed out (Strati & Guillet de Monthoux, 2002) that performance is an expressive style that is difficult to convey in a written text. The script is only one component of the whole. It does not entirely account for the performance: In fact, Steyaert and Hjorth (2002) note that, although the script "creates 'evidence' of organizing aesthetics', . . . it is not without a sense of loss that we relate to the text, having performed the play" (p. 769). In what follows I first describe a performance artifact as it was "acted" within the organizational interactions that it had brought into being. Then, in the following section, I analyze what happened before and after the action in question. The organizational meaning of the performance was not that of artistic creation, but rather the meaning of a teaching device used at a university. It concerned, in fact, the confluence into a "dialogue in act" of a visual and oral counterpoint among:

- Practical knowledge in organizations as discussed during a course on the sociology of work, the focus of which was organizational learning. The course program included practical exercises where the students recorded discursive practices in organizations.
- The norms underpinning the Weberian ideal type of bureaucracy discussed in a course on sociology of organizations.
- A work of art exhibited in a civic art gallery and consisting of an installation divided into two parts: one rigid, solid, and stable, the other melting into soft sinuous movement, which, however, did not deprive the installation of its structuring character.

THE PERFORMANCE AS AN EPHEMERAL ORGANIZATIONAL ARTIFACT

Let us suppose that the reader wants to observe directly, but by means of his or her imagination, the performance that I describe. I refer to a style of organizational ethnography (Strati, 1999) that is used for qualitative empirical analysis in organizational settings much more frequently than has been documented. In order to undertake an ethnographic study of this kind, the participant observer puts him or herself in the place of one of the actors in the process and "constructs" the action and the scenario. But she or he does so on the basis of an activated knowledge that is entirely personal in that it is rooted in his or her personal experiences and based on his or her capacity for imagination and empathy.

The reader should therefore choose a point of observation. This may be very different from the one that I am about to describe, but let us assume that the prompts that follow will suffice to satisfy his or her desire for knowledge. Let us suppose, therefore, that one dreary morning in spring the reader finds him or herself in a small city in northern Italy, in the medieval surroundings of the city center and close to one of the most beautiful cathedral squares in Europe. Standing a few dozen meters away, in one of the main streets, is the university faculty building in which the performance will take place. Outside the faculty building, under persistent drizzle and a gray sky, groups of students are holding a protest meeting with banners, megaphone-amplified slogans, and chants. The reader threads his or her way through the demonstration and enters the faculty building, finding him or herself in a large lobby. On the left is the porters' lodge fitted out as if it were an audiovisual recording studio; on the right is an installation executed by an well-known Italian artist. The reader crosses the lobby, goes up three steps flanked by two large pillars, and follows the temporary signs giving directions to the conference venue. The reader skirts the broad staircase leading to the two upper floors, passes through a large covered courtyard, and heads toward the Main Hall. There the reader takes a seat in a room tiered like a Greco-Roman theater. From his or her seat the reader can see that behind and above the speakers' dais is affixed a large screen on which appear, in sequence, slides of the entrance to the faculty, the room of a German university, and the Main Hall in which she or he is now sitting. The reader listens to the welcoming address and those announcing the theme and context of the event. The reader then leaves the Main Hall and returns to the lobby and to the installation erected therein. She or he is unable to get close to it, however, because of the large number of people assembled to watch the performance. Instead, the reader climbs the main staircase to a vantage point from which she or he can watch and listen.

What the reader hears is a playback of conversations recorded in organizational settings. A female student enters the installation and from its interior, by way of counterpoint, recites phrases taken from the Italian version of the sociologist Max Weber's writings on bureaucracy. The phrases uttered by the student alternate with recordings collected by herself and some other students in the same course for the purpose of studying work and organizational practices in a variety of settings: a railway station, a supermarket, a dance school, and other settings besides. The reader thus witnesses a dialogue between the recorded voices recounting present-day routine in organizations and the live voice reciting the phrases from Weber inside the installation. Merged with these voices is the visual language of the installation, that of the student inside it, and that of the organizational space of the faculty, made up of human bodies and heterogeneous materials, in which the performance is positioned. The reader watches and listens to the performance, but also to the "noise" of the context in which it is taking place. The reader notes that television camera crews are filming the student and the audience, and watches as students enter the lobby, fold their umbrellas, hush their voices and, stooping so as not to block the view, make their way through the watching crowd. The reader can also hear the increasingly distant voices of the demonstrators. Twenty or so minutes pass. The reader then sees the student come out of the installation and, reciting the phrases over again, head toward the Great Hall, accompanied by a lecturer and followed by the audience. The reader thus reenters the lecture hall as enthusiastic applause covers the noise of the participants returning to their seats. One of the speakers briefly introduces the German academic—visible on the screen thanks to the teleconferencing system—who comments on the performance. He is followed by the panel of speakers: lecturers from the faculty, the director of the city gallery of contemporary art, the artist. At the end of the morning, and amid resounding applause on conclusion of the conference, the reader returns to the lobby and inspects the installation—now empty, as is the space surrounding it—and listens to a recording made of the performance that is now being played back at low volume.

The vocal dialogue transcribed in the script that follows was only one aspect of the performance, therefore, for it combined with the "visual" of the installation and of its setting in the university organizational space.

The installation (see Fig. 2.1) occupied a large area to one side of the entrance lobby. It was constructed from materials whereby its linear architecture shifted from rigid and square shapes to fluid and sinuous ones. Thus, although on the one hand the "iron cage" structure gave the impression of solidity, on the other it seemingly melted and collapsed on itself. The squared part of the structure was entirely covered with transparent material and contained a door to the interior. The base of the installation was initially rectangular but then soft, curved, and irregular in shape. The transparent material covering three of its sides created a sharp separation between interior and exterior. But also when the linear structure—the installation's skeleton—became soft, flexible, and bare, it still separated the interior from the exterior and kept the visitor outside the area of the installation or internally to it.

The installation interacted both with the discursive practices of work in organizations and with the norms of the Weberian ideal type of bureaucracy (Fig. 2.2), translating itself into the nonhuman protagonist of a

FIG. 2.1.   Loris Cecchini's installation *Density Spectrum Zone 1.0*. Copyright 2003 by L. Cecchini. Courtesy Gallerie Continua. Reprinted by permission.

FIG. 2.2.   The student Anna Scalfi performing in the entrance to the faculty. Photograph by P. Cavagna. Copyright 2003 by P. Cavagna. Printed by permission.

trialogue among practical knowledge, social science, and art. On conclusion of the performance, the installation was still a protagonist: Though deprived of human presence, it set itself in relation to voices that repeated, over and over again, the following:

> A woman queuing at the station [excerpts from taped conversations in organizational settings]: . . . *because the one behind . . . his train is leaving but he can't go. It's the lady asking as many questions as she wants, of course. But this is also a ticket office and behind her there are people queuing because they need to buy tickets. There isn't an information office anymore, there's no window where you can get information only. This is reorganization as the train company does it, they just cut staff. They cut staff in smaller stations or they ask you to dial this or that telephone number at a rate of . . . 6 or more cents a minute . . . because they're those very expensive numbers, those which used to cost 1400 lire and now cost 60 cents, you're charged on connection. If you go on the Internet it's free, for those who can connect, that is, it's really crazy . . . and a simple thing like the information office has just gone.*

> Student [who has in the meantime entered the installation; excerpts from Weber, 1922, English translation: 1978, pp. 956–1005 and 212–226, and in Mayer, 1956, pp. 125–131]: Modern officialdom functions in the following manner: There is the principle of official *jurisdictional areas*, which are generally ordered by rules, that is, by laws or administrative regulations. This means: The regular activities required for the purposes of the bureaucratically governed structure are assigned as official duties.

> At the supermarket: *bip bip bip 77, 78, 79 . . . 79? 80?*
> —*It's me.*
> —*Yes, please Ma'am.*

> Student: The authority to give the commands required for the discharge of these duties is distributed in a stable way and is strictly delimited by rules concerning the coercive means, which may be placed at the disposal of officials. Methodological provision is made for the regular and continuous fulfilment of these duties and for the exercise of the corresponding rights; only persons who qualify under general rules are employed.

> A woman traveler and a male clerk at the station: *How can the PC keeps track of the previous one?*
> —*I don't know. I don't really know much about computers . . . I was never trained, I only issue tickets.*
> —*Please?*
> —*For technical stuff you need to go to an engineer.*
> —*Without reimbursement you do the . . .*
> —*Ah! The change . . . eh!*

> Student: The principles of *office hierarchy* and of channels of appeal stipulate a clearly established system of super- and subordination in which there is a supervision of the lower offices by the higher ones. Such a system offers the

governed the possibility of appealing, in a precisely regulated manner, the decision of a lower office to the corresponding superior authority.

A woman clerk at the tax office: *If you want, we can check in detail how the payment was made, if it was late and so on. It is very likely that the government will send you, maybe in five years, an order to pay interest because the tax was paid too late. Please consider that the tax is debited directly on . . . OK, the sum clearly goes to the government, instead the government can ask you to pay a penalty. So just to inform you of this I thought it appropriate to let you know . . . by law we have to do it, just in case you receive the penalty notice . . . because it's not one hundred percent sure we are dealing with the specific issue of payments here.*

Student: The management of the modern office is based upon written documents, which are preserved in their original or draft form, and upon a staff of subaltern officials and scribes of all sorts. Office management, at least all specialized office management—and such management is distinctly modern—usually presupposes thorough training in a field of specialization. Official activity demands the *full working capacity* of the official, irrespective of the fact that the length of his obligatory working hours in the bureau may be limited. The management of the office follows *general rules*, which are more or less stable, more or less exhaustive, and which can be learned.

A woman client and a male clerk at the station: *So you want a complete reimbursement? No, no, I'll cancel the transaction because they won't, I'll cancel everything . . . OK, OK, I'll make a complete reimbursement and then do it all over again. I'll do, I should do something else, but I'll do it anyway, when do you need it for? I'll cancel . . . I'll get the seat free and then I'll make a brand-new reservation. Only for the reimbursement, however, and nothing else, then he'll find it, but only for the reimbursement.*
—Any problems?
—Yeah, because it won't accept the change, should I do this way?
—How come the change can't be made?
—Well, let's say that the system is not perfect, let's say
—Please?
—I said the system is not perfect, sometimes it happens that . . . for the 27th you said?

Student: The decisive reason for the advance of bureaucratic organization has always been its purely *technical* superiority over any other form of organization. Bureaucratization offers above all the optimum possibility for carrying through the principle of specializing administrative functions according to purely objective considerations. Individual performances are allocated to functionaries who have specialized training and who by constant practice increase their expertise. "Objective" discharge of business primarily means a discharge of business according to *calculable rules* and "without regard for persons." The peculiarity of modern culture, and specifically of its technical and economic basis, demands this very "calculability" of results.

Woman teacher at the dance school: *Please girls, one hand on the bar . . . stretch in the air and press toward the floor, bend and lift your heel, and down, and stay, and . . . Stretch, and "rond," don't stop, don't stop, continuity, stretch back, the heel brings the leg forward, stretch from far and back.*

Student: When fully developed, bureaucracy also stands, in a specific sense, under the principle of *sine ira ac studio*. Bureaucracy develops the more perfectly, the more it is "dehumanized," the more completely it succeeds in eliminating from official business love, hatred, and all purely personal, irrational, and emotional elements which escape calculation. This is appraised as its special virtue by capitalism.

Clerk and an elderly customer at the supermarket: *bip bip bip 77, 78, 79 . . . 79? 80?*
—Me
—Yes, please Ma'am.
—Here, look, the other day I got a piece of cheese . . . goat cheese, good, really good, but I can't remember which . . . I think, that's it, IS it?
—Is this too much?
—No, there's too much rind.
—Too much rind?
—Oh dear, I'm already too old without . . .

Student: Where administration has been completely bureaucratized, the resulting system of domination is practically indestructible. The individual bureaucrat cannot squirm out of the apparatus into which he has been harnessed. The professional bureaucrat is chained to his activity in his entire economic and ideological existence.

A woman clerk at the tax office: *If you want, we can check in detail how the payment was made, if it was late and so on. It is very likely that the government . . . will send you, maybe in five years, an order to pay interest because the tax was paid too late.*

Student: The whole administrative staff under the supreme authority then consists, in the purest type, of individual officials . . . who are appointed and function according to the following criteria: They are personally free and subject to authority only with respect to their impersonal official obligations. They are organized in a clearly defined hierarchy of offices. Each office has a clearly defined sphere of competence in the legal sense. The office is filled by a free contractual relationship. . . . Candidates are selected on the basis of technical qualifications. . . . They are remunerated by fixed salaries in money, for the most part with a right to pensions. . . . The office is treated as the sole, or at least the primary, occupation of the incumbent. It constitutes a career. . . . The official works entirely separated from ownership of the means of administration and without appropriation of his position. He is subject to strict and systematic discipline and control in the conduct of the office.

Woman teacher at the dance school: *And stretch in the air, and press toward the ground, bend and lift your heel, and down, and stay, and . . . Stretch, and "rond," don't stop, don't stop, continuity, stretch back, the heel brings the leg forward, stretch from far and back.*

<u>Student</u>: In that case every single bearer of power and command is legitimated by that system of rational norms, and his power is legitimated insofar as it corresponds with the norm. Obedience is thus given to the norms rather than to the person.

<u>A woman traveler and a male clerk at the station</u>: *Let's do it again with a different date, can you tell me your name and surname? What should I put in the notes? No, it says I must put it here*
—Listen, but you solve the problem instead of reimbursing it maybe you can convert it into a different ticket to . . .
—Yeah, yeah, I'll make you out a new ticket, it doesn't matter. The system doesn't allow the date to be changed
—The system doesn't allow the change? Date . . .
—If you sign here, then I'll make out another one for the other date, good, good, then we are even, 7 and 28, 7 and 28, here it is
—Thanks.

<u>Student</u>: The purely bureaucratic type of administrative organization . . . is the most rational known means of exercising authority over human beings. . . . The whole pattern of everyday life is cut to fit this framework.

<u>At the butcher's shop</u>: *Cooked beef is, is 1,67, 167, ground is 4,74* [noises], *3,61, 2,47 for sausage*
—Thanks, that's all
—Is that all, madam?
—I'll let you know right away: 2, 3, 4, 5, 6, 7 times, yeah.
—A bit more and that'll do.
—Thanks and good day.
—Bye and thank you again.

<u>Student</u>: Already now, rational calculation, is manifest at every stage. By it, the performance of each individual worker is mathematically measured, each man becomes a little cog in the machine and, aware of this, his one preoccupation is whether he can become a bigger cog. . . . it is horrible to think that the world could one day be filled with nothing but those little cogs, little men clinging to little jobs and striving towards bigger ones. . . . This passion for bureaucracy . . . is enough to drive one to despair.

<u>Woman teacher at the dance school</u>: *Please take care with these movements because otherwise they become mechanical, and end themselves and they become . . . sort of sad. Please, let things start from within, from your soul, from your body, from your heart. And always filter, always, mind, heart, body. You.*

The voice of the woman queuing at the station returns; so does that of the student reciting Weber, and the dialogue between sound artifacts and visual artifacts resumes. But now lacking are the gestures and the gaze of the participants in the event, although there are now those of the people intrigued by the unusual audiovisual artifact placed in the faculty lobby. By moving, using his or her empathic capacity and imagination, among the places of the organizational event, the reader has familiarized him or herself with three of the four organizational spaces in which it took place. These spaces were the following:

1. The faculty lobby in which the installation was positioned, together with the equipment for real-time transmission via Internet and the amplification and recording equipment. The morning light illuminating the scene filtered through the three large glass doors of the entrance, and through them passed to and fro students, lecturers, university personnel, and the television and newspaper reporters. On the opposite side of the lobby, three steps and the broad staircase leading to the upper floors constituted "natural" vantage points for watching the performance. On the side not occupied by the installation, the porters continued with their normal work, given that the performance did not interrupt the faculty's usual activities but was supplementary to them.

2. The Main Hall, equipped for teleconferences and video recording. This was the place where the event began. The attendees were welcomed by the chairman; the two lecturers explained what the event was all about. Then the image of the German academic appeared on the large screen behind the speakers as he commented on the event via teleconference from his university in Germany. It was the place in which the performance was discussed by the Italian lecturers, the German academic, the director of the civic art gallery, the artist, students who had helped with recording the workplace conversations, and some members of the public. It was also the place where the event ended: (a) the performance finished with applause for the female student who had led them vocally through it like the magic piper of the Grimm brothers' fairy tale; (b) both the off-line conference and the teleconference concluded.

3. The street outside the faculty where the students were holding their demonstration, and then moved away from the front entrance so that their banners, slogans, amplified voices, chants, and noise no longer disturbed the performance.

4. The screens of computers logged on to the faculty Web site, both internally and via Internet, and on which events in the lobby or the Great Hall could be watched. Although this place of the performance was obviously a space accessible to anyone, it was not utilized by the reader, by the participants, by the student who did the performance, or even by any of the speakers except for the German academic.

But what led up to the performance? And what happened subsequently to it? This is examined in the section that follows, whereas the conclusions consider the new insights that originate from the performance for the aesthetic understanding of organizational artifacts.

THE PERFORMANCE: ARTIFACT-IMAGERY, ARTIFACT-EPHEMERON, ARTIFACT-SIMULACRUM

I have said that it was the aesthetic sentiment, and the strong emotion aroused by the installation, that fused the student's learning acquisitions from the two courses together. Yet this could not have been anticipated, given that it had not been the artist's intention to represent the sociological problematic of work practices and/or Weber's iron cage. Amid this tangle of sentiments, the performance was—as March (1994) might put it, discussing the "garbage can" model of the organizational decision-making process—a solution looking for a problem: "I could recite the Weber excerpts from inside the installation," the student suggested: "I've studied drama." Should she have been allowed to continue with a study project of such entirely exceptional nature in the faculty—for which, that is to say, there were no socially legitimated practices? The factors that eventually weighed in favor of the performance were the following: (a) the social legitimacy in the faculty of the sociological study of organizational aesthetics as a research topic and an academic subject; (b) the student's past artistic experience, also professional; (c) the fact that there were two faculty courses, rather than only one, involved in the event; (d) the aura of "practice" that surrounded the performance and chimed well with study of organizational practices; and (e) the intention to go ahead step-by-step, seeing how things developed. After all, two of the student's examinations were at stake, and her exploratory work on "what would be beautiful to do" could be assessed as a monographic supplement to the core syllabus.

The occasion that stamped a "style" on this organizational process was the rehearsal of the performance in the art gallery after closing time. The dean of the faculty attended the rehearsal, together with the German professor teaching the course in sociology of art. The dean was impressed by what the female student was trying to do. He understood and admired her work, although everything possible went wrong: The voice recordings were incomprehensible; the student missed cues and forgot part of the script; the emotional support provided by her fellow course members (who had also furnished their own recordings of organizational discourses) did not translate into adequate technical support; the space in which the installation was exhibited was too cramped; and to top it all, the acoustics were dreadful. Despite all these problems, the rehearsal was a success: not because of what could be seen and heard, but because of what was evoked in the lecturers, the dean, and the director of the gallery, viz.:

1. the student possessed the qualities required by the performance: a fine voice, command of gestural communication, and an ability to arouse emotion.

2. the multivoice discourse, the diversity of the work settings in which the voices had been recorded, the swirl of students around and within the installation, all together created a dialogic action with the artwork.

3. the vocal counterpoint between everyday practice in organizations and Weber's sociological reflections was interesting and suited to the faculty's institutional context.

This highlights the aesthetic knowledge on which the lecturers and gallery owners drew: They "felt" that the performance had the potential to become such—in the sense that they had perceived it aesthetically without actually hearing or seeing it. So certain of this perception were they, in fact, that the idea was mooted of organizing a small-scale conference around the performance in order to enhance its value as a didactic innovation. The episode of the rehearsal was thus translated into a course of organizational action of much greater organizational weight: creating space for the innovation in the faculty's teaching program, starting collaborative relations between the faculty and the art gallery, and constructing a scientific debate by holding a conference.

It was thus that the installation entered the university. It was too large to be placed in the Great Hall without removing some of the seats. The only feasible space was the faculty's entrance lobby, the equipping of which to accommodate the performance required involvement of the faculty's IT (information technology) center, the university's multimedia laboratory, and an external technician. But compared to the Great Hall, the lobby had one special advantage that concerned the concept itself of "performance": It did not isolate the performance from the quotidian context, embalming it as a specimen of theatrical recital. On the contrary, precisely because of the lobby's nature as a space through which people entered and left the faculty, even if they did not participate in the performance, it exalted the latter's significance as practice in complex organizational settings. Moreover, the entrance lobby symbolized the temporariness of the performance-as-artifact.

This latter consideration introduces the theme of the ephemeral and of the reproducibility of artifacts. What remained after the performance? The simulacrum of it did (Baudrillard, 1978, 1997), "constructable" from materials that were heterogeneous because they were artifacts from different organizations. These materials were:

- Accounts of the performance published in the local press and broadcast on the local television news.
- The audio and video recordings available at the faculty's web page.
- The audio and visual recording of the teleconference.

• The films and photographs taken by professional television film crews and press photographers, as well as the amateur ones taken by friends and students.

These were the multimedia materials that—enhanced by the memories that they evoked—the student reworked for her degree thesis (Scalfi, 2003), which consisted of a written text and a hypertext CD-ROM. While the student was preparing her thesis, a second artifact was constructed (Gherardi & Strati, 2003): a film of the performance in VHS, DVD, and CD-ROM format, with subtitles in English. The last feature was the quality of the artifact that completed, closed, and stabilized the continuous translation and transmutation of the performance through organizational negotiation. There have, in fact, been no subsequent stagings of the performance and it has been used in its actual form at international conferences—for which purpose the English subtitles were added—and on courses in sociology of organizations and sociology of work (for which the English subtitles are superfluous, given that the courses are taught in Italian).

NEW INSIGHTS INTO ARTIFACTS AND AESTHETICS

The first insight gained from the performance is that its script emphasizes (by default) the importance of the material cultures and artifacts required by its being-in-act for its aesthetic, emotional, and symbol-evocative enjoyment (H. S. Becker, 1982; Fineman, 2000; Linstead & Höpfl, 2000; Rafaeli & Pratt, 1993; Strati, 1999) through the senses (Baumgarten, 1750–1758), through the imagination (Vico, 1725/1968), through taste (Kant, 1790/1968), and at the level of formativity (Pareyson, 1954). But those who rely on writing (as I do in this chapter) are able to evoke the aesthetic that gave rise to the performance by illustrating the artifact as "situated in the practice" of the interactions that it engendered and that themselves imbued it, as well as the scenarios that it depicted and configured for the future.

A second insight furnished is that aesthetic experiences are not invariably of the same intensity, the same strength; they do not have the same capacity to mobilize and connote organizational interaction. It was an aesthetic experience that catalyzed the student's motivation to produce the artifact-performance: It did so because, regardless of the artist's intentions, the artwork in the gallery evoked Weber's iron cage of bureaucracy for her. When the structure of the installation became sinuous and austere, it reminded her of what she had discerned in the recorded workplace conversations: namely, that it is practice that prevails over rule; practice consisting not only of regulations but also of activities that, too, have social legitimacy but are at odds with the regulations, and that indeed circumvent, flout, and make a mockery of them.

Another insight is that, with her initially vague intent to "do something," the student communicated an aesthetic sentiment and an emotion to her fellow students, teachers, and other actors in the performance. They were thus involved, not in "doing" art, but in giving new form to academic work, even though the catalyst had been an aesthetic experience. In other words, this was not a matter of "forming for the sake of forming," as happens in art even at the dilettante level, but of the more general aesthetic experience theorized in Pareyson's (1954) phenomenological and hermeneutic philosophy as "giving shape" to something that does not yet exist in that particular form and corresponding to the interpretative activity of the persons involved. In the case illustrated here, "shape" was given to a dialogue performed visually and vocally and constituted by languages both academic and organizational, as well as being artistically expressed by the installation and the performance.

Described in these terms, it may appear that the process was entirely straightforward and that it uncontroversially yielded only positive outcomes. Instead, mention should be made of certain aspects that show how the beauty of artifacts may conceal the imperfections of the organizational process by which they have been constructed (Strati & Guillet de Monthoux, 2002). In particular:

- The artifact-performance had been socially and collectively constructed by several actors who from time to time gave new form to it, also collectively, in often anarchic and random manner.

- It highlighted the faculty's lack of technical equipment and professional expertise (an outside technician had to be called in), revealed the underfunding of the multimedia laboratory, and led to negotiations whereby, for example, the expense of the recording engineer was shared between the dean's office and one of the teachers.

- It provoked fierce conflict in the multimedia laboratory, because of the professional jealousies caused by the fact that some of the audiovisual technicians, having initially perceived the performance as a minor student work, did not want to participate. Once the performance had grown from a minor event into an artifact that gave professional visibility, they found themselves excluded from it, and clashed with their colleagues who had instead been involved in the social construction of the artifact.

- It disappointed when it was addressed along a single dimension: that of the artist student's performance (as it was perceived by the newspapers, e.g.), Weber's iron cage, practice in organizational life. From heterogeneity and multidimensionality, from evocation on several levels, although constituted of numerous performances, the performance was, to paraphrase Marcuse, reduced to a "one-dimensional artifact."

References

Baudrillard, Jean (1978). *La précession des simulacres*. Paris: Editions de Minuit (Eng. trans.: *Simulations*, New York: Semiotext(e), 1983).

Baudrillard, Jean (1997). *Art and Artefact*. London: Sage.

Baumgarten, Alexander Gottlieb (1750–58). *Aesthetica*. Vol. I–II. Frankfurt am Oder: Kleyb. (Photostat: Hildesheim: Olms, 1986).

Becker, Franklin D. (1981). *Workspace: Creating Environments in Organizations*. New York: Praeger.

Becker, Howard S. (1982). *Art Worlds*. Berkeley: University of California Press.

Cairns, George (2002). Aesthetics, morality and power: Design as espoused freedom and implicit control. *Human Relations*, 55, 7, pp. 799–820.

Callon, Michel (1980). *Struggles and Negotiation to Define What is Problematic and What is Not: The Sociology of Translation*. In K.K. Cetina, R. Krohn and R. Whitley (eds), *The Social Process of Scientific Investigation*. Boston: Reidel, pp. 197–219.

Ciborra, Claudio (1996). *Introduction: What does Groupware Mean for the Organizations Hosting it?* In C. Ciborra (ed.), *Groupware & Teamwork*. Chichester: John Wiley & Sons, pp. 1–19.

Derrida, Jacques (1967). *De la Grammatologie*. Paris: Minuit (Eng. trans.: *Of Grammatology*, Baltimore, MD: Johns Hopkins University Press, 1974).

Ehn, Pelle (1988). *Work – Oriented Design of Computer Artifacts*. Stockholm: Arbetslivscentrum.

Fineman, Stephen (2000). *Emotion in Organizations*. Second edition. London: Sage.

Gagliardi, Pasquale (ed.) (1990). *Symbols and Artifacts: Views of the Corporate Landscape*. Berlin: de Gruyter.

Gherardi, Silvia and Strati, Antonio (eds) (2003). *The Iron Cage. Dialogues from Max Weber about Loris Cecchini's installation 'Density Spectrum Zone 1.0'*. Performance by Anna Scalfi, April 2. Trento, Italy: Faculty of Sociology. DVD/VHS, 19'.

Guillet de Monthoux, Pierre (2000). Performing the absolute. Marina Abramovic organizing the unfinished business of Arthur Schopenhauer. *Organization Studies*, 21, 0, pp. 29–51.

Guillet de Monthoux, Pierre (2004). *The Art Firm. Aesthetic Management and Metaphysical Marketing*. Stanford: Stanford University Press.

Hamilton, James R. (2001). Theater. In B. Gaut and D.M. Lopes (eds), *The Routledge Companion to Aesthetics*. London: Routledge, pp. 557–68.

Hatch, Mary Jo (1997). *Organization Theory. Modern, Symbolic and Postmodern Perspectives*. Oxford: Oxford University Press.

Heath, Christian and Button, Graham (eds) (2002). *Workplace Studies*. Special Issue of *British Journal of Sociology*, 52 (2).

Höpfl Heather and Linstead, Stephen (1993). *Passion and Performance: Suffering and the Carrying of Organizational Roles*. In S. Fineman (ed.), *Emotion in Organizations*. London: Sage, pp. 76–93.

Jauss, Hans Robert (1982). *Ästhetische Erfahrung und literarische Hermeneutik* Frankfurt am Main: Suhrkamp Verlag (Eng. trans.: *Question and Answer: Forms of Dialogic Understanding*, Minneapolis, MN: University of Minnesota Press, 1989).

Kant, Immanuel (1790). *Kritik der Urteilskraft*. In I. Kant, *Werke in zwölf Bänden*. Vol. X, ed. by W. Weischedel. Frankfurt am Main: Suhrkamp, 1968 (Eng. trans.: *The Critique of Judgement*, Oxford: Oxford University Press, 1952).

Knorr, Cetina Karin (2003). Posthumanist Challenges to the Human and Social Sciences. *The Role of Humanities in the Formation of New European Elites*, Venice, Italy, September.

Latour, Bruno (1992). *Where are the Missing Masses? Sociology of a Few Mundane Artifacts*. In W. Bijker, J. Law (eds), *Shaping Technology-Building Society: Studies in Sociotechnical Change*. Cambridge, MA: The MIT Press, pp. 225–59.

Law, John and Hassard, John (eds) (1999). *Actor Network Theory and After*. Oxford: Blackwell.

Linstead, Stephen and Höpfl, Heather (eds) (2000). *The Aesthetics of Organization*. London: Sage.

Mangham, Iain L. (1996). Beyond Goffman: Some notes on life and theatre as art. *Studies in Cultures, Organizations and Societies*, 2, 1, pp. 31–41.

March, James (1994). *A Primer on Decision Making. How Decisions Happen.* New York: The Free Press.

Mayer, J.P. (ed.) (1956). *Max Weber and German Politics. A Study in Political Sociology.* London: Faber & Faber.

Montuori, Alfonso (2003). The complexity of improvisation and the improvisation of complexity: Social science, art and creativity. *Human Relations*, 56, 2, pp. 237–55.

Nicolini, Davide, Gherardi, Silvia and Yanow, Dvora (eds) (2003), *Knowing in Organizations: A Practice-Based Approach.* Armonk, NY: M.E. Sharpe.

Pareyson, Luigi (1954). *Estetica. Teoria della formatività* (Aesthetics. Theory of Formativeness). Torino: Giappichelli. Reprinted in 1988, Milano: Bompiani.

Polanyi, Michael (1962). *Personal Knowledge. Towards a Post-Critical Philosophy.* London: Routledge & Kegan Paul.

Putnam, Linda, Phillips, Nelson and Chapman, Pamela (1996). *Metaphors of Communication and Organization.* In S.R. Clegg, C. Hardy and W.R. Nord (eds), *Handbook of Organization Studies.* London: Sage, pp. 375–408.

Rafaeli, Anat and Pratt, Michael G. (1993). Tailored meanings: On the meaning and impact of organizational dress. *Academy of Management Review*, 18, 1, pp. 32–55.

Scalfi, Anna (2003). *Performance, estetica e studi organizzativi* (Performance, Aesthetics and Organization Studies). Trento, Italy: Facoltà di Sociologia, University of Trento.

Serres, Michel (1974). *La traduction. Hermes III.* Paris: Editions de Minuit.

Steele, Fred I. (1973). *Physical Settings and Organization Development.* Reading, MA: Addison-Wesley.

Steyaert, Chris and Hjorth, Daniel (2002). 'Thou art a scholar, speak to it...' – On spaces of speech: A script. *Human Relations*, 55, 7, pp. 767–97.

Strati, Antonio (1992). Aesthetic understanding of organizational life. *Academy of Management Review*, 17, 3, pp. 568–81.

Strati, Antonio (1996). Organizations viewed through the lens of aesthetics. *Organization*, 3, 2, pp. 209–18.

Strati, Antonio (1999). *Organization and Aesthetics.* London: Sage.

Strati, Antonio (2000). *Theory and Method in Organization Studies. Paradigms and Choices.* London: Sage.

Strati, Antonio and Guillet de Montoux, Pierre (2002). Organizing Aesthetics. Introduction to the Special Issue. *Human Relations*, 55, 7, pp. 755–66.

Suchman, Lucy, Trigg, Randall and Blomberg, Jeanette (2002). Working artefacts: Ethnomethods of the prototype. *British Journal of Sociology*, 53, 2, pp. 163–79.

Turner, Barry A. (ed.) (1990). *Organizational Symbolism.* Berlin: de Gruyter.

Vico, Giambattista (1725). *Principi di una scienza nuova.* Napoli: Mosca. Third edition, 1744 (Eng. trans.: *The New Science of Giambattista Vico*, ed. by T.G. Bergin and M.H. Fisch, Ithaca, NY: Cornell University Press, 1968).

Weber, Max (1922). *Wirtschaft und Gesellschaft. Grundriß der verstehenden Soziologie.* Tübingen: Mohr (Eng. trans.: *Economy and Society: An Outline of Interpretive Sociology. I-II.* Berkeley: University of California Press, 1978).

Whalen, Jack, Whalen, Marilyn and Henderson, Kathryn (2002). Improvisional Choreography in Teleservice Work. *British Journal of Sociology*, 53, 2, pp. 239–58.

[15]

Management Learning
Copyright © The Author(s), 2009.
Reprints and permissions:
http://www.sagepub.co.uk/journalsPermissions.nav
http://mlq.sagepub.com
Vol. 40(2): 115–128
1350-5076

Introduction

Silvia Gherardi

University of Trento, Italy

Introduction: The Critical Power of the 'Practice Lens'

Managerial and organizational studies have rediscovered the concept of practice in recent years. The term has spread in such a rapid and unnoticed way that it has generated a body of research bearing the acronym PBS (Practice-Based Studies) almost from nothing. In this introduction I shall treat the rapid diffusion of the practice concept as evidence of the power intrinsic to the central concept of practice. In fact, the greater diffusion and acceptance of Practice-Based Studies (PBS) has been accompanied by concerns about the loss of critical power of the practice concept to more orthodox accounts shaped by assumptions of rationalism and cognitivism in organization studies. We often find the term 'practice' being assumed to be synonymous with 'routine', or taken to be a generic equivalent of 'what people really do', without addressing the link between practice and knowledge, its original and distinctive critique of the modernist conceptions of knowledge (i.e. practice as the generative source of knowledge), and the methodological problems that its use implies. It was with these concerns in mind that the call for papers was made for this special issue.

How the conception of practice as epistemology constitutes a critical approach to the modernist conceptions of knowledge dominant in organization studies can be better understood if we recall the distinction drawn by Ira Cohen (1996) between theories of action and theories of practice. We may say that while the former theories privilege the intentionality of actors, from which derives meaningful action (in the tradition of Weber and Parsons), the latter locate the source of significant patterns in how conduct is enacted, performed or produced (in the tradition of Schutz, Dewey, Mead, Garfinkel and Giddens). Hence theories of practice assume an ecological model in which agency is distributed between humans and non-humans and in which the relationality between the social world and materiality can be subjected to inquiry. While theories of action start from individuals and from their intentionality in pursuing courses of action, theories of practice view actions as 'taking place' or 'happening', as being performed through a network of connections-in-action, as life-world and dwelling.

DOI: 10.1177/1350507608101225

Practice: A Polysemic Concept

It appears that practice has become a buzz-word in organization studies, and the aggregate of voices under the label 'practice-based studies' is rather polyphonic. When we leave aside the commonplace use of the word 'practice' and assume that reference is being made to practice as epistemology, we can see how practice-based studies converge on a common interest in understanding the production/consumption of knowledge and its circuit of reproduction. 'Practice', Schatzki (1996, 2001) argues, is a term that seems to be descriptive of fundamental phenomena of society, as encountered, for example, in the writings of philosophers and sociologists such as Bourdieu (1972), Lyotard (1979), Foucault (1980), Taylor (1995), as well as in ethnomethodology (Garfinkel, 1967). In Bourdieu's case the deeper-lying structures that organize general social practices are self-reproducing dispositions; in Lyotard discursive moves or language games; in Foucault genealogies of practice; in Taylor the vocabulary embedded within the practice marks its range of possible actions and meanings, while in Garfinkel the reflexive tendency of social interaction provides for its own constitution through practices of accountability and scenic display.

In organization studies, the influence of practice theorists has been seen as more important as an epistemology for the study of working practices and the kind of practical and 'hidden' knowledge that supports them. Paradoxically, the term 'practice' has the connotation of being something transferable, teachable, transmittable, or reproducible (Turner, 1994), but at the same time, practices are difficult to access, observe, measure or represent because they are hidden, tacit, and often linguistically inexpressible in propositional terms. The problem of representing practices is well illustrated in the contributions in this special issue by Blacker and Regan, Geiger and Nicolini.

In both scientific and ordinary language, the term 'practice' relates to a plurality of semantic fields. Although this may be a limitation, it also has the advantage that 'practice' is a malleable term which can be put to numerous uses and employed to denominate many aspects of the phenomenal reality under study. The numerous phenomenal aspects comprised in a practice can be studied in relation to their recursiveness, socially sustained habits, the knowledge implicit in a dominion of action, the values that give social accountability to action, and the shared ways of accomplishing any practice. The challenge raised by the current recovery of the concept of practice within organization studies is to conjecture whether it is possible to consider the set of all these aspects in their phenomenal occurrence and in their temporality. If this challenge is taken up, the 'growing calls to get close to work/organizational practices happening' (Samra-Fredericks and Bargiela-Chiappini, 2008: 654) would constitute an objective attainable with rigorous theorization and methodology.

Practice from Outside and Practice from Inside

The difficulty of defining what is meant by 'practice' is due not only to the polysemy of the term but also to the various epistemic positioning of different researchers. Applying the fundamental distinction in sociology between object-ivism and subjectivism (Bourdieu, 1990), or in Evered and Louis's terms (1981) between 'inquiry from outside' and 'inquiry from inside', yields different concep-tions of practices and different methodologies for studying them.

When practices are read 'from outside', the inquiry concentrates on their regularity, on the pattern which organizes activities, and on the more or less shared understanding that allows their repetition. The recursiveness of practices (Giddens, 1984) is the element which enables both practitioners and researchers to rec-ognize a practice as practice, that is, a way of doing sustained by canons of good practice (a normative accountability) and beautiful practice (an aesthetic account-ability). Therefore a practice becomes such when it is socially recognized as an institutionalized doing. When a practitioner tells a colleague that from 10 to 12 o'clock she or he will be doing 'X', the expression is intersubjectively meaningful as indexing a specific work practice that is different from others, not only because of the use of specific technologies and tasks but also because of the set of rela-tions activated to produce that practice and to sustain its legitimacy and value. In this case knowledge about the practice is anterior to the practitioner who will put it into practice, that is, perform it as situated activity complying with the logic of the situation. When researchers read practice 'from outside' their knowledge interest will be driven by questions such as: How does the object of the 'X' practice emerge from the recursiveness of the activity? Reading practices from outside enables them to be analysed as an 'array of activities'. It is this epistemological position that links the analysis of practices with the analysis of routines—as conducted, for instance, by Feldman and Pentland (2003) and by Feldman (2000), who propose a reading of routines as practices in order to move from the analysis of routines as programmes of action to that of routines as performances. In these studies, the tradition of inquiry into routines initiated by March overlaps with a new research programme concerned with the dynamic aspect of the recursiveness of organizational actions, although it maintains the function of routines and practices as uncertainty reduction devices. This reflects an increasingly common interpretation of organizing in terms of 'recurrent action patterns' (M. Cohen, 2007) and a resumption of interest among organization scholars in Dewey and pragmatism (Elkjaer, 2003) and in Heidegger and pheno-menology (Chia and Holt, 2006).

Let us go 'inside' practices. A second reading can be conducted 'from within', that is, from the point of view of the practitioners and the activity that is being performed, with its temporality and processuality, as well as the emergent and negotiated order of the action being done. This perspective is discussed and illu-strated in the articles by Geiger and Nicolini in this issue. Seen from the inside, practice is a knowledgeable collective action that forges relations and connections among all the resources available and all the constraints present. Performing a practice therefore requires knowing how to align humans and artefacts within a sociotechnical ensemble and therefore knowing how to construct and maintain an action-net (Czarniawska, 2004), which is interwoven and deployed so that every element has a place and a sense in the interaction. From this definition it follows that knowing is a situated activity and that knowing-in-practice is always a prac-tical accomplishment.

Knowing is something that people do together, and it is done in every mundane activity, in organizations when people work together, and also in academic fields. To know is to be able to participate with the requisite competence in the complex web of relationships among people, material artefacts and activities (Gherardi, 2001). Acting as a competent practitioner is synonymous with knowing how to connect successfully with the field of practices thus activated.

Empirical studies, which analyse practice from inside, consist in the study of the practical organization of knowledge, taking the form of methods of seeing, listening, reasoning and acting in association with human and non-human elements. In fact, objects and their material world can be construed as material-ized knowledge and matter, which interrogate humans and interact with them. And practical reasoning can be considered as a mode of ordering and deploying the interweaving between knowledge and power (Foucault, 1980). In this sense, practice from inside constitutes an epistemology that can be called 'post-humanist' in that it seeks to decentre the human subject (as in the object-centred sociality of Knorr-Cetina, 1997) or to reconfigure agency (Latour, 2005) as a capacity real-ized through the associations of humans and materiality.

The article by Bjørkeng, Clegg and Pitsis in this special issue proposes an apt neologism to convey the duality of the researcher's practice and positioning. 'Becoming (a) practice' comprises both the message that the object of empirical study of practices is *a* practice, that is, identification by the researcher of the empirical object of study, and the sense that the emergence of a shared way of doing becomes a shared practice (i.e. a habit) through a series of social processes which the authors identify in authoring boundaries, negotiating competences and adapting materiality. Their empirical study responds to the question: How are practices born?

Practice and its Effects

Within an ecological model, practice can be described and analysed as a texture of connections in action (Gherardi, 2006), delineating a third analytical level in ad-dition to those of practices 'from outside' and 'from inside', a level that involves analysis of practices in terms of their deliberate and non-deliberate consequences as and when they are being practised. Hence, practice is viewed as the effect of a weaving-together of interconnections in action, or as a 'doing' of society. Such a third reading of practice considers the social effects of a single practice in relation to its being practised within society. This is the level of the reflexivity of prac-tices and the reproduction of society. Ethnomethodologists talk of the inevitable reflexivity of practices to show that every practice creates its context: 'Reflexivity refers to the dynamic self-organizational tendency of social interaction to provide for its own constitution through practices of accountability and scenic display' (Flynn, 1991: 28). Bourdieu (1972) speaks of 'circuits of reproduction', that is, the reciprocal, cyclical relationships through which practice creates and re-creates the objectified social structures and the conditions in which it occurs. At this analytical level the researcher asks: What is it that doing the practice does? And it is the level at which ethical questions can be asked and at which the emancipatory or exploitative effects of a social practice may be questioned. Mathieu's contribution in this issue illustrates this third level of analysis. In his article Mathieu illustrates how gender is a social practice that cuts across other practices (of work and organization) and produces inequality effects rooted in the unintentional doing of actors.

The theme of the effects of practices, of the morality associated with their accomplishment, and of the applications of theories of practice in action research, is introduced in this special issue by Blackler and Regan, who present an example of intervention interpreted from within activity theory: that is, from a theoretical point of view originating in cultural psychology which uses the concept of system of activity rather than practice. This preference has historical and disciplinary origins, which the article clearly describes and which, interestingly, represent the other extreme of the concept of practice. In fact, we may say that the term 'practice' is an in-between concept which relates on the one hand to the semantic domain of habit and of habitual action (and therefore, as we have seen, to routine as an uncertainty reduction device), and on the other, to the domain of deliberate action. Practice contains elements of both domains, but it coincides with neither of them. Blackler and Regan's article is particularly efficacious in its discussion of intentionality and agency in theories of practice, and it also addresses the question of the usability of PBS in relation to organizational change. The essays by Bjørkeng, Clegg and Pitsis and by Blackler and Regan respond to the following questions: Why study practices? What relationships do they entertain with change and organizational stability? What should the researcher's relationship be with the moral accountability of the practices that he or she studies?

These are questions which have been variously addressed in the main fields of study that have employed practice as a lens, and which I now outline in order to show how PBS are mainly concerned to develop a politics of knowledge while criticizing the representationalist conception of knowledge.

When Practice Is Used as a Lens

The complex map of PBS can be presented in many different ways; delineating a map is always an arbitrary operation. I have done so previously in relation to the intellectual traditions converging in the study of knowing-in-practice (Gherardi, 2001) and in relation to the so-called paradigm of situated action (Gherardi, 2008). My approach here is to point up its most salient themes, when practice has been used as a lens, to employ the apt metaphor coined by Wanda Orlikowski (2000). I shall therefore describe the ways in which the concept of social practice has been critically appropriated as a critique of representationalist conceptions of knowledge:

1. within studies on science to show how scientific knowledge is the situated product of laboratory practices;
2. within organizational learning to problematize what is meant by knowing in its everyday use;
3. within studies on technology (computer supported cooperative work, information systems, workplace studies) to direct attention to 'real' work practices,

to the knowledge performed within them, and to participatory design of work and technologies;
4. within gender studies in order to 'read' gender as a social practice and a politics of knowledge.

These are complex debates in terms of both the topic and the number of authors involved. I am therefore aware that my treatment will be limited[1] and will not do justice to the richness of the contributions. What do all these strands of inquiry have in common? Intuitively, we can see that abstract and universal concepts, in the case of both science and gender, are inscribed in a distinct temporality and spatiality. 'Science' is what scientists 'do' in their laboratories and which institutional practices transform into 'science'; 'gender' is what people in interaction 'do', 'say', 'think' so that 'gender' is produced as a social effect. The same holds for the appropriation of technology and of practical knowledge. This is therefore an intentional 'doing' (as in the work practices of scientists), but also an unintentional one (as in the gendering of scientific occupations). It is a 'doing' which is productive, but simultaneously reproductive because it is a 'doing of society'. I shall now briefly describe each of the foregoing strands.

Science as Practice

The roots of 'science as practice' can be traced back to the 1970s and the advent of a new approach to science within the sociology of scientific knowledge (Pickering, 1992). It was argued that scientific knowledge—much as technology—is intrinsically social. It must therefore be understood as such and studied as a set of historically situated social practices. The 1970s and 1980s saw flourishing ethnographic studies of scientific laboratories (Latour and Woolgar, 1979; Knorr-Cetina, 1981). In the USA, ethnomethodologists applied themselves to laboratory life and to mathematics (Lynch et al., 1983; Lynch, 1985; Livingstone, 1986), whilst the 'Tremont group' in California continued the tradition of symbolic interactionism in the study of science (Star and Griesemer, 1989; Fujimura, 1992, 1995), and in England there arose the discourse analysis developed by Gilbert and Mulkay (1984) and by Ashmore (1989) on reflexivity.

Scientific knowledge was thus removed from the pedestal erected for it by positivism, and science could be seen as a culture much as every other form of knowledge and, as such, subject to implications of social control and social interests. The connection between the micro-social (laboratory practices) and the macro-social (science in society) was thematized together with issues concerning ethics and social change. The metaphor of 'ecologies of knowledge' (Star, 1995) was proposed to locate the production of knowledge within an ecosystem that rejects the dichotomies of functionalist thought between nature and society and between the social and technical. It is argued that science and technology become 'monsters' when they lose their connections with the social conditions of their production (Law, 1991; Haraway, 1992). We may say therefore that this field of studies conducted a critique against positivism and focused on the circuit of knowledge reproduction and its societal effects.

Organizational Learning and Knowing in Practice

The concept of practice gained ground in studies of organizational learning through a critical approach to learning as cognition, on the one side, and to change on the other. The strong criticisms provoked by the concept of 'community of practice' (CoP), especially in its managerialist version (Wenger et al., 2002), have changed the setting in which the conception of knowledge is delineated (Fox, 2000, 2006). Authors who have criticized the concept of community of practice (Contu et al., 2003; Cohendet et al., 2004; Elkjaer, 2004; Lindkvist, 2005; Handley et al., 2006; Roberts, 2006) have done so mainly to move from the absence of conflict to the absence of power in the concept of CoP.

Now that the fashion has passed, and with it the persuasive power of the rhetoric associated with the label CoP, several authors (Gherardi et al., 1998; Brown and Duguid, 2001; Swan et al., 2002; Roberts, 2006; Gherardi, 2009) have proposed reversing the emphasis between the two terms—from community of practice to practices of a community. Stressed in the former case is that community constitutes the container of knowledge and the community pre-exists its activities. In the latter, it is the activities themselves that generate a community, in that they form the 'glue' which holds together a configuration of people, artefacts and social relations. In this case the attention is directed at the practical knowledge contextually enacted during performance of a practice and at the knowing coming from the senses (Strati, 2007). Knowledge, therefore, is not an 'asset' of the community, but rather an activity (a 'knowing'), and an activity that itself constitutes the practice ('knowing-in-practice').

Fox (1997, 2000) and other authors, such as Contu and Willmott (2003) and Gherardi (2001), have pointed out the ambiguity between realist and constructionist assumptions, with respect to consideration of the context as sometimes pregiven and sometimes emergent. The criticism of the conception of 'context' consists in showing how practices are tightly interwoven to constitute a field of practices or a network of more or less closely connected practices enduring over time, variously sustained by power, and anchored in materiality. The community is one of those effects, as well as being a device for the reproduction of the field of practices. It is therefore through the conceptions of power and materiality in actor-network theory, that the epistemology of knowledge as an object or an asset is displaced in favour of an epistemology of knowing in practice. It is in this field of studies where PBS have most contributed to a critique of the power effects of organizational learning (and knowledge management) as a managerial ideology.

Critical Studies of Technology and Technology as a Social Practice

Technology, knowledge-sharing and coordination as an emergent phenomenon can be considered the themes which unite strands of inquiry—such as computer-supported cooperative work, critical information systems, and workplace studies—which, although highly diversified, are jointly considered here for the sake of brevity.

Particularly influential in this area has been Lucy Suchman's book (1987 first edition, 2007 second) based on a symbolic interactionist framework and which criticized the concept of *ex ante* rationality in the form of plans assumed to regulate action, indicated by the notion of 'situated rationality' in contrast to the rationality of plans and programs. Before action takes place, plans serve only a predictive or organizational purpose; after that action, plans serve to justify the actions undertaken. Central to the paradigm of situated action are interactions with others, situated communication, the construction of situations, the relationship with the physical environment and the objects in it, but above all the idea that these elements are 'held together' by and express a situational rationality.

The theme of situated rationality is taken forward by workplace studies (Heath and Luff, 2000; Luff et al., 2000; Heath and Button, 2002) that are anchored in an ethnographic and ethnomethodological framework, which seek to determine how the verbal, the visual, and the material take shape through practice (and discursive practices) during the production and coordination of interaction. The terms 'technology-in-use' (Orlikowski, 1992) and 'technology as social practice' (Suchman et al., 1999) have been coined to distinguish this approach to technology.

The studies by Wanda Orlikoswki (2000, 2002, 2007) on technological practices are exemplary for their adoption of the theoretical framework of 'structuration' (Giddens, 1984) to connect agency and structure. There arose ethnographic methods of investigation (Brown and Duguid, 1991; Blomberg et al., 1993; Barley, 1996; Carlile, 2002; Østerlund and Carlile, 2005) which set the study of situated working practices in opposition against the positivist methods then current in order to emphasize user requirements (Richardson et al., 2006). There ensued reflection on the methods adopted by researchers to represent work practices and on the need for reflexivity by researchers, who should conduct ethnographic research upon themselves, given that they are 'knowledge workers' who study other knowledge workers (Schultze, 2000).

Gender as a Social Practice

Since the publication of West and Zimmerman's (1987) article on 'doing gender', drawing on Garfinkel's (1967) classic account of Agnes, many articles and books about gender as *actions* that people *do*, not only who/what they are, or the positions they occupy, have fostered insights about how gender is accomplished through interaction (Bruni and Gherardi, 2001; Martin, 2001; 2003; Ashcraft and Mumby, 2004; Poggio, 2006). 'Gender practices', 'gendered practices' and 'gendering practices' stand for a class of activities that are available—culturally, socially, narratively, discursively, physically—to be done, asserted, performed in social contexts. How we do gender (and how we can do it differently) is still a question central to micro-politics between the sexes, in the social construction of the everyday reality of our society and culture, an assertion that presupposes that gender is a social practice that anchors other practices, in other words, it is a methodical and recurrent accomplishment. Following the line of 'gender as social practice', Mathieu's contribution in this issue illustrates this stream of research in PBS, and I therefore refer the reader to his presentation.

The Limits of the Visual Metaphor and the Limits of Language

The metaphor of using practice as a lens through which to examine social phenomena is highly efficacious because it evokes a mental image of the researcher as a Sherlock Holmes intent upon the close scrutiny of a reality. However, it is also misleading because it simultaneously activates an image in which the researcher is disconnected from the field of study, which exists independently from him/her, 'out there'. The role of language in the construction of social phenomena is too well known to require treatment here. I shall therefore merely point out that the 'practice turn' was preceded by a 'linguistic turn' (Deetz, 2003) in organization studies as well, so that the concept of practice can be used as much within a positivist epistemology and a realist empiricism, as within a social constructionist epistemology. In this context, the notion of the critical power of PBS makes implicit reference to a constructionist epistemology, which conceives practices only in relation to their practitioners, and the accountability practices that have constituted them as socially sustained modes of practising. The definition of something as ' a practice' is therefore itself the result of a discursive practice that has intersubjectively created a feeling and a doing around a socially recognized and recognizable modality of collective doing. All the contributions to this special issue are committed, in various ways, to describing the discursive construct which drives the emergence and unfolding of a practice over time and its ruptures and disconnections.

The limitation of the metaphor of the lens is that it obscures the fact that researchers—as well as practitioners who talk about their knowing—discursively construct the phenomenon which they study and describe. Consequently, the representation of practices is the crucial issue for PBS and for the methodologies available to talk and write about knowing in practice. This theme is developed in this special issue by the article by Nicolini. The theme is crucial for several reasons, and Nicolini's article comes last in this special issue because it links with the first article, in which Geiger poses the problem of whether practices should be defined as patterns of activity, or vice versa; whether they should be defined in their being socially sustained by a normative accountability. If the former definition is favoured, the methodologies for the analysis of practices seek to describe the tasks making up practice in analytical and routine-like manner. If the latter definition is preferred, the activities making up practice are viewed as the tip of an iceberg: they emerge and become visible because lying beneath them is a mass of practical knowledge and discursive (material-semiotic) practices that justify practices as morally and aesthetically acceptable. In this sense, practice discloses its aspect as an institution, the product of a negotiated order which has momentarily crystallized a shared mode of doing and sustains it while the premises for its change are being set.

These two authors suggest two topical moments in which to study practices. Geiger suggests looking at breakdowns and the discursive forms of practice repair in order to direct attention to the moments in which practices constitute an uninterrupted flow (a life-world) and the moments in which practitioners reflect upon and negotiate practices. Nicolini instead proposes accessing practices through the discursive practices of the practitioners that make practices accountable for the researcher through a projective technique.

Methodological questions in the empirical study of practices raise crucial theoretical issues because, on the one hand, theories of practice start from the assumption that practical knowledge is observable and describable without the need for categories such as intentionality, values or knowledge (one therefore understands why ethnomethodology is one of the most influential theories of practice within PBS), and on the other, because they fully endorse the contention of both Bourdieu and Polanyi that practical knowledge is personal knowledge: it is ineffable, and hence our re-presentations of practices are always 'poor' because, as Polanyi puts it, we know more than we can tell. Language thus reveals its limitations, showing that human knowledge is also pre-discursive, sensorial and embodied (Strati, 2007). We know through the body and sensorial experience that knowledge is not only individual but is also collectively elaborated in the form of taste-making. The question of what socially sustains practices and how practices are reproduced and in being reproduced change over time—intentionally and unintentionally—is more challenging for opening a critical stance on society and the social effects of consolidated practices than the study of practice as a recurrent pattern of action. The shifts from organization to organizing and from work to working entail consideration not only of temporality and becoming, but also of (temporary) permanence, and therefore of practices as order-generating mechanisms.

Where is the Critical Power?

The 'practice turn' in organizational studies is at odds with cognitivism and rationalism because it defines knowledge as a practical and situated activity. It propounds a vision of organizing as knowledgeable collective action within an ecology of humans and non-humans. PBS therefore constitutes both a sociology and a politics of knowledge in its everyday use. In summary, practice as epistemology articulates knowledge in and about organizing as practical accomplishment, rather than as a transcendental account of a decontextualized reality done by a genderless and disembodied researcher.

The knowledge interest of critical PBS in regard to work and organizations is determining how practitioners do what they do and what doing does; how working and organizing practices become institutionalized because they are sustained by a 'working consensus' (an institutional work) and a moral and aesthetic order; and on how practising is interactionally sustained by a pre-verbal understanding, a mutual orientation and a production of mutually intelligible artefacts. Theories of practice furnish the theoretical and methodological bases for the construction of middle-range theories which flank the vision of organization as planning and design (rationality from outside) with the vision of organization as an unstable accomplishment in becoming, but based on widespread social intelligibility (contingent and plural rationalities).

Note

1. I shall not refer to the large stream of 'strategy as practice' since in this case practice is used to refer to processes (i.e. strategizing) rather than to practices of knowledge

production. While the debate is critical of the prescriptive ethos in strategy studies, seldom has it a critical stance toward cognitivism and positivism.

References

Ashcraft, K. and Mumby, D. (2004) *Reworking Gender.* London: SAGE.

Ashmore, M. (1989) *The Reflexive Thesis: Writing Sociology of Knowledge.* Chicago, IL: University of Chicago Press.

Barley, S. R. (1996) 'Technicians in the Workplace: Ethnographic Evidence for Bringing Work into Organizational Studies', *Administrative Science Quarterly* 41(3): 404–41.

Blomberg, J., Giacomi, J., Mosher, A. and Swenton-Wall, P. (1993) 'Ethnographic Field Methods and Their Relation to Design', in D. Schuler and A. Namioka (eds) *Participatory Design: Principles and Practices,* pp. 123–55. Hillsdale, NY: Lawrence Erlbaum.

Bourdieu, P. (1972) *Outline of a Theory of Practice.* Cambridge: Cambridge University Press.

Bourdieu, P. (1990) *The Logic of Practice.* Stanford, CA: Stanford University Press.

Brown, J. S. and Duguid, P. (1991) 'Organizational Learning and Communities of Practice: Toward a Unified View of Working, Learning and Bureaucratization', *Organization Science* 2(1): 40–57.

Brown, J. S. and Duguid, P. (2001) 'Knowledge and Organization: A Social-Practice Perspective', *Organization Science* 12(2): 198–213.

Bruni, A. and Gherardi, S. (2001) 'Omega's Story: The Heterogeneous Engineering of a Gendered Professional Self', in M. Dent and S. Whitehead (eds) *Managing Professional Identities. Knowledge, Performativity and the New Professional,* pp. 174–98. London: Routledge.

Carlile, P. R. (2002) 'A Pragmatic View of Knowledge and Boundaries: Boundary Objects in New Product Development', *Organization Science* 13(4): 442–55.

Chia, R. and Holt, R. (2006) 'Strategy as Practical Coping: an Heideggerian Perspective', *Organization Studies* 27(5): 635–55

Cohen, I. J. (1996) 'Theories of Action and Praxis', in B. S. Turner (ed.) *The Blackwell Companion to Social Theory,* pp. 111–42. Cambridge, MA: Blackwell.

Cohen, M. (2007) 'Reading Dewey: Reflections on the Study of Routines', *Organization Studies* 28(5): 773–86.

Cohendet P., Creplet, P., Diani, M., Dupouet, O. and Schenk, E. (2004) 'Matching Communities and Hierarchies Within the Firm', *Journal of Management and Governance* 8(1): 27–48.

Contu, A. and Willmott, H. (2003) 'Re-embedding Situatedness: The Importance of Power Relations in Learning Theory', *Organization Science* 14(3): 283–96.

Contu, A., Grey, C. and Ortenblad, A. (2003) 'Against Learning', *Human Relations* 56(8): 931–52.

Czarniawska, B. (2004) 'On Time, Space and Action Nets', *Organization* 11(6): 773–91.

Deetz, S. (2003) 'Reclaiming the Legacy of the Linguistic Turn', *Organization* 10(3): 421–9.

Elkjaer, B. (2003) 'Organizational Learning with a Pragmatic Slant', *International Journal of Lifelong Education* 22(5): 481–94.

Elkjaer, B. (2004) 'Organizational Learning: The "Third Way"', *Management Learning* 35(4): 419–34.

Evered, R. and Louis, M. R. (1981) 'Alternative Perspectives in the Organizational Sciences. "Inquiry from the Inside" and "Inquiry from the Outside"', *Academy of Management Review* 6: 385–95.

126   **Management Learning 40(2)**

Feldman, M. (2000) 'Organizational Routines as a Source of Continuous Change', *Organization Science* 11(6): 611–29.

Feldman, M. S. and Pentland, B. T. (2003) 'Re-conceptualizing Organizational Routines as a Source of Flexibility and Change', *Administrative Science Quarterly* 48(1): 94–118.

Flynn, P. (1991) *The Ethnomethodological Movement.* New York: Mouton de Gruyter.

Foucault, M. (1980) *Power/Knowledge.* New York: Pantheon Books.

Fox, S. (1997) 'Situated Learning Theory Versus Traditional Cognitive Theory: Why Management Education Should not Ignore Management Learning', *Systems Practice* 10(6): 749–71.

Fox, S. (2000) 'Communities of Practice, Foucault and Actor-Network Theory', *Journal of Management Studies* 37(6): 853–67.

Fox, S. (2006) 'Inquiries of Every Imaginable Kind: Ethnomethodology, Practical Action and the New Socially Situated Learning Theory', *The Sociological Review* 54(3): 426–45.

Fujimura, J. (1992) 'Crafting Science: Standardized Packages, Boundary Objects, and "Translation"', in A. Pickering (ed.) *Science as Practice and Culture,* pp. 168–214. Chicago, IL: University of Chicago Press.

Fujimura, J. (1995) 'Ecologies of Action: Recombining Genes, Molecularizing Cancer, and Transforming Biology', in S. L. Star (ed.) *Ecologies of Knowledge,* pp. 302–46. Albany: State University of New York Press.

Garfinkel, H. (1967) *Studies in Ethnomethodology.* Englewood Cliffs, NJ: Prentice Hall.

Gherardi, S. (2001) 'Practice-based Theorizing on Learning and Knowing in Organizations: An Introduction', *Organization* 7(2): 211–23.

Gherardi, S. (2006) *Organizational Knowledge: The Texture of Workplace Learning.* Oxford: Blackwell.

Gherardi, S. (2008) 'Situated Knowledge and Situated Action: What Do Practice-Based Studies Promise?' in D. Barry and H. Hansen (eds) *SAGE Handbook of the New & Emerging in Management and Organization,* pp. 516–25. London: SAGE.

Gherardi, S. (2009) 'Communities of Practice or Practices of a Community?' in S. Armstrong and C. Fukami (eds) *Handbook of Management Learning, Education and Development,* pp. 514–30. London: SAGE.

Gherardi, S., Nicolini, D. and Odella, F. (1998) 'Towards a Social Understanding of how People Learn in Organizations', *Management Learning* 29(3): 273–98.

Giddens, A. (1984) *The Constitution of Society.* Cambridge: Polity.

Gilbert, G. and Mulkay, M. (1984) *Opening Pandora's Box: a Sociological Analysis of Scientists' Discourse.* Cambridge: Cambridge University Press.

Handley, K., Sturdy, A., Fincham, R. and Clark, T. (2006) 'Within and Beyond Communities of Practice: Making Sense of Learning Through Participation, Identity and Practice', *Journal of Management Studies* 43(3): 641–53.

Haraway, D. (1992) 'The Promises of Monsters: A Regenerative Politics for Inappropiate/ d Others', in P. Treichler, C. Nelson and L. Grossberg (eds) *Cultural Studies Now and in the Future,* pp.295–337. New York: Routledge.

Heath, C. and Button, G. (2002) 'Special Issue on Workplace Studies: Editorial Introduction', *The British Journal of Sociology* 53(2): 157–61.

Heath, C. and Luff, P. (2000) *Technology in Action.* Cambridge: Cambridge University Press.

Knorr-Cetina, K. (1981) *The Manufacture of Knowledge.* Oxford: Pergamon Press.

Knorr-Cetina, K. (1997) 'Sociality with Objects: Social Relations in Post-Social Knowledge Societies', *Theory, Culture and Society* 14(4): 1–30.

Latour, B. (2005) *Reassembling the Social.* Oxford: Oxford University Press.

Latour, B. and Woolgar, S. (1979) *Laboratory Life: The Social Construction of Scientific Facts.* Beverly Hills, CA: SAGE.

Law, J., ed. (1991) 'Sociology of Monsters? Power, Technology and the Modern World', *The Sociological Review Monograph* 38. London: Routledge and Kegan Paul.

Lindkvist, L. (2005) 'Knowledge Communities and Knowledge Collectivities: A Typology of Knowledge Work in Groups', *Journal of Management Studies* 42(6): 1189–210.

Livingstone, E. (1986) *The Ethnomethodological Foundations of Mathematics.* Boston, MA: Routledge and Kegan Paul.

Luff, P., Hindmarsh, J. and Heath, C., (eds) (2000) *Workplace Studies.* Cambridge: Cambridge University Press.

Lynch, M. (1985) *Art and Artifact in Laboratory Life. A Study of Shop Work and Shop Talk in a Research Laboratory.* London: Routledge and Kegan Paul.

Lynch, M., Livingstone, E. and Garfinkel, H. (1983) 'Temporal Order', in K. Knorr-Cetina and M. Mulkay (eds) *Science Observed,* pp. 205–80. London: SAGE.

Lyotard, J. (1979) *The Postmodern Condition.* Manchester: Manchester University Press.

Martin, P. Y. (2001) '"Mobilizing Masculinities": Women's Experience of Men at Work', *Organization* 8(4): 587–618.

Martin, P. Y. (2003) '"Said and Done" Versus "Saying and Doing". Gendered Practices/Practicing Gender at Work', *Gender & Society,* 17(3): 342–66.

Orlikowski, W. J. (1992) 'The Duality of Technology: Rethinking the Concept of Technology in Organizations', *Organization Science* 3(3): 398–427.

Orlikowski, W. J. (2000) 'Using Technology and Constructing Structures: A Practice Lens for Studying Technology in Organizations', *Organization Science* 11(4): 404–28.

Orlikowski, W. J. (2002) 'Knowing in Practice: Enacting a Collective Capability in Distributed Organizing', *Organization Science* 13: 249–73.

Orlikowski, W. J. (2007) 'Sociomaterial Practices: Exploring Technology at Work', *Organization Studies* 28(9): 1435–48.

Østerlund, C. and Carlile, P. (2005) 'Relations in Practice: Sorting Through Practice Theories on Knowledge Sharing in Complex Organizations', *The Information Society* 21(2): 91–107.

Pickering, A. (1992) *Science as Practice and Culture.* Chicago, IL: University of Chicago Press.

Poggio, B. (2006) 'Editorial: Outline of a Theory of Gender Practices', *Gender, Work and Organization* 13(3): 225–33.

Richardson, H., Tapia, A. and Kvasny, L. (2006) 'Introduction: Applying Critical Theory to the Study of ICT', *Social Science Computer Review* 24(3): 267–73.

Roberts, J. (2006) 'Limits to Communities of Practice', *Journal of Management Studies* 43(3): 623–39.

Samra-Fredericks, D., Bargiela-Chiappini, F. (2008) 'Introduction to the Symposium on the Foundations of Organizing: the Contribution from Garfinkel, Goffman and Sacks', *Organization Studies* 29(5): 653–75.

Schatzki, T. R. (1996) *Social Practices: A Wittgensteinian Approach to Human Activity and the Social.* Cambridge: Cambridge University Press.

Schatzki, T. R. (2001) 'Introduction. Practice Theory', in T. R. Schatzki, K. Knorr-Cetina and E. von Savigny (eds) *The Practice Turn in Contemporary Theory,* pp. 1–14. London and New York: Routledge.

Schultze, U. (2000) 'A Confessional Account of an Ethnography about Knowledge Work', *MIS Quarterly* 24(1): 3–41.

Star, S. L. (1995) *Ecologies of Knowledge.* Albany: State University of New York Press.

Star, S. L. and Griesemer, J. (1989) 'Institutional Ecology, "Translations", and Coherence: Amateurs and Professionals in Berkeley's Museum of Vertebrate Zoology, 1907–1939', *Social Studies of Science* 19: 387–420.

Strati, A. (2007) 'Sensible Knowledge and Practice-Based Learning', *Management Learning* 38(1): 61–77.

Suchman, L. (1987) *Plans and Situated Action: The Problem of Human–Machine Communication.* Cambridge: Cambridge University Press.

Suchman, L. (2007) *Human–Machine Reconfigurations: Plans and Situated Actions.* Cambridge: Cambridge University Press.

Suchman, L., Blomberg, J., Orr, J. E. and Trigg, R. (1999) 'Reconstructing Technologies as Social Practice', *American Behavioural Scientist* 43(3): 392–408.

Swan, J., Scarbrough, H. and Robertson, M. (2002). 'The Construction of "Communities of Practice" in the Management of Innovation', *Management Learning* 33(4): 477–96.

Taylor, C. (1995) *Philosophical Arguments.* Cambridge, MA: Harvard University Press.

Turner, S. (1994) *The Social Theory of Practices.* Chicago, IL: The University of Chicago Press.

Wenger, E., Mc.Dermott, R. and Snyder, W. M. (2002) *Cultivating Communities Of Practice.* Boston, MA: Harvard Business School Press.

West, C. and Zimmerman, D. (1987) 'Doing Gender', *Gender and Society* 1(2): 125–51.

Contact Address

Silvia Gherardi is professor in the Department of Sociology, Universita Degli Studi Di Trento, Piazza Venezia 41, Trento, I 38100, Italy.
[email: silvia.gherardi@soc.unitn.it]